# THE LANDING!

What happened next, many would consider Divine Providence. Others would call it just plain luck. As for me? I was more anthropomorphic. I viewed Antarctica as a majestic female. She was cold-hearted, and she was hot-tempered. She caught me when I wasn't expecting it, and she intended to hurt me. She had killed many others in the past. I thought she would cut me some slack, but in the end, she was just toying with me.

As I was about to pitch the nose up for landing, the wind died briefly, and I did not need any crosswind controls. I lowered the aircraft gently on the slick, icy runway. We were down, but Antarctica wasn't finished with us. Upon landing, I pulled the throttles to reverse. I gave my copilot control of the yoke, allowing me to move my left hand to the nosewheel steering to monitor its movement. The aircraft began to slide to the right.

I've heard people talk about how time slows down when they're under a great deal of pressure. It certainly slowed down for me. One at a time, I considered my options and tried them. The rudder was still effective at higher speeds, so I stepped on the left rudder to correct back to the centerline, but it had no effect. Next, I relieved pressure on the right brake and kept the pressure on the left brake. It had no effect. I tried turning the nosewheel, but it did not affect our path on the slippery runway.

There was only one remaining option. I began to manipulate the throttles. I pushed the #3 and #4 engines over the flight idle gate. The aircraft began to correct back to the centerline, but it wasn't enough. I was running out of room. The aircraft turned, and for a moment, I thought I was in the clear. I needed to stop, so I brought the throttles back to reverse, but the aircraft began to turn and drift right. So, I made a more aggressive correction. We passed the tower as we traveled down the runway. The visibility was low, so the tower operators were convinced we were spinning in 360-degree circles down the runway.

When the aircraft began turning right a third time, I knew I was out of room. The end of the runway was fast approaching. I estimated I had less than one thousand feet remaining and only seconds to stop the aircraft.

I pulled the throttles into reverse again, and instead of correcting the turn, I stepped on the right rudder and the right brake to increase the turn rate. The aircraft spun to the right, and the aircraft's nose was pointing in the opposite direction. We were still moving down the runway, but now we were traveling backward, so I added power with the throttles to stop the backward momentum. It worked! Finally, we stopped only a few feet from the runway's end.

# SKI BIRDS

## ADVENTURES OF THE RAVEN GANG

JOSEPH P. HATHAWAY
LIEUTENANT COLONEL USAF (RET.)

SOUTHWESTERN
LEGACY PRESS

PUBLISHERS ACKNOWLEDGMENTS:
Publishing and Design Services: Martin Publishing Services

LANDSAT Photo use permitted and courtesy of NASA and National Science Foundation
Skylark Photography – Gabriel Enders, Owner – Email: skylarkphotography518@gmail.com
Collaborator: Stan Corvin, Jr. – Author of *Vietnam Saga: Exploits of a Combat Helicopter Pilot*

ISBN: Paperback: 978-1-7366245-0-0, Hardback: 978-1-7366245-1-7,
eBook: 978-1-7366245-2-4

PUBLISHED BY: Southwestern Legacy Press, LLC
P.O. Box 1231
Gallatin, TN 37066
Email: swlegacypress@gmail.com

Bulk Sales: Special discounts are available to civic groups, military and veterans' organizations, and others by contacting Southwestern Legacy Press, LLC at its email address shown above.

LIBRARY OF CONGRESS CATALOGING NUMBER (LCCN): 2021935666
LIBRARY CATALOGING:
Names: Hathaway, Joseph P. (Joseph Hathaway)
*"Skibirds: Adventures of the Raven Gang"*
454 pages, 23cm × 15cm (9in. × 6 in.)
DESCRIPTION: Written by Lt. Col. Joseph P. Hathaway USAF (Ret.), "Skibirds: Adventures of the Raven Gang" is the fascinating history and story of the 109th Airlift Wing, a unit of the New York Air National Guard, stationed at Stratton Air National Guard Base, Schenectady, New York.
The wing's mission is to provide airlift support to the National Science Foundation's Arctic Circle and South Pole research program. They fly LC-130H Hercules airlifters, equipped with wheel-ski landing gear, to their Arctic and Antarctica operations. The 109th Airlift Wing is the only unit in the world to fly these aircraft.
Using numerous anecdotal stories, the book tells of dangerous missions carrying civilian scientists, survival experts, and their equipment to some of the most remote locations in the Arctic and Antarctica. Frequently, unable to see the snowy "skiway" and landing on ski-equipped LC-130s, they fly inside what Lt. Col. Hathaway describes as the "ping-pong ball." It is a term he uses to describe the inability to tell the ground from the clouds when landing on the snowfield.
KEY TAG WORDS: 109th Airlift Wing, New York Air National Guard, Stratton Air National Guard Base, Schenectady, New York, LC-130H Hercules, National Science Foundation, Arctic Circle, Antarctica, McMurdo Station, Ross Ice Shelf, South Pole, Christchurch, New Zealand, Greenland, Polar Ice Caps.

# CONTENTS

## *Publisher's Notice*

Extensive effort has been made to obtain name and image release forms from everybody mentioned in this book; however, some people have been impossible to locate, and a few refused to sign the form. Therefore, those individuals' names have been changed, are fictitious, and are not included in the index.

—Southwestern Legacy Press, LLC

## DEDICATION

This book is for all the men and women who flew
and maintained the LC-130 airplanes through the years.
I salute your dedication and magnificent efforts
to overcome the unique challenges of
the Arctic and Antarctica.

—Joe Hathaway

# THANKS

All our stories will be forgotten over time without a written record of them. I owe a great deal of thanks to the Raven Gang, past and present. In some cases, I wish I had more details for the stories, but some memories are no longer accessible. They are gone forever.

There are also many people whose stories are not in this book. I want to thank some of them here. Tracking people down through the decades has been a challenge, especially the maintenance people. I owe a great deal of thanks to retired Brigadier General Ed Kinowski, retired Chief Master Sergeant Charlie Del Toro, and Master Sergeant Joe Archambeault. Ms. Colleen Connor and retired Senior Master Sergeant John Panoski, Sr. helped me find aircrew members from the past.

Senior Master Sergeant Willie Gizara played a big part by converting many people's old photos and videos from the 1980s into a digital format. And he allowed me to spend countless hours in his 109th Airlift Wing audiovisual office, digging through historical records to find information for these stories.

Thank you, Frank Mendicino, for reviewing the Navy chapters. I appreciate all of you sending me pictures.

I owe a great deal of thanks to CW-2 Cecil C. Hathaway, U.S. Army (Ret.), and his wife Mary, my parents for their love, generosity, and direction through the years. Instead of enlisting in the U.S. Army, like my father, I became an officer and a pilot in the U.S. Air Force.

Kathy Mitchell, big sister, thank you for your wisdom in explaining how to self-publish. Stan Corvin, Jr., I can't thank you enough for editing, publishing, and publicizing the book. I've learned a lot from you. Melinda Martin, you have done a wonderful job on the design of the book and its cover, thank you. Dan Hankiewicz, thank you for narrating the audiobook.

Finally—most of all—thank you, Marlene.

—Joseph P. Hathaway
Lt. Col. USAF (Ret.)

# PROLOGUE

Have you ever wondered how scientists travel to Antarctica or Greenland? How they got their science projects to the ice cap? How they came back home? The New York Air National Guard's 109th Airlift Wing "Raven Gang" aircrews fly to Greenland and Antarctica in their LC-130 aircraft and support the National Science Foundation. They are the scientists' primary means of transportation and are the only squadron in the world that flies the large Lockheed Martin four-engine turboprop aircraft with ski-equipped landing gear.

The intent of this book is to explain their missions, describe their airplanes, and tell of the other squadrons that flew alongside them. I use short stories to explain the details and challenges of the ski mission. In most cases, a foreword to the short story is the prior chapter. This foreword is a history or explanation of the short story that follows. The story may be written chronologically or adapted to more of a narrative storyline.

I begin the book with a brief mission history and its purpose. Following World War II, the United States needed to respond to the Soviet Union's nuclear bomb testing. However, the short story that follows does not follow the format of the rest of the book, as I described above. Instead, I explain the phenomenon called flying "inside the ping-pong ball." It is told as a conversation between two pilots, and I frequently refer to this strange phenomenon throughout the book.

The ski missions won't continue forever. The aircraft are old, and there are efforts within the Department of Defense to restructure the ski missions, perhaps with different aircraft. The Raven Gang's unique story, and the others that flew these incredible aircraft, needs to be written before they are forgotten. So, I've accepted the challenge to write their history and many of their stories before the aircrews "Fly West" one last time, and the memory of these events is lost forever.

Finally, this book's writing has been the culmination of many years of research as I endeavored to document The New York Air National Guard, 109th Airlift Wing, "Raven Gang's" remarkable history.

# INTRODUCTION

## The Raven Gang

Once a year in Valatie, New York, a small group of old aviators converge to relive old stories. Many are in their 80s now; most are in their late 70s, several are in their 60s. I'm a new addition. I'm in my late 50s. No one understands our stories but us. We are the retired aircrew members of the Raven Gang.

Many of the experiences of the 1980s on the Greenland ice cap preceded me. I joined the Raven Gang in February 1996. So, I listen to the challenging, often harrowing, tales of these people and laugh. The gathering is all about laughter. Old conflicts arise when emotions are stirred, but it's fleeting.

The flying organization these people created is unique, and it's an honor to be among their ranks. There is no flying organization that can compete with their illustrious history. But there is no one to tell their story. Families don't understand. We share our stories, but they're often incomprehensible to them. Years are spent learning to fly. The military has a language of its own; usually, it's a bunch of acronyms. But the ice cap has a life of its own.

The ice cap tells you what you need to know. The snow, sunlight, sun angle, cloud cover, wind, elevation, and temperature, tell you everything you need to succeed on the ice cap. Interpreting what it has to say is the challenge.

The culture these aviators created was one of excellence. The lessons they learned were passed to the next generation of ski mission aviators. Mistakes have rarely been repeated through the years. Not everyone that came through the doors of the Raven Gang's squadron stayed. A group of ravens is appropriately called an unkindness. It's a fitting term for these aviators. They are harsh in their criticism but laugh at the bar at the end of the day.

# Air National Guard

For those unfamiliar with the National Guard, they are a state governor's military arm. The governor is their commander and chief. In times of need, the governor loans these people to the federal government.

After World War II, the United States Air Force became a separate branch of the military, and the Air National Guard became an independent branch of each states' military. In 1948, Schenectady's 139th Fighter Squadron became one of the country's original Air National Guard units. For a dozen years, they were fighter pilots who flew P-47 Thunderbolts, then P-51D Mustangs, F-94B Starfires, and F-86H Sabers.[1]

In 1960 they received their first C-97 Stratofreighter. This was a significant change. No longer fighter pilots, they moved cargo and had enlisted aircrew members. In 1961, Nelson Rockefeller, the governor of New York, allowed his Air National Guard unit at Schenectady to be federalized to support the Berlin Crisis. For the next year, these C-97 aircrews flew around the world and delivered people and cargo where needed.

In March of 1971, the C-97s were replaced with old C-130A Hercules aircraft. The aircrews became experts in these aircraft. In 1975 they got the C-130D model. These were similar to the C-130A aircraft, but their landing gear were equipped with skis. Their mission was to support the distant early warning sites on the Greenland ice cap. This ended in 1989, and the flying squadron took over the Operation Deep Freeze mission from the Navy in 1996, which supported the National Science Foundation.

Most of the people in an Air National Guard unit are from local communities. Frequently, they returned to their hometown after serving in the active-duty military and joined their local guard unit. Many others are young people working in the shop next door. They joined their local guard unit to fly airplanes or work on them, or because they wanted to serve their country, state, and their community.

Many early Skibird aircrew members and maintenance people in the Schenectady Guard unit grew up on farms. It was a perfect complement for this unique mission. Repairing aircraft in an open snowfield was different than fixing a tractor in a cornfield. Still, there were enough similarities for these farmers to adjust or adapt to the environment. Both challenges required common sense and a little know-how.

CHAPTER 1

# DEW LINE MISSION

The Soviet Union first tested an atomic bomb in 1949. In response, the United States reassessed their air defenses and realized they needed an early warning system for Soviet bombers flying over the Arctic. Construction of a line of distance early warning stations, DEW stations[2], or the DEW line was built from western Alaska across Canada's northern frontier. On 13 August 1957, the DEW line became operational.

These DEW stations and other stations along the Aleutian Island Chain were equipped with a Raytheon AN/FPS-19 radar having a range of about one hundred and sixty nautical miles. Each station was located so that the radar from stations on either side could still provide complete coverage if any site went down. In other words, every second site could be down, and the northern frontier would still be covered.[3]

On 20 March 1958, Denmark agreed to extend the DEW line across Greenland. This allowed the United States to construct four additional radar sites across Greenland, and a fifth in Keflavik, Iceland. The United Kingdom picked up the radar surveillance from Iceland to the British Isles. The DEW line stations were organized in groups of four or five stations and given a call sign. The group extending across Greenland and Iceland was given the call sign "DYE" after the primary station located at Cape Dyer on the eastern tip of Baffin Island, Canada. The DYE stations closed the radar coverage gaps across the Davis Strait, Greenland's ice cap, and the Denmark Strait.

By the end of 1959, DYE-1, DYE-4, and DYE-5 were completed; however, the building of DYE-2 and DYE-3 on the Greenland ice cap posed unique challenges. Massive single structures were designed in place of the multiple buildings at other DEW stations. They would serve as the workstations and living quarters for those employed there.[4]

DYE-1 was located in Sisimiut, on the west coast of Greenland. Its tactical call sign was "Red River." Its coordinates were North 66°38' West 52°51'. Its elevation was 4,789 feet. DYE-2 was built approximately one hundred miles east of Sondrestrom Air Base on the Greenland ice cap. Its tactical call sign was "Sea Bass." Its coordinates were North 66°29' West 46°18'. Its elevation was 7,650 feet. DYE-3 was approximately one hundred miles east of DYE-2. Its tactical call sign was "Sob Story." Its coordinates were North 65°11' West 43°50'. Its elevation was 8,700 feet. DYE-4 was located at Kulusuk Island, on the west coast of Greenland. Its tactical call sign was "Big Gun." Its coordinates were North 65°32' West 37°10'. Its elevation was 1,000 feet. DYE-5 was at Rockville Station near Keflavik, Iceland. Its coordinates were North 64°02' West 22°39'.

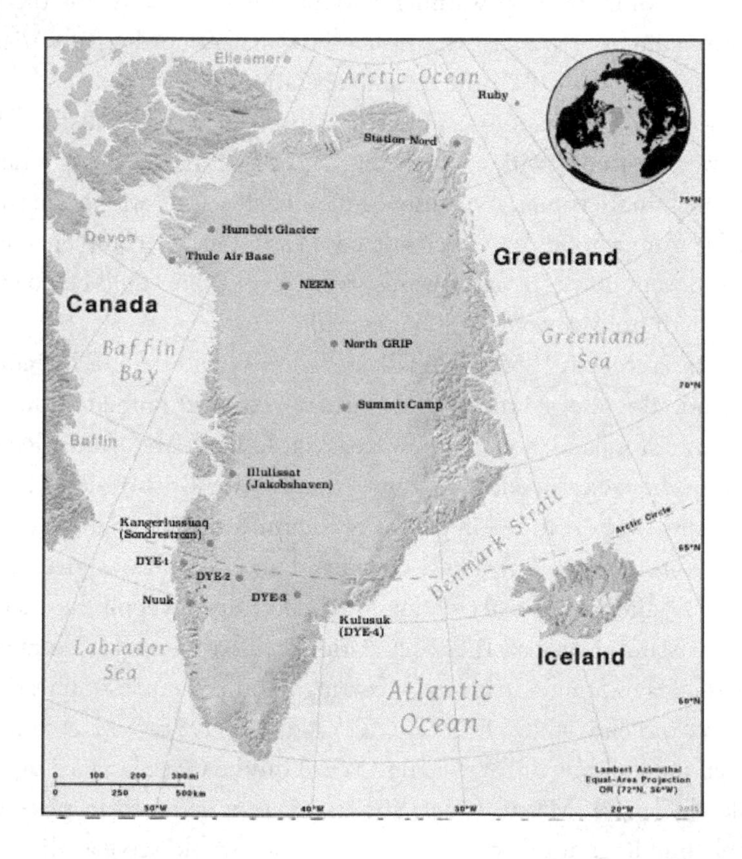


*Greenland Map (Approximate Locations)*

# 61st Troop Carrier Squadron

Initially, Douglas C-47 Skytrains, then Fairchild C-123 Provider aircraft, both equipped with skis, were used to fly equipment and material to the Greenland ice cap's DEW locations, but they proved inadequate. Larger aircraft were needed. Lockheed Corporation designed and built a multi-engine turboprop airplane called the Hercules that fulfilled the need. This aircraft was called the C-130D. It was the original C-130A model, with skis. Later models of the ski-equipped C-130 would be designated as the LC-130.

The first C-130 with skis was tail number 55-0021. On 29 January 1957, its initial flight was piloted by Lockheed's chief engineering test pilot. It was a quick flight around the local Marietta, Georgia, area. In February, ski landing tests took place in Bemidji, Minnesota. The test project was called Task Force Slide. Results of the initial tests showed modifications to the skis were required. Once the changes were made, the aircraft was turned over to the Air Force's Wright Air Development Center who scheduled more testing during the next snow season. The results of these tests determined the standard design for the C-130D skis.[5] Tail number 55-0021 eventually had its skis removed and was given to the Navy.

Twelve aircraft, tail numbers 57-0484 through 57-0495, were modified with skis and delivered to the 61st Troop Carrier Squadron at Sewart Air Force Base in Smyrna, Tennessee.[6] They went to Bemidji, Minnesota, for five weeks in February and March 1959 for intensive training on operating in Arctic conditions. Each aircrew accomplished five ski landings to familiarize themselves with radar approaches and cold weather survival school.[7]

On 19 March 1959, the 61st Troop Carrier Squadron deployed to Sondrestrom Air Base, Greenland. For the next two years, they flew to the ice cap and delivered construction materials to build DYE-2 and DYE-3. Steel beams were fabricated in the United States and shipped to a port, loaded on ships, and sailed to Greenland. When they arrived at Sondrestrom, they were loaded on the C-130Ds and flown to the ice cap. The flying squadron had many challenges ahead.

During the first two weeks, several aircraft were seriously damaged by rough landings on the ice cap. Something needed to be done to mitigate the damage on future flights. The obvious answer was to try to prepare a smoother surface upon which the aircraft could land. Until then, all landings were conducted in the open snowfield. Before the next flight, a "skiway" 6,000 feet long and 200 feet wide was groomed at each location. Flights immediately became more reliable.[8]

## The Firebirds

On 1 October 1960, these specialized aircraft were transferred to the17th Troop Carrier Squadron in Dyess Air Force Base in Abilene, Texas. For the next fifteen years, their mission was an annual fuel resupply mission to the DYE sites between April and May.[9] The Air Force saw no need to keep twelve C-130Ds. In 1962, six of these aircraft had their skis removed, tail numbers 57-0484 through 57-0489. These aircraft were re-designated, C-130D-6 models.

On 1 April 1964, the 17th Troop Carrier Squadron transferred from Texas to Elmendorf Air Force Base in Anchorage, Alaska.[10] The Inuit people of Greenland were the first to give them their name. They called the aircraft "Firebirds" because of the extra flames and smoke produced when they lit off the assisted takeoff bottles called ATO. The aircrews adopted the name.

*Firebird at DYE site*

For the next ten years, aside from the annual refueling missions from April through May and the infrequent movement of construction materials, the Firebirds maintained at least two aircraft and aircrews at Sondrestrom for two-week tours throughout the year.[11] Their purpose was to be available in case of an emergency at one of the DYE sites. The flying was very limited, and the aircrews had difficulty maintaining proficiency in the ski mission. They damaged several aircraft, but the maintenance teams were outstanding and could always bring the aircraft home until 5 June 1972.

At 6:55 a.m., aircraft 57-0495, "Frozen Assets," stalled while landing at DYE-3 during a routine supply flight.[12] The copilot was flying the aircraft. An instructor pilot in the left seat was giving him instruction. The copilot followed the landing approach guidance from the navigator. On final approach at DYE-3, he zig-zagged through the centerline to align the aircraft with the skiway for landing. On short final, he slowed the aircraft to 102 knots, his target runway threshold crossing speed. At about fifty feet off the snow, he was right of course. He used his left rudder to correct to the centerline, putting the aircraft in a right sideslip.[13]

Their altitude was low. The instructor pilot didn't think the copilot had time to correct the situation, so he ordered a go-around. A go-around required the copilot immediately to add power and start a climb to a higher altitude and start the approach again. It was a routine call, but the copilot added power before taking his foot off the rudder pedal, which sealed their fate.[14]

The pilots lost control of the rudder. The high-power setting at the slow airspeed locked the rudder in a right sideslip. It seemed counter-intuitive to reduce the engine's power, but this was the only thing they could have done to regain control of the aircraft. The locked rudder condition was known as a rudder fin stall. The flight engineer yelled, "Ninety knots." The aircraft stalled soon after that and fell out of the air. There was extensive damage upon impact with the snow, and the navigator was injured. The #2 propeller was torn from the engine on impact and ripped through the aircraft cargo compartment, severely injuring a passenger sitting in the back. He died a few hours later.

The Firebirds kept an aircrew on alert status at Elmendorf Air Force Base. Captain Graham Pritchard received a phone call while he was sitting at home. *"There's been an accident in Greenland. Pack your bags; you are leaving for Sondy in two hours."* Pritchard and his aircrew flew aircraft 57-0486 out of Elmendorf on 6 June 1972. Also on board was a hastily appointed accident investigation team. The weather was bad at Sondrestrom upon their arrival, so Pritchard diverted to Thule, two hours north. The following day they flew to Sondrestrom.

On 8 June 1972, the accident investigation team flew to DYE-3.[15] The aircraft was in pieces and beyond recovery. All four props were sheared off. The landing gear and skis, both pylon tanks, and the number one engine were torn from the aircraft by the impact. Twelve feet of the left wing and six feet of the right wing were sheared off from the airplane. The remainder of the left wing and the number two engine were destroyed by fire. The left side of the fuselage from the wing's leading edge to the left paratroop door was severely burned. The fuselage skin aft of the paratroop door to the horizontal stabilizer's leading edge was also burned. The tail assembly had rotated. The cargo of steel beams damaged the interior of the cargo compartment.[16] Pritchard's first impression when he arrived at DYE-3 and saw aircraft 57-0495 was, *"It's one sad-looking skibird on the icecap that would never fly again."* Valuable components were salvaged before an Air Force demolition team destroyed the remains of the aircraft.[17]

*Raven 95 Buried at DYE-3, 1972*

The Firebirds' Sondrestrom Daily Log, on 18 July 1972, noted:

> *"70495 has been burned, and remains were dragged to DYE site dump. Pieces of engines were pushed into the hole created from burning fuel and covered with snow. Salvage team ready to return to Sondy. Will pick team up tomorrow."*[18]

The remains of the aircraft were eventually covered by blowing snow.

The following year, the Air Force began considering replacing the Firebirds' two-week rotations with a civilian carrier. Greenlandair was contracted for one year, and they subcontracted Bradley Air Service, located at Carp, Ontario, Canada. They operated and maintained ski-equipped De Havilland Twin Otter aircraft or DHC-6s.

The test was successful, with one exception. DYE-3's elevation was 8,700 feet. If a fully loaded Twin Otter lost an engine, the maximum altitude it could reach was 9,500 feet. According to international flight rules, the minimum instrument en route altitude over DYE-3 was 10,200 feet; 1,500 feet above the surface. Danish Civil Aviation Authority controlled the airspace over Greenland, and they considered the 700-foot discrepancy a minor issue and granted them a waiver. The Twin Otters took over the emergency standby mission.

The end of the Alaskan Skibird mission was approaching. The only use for the C-130Ds was the annual April through May fuel resupply mission for DYE-2 and DYE-3. The Firebirds also supported the Alaskan DEW stations. These sites had gravel airstrips that damaged the bottom of the C-130D's skis, so only the C-130D-6s, the wheeled aircraft, were used.

The coup-de-grace came when the Air Force ordered ten new C-130E aircraft. These aircraft would resupply the DEW line sites in Alaska; however, none of them had skis. The Air Force transferred Alaska's remaining five C-130Ds and six C-130D-6s to the Air National Guard. The C-130D ski mission only required limited springtime support. The Air Force determined a part-time Guard unit would serve the mission's purpose more effectively.

CHAPTER 2

# PROFESSIONAL VIRTUE

*Author's Note: The following story isn't about the Raven Gang, but I want to describe a unique weather phenomenon. There are insidious and dangerous challenges on the ice cap. Flying inside the ping-pong ball is one of the most challenging. In Antarctica, there is still a crashed Twin Otter aircraft on the side of a mountain. There was an investigation with no clear answers about what happened, but it presented some interesting speculation.*[19] *The investigators' believed the pilot flew into clouds and turned into a mountain. But I'm not satisfied with this explanation.*

It's tragic. I never knew the pilot. I don't even know his name. Perhaps I saw him and gave him a nod as we passed on the aircraft parking ramp. Maybe we sat in the dining hall and shared a meal. We shared a similar life and many of the same challenges.

Antoine de Saint-Exupery described the work of the professional pilot as the following:

> *"There exists a quality which is nameless. It may be gravity, but the word does not satisfy me, for the quality I have in mind can be accompanied by the most cheerful gaiety. It is the* quality *of the carpenter face to face with his block of wood. He handles it, he takes its measure. Far from treating it frivolously, he summons up all his professional virtues to do it honor."*[20]

I believe the Twin Otter pilot was a professional, and below is my interpretation of what occurred.

# Inside the Ping-Pong Ball

**Cynic:** "Why did a pilot with 22,000 flight hours fly into the side of a mountain in VMC (Visual Meteorological Conditions) weather in the middle of the day? It's inconceivable. Perhaps his home life was falling apart. Perhaps he just found out he had a terminal illness. Perhaps if we could look into his psyche, we could find the answer."

**Ski Pilot:** "No, he wasn't suicidal. He was a pilot doing his life's work. He was doing what he loved to do. We can speculate on these other things, but there is one unusual factor that sets this mishap apart from many others; he was flying in Antarctica. He had flown the route from the South Pole to Terra Nova Bay multiple times over the years, but this didn't give him everything he needed to know."

**Cynic:** "Need to know? The man had 22,000 flight hours. After that many flying hours, what could he possibly learn? He had flown to locations all around the world. He had flown in Greenland. He'd been going to Antarctica for eight years. He's been challenged with emergencies, some unique. He's instructed scores of pilots throughout his illustrious career. He was the best of the best."

**Ski Pilot:** "Listen, I get it. I understand your exasperation. I understand why you're questioning this. But Antarctica's a special place. Perhaps he didn't see the mountain."

**Cynic:** "Ha-ha, you're joking. How could he possibly have missed it? This is a joke, right? It was the middle of the day. VMC means visual meteorological conditions. It was a beautiful day. He had a 13,000-foot cloud ceiling and good visibility throughout his route of flight. If he hit bad weather, he would have turned around. He reported in forty minutes before the crash. Everything was normal. The man knew his job. He was a professional. He had to see the mountain unless you're speculating he was asleep—but he wasn't asleep. I know because I read the transcripts of the investigation. He turned into the mountain. Unless you think the copilot was suicidal, and he did it while the pilot was asleep."

**Ski Pilot:** "No, I don't think the copilot was suicidal, nor do I think the pilot was asleep. The crew did their job just as they did every day. They were flying down the Beardmore Glacier in the Trans-Antarctic Mountains. The mountain tops are up to 14,000 feet high. He had options. Perhaps he was trying to pop over the mountain, but he didn't have the climb performance to make it over the top. But he wouldn't have done this. As you stated, the man was a professional and knew his job. He had been flying the same type of aircraft for over twenty years. He knew the performance of the airplane. He would have known whether he was going to make it or not. No, the pilot needed to continue down the glacier until the end, then make a left turn to get to his destination. But he turned early. He didn't see the mountain."

**Cynic:** "Ridiculous. I told you it was a beautiful VMC day, perfect for flying. The pilot wasn't blind. Are you suggesting the mountain just popped up in front of him? Is Antarctica a fairyland where mountains just pop up in front of you? You're speaking nonsense."

**Ski Pilot:** "Let me explain. There are documented cases of pilots flying their airplanes into the ocean on a beautiful moonless, VMC evening. The skies were clear, and the winds were light. At first, investigators couldn't understand it. They asked the same questions you're asking. Suicide? Incompetence? There are easier ways to kill yourself than to take an aircraft into the air, with another pilot on board who could defeat your purpose of crashing into a mountain or the ocean. It wasn't suicide. Investigators figured it out. Flying a few hundred feet over the ocean on a clear, beautiful, moonless evening can give you some very unusual sensations. The stars are wondrous. You get lost looking into the sky. And that is why they crashed."

**Cynic:** "Wait…hold on…they were looking at the stars, so they died. Is that what you're saying?"

**Ski Pilot:** "Yes. The stars were reflecting off the ocean. There were no waves on the water. The reflection looked the same as the stars. It was a beautiful evening. It was VMC weather. But the pilot couldn't tell the difference between the water and the sky. He could see it all. He wasn't blind. But it all blended together. Sit down in a room someday. Turn out the lights. Remove as many sensory inputs as possible. Close your eyes and imagine floating in your tube with wings, hundreds of feet over the ocean. The stars are shining off the ocean waters. If you were upside down, could you tell the difference? Gravity will push you down, but gravity doesn't give you any sensation on your way down. The only sensation you'll feel is when you hit bottom. And if you're falling from several hundred feet, you probably won't have time to feel the sensation before you die. You'll never know what happened."

**Cynic:** "Okay. I can almost imagine that. But it's morbid. I don't like to think about crashing. I'm a better pilot than that. And it certainly doesn't explain why a 22,000-hour pilot didn't see the mountain."

**Ski Pilot:** "Okay. I concede. He did see the mountain. He just couldn't differentiate the mountain from the sky. He was flying inside the ping-pong ball."

**Cynic:** "Inside the ping-pong ball?"

**Ski Pilot:** "Let me start from the beginning. Before takeoff from the South Pole, a 9,300-foot field elevation, the aircrew pre-flighted their aircraft. There's no evidence to suggest they were aware of the failure of their cockpit voice recorder. They knew a terrain warning system was not required under existing regulations because they weren't flying passengers. They had one, and it was capable of looking forward along the aircraft's flight path relative to the terrain database to provide an alert. But, the instrument's database didn't cover Antarctica. It didn't cover terrain below seventy degrees south latitude. However, they did have an aircraft warning system capable of visual warnings concerning terrain proximity. They had functioning oxygen available if they needed it. The airplane's status was acceptable, per all existing regulations. The weather was forecast to be VMC over the route of their flight for the duration of their flight. Once airborne, they flew over the ice cap at 11,000 feet for at least an hour. The Antarctica ice cap landscape is featureless. If there was a solid cloud deck above, it would be difficult to differentiate between the sky and the surface. Everything would be a dull white color. Everything would blend together. They would be flying 'inside the ping-pong ball.' After an hour of flying, they arrived at the Trans-Antarctica

Mountain Range. They reported in with the South Pole to let them know operations were normal. At the Trans-Antarctica Mountain Range, they proceeded down the Beardmore Glacier, which took them right of course. Do we disagree on any of these points?"

**Cynic:** "No. Go ahead."

**Ski Pilot:** "Beardmore Glacier is several miles wide. It is a frozen river that flows very slowly. The source of this river is the Antarctica ice cap that spills through the mountain valleys. The top of the river begins at about 9,000 feet and flows down to the Ross Ice Shelf, near sea level. The length of the Beardmore Glacier is one hundred miles or more. When they arrived at the mountains, they weren't high enough to clear the terrain. They could have gone on oxygen and climbed into the clouds to clear the mountains, but that wasn't their intention. They wanted to stay in visual conditions. They planned to fly down the Beardmore Glacier. At the end of the glacier, they intended to make a slight left-turn course correction and continue directly to their destination, Terra Nova Bay Camp.

*Approaching Beardmore Glacier, Over Transantarctic Mountains*

"The Beardmore Glacier flows through the Trans-Antarctica Mountains that rise above 14,000 feet in some locations, specifically Mount Elizabeth.

The investigators believe the cloud ceilings were about 13,000 feet; therefore, the pilots couldn't see the mountain's top. There were no reflections from the sun on the ice below. There were no shadows because, again, the sun was hidden above the cloud deck. There was no discernable horizon. Looking down the glacier, the crew couldn't tell the sky from the ground. But they knew they were at 11,000 feet, and they knew the ground was falling away into the Ross Ice Shelf. They were in VMC weather conditions. When they started down the glacier, they were about three hours from their destination.

"Beneath the Antarctica ice cap, the snow has accumulated high enough to bury mountains. But it hasn't happened yet in the Beardmore. However, over many years, snow accumulated on the bottom of the mountains and built up thicker on the sides, and hid the terrain features. Without direct sunlight, there are no shadows. It becomes very hard or impossible to discern the sky from the surface of the glacier or mountains. Have you seen a picture of Mount Elizabeth? Snow rises along the side of the mountain above 13,000 feet.

"As they started down the glacier, they would have lost sensory input, much like they did when they were flying over the ice cap. By now, they were clearly inside the ping-pong ball. The investigators reconstructed the aircraft's track. It shows the pilot was cheating left, closer toward the mountains. I suspect he was edgy. He wanted to find land features to provide him some comfort. He had been flying for twenty minutes down the glacier and couldn't see anything, but he knew he was still clear of the clouds. He had probably seen these conditions before, but he had not seen it hide the mountains."

**Cynic:** "Reconstructed weather models suggest he was in the clouds. After the crash, an LC-130 search and rescue aircraft flew over the vicinity of Mount Elizabeth. There was a solid cloud deck with tops at approximately 16,000 feet. High winds over the mountains would have created mountain wave turbulence. He was desperate, so he tried to pop over the ridgeline."

**Ski Pilot:** "I knew you'd eventually question his judgment. Think about it. I don't have half as many hours as he had. You have fewer hours than me. Even with the hours we have, we are considered old by our peers, and we are too experienced to do something like that. He was ancient by our standards.

He wouldn't do it. He had been flying the aircraft for over twenty years. He knew his aircraft's performance capabilities. He wouldn't just try to pop over the ridge and hope for the best. No, he was a humble man in the aircraft. Time had done it to him. Perhaps he was reckless in his youth, but, by now, he had seen too much. He had seen friends, or at least they were peers, die; others were injured, and others were just damn lucky and walked away from the flying profession. He had experienced the inexplicable and the indescribable. Every day he walked to the aircraft, he thought of his mortality. And every time he sat in the aircraft, a peacefulness would settle in his soul. He was home."

**Cynic:** "You talk like you knew him."

**Ski Pilot:** "I know his soul."

**Cynic:** "Mumbo-jumbo crap. Is that your explanation?"

**Ski Pilot:** "No, let me finish. He wasn't in the clouds. He had too much experience; he was too old, he had too much respect for his profession to do something that sophomoric. You suggest he flew into a cloud then turned into a mountain. That sounds ridiculous to me. The LC-130 aircraft reported turbulence in the area after the ancient one's aircraft disappeared. This aircraft is much larger than the ancient one's aircraft. If the turbulence was bouncing around the larger aircraft, the ancient one's smaller aircraft would have really been rocking around.

"The bumps due to turbulence would affect his inner ear, but there wouldn't be coinciding visual cues inside the ping-pong ball. This may have made him nauseous or at least uncomfortable, but it wouldn't make him reckless. Mount Elizabeth is at the end of the Beardmore Glacier. It may have blocked the high winds as he approached it. Perhaps he interpreted the smooth air as passing beyond the glacier and over the Ross Ice Shelf. This is speculation, though. The LC-130 flew over their location five hours later. Anyone flying in Antarctica knows how rapidly the weather changes."

**Cynic:** "All you are offering is speculation."

**Ski Pilot:** "No one knows what really happened. Here are the facts. The aircraft was most of the way down the glacier. The aircraft's turn in the final minutes would have led directly to his destination, but he wasn't clear of Mount Elizabeth. This suggests to me he was clear of clouds and thought he was clear of the mountain.

"No performance anomalies were indicated with the aircraft or the GPS, which was accurate to within ten feet. At forty-five seconds before the impact, the pilot began a climb. His terrain advisory system was probably giving him visual cautionary advisories. Aircraft performance would have allowed an estimated 700-feet-per-minute climb. I don't believe the pilot understood his situation. He didn't understand the effects of the ping-pong ball anomaly. He couldn't see any terrain in front of him. He thought he was over the Ross Ice Shelf. Without question, with forty-five seconds remaining, he had options. He could believe what he saw and continue forward, he could turn away and spiral up into the clouds and then press on to his destination, or he could turn back to the South Pole. He believed what he saw, and Antarctica killed him."

*Ping Pong Effect (Skylark Photography)*

CHAPTER 3

# DYE SITES

Colonel Stanley Hemstreet wondered whether his quiet little Air National Guard unit would remain open following the Vietnam War. He knew the United States Congress would draw down its military forces and reduce the size and numbers of bases.[21] He knew his base would be on the chopping block through the Base Realignment and Closure (BRAC) process. Nothing set them apart from the rest.

In the early 1970s, New York State had two active duty Air Force bases, Griffiss and Plattsburg; five Air National Guard bases, Niagara Falls, Schenectady, White Plains, Syracuse, and Westhampton; the Northeast Air Defense Sector; and Air Force Reserve units.

Hemstreet's 109th Tactical Air Group had twelve-year-old C-130A model aircraft located at Schenectady County Airport, in Upstate New York. In 1974, the New York State National Guard's Adjutant General asked Hemstreet if he wanted to take over the active-duty Air Force's ski mission. Hemstreet jumped at the opportunity.

At first, he didn't understand. Hemstreet thought he was being offered new C-130E station keeping equipment, SKE, aircraft.[22] SKE allowed aircraft to maintain formation with other SKE-equipped aircraft while in poor weather conditions. Getting new aircraft was a signal his base would remain open during the draw-down.

The Adjutant General clarified he was offering Hemstreet the ski mission, not the SKE mission, with 1957 vintage C-130D model aircraft, which were C-130A's with skis. Hemstreet knew he couldn't say no. His airbase was being offered a lifeline to remain open. Rejecting the general's offer risked no longer receiving support from him in the future.

Hemstreet agreed to take the mission, but he still needed to go to the National Guard Bureau in Washington D.C. to secure it. It was a formality. There were many benefits to moving the Greenland ice cap resupply mission to Schenectady. Location was perhaps the biggest one. Schenectady was only a six-hour flight to Sondrestrom Air Base in Greenland.

*Schenectady Guard Ramp, circa 1971*

In 1975, the 109th Tactical Airlift Group's C-130A aircraft were transferred to other bases around the country, and five C-130D and six C-130D-6 aircraft were transferred to Schenectady County Airport. The six C-130A aircraft at Schenectady were transferred to different locations. One went to Oklahoma, three went to Nashville, one went to Memphis, and one went to Martinsburg, West Virginia.

There would be a steep learning curve for the aircrews. Planes got banged up, and the maintenance people learned how to fix them. It took a commander like Hemstreet to understand his people were doing their best and things don't always go as smoothly as they wished. He held old school clearly defined principles. He believed that if you damaged an aircraft in your country's service, it was forgivable. The cost could top over a million dollars, but he always supported his aircrews as long as it was in the line of duty. However, cheat five dollars on your travel voucher, and you were fired.[23] Hemstreet led a highly experienced, flexible aircrew on the Greenland ice cap for the next ten years. This was the Golden Age of the 109th Tactical Airlift Group's ski mission.

## DYE-2 and DYE-3

A Metcalf & Eddy structural engineer designed the DYE-2 and DYE-3[24] radar stations. They were 3,300-ton, 126-foot-high buildings with a radar dome on top. They had 145,000 square feet of living, working, and storage space. There were five DYE sites, six including Cape Dyer, all equipped with a Bendix AN/FPS-30 radar, having a range of two hundred nautical miles with an overlapping capability in case one of the DYE sites went down.[25]

The DYE-2 and DYE-3 buildings were built around four large trusses suspended from eight metal columns, two per truss. Each column had a jacking system capable of raising the building higher to keep pace with the snow accumulation and the sinking of the building from its weight, melting the snow beneath each column, then refreezing, known as regelation.

At the base of each column, thirty feet below the snow surface, a steel and timber spread-footing was designed to distribute the weight of the heavy columns. Sub-surface trusses braced the columns so they wouldn't splay apart in the snow. The sub-surface steel trusses were isolated from the surrounding snow by timber and steel truss enclosures. If the snow backfilled around the sub-surface steel trusses, the Greenland ice cap would create gigantic stress-loads on this support system, and it would fail in short order. However, damage to the protective timber and steel truss enclosures was expected, and they could be repaired when necessary.

Construction of DYE-2 and DYE-3 stations was completed in mid-1960. Their elevations on the ice cap were about 7,650 feet and 8,700 feet, respectively. The U.S. Army Corps of Engineers, Cold Regions Research and Engineering Laboratory or CRREL, structural engineers were hired to monitor the multi-faceted series of stresses on the DYE sites' columns. These engineers determined measurement points on the buildings and installed equipment to monitor the DYE sites' sub-structure.

*DYE site*

Wayne Tobiasson, 6'10" and thin, was a fresh-out-of-college engineer-in-training when he first started work at DYE-2 and DYE-3. Over time he became a co-investigator of the DYE sites, and as the years went by, he became the sole principal investigator for CRREL in Hanover, New Hampshire. It became painfully evident to him that the "Greenland Icecap was not a harmless sleeping giant as it appeared to the casual observer, but rather a giant, moving in slow motion."[26]

Snow existed from the surface of the ice cap down to a depth greater than one hundred feet. As the snow's density increased below one hundred feet, it became, by definition, glacial ice to the bottom of the ice cap, thousands of feet below. As the DYE sites were raised, the sub-structure sank deeper in the snow.

DYE-2 and DYE-3 were designed to meet ten-year design life, but the Air Force wanted them to last longer, so CRREL and Metcalf & Eddy engineers worked together to develop solutions to extend the useful life of these DYE sites. This often proved quite difficult. The design of the truss enclosure was based on the principles of soil mechanics. Tobiasson determined the snow densified laterally and vertically on the truss-enclosure at twice the draw-down loads of those anticipated on the original design. He designed and installed a pressure plate to measure the lateral loads at depth.[27]

Tobiasson also found the snow's vertical draw-down loads on the truss enclosure were uneven. This caused the eight column-footings to tilt away from the center of the building and settle at different rates. The ice cap's downslope movement caused the squared array of footings to distort into a rhombus, causing secondary stresses to accumulate within this complex framework. To measure these secondary stresses and track their steady growth, CRREL developed instrumentation to monitor them.[28] Over the years, no steel beams of the main structure ever failed, some were overstressed, but they never failed.

## Changing of the Guard

When Tobiasson heard that the ski-equipped C-130s had been transferred to an Air National Guard unit at Schenectady County Airport, New York, he was deeply concerned. During the Cold War, failure to keep these overworked aircraft flying would impact the Western Hemisphere's air defense capability. He couldn't imagine these Air National Guard "weekend warriors" would be able to take over such a dangerous and challenging mission.

His concerns were short-lived. Colonel Stan Hemstreet had found out about CRREL's involvement with the ice cap stations. He contacted CRREL and asked for a contingent of structural engineers to come to Schenectady and brief his people on snow and ice, Greenland, and the DYE sites. Tobiasson thought, *"This was unusual. No other flying organization had ever expressed interest in what they were doing."*

The meeting was an eye-opener. Tobiasson realized this was a serious group of individuals seeking information. They wanted to undertake this unusual mission and do it well. In an Air National Guard unit, the same people would fly this mission for their whole career, spanning twenty to thirty years. Knowledge of the mission wouldn't be lost as aircrew members transferred to other organizations, as done in the active-duty Air Force. Throughout the visit, information was exchanged, and friendships began that lasted decades.

On Monday, 31 March 1975, the initial cadre of New York aircrews arrived in Sondrestrom aboard one of their C-130A aircraft to get familiar with the C-130Ds and get checked out in the ski mission. It was the Firebird's last resupply season. After they were qualified, several New York aircrews spent April and May flying with the Firebirds to get better acquainted with the aircraft and get more familiar with the ski mission. When the resupply was finished, the New York aircrews returned to Schenectady, and the Firebirds and their airplanes went back to Elmendorf Air Force Base.

Later in the summer, Schenectady aircrews picked up the five C-130D and six C-130D-6 aircraft from Alaska and flew them back to New York.[29]

| Transfer Dates | | | |
|---|---|---|---|
| Wheel-Birds | | Skibirds | |
| Tail Number | Date | Tail Number | Date |
| 57-0484 | 18 July 1975 | 57-0490 | 21 July 1975 |
| 57-0485 | 19 June 1975 | 57-0491 | 20 June 1975 |
| 57-0486 | 7 July 1975 | 57-0492 | 2 June 1975 |
| 57-0487 | 31 July 1975 | 57-0493 | 6 June 1975 |
| 57-0488 | 14 July 1975 | 57-0494 | 21 June 1975 |
| 57-0489 | 30 June 1975 | | |

# The Mission

The 109th Maintenance Squadron began work on the aircraft when they arrived. It took several years for the highly experienced maintenance team to repair many of the aircraft's nagging issues. Eventually, they returned these aircraft into a sustainable airlift support apparatus. The engine shop removed and rebuilt the engines and propellers. The engine harnesses were replaced. The skis and landing gear cylinders were overhauled and serviced.[30] The aircraft lasted another ten years.

Schenectady also inherited eight-hundred-gallon Benson fuel tanks, previously used on KC-97 aircraft. They needed to be refurbished. Four Benson tanks fit in the cargo compartment of the aircraft. A metal support structure was created to put two tanks on top of two others. They were welded together and designed to fill and empty in series, with a single tap to fill or empty all four tanks. A fuel hose was connected to a fuel truck or a storage tank outside the aircraft. It took about twenty minutes to fill or empty these tanks once they were hooked up.

*LC-130 Benson Tanks, Courtesy of Bill Heaphy*

From August through October of 1975, the Schenectady aircrews flew to Sondrestrom. The initial cadre of ski mission instructors qualified the rest of the squadron's aircrews. Each pilot watched the first landing, they flew the second landing, and the third landing qualified them as an instructor in the ski mission. The training was a bit of a farce, but it allowed the squadron to start the next resupply season with a fully qualified aircrew force. When April rolled around, the real training took place.

CHAPTER 4

# THE RAVEN GANG

In the Spring of 1976, the aircrews started their first season supporting the Greenland ice cap's DYE sites. As they walked around the local Sondrestrom Air Base area, they found the dump where the Air Force disposed of their out-of-date equipment and supplies. There, they found uses for much of the discarded equipment back in New York for their farms, businesses, and homes. They named their unit, The Raven Gang, after the birds they found scavenging and picking through the dump with them. A group of ravens is called an unkindness of ravens, and these New York aircrews were an independent-minded group of aviators that thrived in this unkind polar environment.

*Sondrestrom Air Base, circa 1985*

Anecdotally, there were times when these farmers knew more about the cargo they were flying around than the Air Force. Major Giles Wagoner's aircrew arrived at Sondrestrom with a D-8 bulldozer in the back of his aircraft. No one on the base knew how to operate it, and undoubtedly not well enough to drive it out of the aircraft except the pilot. Before becoming a Delta Airlines pilot, Wagoner worked his farm and had a small construction business. He was familiar with the bulldozer, so he climbed in the seat and drove it out.

By the end of May, the DYE sites needed enough fuel to last until the following April. The fuel arrived in Sondrestrom during the summer before the resupply season. Over the winter, it cooled. It needed to be cold so the ice cap didn't melt from beneath the fuel tanks and bladders. It was too dark to fly routine missions to the ice cap before April, and the fuel was too warm to deliver to the DYE sites in June. Therefore, they had two months to move about 650,000 gallons of fuel to DYE-2 and DYE-3—3,200 gallons at a time.

Sondrestrom Air Base's air traffic controller created an airspace corridor where the C-130D aircraft could fly unrestricted and without any delays. The corridor was two hundred fifty miles long and one hundred miles wide, extending from the surface to about 16,000 feet. Every day the mission commander assigned each aircrew a specific number of missions to complete. Four lines a day to DYE-2 was very reasonable. Three lines to DYE-3 took about the same amount of time. Their day started after an early breakfast and finished by happy hour.

Their success was noted in their local publication, "Transport Topics," in June 1976:

> *"The first contingent from the 109th TAG arrived in Sondrestrom on 10 Apr 76 to begin the POL Replenishment mission for the first time—at least our first time. The schedule that operations set was a tight one. It called for a start on 10 Apr and the finishing load on 22 May.*
>
> *"The mission was completed over two weeks early…by 6 May, the last of the 636,000 gallons of fuel had been ferried and placed in the under-snow tanks of DYE 2 and 3…377*

*flight hours were spent on the cap—an average of 9.9 sorties per flying day. In fact, one fine day, a total of eighteen sorties were flown; this will be considered a record until next year."*

The aircrews needed to average twenty-five flights a week for eight straight weeks. If the weather was perfect and the aircraft were healthy throughout the season, this was possible. However, this rarely worked out. Every week on the ice cap, aircrews pushed to complete as many missions as possible. There was never too much flying.

On a bad week, the mission was plagued with poor weather for days at a time, and sometimes aircraft broke. Often, aircraft repair parts were needed from Schenectady, which delayed the maintenance team's ability to repair the planes for the following day's mission. Therefore, very few missions would be completed during these weeks.

On good days when the weather cooperated, the Raven Gang averaged 6–8 lines a day, sometimes more. For example, between May 4–9, 1980, three aircrews flew thirty-nine missions to DYE-3 and ten missions to DYE-2. They didn't do more because the fuel truck at Sondrestrom stopped delivering fuel to the aircraft at 5:30 p.m.

Each season, over two hundred missions were flown, despite poor weather and broken aircraft. By the end of every May, they were completed. They turned this flying into a game. It was a race to the bar at the end of the day.

# Aircraft Problems

The Raven Gang was a Guard unit with fifteen volunteer aircrews who went to Greenland when their full-time job allowed. They were a collection of farmers, airline pilots, mechanics, businessmen, and other volunteers from around Schenectady, New York. Many of these aviators were veterans of the Vietnam War. The ski mission had many challenges ahead, but the Vietnam experience gave them insight into handling the unknown.

On 22 April 1980, Raven 90 took off from Sondrestrom Air Base, Greenland, transporting 3,200 gallons of fuel to DYE-2. As Captain Dennis

Zicha rotated the aircraft's nose off the surface of Runway 11, he noticed a loss of power. Senior Master Sergeant Warren Swatling, Zicha's flight engineer, noticed it too. Swatling was a previous crew chief. During the Vietnam war, he was in Japan, maintaining and repairing B-25 aircraft. He had a solid background in aircraft systems before he joined the Raven Gang's flight engineer section.

Swatling had leaned forward in his seat to push up the #1 throttle because the power looked low. As he did so, all four engines had an immediate torque loss. Zicha had no choice but to continue the takeoff while Swatling worked on the problem.

Seconds later, Swatling noticed the right center-wing overheat warning, and #4 generator failure lights had illuminated. He suspected there was a serious bleed air leak on the right wing, so he closed all four engine's bleed-air valves. Closing the valves blocked the 600° Fahrenheit bleed air from the aircraft engines to the wings' bleed air ducting.

Captain Will Merwin declared an emergency with Sondrestrom Tower, and he told the controller they were turning back to land at Sondrestrom. There could be no delay. Zicha made a 180° turn back to the field. He was thinking, *Gotta love that barn door rudder,* as he spun the aircraft around. He landed on Runway 29, stopped the aircraft on the runway, did an emergency shutdown of the engines, and his aircrew evacuated the aircraft. As Zicha exited the aircraft, he noticed the wing's leading edge, usually gray, was a sickly yellow color. That's when it hit him, and he was scared.

The maintenance guys towed the aircraft off the runway and inspected it. They found a six-inch rupture of the bleed air duct between #3 and #4 engines. There was severe structural damage to the wing's leading edge, and insulation burned off two electrical wire bundles. The center wing fuel tank, located immediately behind the bleed air duct, showed signs of structural failure, structural supports and panels were warped, and riveted joints were leaking fuel. Swatling's quick analysis and immediate response prevented an inflight explosion and probable loss of the aircraft and aircrew. Any hesitation would have been fatal.

A couple of years later, Captain Jon Adams had his own unique experience on the ice cap. He had five years of experience in the active-duty Air Force, including flying missions in Vietnam. He had been flying the ski mission for the last seven years. Recalling an adventure thirty-seven years later, he reflected:

> *"The lesson learned was every day, every mission held unknown challenges. I never figured out what I would do differently, and I was arguably at my peak performance."*

CHAPTER 5

# DYE LANDING SITES

Sunday, 12 September 1982, was a standard Greenland launch from Schenectady County Airport. Raven 94 departed at 9:00 a.m. for Goose Bay Air Base, Canada, with two aircrews and a maintenance team. They landed at Goose Bay at 1:20 p.m. local time. Goose Bay was a fuel stop before reaching their final destination. It was a three-hour and twenty-minute flight with a one-hour time zone difference between New York and Goose Bay. The aircraft was refueled, and they departed from Goose Bay at 2:45 p.m. for Sondrestrom Air Base, Greenland. They arrived at 7:35 p.m. local time, a three-hour and thirty-five-minute flight, and another one-hour time zone difference. The day of flying was uneventful.[31]

Many of the aircrew members were on the last weekly rotation to Sondrestrom, from 29 August to 3 September. The majority of these people had a full-time job around the Albany-Schenectady area, i.e., traditional guardsmen. Some of them had a full-time job at the airbase as federal civil servants, also known as federal air reserve technicians or technicians. And a few of them had no job aside from flying for the base, "guard bums." But they were all part-time guardsmen. Greenland was beautiful, the flying was challenging, and the pay was good, so they took time off from their full-time job whenever possible to fly the ski mission.

Major Tom Noel was the mission commander for the week. He had a thin frame and a big smile with a perfectly groomed head of red hair, going gray. He was a perfectionist. His primary mission for the week was to remove cargo from DYE-2. When the weather was poor, there were always secondary missions to DYE-3 or DYE-4 that needed to be completed. The Raven Gang was the only airlift unit in the world aside from the U.S. Navy's VXE-6 squadron capable of providing the immense amount of materials, tools, and provisions needed on top of the Greenland ice cap. Raven 91 and Raven 92 had remained in Sondrestrom from the previous Greenland rotation, so Noel had three aircraft for his two aircrews. Raven 92 and Raven 94 were the primary aircraft for the week. Raven 91 was a backup. Noel paired his aircrews and assigned them an aircraft for the week. A member of the mobility aerial port flight was acting as the second loadmaster on Raven 94's flight. He would fly along as a working passenger to help Senior Airman Ray Morgan throughout the week aboard Raven 94. Raven 92's second loadmaster was from the 137th Tactical Airlift Wing, Oklahoma Air National Guard.

With the week planned out, Noel had his administrative assistant prepare the flight orders for the morning's flights to the Greenland ice cap. He ensured flight plans were ready for the pilots' signature, any restrictions to the airfields were provided, and a weather forecast was ready when the aircrews arrived in the morning.

### DENNIS ZICHA'S STORY ABOUT A PRANK

Tom Noel was a special person. Zicha learned a lot from him, and they were close friends. They tried to fly together whenever they could. Noel was always up for an adventure of some sort and was curious about everything. He got it in his head that he wanted to visit the town of Holsteinsborg. He pestered everyone looking for someone to go with him, but nobody bit. A lot of people asked him, "How ya gonna get there?"

It's a generally accepted belief that all aircrews were, and are, rogues. They concocted a story, and Noel believed it. They told him there was a bus that went from Sondrestrom to Holsteinsborg a couple of times a week, and the pickup point was down by the port at the end of the road.

One fine day Noel's curiosity got the better of him, and off he went to the port to catch the bus to Holsteinsborg. He came back after more than four hours with a tale to tell. A few Danes were working at the port and got suspicious of the American hanging around there. They approached Noel and asked him what he was doing. When Noel told the Danes he was waiting for the bus to Holsteinsborg; they broke out in laughter.

There was a lot of laughter among the aircrews after Noel returned and told his story. There are very few roads in Greenland, the longest is about eleven miles, and none lead from Sondrestrom to Holsteinsborg more than eighty miles away. The prank has found many new aircrew members and maintenance folks at the bus stop through the years.

Since the original Holsteinsborg prank, the story has become more sophisticated. The Danish civilians at the hotel are aware of it and play a part in it now. Unsuspecting Americans can purchase tickets for the bus ride to Holsteinsborg when they check-in and get their room.[32]

Noel rarely got angry and loved a good prank. Through the years, he has been the instigator of his own pranks. Frequently, he had his copilots note the coordinates of dozens of the hundreds of icebergs while flying above them. He even created an iceberg reporting form to track their coordinates to file after a flight from Greenland. According to Noel, the form was sent to ships in the area to know of these hazards. In reality, no one else knew what the form was, and it was thrown in the garbage after each flight.

# Raven 92

On Monday, 13 September 1982, the forecasted weather for DYE-2 was poor. The winds were high, the cloud ceiling and visibility were low, so Noel turned his focus to DYE-3. Raven 94 was the first aircraft to go. Captain Rich Danzer and the rest of his aircrew walked to base operations, gathered their cold-weather gear, and prepared for the day ahead.

They flew to DYE-3 to give twenty passengers time to look around the site, and they returned to Sondrestrom later in the day. Master Sergeant Armand "Red" LaFerriere, Danzer's flight engineer, refueled the aircraft, and Ray Morgan loaded it full of cargo. They took off again, this time headed for Kulusuk, or DYE-4. The weather at Kulusuk was clear, and the winds were calm. Throughout their two-hour flight, they listened to radio traffic about Raven 92's difficulties at DYE-3. When they returned to Sondrestrom at 5:05 p.m. local time, they got the details.

Earlier in the day, Captain Jon Adams aircrew had flown a mission to DYE-3. Upon their return to Sondrestrom, the weather was beautiful, and the winds were forecast to be light, a gorgeous Greenland day. Master Sergeant Lou Ott, Adams' flight engineer, looked the aircraft over. After the fuel truck pulled away, Master Sergeant Dennis Morgan loaded twenty empty fifty-five-gallon drum barrels in the aircraft's cargo compartment.

Adams' second flight to DYE-3 was uneventful until landing. "Sob Story," the call sign for DYE-3, reported light winds. The approach was routine. Upon landing, a high gusty wind began to blow, and the aircraft pitched to the left. Adams was able to correct back to the centerline of the skiway by using the right rudder and differential power, adding more power to the engines on the left side of the aircraft than the right side.

As he slowed, the aircraft pitched to the left again, and things went squirrely. As he tried to correct back a second time, the aircraft drifted further to the right side of the skiway. The right ski slipped off the groomed firm surface of the skiway and dropped into the soft snow. The left wing rose, and the right wing dipped into the snow. The right pylon fuel tank, below the right wingtip, saved the aircraft from cartwheeling. The #4 propeller sheared off the engine. The aircraft swung uncontrollably to the right and departed the skiway. Ott reached forward and pulled all four condition levers to the full aft position, which feathered the propellers and shut down the engines. The #4 propeller came to rest on the snow, alone like a garden ornament.[33]

Raven 92 stopped 5,000 feet down the skiway and off the right side of Skiway 34, with the aircraft facing a 120-degree direction. The nose ski was cocked thirty degrees to the right when the aircraft came to a stop. No one was injured.

Dennis Morgan said, “I jumped out the right paratroop door, ran around the back of the aircraft, opened the crew entrance door, and Louie Ott met me at the door. He had sweat running off his nose.”

Adams made a radio call to Sob Story to let them know everyone was unharmed and asked the radio controller to notify Sondrestrom about what occurred. The aircrew collected their gear and went into the radar site. The aircraft needed to be repaired before they could leave. They stayed the night at DYE-3. When Tom Noel received the news from Sob Story, he contacted the Sondrestrom base commander and the Sondrestrom safety officer. Next, he called Lt. Col. Karl Doll, the deputy commander for the $109^{th}$ Tactical Airlift Group in New York. In turn, each of these people notified the appropriate agencies to start an investigation into the incident.

*Prop Lawn Ornament, 109th Pic*

# Raven 94

To get everything maintenance needed to fix Raven 92, Noel planned a double-shuttle to DYE-3. On Tuesday morning, he flew the first shuttle to the DYE site with Danzer's aircrew. He wanted to take a look at the situation. He left Sondrestrom with engine stands, tools, and a five-person maintenance team. A base photographer and the chief of safety from Sondrestrom Air Base also accompanied the aircrew to start the investigation.

The weather was good when Raven 94 arrived at DYE-3. Noel landed in the open snow due to Raven 92 being so close to the skiway. The snow was smooth when the aircraft touched down. Noel taxied to the left side of Raven 92 and dropped off the maintenance team. Ray Morgan unloaded the cargo in the back of the plane.

They kept the engines running during the offload of cargo. When they were finished, they loaded Adams and his crew. Ray Morgan closed the back of the aircraft. Noel taxied into the open snow. He then pointed the nose of the aircraft into the headwind and pushed up the throttles to accelerate. The aircraft bogged down and didn't have enough speed to get airborne due to the soft snow. After a couple of miles, Noel pulled the throttles back and slowed. He turned the aircraft around and again tried to take off in the opposite direction. No success.

He kept going back and forth, packing down the snow to create his own skiway. Finally, Raven 94 got airborne on the fourth try, and the flight back to Sondrestrom was uneventful. However, they still needed to get an engine and a propeller to DYE-3. Upon returning to Sondrestrom, Danzer took over the mission and flew in Noel's place. Noel debriefed Danzer on the proximity of Raven 92 to the skiway. He also told Danzer the general vicinity in the open snow where he found good snow to take off from. He then returned to his mission commander duties.

It was another routine flight to DYE-3. The skies were cloud-covered, but overall the weather was good. Danzer chose to land in the open snow, in the same area from which Noel took off. As Danzer descended, there was no definition in the snow. The sky, the horizon, and the surface were all the same color, pale white, and there were no shadows to define Noel's tracks in the snow. He was inside the ping-pong ball.

The main skis touched down in the snow, but when Danzer lowered the nose ski, it hit hard. He landed perpendicular to Noel's deep tracks instead of parallel. Ray Morgan heard a loud *bang* and *thump*. That wasn't good. As he slowed, Danzer had problems steering so, he used the throttles and asymmetric thrust to maneuver the aircraft. He taxied to the DYE-3 parking area, stopped the aircraft to the left side of Raven 92, and shut down the aircraft engines.

Ray Morgan was one of the first crewmembers outside the aircraft. The nose of the aircraft was low. He poked his head underneath and saw the strut of the nose gear had snapped and was behind the nose gear tire, buried in the snow under the belly of the aircraft. The tire was carrying the aircraft's weight in the aft portion of the nose wheel well area.

There was nothing more to do. The engine and propeller were offloaded, and the maintenance folks began repairs on Raven 92. Danzer relayed to Sondrestrom that the aircraft was broken. He and his crew remained at DYE-3 overnight. DYE-3 was beginning to look like an aircraft graveyard.

## Weather Issues

For the next two days, there was no flying. Sondrestrom had poor weather. It remained below landing minimums throughout the day. The weather at the DYE sites was below approach minimums. Visibility at DYE-2 was one-eighth to one-quarter of a mile due to ice fog. The weather at DYE-3 was worse. All day Wednesday, the winds were howling at 30 to 40 knots. Blowing snow created drifts along the skiway. Drifting snow built up around all of the aircraft equipment. The snow had drifted so high around the aircraft Ray Morgan could rest his hand on the wingtip. No maintenance work on the aircraft was accomplished.

Things looked a little better on Thursday. Raven 91 had been sitting in Sondrestrom for the last couple of weeks. It took a lot of effort to get the aircraft airborne. Maintenance took their time. By the end of the day, Adams' crew accomplished a couple of missions to DYE-2.

*Ray Morgan with Hand on Wingtip of Raven 92*

On Friday, the weather at DYE-3 remained poor for most of the day. With the continued high winds and blowing snow, the maintenance folks didn't accomplish any work on Raven 92 until late in the afternoon. Their people and aircrews were going nuts inside of DYE-3. For three days, there was little for them to do except watch movies, played a lot of pool, and read books from the DYE site's library.

Senior Master Sergeant Wally Dillenback helped the cook lay tile down on the kitchen floor. The cook was having a great deal of difficulty with it. The floor and tiles were too cold for the tiles to seal to the floor. Dillenback took the heating unit from the DYE site's sauna and brought it into the kitchen. This did the trick.

The weather at Sondrestrom was below landing minimums until late in the afternoon, so all flying was canceled. Fortunately, it improved long enough for the arrival of a spare aircrew from Schenectady. Raven 86, an aircraft without skis, arrived at 5:45 p.m. He brought the nose gear and ski assembly off Raven 90 in New York to install on Raven 94 at DYE-3.

| Raven 86 Aircrew | |
|---|---|
| **Pilot:** | Captain John Mitchell |
| **Copilot:** | Captain Harry "Nick" Tredennick |
| **Navigator:** | Major Ernie Meyer |
| **Flight Engineer:** | Technical Sergeant Mike Cristiano |
| **Loadmaster:** | Technical Sergeant Bob Macauley |

The weather was a little better at Sondrestrom on Saturday, although there were still a few light snow flurries. Weather at both sites had improved. DYE-2 had three-miles visibility, so Adams' crew completed four more shuttles.

DYE-3 had improved to three-quarters mile visibility with blowing snow. This was good enough to allow Dillenback, Senior Master Sergeant Floyd Kilmartin, and the rest of the maintenance team the opportunity to remove and replace the engine and propeller on Raven 92. Dillenback and Kilmartin had known each other as children in first grade. They grew up together in the small town of Palatine Bridge, New York. They eventually parted ways when Kilmartin's family moved away, but they reunited again when they both joined the Guard unit at Schenectady.

This wasn't their first engine and propeller change on the ice cap. They had changed the #4 engine and propeller on the right wing of Raven 93 at DYE-2 a couple of years before. The pilot had taxied the aircraft's right wing along the edge of the skiway, and the #4 propeller hit a post. On that adventure, when they went out there to repair it, Dillenback shook one of the damaged propeller's blades, and the propeller fell off into the snow. There were always surprises on the ice cap.

The weather held, and repairs progressed well at DYE-3. Dillenback contacted Tom Noel, and he let him know Raven 92 would be ready to return to Sondrestrom the following day at 4:00 p.m.

## Raven 92 Recovery

It was Sunday, and there was no pause in the work. At Sondrestrom, Master Sergeant Lou Ott walked around Raven 92 and went through a series of preflight checks and engine runs. Technical Sergeant Dennis Morgan loaded the maintenance team and thc nosc gear and ski assembly for the repairs of Raven 94 in the back of the aircraft. After the pre-flight and loading were completed, maintenance people mounted four ATO bottles to each side of the aircraft.

| **Raven 91 Aircrew** | |
|---|---|
| **Pilot:** | Major Tom Noel |
| **Copilot:** | Captain Dick Bayly |
| **Navigator** | Major Ernie Meyer |
| **Flight Engineer:** | Master Sergeant Lou Ott |
| **Loadmaster:** | Technical Sergeant Dennis Morgan |

Major Tom Noel flew with Adams' aircrew. They departed Sondrestrom at 9:30 a.m. for DYE-3. Captain Dick Bayly contacted Sob Story and let them know they were coming in. Noel landed in the open snow. After slowing, he taxied Raven 91 up to the DYE-3 camp, around the two broken aircraft. When they stopped, Bayly shut down the aircraft engines.

Noel knew Raven 92 wouldn't be ready until 4:00 p.m., but he wanted to arrive early. The weather was good, and he wanted to ensure he got Danzer's crew back to Sondrestrom before the poor weather moved in again. Dennis Morgan offloaded the cargo to repair Raven 94 and loaded the damaged engine and propeller from Raven 92 into the back of the aircraft. Ott walked around the aircraft and looked it over, then installed the ignitors into the ATO bottles. When they were finished, Noel turned over the aircraft to Danzer's aircrew.

Danzer started the engines and taxied Raven 91 into the open snow, and as he accelerated, he directed Red LaFerriere to fire the ATO bottles. They broke at DYE-3 on Tuesday, and on Sunday, they were airborne again. They landed at Sondrestrom about 1:00 p.m. with a nose ski problem.

Noel and his aircrew remained at DYE-3, waiting until the maintenance people completed repairs to Raven 92. He seemed to be the only pilot on the island not having problems throughout the week. When Dillenback's maintenance team completed their work, the aircrew started theirs. Lou

Ott and Dennis Morgan finished pre-flight checks on the aircraft with the assistance of the maintenance personnel. Morgan loaded Dillenback's maintenance team, and the engine stands in the back of the aircraft.

Before becoming a pilot, Dick Bayly worked in the maintenance squadron as a hydraulic specialist. He knew the aircraft had stopped while the nose ski was in a 30-degree turn, so he poked his head underneath the aircraft's nose and noticed one of the nose tires was flat. Fortunately, Sob Story had an air hose. The aircrew jumped in their seats, started the aircraft engines; Noel taxied closer to the station, and they shut down the engines again.

Ott walked to the DYE site and stretched out an air hose, and filled the tire. He then suggested they delay going airborne and wait and see if the tire leaked. After waiting half an hour, he was satisfied. The aircrew started the engines again, and Noel taxied out to the open snow for takeoff. Raven 92 was airborne at 7:30 p.m. Soon after takeoff, the utility hydraulic system dumped all of its fluid. Dick Bayly shut off the switches on the hydraulic panel. The aircraft lost its utility hydraulic pressure. Morgan crawled under the flight deck to look out the inspection window at the nose ski. It was drooped, and it appeared as if the left nose gear tire was flat again.

As he approached Nav Rocks, near the edge of the ice cap, Noel jettisoned the eight ATO bottles from the side of the aircraft. He declared an emergency with Sondrestrom Tower, and upon landing, he had difficulty controlling the aircraft. The nose ski began to shimmy left and right excessively, so he stopped on the runway and shut down the engines. Maintenance towed the aircraft to the parking ramp. Raven 92 was back in Sondrestrom. The second maintenance team remained at DYE-3 to replace the nose gear and ski assembly of Raven 94.

Technical Sergeant Charlie Lucia and the rest of the maintenance team spent the day fixing Raven 94. They used a modular lift device, a heavy-duty balloon attached to a compressor. They put the uninflated balloon beneath the nose of the aircraft. Then, they inflated the bag and raised it. When the nose was high enough, they installed jacks to steady the aircraft. The jacks were strapped to loading pallets sitting in the snow. It required a lot of coordination, but they were able to remove the broken nose gear and ski.

Lucia needed to inflate the bag further to raise the nose higher for his team to slide the replacement nose gear and ski assembly into place. When they were ready, they slowly deflated the bag and lowered the nose down until the strut sat in the aircraft's bearing saddles. They finished the installation of the nose gear and removed the balloon and the jacks. The aircraft was ready to fly.

# Raven 94 Recovery

On Monday, 20 September 1982, the Raven Gang changed out aircrew members in Sondrestrom, and Raven 93 brought fresh people from New York. Noel returned to Schenectady aboard Raven 86, and Lt. Col. Jeff Slovak became the mission commander. Slovak lived in Lake George. He flew corporate jets out of New Hampshire and Boston. He loved to laugh, and within the Raven Gang, he was famous for his quote, *"There is a lot of profit to be made in confusion."* Had he been in Greenland the week before, he would have been a rich man.

Slovak's first task was to recover Raven 94 from DYE-3. The aircraft maintenance problems continued. Raven 94 was broken at DYE-3; Raven 92 was in an aircraft hangar going through a series of gear retractions after repairing it, following Noel's landing the evening before; and Raven 91 needed a nose ski change.

The following morning Slovak had one aircraft available, Raven 93. He wanted to send an aircrew to DYE-2 to offload fuel, but the aircraft had a bleed air leak. By late morning the maintenance team was able to repair it. At 10:00 a.m., the maintenance folks at DYE-3 called Slovak and told him Raven 94 was ready to return to Sondrestrom. He decided to fly the mission. Major Jay Fuller and his crew rode in the back of the aircraft. They would fly Raven 94 back to Sondrestrom.

Fuller was a former Vietnam helicopter pilot. After the war, he left active duty and joined the Syracuse, New York Air National Guard unit and flew fixed-wing A-37 aircraft, but like many veteran pilots, the Raven Gang had a more unconventional mission that fit his flying style. He was an outstanding aircraft commander with a quiet, pleasant demeanor who was awarded over fifty air medals throughout his career.

Things began to click after more than a week of aircraft maintenance challenges for the aircrews and maintenance teams. The weather was good. Slovak got airborne and flew out to DYE-3 without incident. Both aircrews spent 2½ hours on the snow at DYE-3, loading both the aircraft full of equipment and tools, the damaged nose gear and ski assembly, and the maintenance team. Technical Sergeant Red LaFerriere did a preflight inspection on Raven 94. The aircrew climbed in the aircraft when he was finished.

Major Wolfgang Walther, Fuller's copilot, called DYE-3 and told them they were starting their engines. Once they were started, Fuller let the engines and propellers warm up for a while. The aircraft had been in extreme temperatures for about a week. He wanted to ensure the propeller seals were flexible enough to prevent any leaks. When he was satisfied, he taxied to the skiway. On Fuller's first takeoff attempt, Raven 94 wouldn't accelerate, but he had LaFerriere fire the ATO bottles on his second attempt and got airborne. Slovak and Raven 93 followed a short time later.

CHAPTER 6

# TIME AND NEW TECHNOLOGY

From 1960 to 1989, the Air Force contracted employees from the Federal Electric Corporation to live and work in the DEW line sites year-round; fifteen to twenty people total, per site. Six or seven of them were electronic technicians, called radicians. The rest were support personnel; mechanics, cooks, and administrators.

*DYE Site*

These contractor positions were highly sought-after jobs. The minimum contract length was one year, but people were allowed to go home for a two-week hiatus after spending six months at the sites. The pay was two to three times the standard income in the United States and Canada. The room and board were free, so everyone banked about ninety-five percent of what they earned.[34]

During the summer months, structural engineers from CRREL arrived to analyze the DYE sites' stability. Danish construction workers arrived when maintenance or construction was required, and National Science Foundation personnel arrived to conduct science projects.

## The Big Move

The DYE sites were designed to be jacked up higher as snow accumulated around the station. By the end of 1975, DYE-2 had been raised 50.5 feet, and DYE-3 had been raised 79.2 feet. Two three-hundred-fifty-ton jacks were installed in the eight columns to raise them. Every time changes or movements were made to the DYE sites, contractors, supplies, and heavy equipment were needed for it to happen.

The life of these structures could not be extended forever by simply lengthening the columns and raising the building.[35] After years of raising them, they were becoming unstable. A 1974 study concluded the best way to save the DYE sites was to move them sideways onto a new foundation. This engineering feat was CRREL's Wayne Tobiasson's idea. His brother worked at a naval shipyard. He knew it was possible to move the DYE sites laterally, using a similar method the Navy used to bring ships into dry dock.

The plan was for the DYE site, above the snow surface, to be cut from the subsurface structure which braced it. Before it was cut, a brace structure was designed and added above the snow to prevent the DYE site from collapsing while it moved along Tobiasson's rail system.[36] The rail structure was much like train tracks. The DYE site rested on rollers on these rails, and jacks pulled the building along the rails.

He conducted multiple tests to ensure its success. When the tests were completed, the DYE-3 Site Extension Project's $7,000,000 contract went to the Danish Arctic Contractor. The project needed to be completed within three hundred man-days. It did not include the backhaul of equipment or the DYE site's waste material after the work was completed.[37]

From April through May, the Raven Gang moved about 650,000 gallons of fuel to DYE-2 and DYE-3. When they were finished, they changed focus to "The Big Move." They airlifted 3,000 tons of steel, wood, equipment, and miscellaneous items to DYE-3. It required more than 250 flights for the contractors to build the rail system.

As the cargo arrived at DYE-3, the Danish Arctic Contractor personnel went to work. Rollers and hydraulic jacks were installed on the rails, and the jacks were attached to the DYE site's columns. When the building's full weight was on the rollers, contractors cut away each column's section one foot below the rollers.

The jacks pulled the 3,300-ton structure along the rails in six-foot increments. When the station was 210 feet from its original location, the contractors secured it on eight new footings. Tobiasson was on-site to observe and document the work. When "The Big Move" was finished, the Danish Arctic Contractor hosted a great Scandinavian feast.[38]

*Building Rail System to Move DYE Site, Ray Morgan pic*

The following year DYE-3 was jacked twenty-seven feet higher. Tobiasson was challenged to move the DYE site, and he did it while it remained operational. Five years later, this immense airlift requirement was duplicated on DYE-2. At 6:45 p.m. local time, on 23 August 1982, DYE-2 moved. By the end of the day, it was 210 feet from its original location. DYE-2 was raised twenty-seven feet in the following year.

## New Aircraft

The first indication the Raven Gang was interested in Antarctica came in 1982. Colonel Stan Hemstreet made a trip to McMurdo to observe the Navy's Operation Deep Freeze mission. He thought the Raven Gang had something to offer. However, he realized the limitations of the C-130D aircraft could only provide marginal support.

Hemstreet worked with Congressman Sam Stratton of New York, who chaired the U.S. House of Representative Procurement Subcommittee, to secure funding for new aircraft. They had an excellent relationship, and Hemstreet's timing was perfect. By late 1983, restrictions were put on the C-130As due to failures of floor bulkhead end fittings or pork-chop fittings that provided structural support for the landing gear in the floor of the aircraft. This restriction included the skibirds because they were a variant of the same model of aircraft.

On 22 September 1983, the Air Force put restrictions on C-130As when the aircraft was pressurized while flying above 10,000 feet. On 11 October 1983, the 109th Airlift Wing requested a waiver to the restriction. The Air Force contractors at DYE-3 required 102,400 gallons of fuel, thirty-two sorties, by 15 January 1984, to ensure the radar site's survival. The waiver was denied.

On 25 October 1983, they tried a new tactic. They requested to do the needed repairs on two of their aircraft, 57-0490 and 57-0493, at Schenectady County Airport instead of waiting for depot-level repairs. Doing so would allow them to deploy these aircraft to Greenland and provide the needed fuel to the DYE site. This was approved, and the fuel resupply was completed.

In April 1984, enough ski aircraft were available to complete the rest of the DYE sites' fuel resupply. Maintenance issues continued to plague the mission, but there was a long-term fix in place. On 27 October 1984, the 109th Tactical Airlift Group received their first of eight new aircraft from the Lockheed assembly line. The twenty-five-year-old C-130Ds and C-130D-6s were retired, and eight new aircraft were purchased; four LC-130H2s and four C-130H2s.

The pilots didn't like the H-model aircraft because it was sluggish and less maneuverable. A pressure reducer had been added to the aileron hydraulic system, decreasing the pressure to the ailerons from 3,000 psi to 2050 psi. Although the pilots didn't like the new planes, the maintenance people loved them. New aircraft didn't break as often. By comparison, the H-model aircraft had four-bladed propellers, instead of the very loud three-bladed propellers on the D-model. The ATO mounts on the sides of the aircraft could no longer eject the bottles. Landing gear weight restrictions limited the weight of the C-130D to 124,200 pounds. The strengthened landing gear increased the maximum weight of the H-model to 155,000 pounds. The H-model had auxiliary fuel tanks built into the center wing section.

*C-130D (gray) and LC-130H (green)*

The Raven Gang had some serious concerns on how these 30,000-pound heavier aircraft would function in the snow. Although the Navy had been operating their C-130BL aircraft at 155,000 pounds, the snow in Greenland was different. It was wetter, which created more drag as the aircraft plowed through the snow. The engines were more powerful, but there was no data that the increased power would offset the increased weight. They needed to test how the increased engine performance would balance out with the aircraft's increased weight.

The maintenance people removed the external fuel tanks from aircraft 83-0490 before going to Greenland to test the aircraft on the snow. This reduced the weight and drag for ski takeoffs and increased cruise performance, but the benefits were offset by the loss of fuel capacity and distance the aircraft could travel.[39]

Major Giles Wagoner did the first ski landing with a new aircraft. At the end of the week, the mission commander, Lt. Col. Graham Pritchard, concluded, "There's no gain in capability but no great loss."[40] After the Raven Gang became more comfortable in their new aircraft, the maintenance team reinstalled the fuel tanks. The aircraft came out of the Lockheed factory with the standard C-130 camouflage green colors. The LC-130 icecap color scheme, light gray with orange flash, wouldn't reappear again until the early 1990s.

Brigadier General Stanley Hemstreet retired in September of 1985. It was a pivotal moment for the Raven Gang. By the time he left, he had built a flight operation capable of succeeding in the harsh environment on the ice cap of Greenland and ensured his vision would continue well into the future with the purchase of new aircraft. On 4 March 1989, in honor of Sam Stratton, the 109th Air Group named their airbase at Schenectady County Airport after him, Stratton Air National Guard Base.[41]

## The Inevitable Conclusion

The DYE sites were built for a ten-year life, but they functioned until the end of the Cold War.[42] The ingenuity of the CRREL structural engineers extended the life of the buildings to nearly thirty years.[43] Cutting the subsurface structure from the rest of the DYE sites created new challenges. DYE-2 began to tilt westward as the ice cap descended and flowed in that direction. DYE-3 had a different problem. One corner of the structure began to compress with the corner on the opposite side, creating a rhomboid formation. This deformation created serious structural problems.

In 1988, nine years after it was moved sideways, two of DYE-2's eight columns were again stressed beyond design limits. Tobiasson reported this to the Air Force as he had done in the past, and he expected the Air Force would handle the issue as they had always done. He expected them to contact Federal Electric Corporation and their contractors to notify them of the issue and let them know Tobiasson and the rest of the CRREL team would develop a strategic plan to respond to this problem over the next year or so.

Instead, the Air Force overstated the problem and alerted Federal Electric Corporation that their employees' safety could no longer be guaranteed. This immediately prompted Federal Electric Corporation to abandon the buildings. They called for the LC-130s, turned off the power to the station, and evacuated DYE-2. Tobiasson was disappointed and protested, *"DYE-2 wasn't a three-legged milking stool. It had eight columns. It was locally overstressed, but it had been overstressed in the past and had proved to be rather tough."* He explained further, *"An eight-legged structure that is locally overstressed according to design guidelines is of concern, but that is not to say that it is about to collapse. All those involved should have paused to discuss this. Unfortunately, that did not happen."*

The Air Force sent the CRREL structural engineers back to the DYE sites to verify their measurements. Tobiasson and his team went to the Greenland ice cap and took new readings. They verified only a couple of the columns were overstressed. It didn't make any difference. The temperature within the empty building dropped below freezing. Utilities were damaged.[44] Once the power was removed and the site was cold-soaked, the Air Force decided to keep it shut down. The Federal Electric Corporation contractors were allowed to return to the DYE sites one last time to collect the belongings they had left behind.

As mentioned before, the DYE sites were designed as an early warning detection system to protect the Western Hemisphere from incoming Soviet aircraft. Over the passing years, they couldn't keep up with the new technology, the intercontinental ballistic missiles threat. They were out-of-date. The information from the DEW line couldn't provide information fast enough to be useful against incoming missiles. To counter this threat, a ballistic missile early-warning system was developed, consisting of three powerful radar installations; one in England, one in Alaska, and one in Greenland.[45] Satellites were also coming of age.

In 1989, coincident with the collapse of the Soviet Union and the end of the Cold War, the Air Force closed the DYE sites. They were no longer needed to counter the "Evil Empire."

The Raven Gang flew their final two missions into DYE-3 on 2 December 1989. When they arrived at the site, the skies were clear, and the visibility was unrestricted, but there was an 18-knot crosswind, so both aircraft landed open snow. There were delays loading the last of the cargo. Lt. Col. Graham Pritchard and Lt. Col. Ray Tousey flew Raven 91. They had loaded 38,000 pounds of cargo and took off in the open snow using ATO. They were airborne on the first slide.

*Tousey (pilot window) and Pritchard at DYE site*

Technical Sergeant Mike Messineo, Raven 90's flight engineer, was a practical man. It was getting dark. It was the last mission before the site was abandoned, so he told the contractor to leave the skiway lights on for the takeoff. The contractor refused. He needed to secure the generator. When the generator stopped, all of the lights, including those on the skiway, turned off. Sob Story's door was locked.

From 1980 through 1989, the Raven Gang had kept a mission commander's book. The final entry said the following: "Last flight 490 with 20,000 pounds miscellaneous cargo and last personnel from site took off with a crescent moon on the southern horizon and the northern lights in full display above. Colonel Terusi and crew used all the runway, slid off into the dark for another thousand feet before leaving the snow and marking the end of an era. Peter D. M. Terusi.

The closure of Sondrestrom Air Base soon followed. The airbase facilities transitioned from the United States to Greenlandic control on 30 September 1992. The town became known by its Inuit name, Kangerlussuaq.

CHAPTER 7

# COLD WAR RESCUE STORY

Below is a true story of a rescue on the Greenland ice cap in 1985. The common enemy of all aircrews flying across the ice cap is what the noted American writer, Jack London, referred to as the white silence. *"Trapped, alone, lack of food and water. The cold sapping your strength and your will to survive."* The F-27 aircrew wasn't prepared for their flight over the Greenland ice cap. Those that survived were fortunate the Raven Gang was in town. The names of the F-27 aircrew have been changed.

The year was 1985, and Ronald Reagan was president. The Soviet Union and its communist ideology were the menaces of the world. Libya was promoting terrorist attacks against Americans. Anti-communist Contras were battling the Sandinista communist government in Nicaragua. Lt. Col. Oliver North was about to become a household name, and the Iran-Contra Affair was about to be exposed. The United States was selling weapons to Iran to release hostages held in Lebanon and fund Nicaragua's Contras.

None of this had anything to do with the events which occurred on the Greenland ice cap in April of 1985, but the F-27 aircrew members got some media attention. It was an interesting mix of people. Aeronica, the government-owned Nicaraguan airlines, had hired a crew in communist-governed South Yemen to ferry the plane to Managua.[46] All of the crew members were well qualified and properly certified for the flight.[47]

The aircraft commander was from India. His name was Nehru. The flight engineer, Santiago, was from the Philippines. There were two copilots aboard; Rashid from Jordan and Hisham from Israel. Both were members of the Palestine Liberation Organization. Both were combat pilots. The navigator was Bo Thomas. He was an American, a Vietnam veteran, and rumored to have been a former employee of the Central Intelligence Agency.[48]

The aircraft, YN-BZF,[49] was purchased by Aeronica. It was a turbo-prop Fokker/Fairchild 27, known as the F-27, and was located in North Yemen. To extend the distance the aircraft could travel, Aeronica installed two 200-gallon auxiliary fuel tanks in the passenger cabin.[50]

**11 April 1985**

YN-BZF departed from Sanaa, North Yemen, for Athens, Greece, via Jeddah, Saudi Arabia, and Cairo, Egypt.

**19 April 1985**

They flew from Greece to Prestwick, Scotland, via Genoa, Italy.

**20 April 1985**

They flew from Prestwick to Reykjavik, Iceland, via Stornoway. They arrived in Iceland at 2:48 p.m. local time.[51] Their next destination was Sondrestrom, Greenland.

They flew this route because their aircraft was unable to cross the Atlantic without refueling. Even with the auxiliary fuel tanks in the back of the aircraft, there were no refueling locations within reach, except for this northern route. During the last part of their journey, the aircrew could not retrieve fuel from the two 200-gallon tanks. During their refueling stop in Reykjavik, they had the system inspected, and experienced F-27 engineers looked at the system. In their opinion, the auxiliary fuel system was *"not very professionally looking,"* and they *"got the feeling that the crew was not quite certain of how to operate it."* The engineers gave the crew some instructions on the operation the fuel system and did a ground run to verify it worked.[52]

# Stranded on the Ice Cap

**4:21 p.m.**

The aircrew left Iceland at 4:21 p.m. local time. The aircraft had no difficulty climbing up into the positive control airspace, or PCA starting at 18,000 feet. While still over the Denmark Strait, which separated Iceland from Greenland, Nehru contacted Iceland Radio. He asked that they extend his thanks to the Icelandic F-27 engineers, and he verified the auxiliary fuel system was working correctly. The rest of the aircraft systems were operating normally except for the flight data recorder and the deicing system in the copilot's right front window.

**5:35 p.m. (Local Time)**

After two hours and fourteen minutes of flying, YN-BZF passed over Kulusuk on Greenland's east coast. Kulusuk was the location of DYE-4. It was the last of four distant early warning, DEW line, radar sites crossing Greenland from the west.

**5:50 p.m.**

Fifty miles west of Kulusuk, Nehru called Big Gun, DYE-4's callsign. Their fuel problems had returned, and the auxiliary fuel system was no longer working. This deprived them of four hundred gallons of much-needed fuel. The headwinds were strong, and they could only achieve a ground speed of 180 knots. They could no longer reach Sondrestrom. Nehru knew he no longer had enough fuel to return to Iceland.

He descended to land at Kulusuk Airport, which had a small gravel runway. It was located on a small, rugged mountainous island off the east coast of Greenland. This island was surrounded by many other small, rugged mountainous islands. It was a difficult runway to find when the weather was good.

The weather was deteriorating as Nehru descended to find the runway. He wasn't comfortable enough with the weather conditions to visually descend into the terrain. Dense fog covered the area and made it impossible to locate the airport for an emergency landing. There was no other runway destination within reach. He decided to attempt to land at DYE-3 on the Greenland ice cap. Most of the DEW line sites had an airfield or skiway for resupply. He declared his intentions to the Danish flight information center. Nehru and his crew were not familiar with the Greenland ice cap. They were not prepared for the extreme cold, and they were about to learn some very harsh lessons.

Nehru climbed his aircraft away from Kulusuk and headed for DYE-3, about one hundred miles west. The flight took about fifteen to twenty minutes. The weather was poor. The Danish Civil Aviation Administration weather forecast for the area fifty miles east of DYE-3 was the following:

- The surface wind was from the north-northeast at about 5 knots
- The visibility was 500 meters to 1500 meters
- There was ice, fog, and light snow in the area
- Vertical visibility was 100 feet to 400 feet above the ground[53]

**6:38 p.m. (Local Time)**

The Danish flight information center notified the Greenlandic rescue coordination center chief that the F-27 aircraft was having fuel problems and may have to attempt an emergency landing at DYE-3.[54]

**6:55 p.m.**

Nehru advised Big Gun he had an estimated forty to forty-five minutes of fuel remaining. As YN-BZF climbed away from Greenland's east coast, the crew didn't notice the ice cap rising to meet them as they flew toward the radar site.

The F-27 aircrew did not have any approaches or other flight navigational guidance for the DYE sites. In lieu of this, Nehru hoped the weather would be clear overhead DYE-3 when he arrived. He wasn't so lucky. From an interview with Hisham, following his rescue, the twenty-seven-year-old PLO copilot said Big Gun responded, *"Stay up. We will send planes which will guide you down safely. In the cockpit, we were looking at each other happily. We were saved! But our windows froze over...suddenly we hit the ice."*

Nehru did not realize DYE-3's field elevation was 8,700 feet. As he started a descent to find the DYE site, the F-27 impacted the ice cap. On the second bounce, the F-27 lost its tail section. On the third impact, the remaining portions of the aircraft came to rest. Fuel vapors exploded, killing Santiago, the Filipino, and severely injuring Rashid. Rashid's lungs were burned. He needed immediate medical attention, but there was none.

The distressed aircrew was alone in the vast expanses of the Greenland ice cap. The silence was unnerving, and they were stranded and alone. The only survival capabilities they had were in the broken pieces of their aircraft and each other.

They performed medical triage on one another and searched for anything to protect them from the frigid temperatures. It was cold, -13 degrees Celsius. They were fortunate the winds were mild. In the waning daylight, they crouched together wrapped in a blanket for warmth.[55]

# Sondrestrom

**7:00 p.m.**

The rescue control center chief at Sondrestrom Air Base notified Lt. Col. Graham Pritchard, from the Raven Gang, of the possible emergency and to prepare for a search and rescue mission. His group of flyers flew C-130 aircraft with snow skis, LC-130s. They were based at Schenectady County Airport in New York, but their mission was to refuel and resupply the DYE sites on the ice cap during April and May of every year.

**7:33 p.m.**

The Danish flight information center received information that Big Gun lost radio and radar contact with the aircraft. Their last recorded altitude was 9,000 feet. The LC-130 aircrews were off duty at the time. It was the beginning of the annual resupply of the DYE sites. The Raven Gang arrived in Greenland on 14 April 1985 to start the two-month marathon fuel airlift to provide DYE-2 and DYE-3 with 650,000 gallons of fuel to run their operations through the year.

Raven 90 and Raven 93 were new aircraft. In March, they were used as the test aircraft to see how they would perform in the snow.[56] Raven 90 had its external fuel tanks removed during the test period to see how it would perform on the ice compared to Raven 93 with the external fuel tanks installed. Raven 90 performed much better. The external fuel tanks created additional drag. At the end of the week, Raven 93 returned to New York with landing gear issues.

On April 20, 1985, the day of the F-27 crash, the same two aircraft were back in Greenland. It was the final day of the week's fuel resupply, and it had been a good week. The Raven Gang was scheduled to return to New York the following day.

**6:15 a.m.**

Major Elliott "Aldo" Marchegiani started his day. He was scheduled to fly a couple of missions to DYE-3, about 200 miles east of Sondrestrom. Then he intended to pack his bags for his return flight home to New York. He grabbed some breakfast and was on the flight line at Raven Operations by 7:30 a.m. His official arrival time for his flight was 8:00 a.m., but he liked to get an early feel for the day before digging deep into mission planning. The weather was forecast to be poor at DYE-3. The backup plan was DYE-2.

**10:10 a.m**

Raven 90, with Marchegiani and his crew, was airborne. The weather was too poor to land at DYE-3, so Marchegiani diverted to DYE-2 and delivered the fuel there instead. DYE-2 was between Sondrestrom and DYE-3. When the fuel was offloaded at the DYE site, he took off and landed at Sondrestrom by noon.

Maintenance personnel refueled his aircraft, and he was airborne again by 12:25 p.m. to again deliver fuel to DYE-3. Again, he diverted to DYE-2 and delivered his fuel there instead.

**2:30 p.m.**

His mission was complete. He was back at Sondrestrom and debriefed maintenance personnel on the status of his aircraft. He then assumed mission commander duties while Major Jon Adams and Lt. Col. Graham Pritchard flew a round trip to DYE-2.

Lt. Col. Ray Tousey was an hour behind Marchegiani all day. His flying day was over by 3:30 p.m.

Adams and Pritchard returned to Sondrestrom at 4:30 p.m.

By 5:30 p.m., Adams and Pritchard completed their maintenance debriefing.

All of the scheduled missions were finished for the day, and it was time to prepare the aircraft for the return to New York. Marchegiani handed over the mission commander duties to Pritchard. He went to the gym and played some paddle ball, swam in the pool, and used the hot tub. He returned to his room and began packing his bags after a very satisfying day.

**7:00 p.m.**

There was a knock on his door. He was told to go to Raven Operations to help with a possible aircraft crash. Pritchard needed two crews to make a search and rescue effort. Marchegiani was at the operations building within fifteen minutes. The aircraft was ready to go, and Pritchard gave the order to launch.

Danish Civil Aviation Administration's aeronautical information service sunrise/sunset tables established sunset at DYE-3 at 6:26 p.m. local Sondrestrom time. Full darkness was at 7:30 p.m.[57]

Aldo Marchegiani was airborne again by 8:00 p.m. aboard Raven 90. His copilot was Jon Adams. His navigator was Major Andrew Ellis. Master Sergeant Mike Cristiano was the flight engineer. Master Sergeant Garry Quick and Staff Sergeant Ray Morgan were the loadmasters in the back of the aircraft, along with a maintenance crew chief, a Danish doctor, and two nurses.

Sob Story reported the last known coordinates of the downed aircraft. They "painted" it on their radar. The aircraft was last seen forty-eight miles east of the site on a 081° true heading.

**9:00 p.m**

Raven 90 arrived at the last known coordinates. Marchegiani descended out of altitude and started searching for the missing aircraft. Tousey was overhead in Raven 93, providing top cover. The top cover aircraft's purpose was to provide a communications link between the aircraft on the ground and the Greenlandic rescue control center.

# Night at the Crash Site

**9:20 p.m.**

Ellis painted a possible target on his radar and directed Marchegiani to the target location. It was twilight at altitude, but as they descended through the low cloud deck, the sun went behind the Earth. About two and a half hours after they crashed, the marooned aircrew heard the C-130 aircraft overhead. Bo Thomas, the American, ran outside and waved a red bag. He could not be seen in the low light because he was too close to the wreckage.

Raven 90 made four passes over the crash site. On the first two passes, they didn't see any of the wreckage. Quick was standing behind the pilot seat, looking out the window. As Marchegiani flew the third pass, the clouds parted enough to let some moonlight provide some shadowing. Quick saw the tracks from the wreckage. The F-27 aircraft was destroyed.[58]

When Raven 90 flew over the wreckage, the aircrew didn't see any survivors in the darkness. They discussed whether they should land. Their ski procedures authorized landing at night with approval, but their approval authority was in New York. It would take too long. So, they did what all aircrews do; they discussed whether it was sunset, twilight, or civil twilight. They were parsing words to justify landing.

The Raven Gang was aware of the hazards of the ice cap. Raven 90's aircrew had no real confidence in how low they could descend due to the poor visibility. Marchegiani's radar altimeter indicated he was about 1,000 feet above the snow. No one on his crew was interested in going lower either. Their concern was the warning in the manual: *"The terrain clearance indications received from the AN/APN-22 are unreliable when operating over large depths of snow and ice since the radar waves will actually penetrate the surface and indicate greater terrain clearances than actually exist."* In other words, their aircraft may be lower than their instruments indicated.

A red survival sled was in the back of the aircraft. It was designed to carry survival gear and be pulled by the aircrew across the snow if needed. They discussed descending lower and dropping it out of the aircraft. No one was airdrop trained or qualified, and no one was sure what would happen to the sled when it impacted the ice cap. It was not designed to be dropped.

Would it fly up and hit the tail of the aircraft?

Would it remain closed when the prop wash hit it?

Would it remain intact when it hit the snow without a parachute?[59]

On the fourth pass, Marchegiani intended to drop it out of the back of the aircraft, but the crash site was engulfed in darkness. They could no longer find the wreckage. They didn't know where the sled would impact the ground below if they let it go, so they decided to keep it inside the aircraft.

Marchegiani couldn't assess the snow conditions well enough to make a safe landing, and he couldn't justify endangering ten more lives. Ellis had marked the exact coordinates of the crash site. The downed aircraft's location was thirty-one miles west of DYE-3. After the fourth pass, they returned to Sondrestrom.

Rashid had spent a lifetime fighting for his people. He was a member of the Palestinian Liberation Army and was a successful military pilot. Yet, in one harrowing night of silence on the Greenland ice cap, he abandoned everything and gave up all hope of survival and rescue. He took off his clothes, climbed out of the wreckage, and walked into the snow. No one stopped him. His last words were to Hisham, *"Turn my head in the direction of Mecca when I die. And tell the world how unmerciful the Hercules aircraft from U.S. Air Force in Sondrestrom was."*[60] Rashid died on the ice cap. When Hisham later found him, the blood in his mouth had frozen to ice. Hisham blamed the LC-130 aircrews. It was irrational, but it was a sign of the times.

## Rescue

**10:30 p.m.**

Marchegiani departed the crash site.

**11:35 p.m.**

Both Raven 90 and Raven 93 were on the ground at Sondrestrom. Maintenance and support personnel were told to have the aircraft prepared for early morning launches. They were going back out to the crash site as soon as the sun came up.

Raven 90 only needed more fuel. Raven 93 had an oil cooler flap actuator that needed to be replaced. The maintenance debriefing was finished by midnight. The maintenance team worked throughout the night to ensure the aircraft were ready. Marchegiani ate midnight chow and went to his room afterward. He didn't sleep very well, wondering if there were survivors at the crash site.

*Warming Up the Aircraft*

**April 21**

**3:30 a.m.**

Both Raven Gang aircrews were at Raven Operations. Pritchard, Marchegiani, and Tousey talked things over. The foreign aircraft crash was now getting interest from the press. Pritchard decided to assign his most experienced pilot on the rescue mission should things go awry. They agreed Tousey should fly the recovery aircraft, Raven 90, with Marchegiani's crew from the night before. Marchegiani would fly top cover in Raven 93.

| Raven 90 Aircrew | |
|---|---|
| **Pilot:** | Lt. Col. Ray Tousey |
| **Copilot:** | Major Jon Adams |
| **Navigator** | Major Andrew Ellis |
| **Flight Engineer:** | Technical Sergeant Mike Cristiano |
| **Loadmaster:** | Master Sergeant Garry Quick |
| **Loadmaster:** | Staff Sergeant Ray Morgan |

| Raven 93 Aircrew | |
|---|---|
| **Pilot:** | Major Elliott Marchegiani |
| **Copilot:** | Captain Richard Saburro |
| **Navigator** | Captain Ginny Reilly |
| **Flight Engineer:** | Master Sergeant Lou Ott |
| **Loadmaster:** | Master Sergeant William Goffi |

**4:05 a.m.**

Tousey was airborne with the doctor and nurses. Marchegiani was ten minutes behind. More information about the F-27 aircraft and the aircrew came in overnight. A Danish police officer and an Air Force security police officer also accompanied Tousey's aircrew.

**5:00 a.m.**

Raven 90 was over the crash site. Tousey had already determined he was going to land. It was the only way to verify whether anyone had survived the crash. He kept his eyes outside the aircraft surveying the ice cap. He studied the snow conditions and the debris field to determine where he was going to land. The visibility was good, and the winds were light. Adams and Quick were the first to see one of the survivors standing in the wreckage waving at the aircraft. It was Bo Thomas, the American.

**5:10 a.m.**

Tousey set Raven 90 down on the ice cap and taxied up to the wreckage. The snow had a hard, crisp surface but was soft and powdery beneath. As Tousey taxied, the aircraft sank deep in the snow. The remnants of YN-BZF's flight deck were nose down in the snow. Tousey stopped beside it.

Bo Thomas and Hisham were ambulatory and walked to Raven 90. Nehru needed to be litter-carried. Tousey, Ellis, Quick, and Morgan each grabbed a handle of the litter and carried him. They sank knee-deep in the snow as they made their way back to their aircraft. It was stressful as they stumbled along their way. At one point, the litter tipped and dropped Nehru off. Tousey yelled at Quick, "Keep the litter straight!" Quick had a few choice words for him in return.

After Nehru was on the LC-130, Tousey and Ellis went back to the aircraft to help retrieve Santiago's body. It was in an awkward position when he died, and he was frozen that way. This added another dimension of difficulty as they carried his body through the deep snow. Quick and Morgan retrieved the naked body of Rashid behind the wreckage of the aircraft. His leg looked like it was broken. He was frozen, and the awkward position of his leg kept them off balance. It was the first time Ray Morgan had seen a dead man's body.

**5:45 a.m.**

They were airborne again with the three survivors and two casualties.

Raven 90 was a new LC-130H model aircraft. It wasn't a year old. The older model C-130Ds were known to have a generator circuit breaker pop open during a rough ski takeoff. Cristiano wanted to ensure all the AC generators remained online, so he kept the auxiliary power unit, or APU, running. By trying to prevent something known to occur on the older model of aircraft, he gave himself a new problem. Snow was packed into the APU intake and caused the fire light to come on.[61] Cristiano pulled the fire handle and discharged a fire suppression bottle into the APU. Thirty-five years later, he was still full of self-incrimination, thinking, *"Stupid decision to leave the APU running."*

Initially, Tousey headed for DYE-3 in case he needed to make an emergency landing. Raven 93 now functioned as a chase plane, but it took Marchegiani a while to catch Tousey's aircraft and check it out. Tousey kept yelling at him over the radio, "Aldo, where the hell are you?" And Marchegiani kept replying, "Closing as fast as I can." As Raven 93 closed in on Raven 90, Tousey asked more emphatically, "Aldo, where the hell are you!?[62] As Raven 93 struggled to overtake Raven 90, Marchegiani initially thought Tousey was on fire. It didn't take long to see it was snow shedding from the aircraft. Snow was streaming from every crook and cranny exposed to the airstream.

Marchegiani flew around Raven 90 and gave it a visual inspection. No smoke was trailing the aircraft. Rich Saburro, Marchegiani's copilot, passed this information to Tousey.

**7:02 a.m**

Tousey's crew talked things over and decided to continue to Sondrestrom, where they landed. Marchegiani landed five minutes later. Everyone was elated but tired. Several rescue crew members had been up for over twenty-four hours, except for three hours of restless sleep, between midnight and 3:00 a.m. The injured survivors were immediately transferred to the hospital.

Maintenance looked over the APU problem. On the ground, the APU door was designed to open thirty degrees from the aircraft's side. When the aircraft was in the air, the door system was designed only to open fifteen degrees. On takeoff from the wreckage site, the air-inlet door closed from thirty degrees to fifteen degrees. Ice and snow were ingested by the APU, which packed the intake plenum chamber with a solid mass of snow constricting the airflow. It took maintenance three hours of heating with a Herman-Nelson heater to melt all the snow. Once the snow was cleared and the fire retardant was washed out, the APU ran fine.[63] The aircrews went back to their rooms and retrieved their bags.

**10:25 a.m.**

They boarded an LC-130 aircraft, and they departed for home. They slept in the back of the aircraft while Pritchard flew the weary aircrews back to Schenectady.

# Fall Out

Weeks later, Bo Thomas called Tousey and thanked him for saving his life. On 23 April, a Danish liaison officer arrived in Sondrestrom to investigate the F-27 crash. The following day Raven 90, commanded by Colonel Pete Terusi, flew the liaison officer, a Danish police officer, a Danish crash investigator, and two Americans to the accident site. At the F-27 wreckage, they found the cockpit voice recorder and miscellaneous papers. The investigators were satisfied they had everything they needed.

The media broke the story. Weeks before the plane crash, a news reporter from Albany, New York's local paper, *Knickerbocker News,* had gone to Sondrestrom. There he met Graham Pritchard and wrote an article about this *"square-jawed, steely-eyed, Arctic aviator"* for his newspaper. He called Pritchard about the F-27 crash. The reporter intended to show weakness in the military air defenses in Greenland because the F-27 had penetrated them.

During the call, Pritchard tried to counter the reporter's hysteria-fueled hyperbolic comments with the crash's factual details, but he couldn't sway him. The reporter wrote an article titled, *"Libyan Link Revealed in Arctic Air Crash."*

> *"Efforts to reach Bo Thomas this week were unsuccessful. A woman who answered the phone at his California home Wednesday—and identified herself as his wife—said Thomas had returned home last Thursday or Friday and left for Guam on Monday. 'He said he was going to deliver a plane to a private individual there. I do not know any details; all I know is it was not for the military. I don't know where he's staying or when he'll be back.' she said. 'I know you must think I must be crazy, but it has been that way for 18 years—when Bo is home, he's home; when Bo's away, he's away."*

Also, in his article, the reporter stated the F-27 was full of classified information. It was rumored to be full of gold, illegal drugs, and Chinese literature. Rashid was wearing a Libyan military uniform in his passport picture. A search of Rashid's clothes found $11,000 in U.S. currency. Pritchard gave the reporter a reasonable explanation for Rashid's money, telling him he assumed it was to refuel the aircraft. As they made their way around the world, Rashid knew few Western banks would accept credit from the Palestinian Liberation Organization. The reporter refused to accept this explanation.

*The New York Times* picked up on the story and wrote an article on 27 April 1985. Tousey was interviewed.

> *"Asked about reports that the Nicaraguan plane carried large amounts of cash, gold, drugs and Chinese literature intended for the Sandinista Government in Managua, Colonel* Tousey *said, 'I saw none of that, but then I wasn't looking for anything like that.'"*

*Knickerbocker News* wasn't finished. The editorial board wrote an article on 3 May 1985. Much of it was a rant of fear and distrust.

> *"The details have the makings of a best-seller:*
>
> *A Nicaraguan airplane develops fuel-valve trouble over Greenland while on a flight that would take it over the United States. It crashes some 50 miles short of a U.S. military installation that is part of an attack-alert network known as the Distant Early Warning (DEW) system. One pilot, an American who says he once worked for the CIA, walks out of the wreck waving a shirt; an Indian pilot and a Jordanian also survive. But the flight engineer, a Filipino, dies on impact, while another Jordanian slowly freezes to death in the Arctic cold. Large amounts of cash, mostly in American and Arab currencies, are recovered, as well as some Chinese literature.*
>
> *"It's not fiction. It was all reported last week by Knickerbocker News, and it has some people asking questions and one American colonel very much on the defensive."*

The "defensive" colonel was Colonel Stanley Hemstreet, the commander of the 109th Tactical Airlift Group. He was trying to calm down much of the media hype but wasn't successful. The editorial ended with the following:

> *"Well, Washington had better start asking questions, and soon. How can such a sensitive network be so easy a target for unfriendly aircraft? What is being done—now—to strengthen security? Finally, why is the colonel turning defensive? Confusing the issue serves no purpose. What happened in Greenland uncovered a serious breach in our security. There's no time to lose in fixing it."*

The media reporting was paranoia. It was a sign of the times.

CHAPTER 8

# ASSAULT TAKEOFFS AND LANDINGS

When the Raven Gang inherited the skibirds, the mission encompassed more than flying on the ice cap. They also flew to other DEW line locations in Greenland and northeastern Canada. By the time the Firebirds gave the skibirds to the Guard, the ski mission had become their ancillary job. There were many DEW line locations in Alaska that needed support. Very little has been written about what these bold aviators did, and it is another incredible C-130 mission that will be lost in time.

## Alaskan DEW Line

Seven of the Alaskan DEW line sites required a special certification process before the Firebirds allowed their crews to fly there. It was a self-imposed certification that other units didn't follow. Four of the locations were one-way sites; landing one direction and taking off in the opposite direction. There was good reason for this, they were on the sides of mountains.

Indian Mountain was a 4,100-foot gravel runway. The slope of the runway averaged 7.3% uphill for landing on Runway 24. It looked like a ski slope with a shallower climb at the beginning of the runway and a much more pronounced climb on the second half of the runway. A successful go-around after the missed approach point was improbable. The missed approach point was at the final approach fix.

Sparrevohn was a 4,200-foot gravel runway. The slope of the runway averaged 4.8% uphill for landing on Runway 34. Its most interesting feature was the approach. A few miles before the runway was a ridge. The pilot needed to clear the ridge and start a rapid descent to land in the first 500 feet of the runway. Few pilots tried. The upslope allowed them to land beyond 1,000 feet down the runway, and they often needed more power to get to the parking ramp. On 28 April 1978, a Firebird crew tried to go around beyond the missed approach point and failed. None of the seven people on board survived, and the aircraft debris is still there.

Cape Newenham was a 3,945-foot gravel runway. The slope of the runway averaged 7.7% uphill for landing on Runway 15. It was on the west coast of Alaska, and the wind and the birds over the ocean made the approach challenging. The missed approach point was two miles from the approach end of the runway. A successful go-around inside the missed approach point was improbable.

*Cape Newenham*

Cape Romanzof was a 3,955-foot gravel runway. The slope of the runway was 2.3% for landing on Runway 02. It was on the west coast of Alaska, and aircrews needed to watch out for birds over the ocean. The winds whipping around the side of the mountain made it a squirrely place to land. In 1985, the wind blew a C-130 off the side of the runway and into a gully.

This happened during the bi-annual Brimfrost exercise. The Firebirds had strict wind limitations for landing at these remote locations and wouldn't go. So another aircrew and aircraft supporting the exercise from the continental United States chose to go. Fortunately, they slid off the runway soon after landing because the gully got deeper as the runway rose up the mountainside. There was significant damage to the left side of the aircraft and minor injuries to some of the people on board.

There were also three special qualification two-way sites that had interesting challenges. Tatalina sat on a knoll. Both ends of the runway dropped off and into the valley below. Tin City was located on the west coast of Alaska. The instrument approach required the aircrew to fly toward the side of a cliff and land on the runway, perpendicular to the cliff and about one hundred feet beyond it. Cape Lisburne was located on the northwest corner of Alaska. The instrument approach procedure was ninety degrees from the landing direction. The approach procedure began over the Arctic Ocean and was flown towards cliffs along the coastline. On final approach and when the runway was in sight, the pilot needed to make a ninety-degree turn and land on the "beach." Frequently in the summer, the water from the ocean splashed onto the runway, making the wet runway more challenging for takeoffs and landings.

## Canadian DEW Line

Most of the Canadian DEW line was supported by the Canadian military, although there were missions flown by the C-130 squadrons in the United States. No takeoffs or landings at any of the locations were easy, but they were the C-130 "bread and butter" mission. These airplanes were designed to land on short dirt strips in the middle of nowhere. But in Alaska, northern Canada, and Greenland, the bitterly cold winters made flying to these locations difficult.

These sites had metal planking called PSP, asphalt, or gravel runways. There were challenges, and the Raven Gang became short field landing experts. Preparation had a lot to do with it. Skill was the rest.

# Greenland

The United States Air Force put a peacetime 3,000-foot minimum runway length restriction for the C-130 operations. It was a good restriction that had the safety of the aircrew and airplane in mind yet allowed the mission to be accomplished. However, a special mission assault takeoff and landing qualification was required for pilots and flight engineers to operate the aircraft near its maximum performance level or maximum effort operations.

Pilots and flight engineers were required to go through the charts during the planning session of the mission to understand the limitations of the aircraft based on the aircraft's gross weight, outside air temperature, pressure altitude, and the surface condition of the runway. Every day was different.

Touching down on the first 500 feet of a 3,000-foot runway and the pilot's application of the brakes immediately after touchdown usually made for a safe landing. However, the takeoff was the challenge. In cold weather, the aircraft's minimum control speed was often above the minimum takeoff speed. This meant the aircraft could get airborne, but if an engine seized shortly before or after takeoff, there was no guarantee the aircraft would continue flying. Pilots understood this and usually planned to pull the asymmetric engine back to counteract the aerodynamic forces at play.

Many other locations along the North American coast and the Greenland coast were short and challenging runways not associated with the DEW line. For example, Nuuk, the capital of Greenland, was 3,117 feet long and 98 feet wide and had an asphalt surface. Typically, only small jet engine aircraft flew into Nuuk. No roads led to the town, and if the runway was blocked, it stopped a major source of transportation in and out of the town. Nuuk was surrounded by several mountains. Twelve miles to the northeast was Sermitsiaq Mountain, which was about 3,970 feet in height. Closer to the airfield were two other peaks, Store Malene was about 2,590 feet in height, and Lille Malene was 1,380 feet in height.

Thule runway in northwest Greenland had other challenges. It was long enough and wide enough for large aircraft, but parts of it were built on permafrost, which softened during the summer months. Therefore, the

American military painted it white so the runway would reflect the sunlight instead of absorbing it. Alert, a Canadian base in Canada's northeast, and Kulusuk, Mestersvig, and Station Nord, a Danish base, all on the east coast of Greenland, also had unique landing and takeoff challenges.

Many of the DEW line locations closed as technology advanced, and there was no need to keep them open. In Greenland, the Raven Gang still required the assault qualification to operate. During their training, the pilots were required to be assault mission qualified before they were ski mission qualified. This was because there were challenges while operating on the ice cap when they needed to take off at stall speed, and the assault training provided them a good background of the risks involved.

CHAPTER 9

# INUIT DOGS

In January of 1988, the dogs in northern Greenland were dying. A distemper epidemic hit the canine population, and it was highly contagious. The primary sources of food for the Inuit communities in this area were hunting, and fishing and the only way to get to their hunting grounds were with dogs pulling sleds. The distemper virus had never affected Greenland dogs in the past, so they had not been vaccinated.

Over seven hundred dogs were infected. This equated to ninety percent of the Inuit dog sled population being wiped out. In some places, vaccinations had started to be carried out, but it was too late to be effective. The native communities of northern Greenland were faced with a severe problem. The United States National Library of Medicine National Institutes of Health reported: *"The spread of canine distemper seems connected with a Canadian outbreak and communicated by foxes. Once established, the further spread apparently was by traveling dog teams."*

Any thoughts of importing dogs from other countries were naive. These were extraordinary animals with their own 4,000-year history and were deeply entwined in the Inuit culture. The lives of the people and their dogs were dependent upon one another. They were hunting partners. The dogs typically found game such as polar bears, musk ox, caribou, or seal and trapped the animal until the human could catch up and kill the quarry for food, fuel, clothing, and other materials necessary for existence.[64]

Every team of Inuit dogs had an Alpha dog. A confident Alpha was an owner's most valuable asset. A strong Alpha could rule for many years with a minimum of bloodshed by preventing or stopping fights among lower-ranking dogs.[65] Inuit dogs were not racing dogs. They were sled dogs, pack animals, and guard dogs. They had been bred for centuries to haul people and cargo, sometimes up to twice their body weight, at times on limited rations, and often under the most adverse weather conditions. These were tough and determined animals with a millennium of working in harsh arctic conditions.[66] No other dogs would do.

# Lions Club

The Inuit populations affected by the distemper virus contacted other Greenlanders, including the communities in Disko Bay, Greenland, through the Lions Club. The Lions Club was a service organization started in Chicago in 1916 and spread around the world. All funds raised by Lions Clubs from the general public were used for charitable purposes projects that benefited local communities of an individual club.

The three Lions Clubs in Greenland, the Danish Lions Club, and Lions International heard about this disaster. More than $29,000 was donated to buy 224 dogs from other Inuit communities and 4,400 pounds of food for the animals.[67] The Lions Club in the town of Ilulissat was the primary disaster response location. All the dogs were bought and vaccinated there.

# Ilulissat

A three- to five-mile-wide fjord along the coastline thrust enormous broken masses out into Disko Bay. These ice masses, or icebergs, originated on the Greenland ice cap and flowed down into the open bay. From the bay, they floated into the open ocean. To the north of this ice flow was a small town. It was the third-largest town in Greenland. Until January of 1979, it was known by its Danish colonial name, Jakobshaven. In 1979, Greenland attained Home-Rule.[68] The town was now known by its native name, Ilulissat.

Just north of the town, 1.7 miles away, there was a small runway. Jakobshaven, or Ilulissat, Airport was a small international airfield serving the entire Disko Bay Region and North and West Greenland. It was the third-busiest airport on the island. Ilulissat was a more southern location than where the dog population had been destroyed. The sea ice had already begun to break up in the area, and the ice fishing season had ended. This was very fortunate because Ilulissat fishermen could now donate some of their dogs to the cause. In the more northern locations, fishing lasted a few months longer. The importation of these dogs to the north meant the animals could begin work immediately. The only problem that remained was how to get the dogs north in time to feed the local Inuit communities.

## The Runway

In March of 1988, the Danes and Greenlanders approached the American Embassy of Copenhagen, Denmark, and asked the Americans if they could transport the dogs. They, in turn, contacted the Headquarters of the United States Air Force. On 15 March 1988, the Chief of Staff of the Air Force approved the dog airlift from Ilulissat to Thule Air Base. It was an American military base located on the northwest coast of Greenland. The Air Force contacted a small New York Air National Guard unit, the 109th Tactical Airlift Group, to see if the Raven Gang could provide the transportation.

On 18 March 1988, Lt. Col. Karl Doll, the Raven Gang operations officer, received a formal message approving the airlift. Since 1975, the Raven Gang was America's Arctic experts who flew throughout the northern coast of North America, resupplying the distance early warning, or DEW, stations. The DEW stations were radar sites that provided an early warning alert if the Soviet Union attacked from over the Arctic.

Doll scheduled the airlift during one of the Raven Gang's regularly scheduled rotations to Greenland. The dog airlift from Ilulissat was not the typical Raven Gang mission. They were better known for flying C-130 aircraft with skis, LC-130s, supporting the Greenland ice cap's DEW stations. This mission didn't require skis; however, it had its own unique challenges.

The C-130 was capable of operations from most of the smooth, relatively hard-surface runways. The question wasn't the aircraft; it was the runway. Ilulissat runway was short. For peacetime operations, the C-130 aircraft operations were restricted to airfields with a minimum length of 3,000 feet. Ilulissat runway was 2,746 feet long and 98 feet wide. The strength of the runway was also unknown. Could it handle the weight of the aircraft? It made no sense to land there if the airplane wasn't capable of leaving after it arrived.

Due to permafrost levels in the ground, finding locations to build runways above the Arctic Circle presented challenges to local Greenlandic communities. The Ilulissat Airport was constructed between 1982 and 1984. It had an asphalt runway. The subsurface of the soils was tested before it was built. There were different levels of clays and permafrost, but it rested on a solid foundation. During construction, the permafrost and other subsurface soils of concern were removed and replaced with rockfill under the runway, taxiways, and the terminal area. This created very stable conditions, and Ilulissat Airport was considered a high-strength airfield.[69]

The remaining question was whether Doll could get a waiver to operate on such a short runway. On 24 March 1988, the Adjutant General of New York, on behalf of the Raven Gang, requested a waiver from the Military Airlift Command, located at Scott Air Force Base, Illinois, to operate on the 2,746-foot runway. Doll provided a point paper explaining the mission's scope with its details and how he intended to carry it out.

The mission parameters were:

- 220 sled dogs
- 4,400 pounds of food
- Seven dog handlers
- Double-shuttle—110 dogs and half the food per flight
- Each dog will be in a separate cage, 35 inches x 27 inches x 28 inches
- The average weight of 90 pounds per dog and cage
- 84,000-pound C-130 aircraft, not an LC-130
- 19,000 pounds of fuel
- 9,900 pounds of dogs and cages
- 2,200 pounds of food
- 1,000 pounds for dog handlers
- 116,100 pounds for the total takeoff weight from Ilulissat

Doll's request was approved.

# Sondrestrom

It was a fortunate coincidence Lt. Col. Ray Tousey, and Major Will Merwin were scheduled for the planned DYE site resupply mission in Greenland. Both were C-130 pilots during the Vietnam conflict. Tousey was the mission commander for the week. On 17 April 1988, the Raven Gang departed Schenectady County Airport. After a six-hour flight, they arrived in Sondrestrom, Greenland. Sondrestrom was considered the Raven Gang's second home. They kept the LC-130 flying operation very simple and very small. A mission commander led a team of flyers, a maintenance contingent, and cargo builders and loaders.

The Sondrestrom local area was notable. The town of Kangerlussuaq was at the end of a wide fjord cut into the mountainous terrain. The terrain had been gouged out when the glaciers receded from the area during the last ice age. The fjord was filled with glacial waters. The waters drained from the Greenland ice cap, down the fjord, and into the open ocean.

The runway was on the east end of the east-west oriented Søndre Strømfjord. The orientation of the runway was east-west. Both sides of the fjord were mountainous. The runway was on the north side of the fjord, and on the final approach to it, the navigational guidance system took the aircraft close to the terrain to line up with the runway. Pilots tended to cheat a little to the right as they flew down the approach to stay away from the terrain. It wasn't necessary, but it made them feel a bit more comfortable. The step-down to altitude was aggressive at specific points. The aircraft needed to clear terrain before the descent could begin. However, any delay in the descent made it almost impossible to be at the proper altitude to land during bad weather conditions.

Known by its colonial name, Sondrestrom Runway, it was about 9,000 feet long and 200 feet wide. It had a noticeable dip at the beginning of Runway 09. If the pilot landed within the first 1,000 feet, it had a sharp incline before leveling off. To the north of the runway was the international portion of the airfield. Scandinavian Airlines had a significant operation there. The north side of the runway also had the airport terminal, the weather briefing location, and the flight planning center. It had a small-town atmosphere with a grocery store and other small businesses. On the parking apron to the southside of the runway, the Danish military had an operations center. The airport tower and fire department were also located there. This was Sondrestrom Air Base, where the Raven Gang operated and parked their aircraft.

South of the airfield, the landscape descended into a small valley. This was the location of the United States military facility. There was a base exchange for buying clothes and other necessities; a commissary; dormitories; a dining hall, an officers' club, a non-commissioned officers club; and the Arctic Hotel only available to official visitors. The town was surrounded by a river that flowed from the ice cap to the east and initially came straight toward the runway, bent to the south, then east again, surrounding the town, and flowed into the fjord. A bridge extended over the river, and beyond it, the terrain rose rapidly. It was a beautiful area for hiking.

*Approach into Sondy*

# Preparations

The humanitarian crisis of the Inuit dogs attracted international attention. Dog cages were flown into Sondrestrom Airport from Denmark by Scandinavian Airlines. Danish and Greenlandic civilian journalists arrived via Scandinavian Airlines, also. Journalists intended to board the LC-130 aircraft and fly from Sondrestrom Air Base to Thule Air Base, via Ilulissat, with the dogs. At Thule Air Base, a media escort would guide them around when they arrived.

During the week, Tousey took his mission commander's vehicle over the Scandinavian Airlines to talk with the people there. It was a very interesting discussion. He was told a similar airlift of dogs had been tried before, and things didn't work out.

Tousey asked, "What happened?"

They replied, "All the dogs were dead when they arrived."

Tousey asked, "What killed them?"

"No one knows."

Scandinavian Airlines personnel had retained the lore from many years ago. It was very useful information. But the dogs dying en route to Thule was very disturbing, and it gave Tousey pause. He mulled this problem over throughout the week. He needed to come up with a plan to get the dogs to Thule Air Base alive. If the dogs didn't survive, the hyped-up media attention was sure to let the world know about it. The real concern, though, was for the people. If the dogs died, the Inuit population in northern Greenland would be in real trouble.

As he thought over the problem, he knew it was typical for these dogs to get intensely agitated with unfamiliar surroundings. Perhaps the heat in the airplane, coupled with the fear of being caged, in a very unfamiliar atmosphere of different noises and smells caused the dogs to hyperventilate. Perhaps the heat, agitation, and heavy breathing caused them to suffocate. It was no longer possible to know what happened to the dogs so many years ago, but Tousey was determined he'd protect the dogs as much as possible.

Tousey was in the active-duty Air Force in the early 1970s. His C-130 unit was based in Taiwan, and they flew missions into Vietnam. There were few restrictions when flying in the jungle. He researched new obstacles ahead of time and addressed them. If he couldn't completely solve the problem, he'd mitigate the risk. He lived by jungle rules, "You find out what works, and you use it." If any additional concerns popped up, he addressed them as they occurred.

| Skier 87 Aircrew | |
|---|---|
| **Pilot:** | Lt. Col. Ray Tousey |
| **Copilot:** | Major Will Merwin |
| **Navigator:** | First Lieutenant Ernie Grey |
| **Flight Engineer:** | Technical Sergeant John Pangborn |
| **Loadmaster:** | Technical Sergeant Bob Macauley |

Major Will Merwin was the copilot for the mission. He also flew C-130 aircraft during the Vietnam conflict and was a reliable, steady pilot on the quiet side. He would be an excellent backup for Tousey.

First Lieutenant Ernie Grey, the navigator, had been qualified in the ski mission for 2½ years, and he was good at what he did. He was a part-time "Guard-baby." Guard-babies were never in the active-duty military. All of Grey's military time had been spent in the Air National Guard. He had a full-time job outside the military working as a civilian electronics engineer.

Technical Sergeant John Pangborn joined the active duty in 1977 but left after six years. He had been flying with the Raven Gang for about four years while he went to school to obtain a college degree. He had a maintenance background and was an excellent flight engineer.

Bob Macauley was a Legacy Guard-baby. Legacy Guard-babies were second-generation guard members. Macauley's father had been in the Guard unit years before. Bob Macauley was an outstanding loadmaster.

The next morning the aircrew put the finishing touches on the plan and walked to the aircraft. Tousey told his crew to keep their cold-weather gear close by; parka, fat boy pants, hat, gloves, and mukluks. He wanted to fly the aircraft unpressurized from Ilulissat to Thule. At altitude in April, an unpressurized flight in northern Greenland meant the aircraft would get very cold. Pangborn could probably keep the flight deck warm, but Tousey intended to keep the back of the aircraft cold. The cold temperature would keep the dogs closer to their natural habitat. In an unpressurized aircraft at 12,000 feet, the air was much thinner than at sea level. The thin air also would make the dogs punky, sleepy and lessen their anxiety.

On 19 April 1988, the only remaining issue was whether the aircraft's landing distance would be adequate when they arrived. Tousey bounced this question off Pangborn. His job was to determine the required takeoff and landing distance and takeoff and landing airspeeds. This was based on the weight of the aircraft and specific environmental conditions. Pangborn told him: "If we go in there lightweight, and if the runway is dry, we shouldn't have a problem."

That was the plan. Tousey intended to land at Ilulissat at a very light weight due to the limitations of the runway. The aircrew already planned to make two trips from Ilulissat to Thule. On the first leg of the trip, Pangborn loaded enough fuel to get to Ilulissat, then to Thule. At Thule, he intended to add enough fuel to fly back to Ilulissat and back to Thule, again. At Thule, the final refueling stop, he intended to add enough fuel to go to Ilulissat then back to Sondrestrom. At each phase of the flight, the aircraft would be as light as possible, with as little fuel needed to operate successfully, without taking from the town's limited fuel supply.

Before leaving Sondrestrom, Pangborn also briefed Tousey on the takeoff out of Ilulissat. This would be the riskiest part of the mission.

Because of the short runway, from the time the aircraft reached the predetermined decision speed of eighty-five knots until it accelerated to the minimum control speed of 106 knots, any directional control failures, such as an engine seizure, could doom the flight. The Air Force flight regulations left the decision to accept this risk or find a better solution with the aircraft commander. One possible solution was to wait for another day when the environmental conditions provided better conditions. However, waiting for another day with better weather conditions wasn't an option. The Inuits needed the dogs before the ice began to melt.

Another possible solution was to limit the cargo and fuel, an option which they had already considered. This lightened the weight of the aircraft and increased the aircraft's acceleration to close the gap between the decision speed and the minimum control speed. This was why two flights were scheduled instead of one. The aircrew talked about all of these issues before departing Sondrestrom. Better planning produced better results. Looking early at the weak points in the plan allowed for better outcomes if things did go wrong.

## The Dog Lift

The Scandinavian Airlines cargo people arrived with the dog cages. Bob Macauley loaded them in the back of the aircraft. Ernie Grey put the coordinates for Ilulissat Airport into the aircraft's inertial navigation systems: North 69°14.59', West 51°3.43'. It was a direct thirty-minute flight to Disko Bay.

Above the Arctic Circle, the magnetic lines of variation grew closer together as they approached the magnetic North Pole, so Grey needed to keep a close eye on the navigation. Later in the day, as they approached Thule, it would be more difficult for the navigation systems to maintain their accuracy. If the weather didn't allow them to proceed visually, Grey intended to convert to true navigation.

Using magnetic-north was the typical form of navigation throughout the world. The magnetic North Pole varied and was somewhere over northern Canada. Navigation using true-north would require manipulating the aircraft's inertial navigation systems. True-north was a fixed point over the Arctic Ocean and easier for the inertial navigation systems to navigate.

When the aircraft was loaded, the aircrew got in their seats and started the engines. Tousey taxied the aircraft to the runway, and Sondrestrom Tower cleared them for departure. It was a cold April day with clear skies. The takeoff was routine. The flight was short. As they descended over Disko Bay, there were large ice masses in the bay, drifting out to sea. The airfield had a non-directional beacon that led them to the runway. Will Merwin contacted the Ilulissat Airfield Tower to notify them of their arrival. The tower controller cleared them to land. Ilulissat runway's magnetic orientation was 080 degrees in one direction and 260 degrees in the other. It was 95 feet above sea level, 350 miles north of the Arctic Circle.

Tousey flew the aircraft along the coastline to let the town know of their arrival. He made the short-field landing look simple. He was an artist in his craft. When the aircraft was parked, they shut down the engines.

Loading the dogs began immediately, after that. The people were interested in the aircraft and began to cluster around it, so the aircrew opened up the doors for the people to walk through.

The townspeople helped cage the dogs. The Ilulissat children had been released from school to say farewell to their animals. There were tears in their eyes. The dogs were valued partners and friends. They were part of the family. The people knew they would never see their cherished pups again. But what they did was necessary for the people's survival in the north.

Tousey thought to himself, *"These people didn't allow a day in school to interfere with the kids' education. There are a lot of people with advanced degrees that missed this course in school."*

Every dog was put in a separate cage. This avoided any fights between the dogs during the flight. It was time to go when the dogs were all in their cages. The people lined the taxiway as the aircraft slowly rolled by. Pangborn was astounded to see all the children waving and cheering as they passed. These people considered the aircrew heroes.

*Inuit Dogs, Tousey Pic*

Tousey taxied the aircraft onto the runway and down to "the last brick" before turning the aircraft around. He wanted the most runway available for the takeoff. The tail of the plane was hanging over the side of a hill. He stood on the brakes as he ran the engines to maximum power. Then he released the brakes, and the aircraft began to accelerate.

At the computed decision speed, Merwin said, "Go." This notified Tousey he could no longer stop within the confines of the remaining runway ahead of him. To stop the aircraft after decision speed would result in skidding off the end of the runway. Therefore, stopping was no longer an option.

There was a twenty-one-knot gap between when Merwin said, "Go" and when the aircraft achieved three-engine minimum control speed. If the aircraft had an engine seizure during this time, the aircrew was still committed to getting airborne. If they managed to get airborne, this didn't guarantee they had the speed to stay airborne. This was a known risk the aircrew accepted.

Tousey kept the aircraft on the centerline of the runway as it accelerated. They were within 500 feet of the end of the runway when he lifted the aircraft off of the ground. The aircraft climbed out smoothly. Grey and Pangborn noted how noisy the dogs were, barking and howling in the back. As the aircraft climbed, it got quieter. Then, for the next two hours, everything was silent in the back.

The flight to Thule was smooth, with no hiccups. Pangborn kept the aircraft unpressurized so the dogs would sleep. The thin air also could put humans to sleep, so the aircrew had an oxygen mask nearby. Oxygen regulators attached to the masks provided the additional oxygen the aircrew needed, and from time to time, they used it to stay alert. When the aircraft was within range of Thule, Tousey started a descent. As the atmosphere provided more oxygen, the dogs began to wake. Soon, it became hard to hear inside the aircraft. Usually, the noise of the engines drowned out any noise within the aircraft. But the dogs were agitated, and they were letting the aircrew know about it. Tousey was relieved. The dogs were alive.

Thule runway was unusual. Built in 1951–1952, it was 10,000 feet long and 220 feet wide. Outside air temperatures in the winter could reach -35 degrees below zero Fahrenheit. The wind chill could get much lower when wind approached hurricane force. In the summer, the permafrost thawing beneath the runway frequently caused large depressions creating hazards for aircraft. Since the 1960s, the runway was painted white with red markings. The light-reflecting white paint was very effective in reducing the thaw of the permafrost. But the slick painted surface created other hazards, such as hydroplaning when the runway got wet.[70]

The weather was clear when the C-130 landed at Thule. It was mid-April, so the ground was still frozen, and the runway depressions were minimal. Tousey taxied to the specified parking location and stopped. Once the aircraft was parked and the engines shut down, a flatbed truck backed up to the aircraft, and the dogs were offloaded.

It was a frenzied and jubilant atmosphere as the people waited to receive their new animals. The dogs barked and howled. As the dogs were distributed to the Inuit families, the handlers tried to keep the same sled teams together. The dogs were tagged to identify the team they had run with all season in Ilulissat. It mattered. Some dogs were enemies. It wouldn't be a good idea to put two dogs that hated each other next to one another. Some dogs were friendlier than others. This had pros and cons. Best friends tend to clown around together, and this also caused issues. The best thing was to put a dog next to another dog that was compatible and was focused on pulling the sled.[71]

The Thule base commander and Danish embassy personnel greeted Tousey and his crew. Tousey was very good at the "meet and greet." He knew how to be an ambassador for his country during such occasions. Handshakes and words of appreciation were expressed to the aircrew for their success in transporting the dogs alive in challenging circumstances. As each Inuit family received their dogs, they harnessed them and headed for home. Some of these people reportedly lived 120 miles away.[72] As they left the airbase, they returned to their familiar arctic environment with their new dog team. Now, it was time to hunt!

Tousey's aircrew closed up the aircraft and returned to Ilulissat. The journalists and others returned with them. Pangborn was a bit amused. It couldn't have been comfortable for the people in the back of the aircraft. The dog cages were still there. The smell of the dogs and their remnants filled the air. Bob Macauley and the maintenance guys cleaned up the back of the aircraft after the dogs left, but it still reeked. Upon arriving at Ilulissat, they picked up the remaining dogs and returned to Thule later in the afternoon.

# Celebration

When the mission was completed, the aircrew returned to Ilulissat one final time. They spent the evening there, and the town held a celebratory dinner in their honor. The mayor attended and, in a speech, praised the aircrew. In the morning, Merwin couldn't find Tousey. He suspected he was up to something, so he grabbed Tousey's overnight bag and flying gear and loaded it on the aircraft. He planned the flight back to Sondrestrom with Grey while Pangborn, Macauley, and the maintenance guys pre-flighted the aircraft.

They were running very late. Merwin knew Tousey would show up eventually. He ran the checklists with Pangborn and the rest of the crew and got the engines running. Then they waited. After a short time, Tousey showed up via dog sled pulled by four dogs in a fan formation, with a beautiful Danish woman mushing them. He said his farewell to the woman and nonchalantly walked to the aircraft.

Merwin was right. Tousey was up to something. On the previous evening, Tousey ran into an old friend, Karun. In the early morning hours, Karun knocked on his hotel door. She told him to get outside. She threw an animal skin over a sled and told him to sit down. She sat in front and began to mush the dogs. Tousey later said, "She took me on a dog sled ride. In the beginning, it was a pleasant ride with eight dogs fanned out in front. I expected to be gone about an hour."

*Karun, Tousey Pic*

As the ride progressed, Karun mushed the dogs into the higher terrain around the town. Eventually, they were on top, and the Inuit dogs began to run. They ran as if possessed. As the dim early morning hours began to transform into a sunny day, the dogs kept running. Boulders popped up in the distance, and Karun directed the fan of dogs in their direction. The dogs closed ranks as they approached. Tousey tightened his grip, wrapping his arms and legs around Karun as she weaved among the rocks to avoid crushing an elbow or kneecap.

After about an hour, Karun slowed and eventually stopped the sled. She climbed off and prepared breakfast. Together they sat and ate biscuits and drank tea. In the distance, Tousey saw the airfield. He knew he was late and wasn't going to get back in time. Pointing to his watch, he told Karun he needed to return. In the early morning hour, they heard the aircraft engines starting. Karun had a shortcut back to the airfield. They climbed back on the sled, and the dogs began to run. As they approached a steep hillside, Karun stopped. She moved the leads of the dogs under the sled and pointed down the hill. The dogs were behind. She climbed back on the sled and nosed the sled over the steep slope with the dogs acting as the brakes.

Tousey said, "Slowly we accelerated; then we accelerated more. Before long, we were out of control. As we sped down the hillside, my butt slipped off the back of the sled. Now it was acting as the brake." They impacted the ground at the bottom of the hill. Everything had gone catawampus. As Tousey lay on the ground, he took stock of his health, fingers, hands, toes, feet, arms, legs, neck, head. All seemed to be in working order. As he did this, he saw four dogs running over the horizon. They had slipped out of their harnesses.

Karun was picking herself up off of the ground. She was doing her health check on herself. The sled was tipped over, so they worked together to set it aright and organized the remaining dogs. With the four remaining dogs, Karun mushed the sled to the aircraft. As Tousey approached the aircraft, he decided to be casual about the situation. He was late. So instead of going to the back of the aircraft and changing into his uniform, he decided to get airborne, wearing his civilian clothes. When he stepped into the aircraft, the rest of the crew knew something had gone wrong. The seat of his pants was utterly shredded. The blue from his denim jeans was gone. Only white strands were holding the seat of his pants together. Tousey had a reputation for flying by the seat-of-his-pants. Apparently, he did the same with everything he did.

CHAPTER 10

# OPEN SNOW OPERATIONS

Leadership at the 109th Tactical Airlift Group knew the DYE sites were aging. To leave the fate of the ski mission with anyone else would have been foolish. They knew they needed to find a new follow-on mission for the Raven Gang. Without one, the base would be closed. Throughout the 1980s, they pursued three options. The first was to support the National Science Foundation in Greenland. Everyone recognized the logic in this, but it created new challenges for the Raven Gang.

The second option was to support the Department of Defense on the frozen Arctic Ocean. Again, this held new challenges. They failed at first, but after the Raven Gang reviewed their failure, they developed new procedures and succeeded for years to come.

The third option was to take over the National Science Foundation's Antarctica support operation from the Navy. This took years of planning and preparation. Initially, it started with supporting the Navy, and eventually, they were given the mission.

## Task Force Slide

Landing a C-130 aircraft with skis in the middle of the barren Greenland ice cap was fraught with hazards.[73] The most obvious one was once you landed, could you get airborne again? Flight tests of the skibirds on a lake in Bemidji, Minnesota, proved it was possible. These tests showed the nosewheel steering was ineffective while the aircraft was on skis, and it could only be used as an assist. Applying asymmetric engine power was necessary to maneuver the aircraft during taxiing.

The test pilot stated:

> *"The use of maximum propeller reversing just after touchdown on all landings resulted in an average landing distance of 1250 feet for all gross weight conditions."*[74]

Further tests were done on the Greenland ice cap. In mid-April 1958, the task force arrived at Sondrestrom Air Base. Four flights, with multiple takeoffs and landings, were conducted.

The first thirty-four ski landings and thirty-three takeoffs were completed without any issues. However, on the thirty-fourth takeoff, the nose gear cylinder snapped when it hit a two-foot-high wave-like ridge of hard snow called a sastruga. In a written statement the test pilot described what happened on the next landing:

> *"When visibility was restored from the blowing snow after prop reversal, it was observed that the aircraft was in a nose low attitude. Investigation revealed that the nose gear had collapsed rearward being pushed up and back into the cargo compartment. The nose of the aircraft was resting on the nose ski."*[75]

The fourteen-person team aboard the aircraft had no idea how long a recovery operation would take, days or weeks until someone figured out how to rescue them? The pilot decided to attempt a takeoff, but first, he removed electrical power and hydraulics to the ski systems. He was successful in getting airborne. He then selectively turned on electrical power. He landed at Sondrestrom without sustaining further damage. The ski tests were terminated and considered a success.

The preliminary report said the following:

> *"The ground handling characteristics on skis of the test aircraft were found to be satisfactory with the exception of the large turning radius required. Ski landings were made using 100% flaps and touching down in a nose high attitude at an indicated airspeed of about 90 knots."*

Some of the optimum pilot recommendations for ski takeoffs at the 10,000-foot level on the ice cap was as follows:

- Flaps set at one-hundred percent.
- Maximum available power applied, and directional control maintained with nose ski steering.

No attempt was made to lift the nose ski until an indicated airspeed of sixty-five knots was reached. Then full elevator was used to lift the nose ski, and the aircraft rapidly accelerated to takeoff velocity."

Lockheed made modifications to the aircraft based upon these tests. The following year, for their first five weeks in Greenland, a test pilot from Smyrna, Tennessee, was assigned as a technical advisor to the 61st Troop Carrier Squadron. The first operational mission was scheduled for 1 April 1959. The squadron was expected to ease into their new mission. They were expected to get some familiarization training on the ice cap mission and take some time to learn their new aircraft.

The 61st Troop Carrier Squadron Commander didn't bother to ease into their new tasks. The first two C-130Ds arrived at Sondrestrom on March 20th and 21st. The first operational mission was flown on 23 March 1959 and landed at the future DYE-2 location coordinates. The next day they flew to the future DYE-3 location. There were no prepared landing surfaces, just the wide expansive ice cap. The aircraft returned to Sondrestrom with ski problems. The main skis weren't fully extending when they were on the snow, or once they were extended, they weren't remaining in the fully extended position, regardless of the aircraft's gross weight.

A Lockheed field service representative was in Sondrestrom. He contacted the company in Georgia, USA, and notified them of the problem. Their solution was to increase the main ski hydraulic pressure from 1,535 psi to 2,000 psi and the nose ski air charge from 1,435 psi to 1,900 psi. They did not understand the problem and had no idea what they had just done. The pilot knew the increased pressures would eliminate the shock-absorbing protection for the main skis. The lack of shock absorption created greater jolts, and this would increase stresses and damage. However, his concerns were ignored.[76]

Both aircraft sustained major damage while landing at DYE-3 the following day. Three days later, the pilot of another C-130D made a normal touchdown at DYE-3 and hit a sastruga. The hard impact on the ice berm sheared the nose gear from the aircraft. The open snow landings continued to take their toll on the aircraft.

# PICO

Supporting the National Science Foundation in Greenland required the aircrews to become proficient in open snow operations.[77] As the name implies, these operations required the Raven Gang aircrews to land the aircraft in the middle of open snowfields without any foreknowledge of the snow's surface conditions. There were no DYE sites at which to spend the night if the aircraft broke down. There was no skiway if the snow was too difficult to get airborne once they landed. Scientists selected all of the locations, and much of their work dealt with drilling ice cores in the ice cap. These ice cores told scientists about the atmosphere of the earth through the ages.

Before 1974, CRREL was responsible for the logistics of the National Science Foundation's shallow ice drilling projects in Greenland. In 1974, this responsibility shifted to the Ross Ice Shelf Project, RISP, operating in Antarctica. The University of Nebraska-Lincoln ran the RISP management office from 1971 through 1979.

The Greenland extension of RISP became known as the Polar Ice Coring Office, or PICO. It provided scientists and their subcontractors' support for operations from Sondrestrom Air Base, Greenland. This included transportation, military clearances, access to airbase facilities, and on-site coordination of field activities. Their field offices provided the link between the National Science Foundation's funds and the scientists' and their subcontractors' needs. They maintained snow vehicles, shelters, radios, and generators and provided the fuel necessary to operate them. PICO's ice drilling operation designed, built, and operated ice drilling equipment for National Science Foundation-sponsored projects. They provided drilling services, drilling equipment to scientific parties, and borehole tracking services for glaciological and geophysical projects.

In 1979, RISP shut down operations in Antarctica, and PICO became a separate National Science Foundation contract focused in Greenland. In 1988, the University of Alaska, Fairbanks, was awarded the contract for ice drilling support operations, and PICO moved to Alaska.[78]

The National Science Foundation owned seven LC-130 aircraft. VXE-6, a Navy squadron out of Point Mugu, California, flew the aircraft and maintained them in support of science in Antarctica. The Navy squadron's primary mission was centered on Antarctica. Their secondary mission was in the Arctic.

In 1979, the Navy had one aircraft in Greenland with forty support people to collect ice cores from the ice cap and fly them to Nebraska. At the end of the week, they returned to the United States with their forty people and the scientists, but they left the ice cores on the ice cap. Fortunately, the Raven Gang was in Sondrestrom flying their resupply mission to the DYE sites. A representative from PICO appealed to them for assistance. Lieutenant Colonel Karl Doll agreed to schedule an aircrew to do it.

Karl Doll was the air operations officer for the 109th Tactical Airlift Group. The Raven Gang's unique mission meant their continued existence was always in doubt. He understood the ongoing operation of the DYE sites was always in question. It was a year-by-year decision made by the Air Force. Doll was always looking for opportunities to expand their operations.

When there was a unique and challenging mission, Lieutenant Colonel Ray Tousey was the pilot schedulers called upon first. He succeeded in getting the ice cores from the Greenland ice cap, and this began a long and close relationship with the National Science Foundation, but there were challenges along the way.

## Raven Gang's Open Snow Challenges

The science support mission was significantly different than operations at the DYE sites. A skiway had been created for landings at the DYE sites, but the locations for the science support missions could be anywhere on the ice cap. The Raven Gang was about to get intimately familiar with open snow operations.

Landing in the open snow was the first part of a continuing battle on the ice cap. Every day the ice cap was different from the previous day. Many different variables impacted the condition of the snow. The temperature was an obvious one. Sun angle and cloud conditions were not so obvious. A temperature of -10° Fahrenheit with direct sunlight made snow conditions soft and wet, and a challenge to ski due to the radiant heat.

There were other variables to consider also. Pressure altitude impacted aircraft engine performance. Humidity impacted the dryness of the snow. Any difference could significantly affect how the pilot managed ground operations, and the management of the ground operations couldn't be determined until landing. The Raven Gang pilots needed to find many techniques to fill their bag of tricks.

Offloading the cargo was the second part of the battle. Getting stuck in thc snow was a real possibility; therefore, pilots didn't want to stop unless it was necessary. To offload the cargo without stopping, the Raven Gang created their own way to offload the aircraft's cargo. They took the standard C-130 combat offload procedure and adapted it to their needs. They sought and received higher headquarters permission to lower the ramp of the aircraft twelve inches above the snow's surface during their offload instead of leaving it parallel as an extension to the floor of the aircraft. During the procedure, they never stopped. They slowed to a crawl until the loadmasters gave the call to accelerate. The pilot then pushed up power. The momentum of the acceleration carried the pallets back until they exited the aircraft. During the 1980 and 1981 Greenland seasons, this technique had not been developed yet. It took years to finally adopted it after much trial and error.

Getting airborne again was the third challenge and often the most difficult. Every pilot had their favorite techniques. Taxiing and taking off in the LC-130 aircraft had challenges similar to a person snow skiing. Snow conditions determine how easy skiing would be that day.

## Humbolt Glacier

The 109th Airlift Wing and the National Science Foundation's relationship expanded through the 1980s, and the Raven Gang found a secondary mission. When the last DYE site on the Greenland ice cap closed in 1989, the science support mission became their primary mission. When Sondrestrom Air Base closed a few years later the Raven Gang moved their operations to Thule Air Base.

*Thule Airbase, circa 1988*

When Lieutenant Colonel Graham Pritchard went to Humbolt Glacier in 1994, the Raven Gang was familiar with the ice cap's open snow challenges. It was a routine mission. The aircrew took off from Thule Air Base and proceeded to Humbolt Glacier, about fifty miles north. It was the widest tidewater glacier in the northern hemisphere.[79] PICO was supporting a NASA project to measure its accumulation and ablation.

It was the end of the current Greenland Season, so on the return flight, Pritchard was scheduled to bring the camp personnel, and all of their science and camp equipment, back to Thule. His aircraft was loaded with fifty-five-gallon drums of fuel on pallets on his flight from Thule to Humbolt Glacier to build a fuel cache for helicopters during the next Greenland Season. Upon arrival at Humbolt Glacier, the outside air temperature was mild. The mission required a lengthy ground time to load the camp equipment, so Pritchard shut down the aircraft engines but kept the APU, auxiliary power unit, running.

The aircrew left the airplane, wandered around the site, and left Lou Ott, Pritchard's flight engineer, on the flight deck to monitor the aircraft systems. Pritchard noticed a sudden loss of the noise and trudged back to the airplane. The APU had shut itself down before Ott could stop it, and he was unable to re-started it. This was a big deal because the APU was needed to start the aircraft engines. A maintenance team from Thule needed to come out.

The aircrew pulled the camp generator from the back of the aircraft, and everyone set up a temporary camp for the night. They pitched tents, and Pritchard got on the HF radio and notified the mission commander in Thule of their situation. Pritchard had planned to meet with a senior PICO representative that evening in Thule. Instead, they had their meeting in the command tent. When they were finished, Pritchard climbed into his sleeping bag. Soon after he fell asleep, he thought he heard a "wop-wop-wop" noise. His initial thought was it was the generator, and it was already time to get up, but he was wrong.

The noise was a Greenlandair helicopter. Master Sergeant Joe Butler, the crew chief of Pritchard's aircraft, had commandeered it from Thule to take him to Humbolt Glacier. He was coming to get his airplane. As Pritchard crawled out of his sleeping bag, he heard a voice with a British accent outside his tent say, *"Knock, knock, I say, could we borrow a barrel of petrol?"* It was the helicopter pilot wanting to refuel and depart.

Pritchard: *"I climbed out of the tent and saw that Joe had already rolled a barrel of fuel over to the airplane and was priming the APU with a wobble pump. First thing you know, the APU roared to life."*

The aircrew broke camp, loaded the camping gear in the aircraft, and started the aircraft engines. The aircraft was heavily loaded, and the snow was sticky.

The aircraft's ski system functioned separately from the landing gear system. Pilots could move the skis while leaving the landing gear in the down position. Throughout the day, Captain Anthony Danielson, Pritchard's copilot, had left the ski switch in the up position, and the weight of the aircraft was put on the landing gear tires. They sank in the snow.

Pritchard directed Danielson to lower the skis. As they lowered, the aircraft rose higher out of the snow as the skis rotated below the landing gear.

Pritchard pushed up power to slide, but the aircraft didn't move. Regardless of how Pritchard manipulated the throttles, the aircraft refused to budge. The skis were welded to the surface of the snow. It was time to break out the shovels and start digging. They shut down the aircraft engines again. Ott kept a closer eye on the APU. When they thought they had cleared enough snow from around the skis, they climbed back in their seats, started engines, and tried to move again without any luck. They shut down engines and repeated the process.

Digging an LC-130 aircraft out of the snow was an art. The aircrew filled the holes between the skis that the tires created. Danielson then raised the skis again, and the tires lowered back into the snow. Each time he raised the skis, the holes created from the tires were more compacted. Experience told the loadmasters to bring shoring, planks of plywood on their flight. They put the shoring between the skis to create a solid platform for the tires when they were finished digging.

They got in their seats and started the engines again. Danielson lowered the skis as Pritchard added power. The skis broke free of the ice, the tires rolled along on the shoring, and the aircraft moved through the snow. It had taken several hours to break free, but now they had another problem. A piece of the shoring attached itself to the aircraft's left main skis. The aircraft wanted to taxi in circles.

If Pritchard added full power, he couldn't go straight, so he kept the #3 and #4 throttles pulled back. However, with #3 and #4 pulled back, he couldn't accelerate enough to get airborne. He continued to taxi around the campsite turning left and right. The last thing he wanted to do was to stop the aircraft again.

The shoring finally broke free of the aircraft. Pritchard pushed up the throttles, the aircraft accelerated, and they got airborne. It was late in the evening when they returned to Thule Air Base, which was another problem. Thule airfield had specific flying times when aircraft could come and go. The runway was closed. Opening the runway was going to take time, and no one would clarify how much time.

Pritchard had used much more fuel than he intended at Humbolt Glacier. The aircraft needed to land, so Pritchard diverted to North GRIP, a remote European camp on the Greenland ice cap. North GRIP had fuel.

The weather was reported to be good, and it was about an hour flight. As they approached the camp, the weather worsened and was too low to land. Pritchard flew an approach to the skiway, but he couldn't see anything. He climbed the aircraft back up to altitude and proceeded northbound to an area the aircrew noted earlier had clear weather conditions. They found a clear spot, and Pritchard set the aircraft down in the open snow. The engines were running on fumes. They shut them down and kept the APU running. It had been a very long day. Pritchard called Thule and notified Raven Operations of his status and the coordinates of his location.

It took a couple of hours for Raven Operations to get another aircraft ready at Thule. Lt. Col. Jon Adams, the mission commander, flew out to give Pritchard fuel as soon as the Thule opened their runway. He found Pritchard on the ice cap and landed. Both aircrews dragged the hoses from the fueling pallet in the back of Adams aircraft, connected and extended them, and refueled Pritchard's aircraft from Adams' fuel tanks, an aircraft-to-aircraft refueling. When they finished, the hoses were put back on the pallet, and both aircraft took off and returned to Thule.

The Humbolt Glacier mission was far from routine. However, many of the crewmembers had been flying the mission since 1975. The Raven Gang began open snow operations to support the National Science Foundation in 1980. Through trial and error, they wrote their own rules. It didn't make their day any easier, but fourteen years later, they were better prepared than when they first began.

CHAPTER 11

# OPEN SNOW TECHNIQUES

How much snow is on the Greenland ice cap? To determine the mass of the Greenland ice sheet, researchers from the Ohio State University needed airlift support for their cluster project, better known as the Greenland Ice Sheet Project, or GISP.[80] The researchers wanted to measure the surface elevation and velocity changes on the ice sheet. They intended to make geodetic and other geophysical measurements at cluster sites using seven Doppler satellite-tracking receivers, two of them tied to Doppler receiver base stations in Sondrestrom and Nuuk, Greenland.[81]

Since the snow didn't uniformly thicken and thin, sensors needed to be put in different locations around the ice cap. They intended to return in subsequent years and measure whether the snow was thickening or thinning and determine how climate change affected the ice cap.

Supporting GISP proved to be an interesting challenge for the Raven Gang. Until then, they were exclusively supporting the DYE sites. Landing in open snow locations in the middle of the Greenland ice cap created new opportunities and new problems.

In 1980, there were two preferred locations where the scientists wanted Raven Gang support. One was located seventy miles southwest of DYE-2 and was referred to as the Lower Cluster and later was known as the Western Cluster. The other location was east of Jakobshaven Glacier, 180 miles northeast of Sondrestrom, and was referred to as the Upper Cluster.

The Upper Cluster was intended to be nearer the glacier. Scientists wanted a close look at the edge of the ice cap breaking up along the coastline. The Raven Gang's aerial reconnaissance flight, the day before the Upper Cluster mission, revealed multiple crevasses in the area. After a discussion with the scientists, they moved the location further east.

# Lower Cluster, 1980

On 17 June 1980, the original date for the Lower Cluster flight, the Danish government closed down the project. Neither the Raven Gang, PICO contractors, nor the National Science Foundation notified the Danish government of their intentions. It looked like there would be significant delays; however, the Danes approved the flights the following day. It was a lesson that approval was necessary.

Landing in the open snow at a remote location other than the DYE sites was a different and interesting challenge for the Raven Gang. Major Graham Pritchard and Major Ray Tousey were the aircraft commanders for these missions. Their flying styles were significantly different. Both men were skilled and knowledgeable. Pritchard had a more rigid philosophy. He operated by the book. Tousey was more unconventional. He called it "jungle rules." Much of the flying on the ice cap had unique problems to solve. It wasn't always written in the book. Both philosophies were necessary to succeed in the ski mission.

Pritchard was a former active duty Firebird pilot stationed in Alaska flying the Greenland ice cap's ski mission in the early 1970s. After three and a half years, he left active duty service, moved from Alaska to West Virginia, and joined the Air National Guard. He wanted to pursue an airline career, but the 1973 oil embargo made airline jobs hard to come by. Pilots were being furloughed. Instead, in 1975 Pritchard became an air traffic controller, and his first assignment was in Syracuse, New York. During his first week at Syracuse Tower, he saw one of the skibirds flying around. His supervisor told him Alaska transferred their C-130Ds to Schenectady, New York. The next day Pritchard transferred from the West Virginia Air National Guard to New York Air National Guard.

Tousey's military flying career started in Taiwan, flying missions into Vietnam during the war. He flew challenging missions without much guidance, using jungle rules. He figured out what worked, then used it to get the mission done. After the war, he came home to New York and joined the Air National Guard at Schenectady. On the ice cap, he felt right at home. It was a mission without much guidance, and he was a seat-of-the-pants type of flyer that used ingenuity to get the job done.

Pritchard flew Raven 90 for the first open snow landing at the future Lower Cluster location. He was familiar with open snow work due to his time in the Firebirds. Tousey in Raven 93 orbited overhead, flying air patrol to monitor Pritchard's situation. His aircraft was a radio link with Greenland air rescue services if their services became necessary.

The location for the Lower Cluster was near an ablation zone of the ice cap. The snow conditions were perfect. Pritchard touched down on the snow and slowed the aircraft to a stop. Brian Meaney, his loadmaster, offloaded the science team and their cargo. His first takeoff slide was successful. The mission went flawlessly.

## Upper Cluster, 1980

The next day at the Upper Cluster location, Ray Tousey's aircrew did the open snow work while Pritchard orbited overhead. It was time for jungle rules. When Tousey landed, his aircraft sank three feet in the snow. The belly of the aircraft was riding on it. *Holy crap!* The powdery snow created a bow wave over the wings, and the aircraft decelerated rapidly. He pushed the throttles forward to prevent the aircraft from coming to a complete stop. *Now, what?*

Chief Master Sergeant Bill Pickney, Tousey's flight engineer, got out of his seat and went to the back of the aircraft. He opened the right para-troop door to check the snow's depth. The aircraft was taxiing on its belly. He returned to his seat and ensured the throttles remained full forward. Due to their high altitude, they couldn't achieve maximum torque. He knew if Tousey pulled the throttles back, even a little, the aircraft would stop, and they were stuck.

Tousey made a wide 180-degree turn. He kept the throttles full forward in the takeoff position but couldn't accelerate more than thirty knots. He knew if he stopped, the aircraft would be stuck in the snow. There was no guidance on how to deal with this situation.

Tousey explained the situation to the scientists. He told them he wasn't going to stop the aircraft. He also explained another aircraft might not be able to return once he left. They still wanted to be offloaded. They said they would find an alternate means to get back. They had snowmobiles, and their science project would take them to several locations around the ice cap.

The loadmasters opened the back of the aircraft. The ramp was parallel to the surface of the snow. They attached the vehicle loading ramps to the back of the ramp. They then lowered the vehicle loading ramps into the snow. Tousey taxied the aircraft very slowly, in circles, to keep the cargo somewhat close together for the scientists. Each time he approached the same location, he told the loadmasters to offload a pallet. They pushed the pallet, and it shifted toward the back of the plane and down the vehicle loading ramps into the snow.

The three snowmobiles rolled over in the snow when they hit it. Soon afterward, the snow grabbed the vehicle loading ramps and pulled them out of the aircraft. The loadmasters didn't see much else they could do except to continue to offload the cargo. The science equipment, camp gear, and fuel barrels ended up all around the spirals. On one pass, the science team sat on the ramp of the aircraft. Tousey kept the aircraft taxiing very slow, and the people jumped out of it as they came near their cargo. It wasn't graceful, and many of them face-planted in the snow. The loadmasters then jumped out of the aircraft, found the vehicle loading ramps, and threw them in the aircraft on Tousey's next passed. They chased the aircraft, jumped back in, and closed up the back.

*Upper Cluster, Ray Tousey*

Tousey's next challenge was to get the aircraft airborne. ATO bottles were loaded on the outside of the aircraft, but the igniters weren't installed. They didn't foresee this problem in Sondrestrom before they left. Aircrews didn't fly around with ignitors in the bottles to limit the potential for a misfire of the bottles inflight. If Tousey wanted to use the ATO, he needed to stop the aircraft, and he couldn't stop without getting stuck in the snow. Overhead, Pritchard was searching for answers also. He agreed that stopping the aircraft was a bad idea, too many risks. Tousey pointed the nose of the aircraft into the wind and began the takeoff slide. The aircraft still wouldn't accelerate even at the lighter weight, so he reversed course and taxied back along his tracks and tried again. He intended to create his own skiway by packing down the snow. He worked on this idea for about an hour. He didn't achieve much success, and he burned up a lot of fuel.

It was time for Plan B. DYE-2 was about one hundred miles away. Tousey pointed the nose of the aircraft in that direction. He was in search of faster snow. Snow conditions varied on the ice cap, and better snow conditions would allow him to accelerate. If he could raise the nose of the aircraft out of the snow, he knew he'd get airborne. An empty aircraft meant a forward center-of-gravity, not so good. However, as the aircraft burned fuel, the center-of-gravity shifted aft. He needed between sixty-five and seventy knots, due to the center of gravity of the aircraft, before the airflow over the wings would allow him to pull the nose of the aircraft off the snow and pop a wheelie.

It would take at least three hours at his current speed to taxi to DYE-2 with maximum power, but the aircraft didn't have enough fuel to go the distance. Pritchard coordinated with Raven Operations in Sondrestrom to prepare fifty-five-gallon fuel drums for Tousey's crew. He intended to return to Sondrestrom, pick up the fuel drums, land at DYE-2, and taxi to Tousey.

As the miles passed, the aircraft got lighter, and it accelerated. After the first thirty-five miles of taxiing, the snow conditions began to firm up. Raven 93 accelerated. It was enough for Tousey to pull the aircraft's nose off of the snow. With the nose ski no longer plowing through the snow, Raven 93 accelerated even more.

Tousey needed at least stall speed to pull the aircraft off the snow. Stall speed was the minimum speed the aircraft would fly, but it didn't guarantee directional control. It meant the aircraft had enough lift under the wings to go airborne. If Raven 93 got airborne and had an engine failure immediately after takeoff, Tousey wouldn't have directional control of the aircraft. This could lead to some serious consequences. The upside was the ice cap was a big landing strip.

Another five miles passed before the aircraft accelerated to eighty knots. It was at stall speed. If Tousey delayed pulling the aircraft off of the snow, he might hit a bad patch of snow and slow again, so he pulled. Raven 93 rose out of the snow, and Tousey immediately lowered the nose to keep the aircraft in ground effect. Ground effect was an aerodynamic phenomenon that created a thick cushion of air that was about half of the wing's length or Raven 93's case, from the surface to about fifty feet above the snow. The aircraft rode ground effect as it accelerated. There were no obstacles to hit on the Greenland ice cap, so Tousey could ride this cushion of air all the way to DYE-2, if necessary.

Aerodynamic factors caused the aircraft to yaw to the left at Raven 93's slow airspeed, regardless of Tousey's efforts. His major concern was robbing the #2 engine, the left wing's inboard engine, of air. Without airflow, the engine would stall. But, after a short time, Raven 93 accelerated to one hundred knots. Tousey gained directional control, and he counteracted the yaw by stepping on the right rudder pedal. He climbed to 10,000 feet and turned toward Sondrestrom. The rest of the flight was uneventful, but a lot of knowledge was gained. The mission was a success, but the scientists weren't pleased with getting dumped from the moving aircraft. The following year, the Raven Gang tried something different.

## One Year Later

The scientists had a new location in mind for the following year. The Lower Cluster was at the same location but now was referred to as the Western Cluster. DYE-3 was the Eastern Cluster location, but now the researchers wanted to form a Central Cluster between the two other clusters. On 7 June 1981, Raven 94 picked up ten people from DYE-3 and flew over the Western Cluster location for the Ohio University researchers. They found the reflectors they had left there the previous year. Raven 94 didn't land but instead returned the people to DYE-3.

On June 10th, Raven 94 picked up the same ten people. This time they filled the cargo compartment with snowmobiles, sleds, and three pallets of supplies and equipment. They took off and flew to the Western Cluster, where Raven 92 was already orbiting overhead. They identified the site again and landed just beyond it. The snow conditions were perfect. The offloading went without an issue. Things went so smooth the aircrew didn't use ATO to get airborne. Both aircrews returned to Sondrestrom in time for breakfast.

Two weeks later, the snow conditions were very different. Two aircrews arrived in Sondrestrom from New York on Friday, 26 June 1981. On Saturday, they spent the day adjusting their circadian rhythm to night flying. Captain Dennis Zicha was a man of average size, thin, with light brown hair. He was a civil engineer for New York State. Over the last couple of years, he spent a lot of time in Greenland flying the mission. This was his first week as the mission commander.

It never got dark at this time of year. The sun was always up in June at Sondrestrom. He intended to take advantage of the morning's cooler temperatures. Zicha planned to take off at midnight on Sunday. His mission was to pick up the people at the Western Cluster who were dropped off two weeks earlier. On Monday, Zicha planned to have Captain Phil Bradley land and drop people off at the Central Cluster. Bradley came to the Raven Gang from active duty. He was thin with auburn hair, and he loved to play. He would need his sense of humor for the mission ahead of him.

If all went well, Zicha planned to have everyone back in New York by dinner time on Tuesday. On Sunday morning, the weather was good at DYE-3. Bradley, flying Raven 93, departed Sondrestrom at 12:45 a.m., with four passengers and 10,000 pounds of cargo. They dropped off people and cargo at DYE-3. Next, they were scheduled to support Zicha in Raven 90 as top cover over the Western Cluster.

Bradley had a hard time getting Raven 93 off of the snow at DYE-3. He aborted his first takeoff attempt. Something didn't feel right in the nose of the aircraft. He stopped, and Bradley's flight engineer and systems expert, Master Sergeant Frank Murray, went outside the aircraft to look. He found a broken hydraulic line in the nose ski. He went to the back of the aircraft.

It took Murray over an hour to cannibalize a hydraulic line from the ramp of the aircraft. He, then, was able to repair the ski. Six more unsuccessful takeoff runs later, Bradley finally got airborne.

Raven 90 departed Sondrestrom at 1:15 a.m. with twenty passengers and one thousand pounds of cargo. They were on their way to DYE-3. After DYE-3, Zicha intended to pick up the people and cargo at the Western Cluster. The flight went smoothly, and he was airborne out of DYE-3 before Raven 93 was repaired.

Once Raven 93 was airborne, both aircraft proceeded to the Western Cluster, and Zicha landed. The top eight to ten inches of the snow was firm, but beneath it was slush. It was summertime, and the sun was always shining. The snow was getting soft. Zicha shut down the aircraft engines. Master Sergeant Doug Sargent, Zicha's loadmaster, loaded the people and cargo. When he finished, the aircrew started the aircraft engines. The aircraft accelerated slowly through the snow, so Zicha directed Technical Sergeant Red LaFerriere, his flight engineer, to fire the ATO bottles. They were airborne from the Western Cluster at 6:40 a.m. Both aircraft returned to Sondrestrom. Raven 90 landed at Sondrestrom at 7:25 a.m. Raven 93 landed ten minutes later. They were in time for breakfast of scrambled eggs at the Roost, the Raven Gang's clubhouse.

## Weather Delays

The intended Central Cluster location was fifty-three miles west of DYE-3. On Monday, 29 June 1981, its weather was forecast to be good. The radar site reported they had a 5,000 overcast cloud ceiling and fifteen miles visibility. Bradley was scheduled to land at the Central Cluster. Due to the previous problems with Raven 93, he flew Raven 90. He was airborne out of Sondrestrom at 2:05 a.m., with nine passengers and twenty thousand pounds of cargo.

Zicha flying Raven 93, was airborne at 2:30 a.m. for top cover. He also intended to go to DYE-3 after Bradley got airborne out of the Central Cluster. Bradley descended to one thousand feet above the snow, but he didn't break out of the cloud cover. He had no ground contact. There was a warning in the aircraft's technical manual that stated: *"The terrain clearance received from the AN/APN-22 are unreliable when operating over large depths of snow and ice since the radar waves will actually penetrate the surface and indicated greater terrain clearances than actually exists."*

Bradley didn't descend any further. He returned to Sondrestrom. Zicha went to DYE-3. There the weather was poor. He made two box patterns overhead. On his first approach, he didn't see enough to land. He saw less on his second approach. He returned to Sondrestrom and landed at 4:35 a.m. The day was a big bust.

After debriefing the aircraft issues with the maintenance team, Zicha went to his mission commanders' office. DYE-3 called and told him they had scattered clouds at seven thousand feet and fifteen miles of visibility.

Zicha noted in the mission commander's book:

> *"How nice. Unable to get fuel before 0600 without prior advance notice. Also, out of ATO bottles. By the time we get all this stuff—no crew day. Will try tomorrow... Not too good a day looks like we extend one."*

He called New York and notified the squadron they would remain in Greenland another day.

On Tuesday morning, the weather was supposed to be good. Zicha was airborne at 2:10 a.m. aboard Raven 93. He was the weather ship. His aircraft had a heavy load of cargo and not much gas. He wanted to look at the Central Cluster before Bradley arrived and then go to DYE-3 to drop off his cargo. When he arrived, he already knew the day was going to be another bust. He descended over the Central Cluster to see if Bradley had a chance to land. He descended to four hundred feet and still couldn't get visual contact with the snow. Bradley was airborne out of Sondrestrom fifteen minutes after Zicha, with the same nine passengers and twenty thousand pounds of cargo as the day before. When he got Zicha's weather report, he returned to Sondrestrom.

Zicha went to DYE-3 to drop off his cargo. There were twenty-five knots of wind when he arrived, with a sixteen-knot crosswind. A fifteen-knot crosswind was the limit for landing, so he avoided the skiway and landed in the open snow, which allowed him to land in the direction of the wind. Once he was on the snow, he had a hard time taxiing to the ramp. He offloaded the four thousand-pound fuel bladder without stopping, and he refused to pick up the passengers and cargo waiting for him. A snowstorm was rapidly approaching, and the visibility was going down. He needed to get airborne immediately before he got trapped there. He returned to Sondrestrom and landed at 6:05 a.m. He had some eggs at the Roost and returned to the office.

Zicha added another note to the mission commander's book:

> *"Don't know how we could do this mission without the Roost. Supposed to go home today, but we still have cargo and people (they are getting upset) to bring back from DYE-3, plus the put-in at Central Cluster. Called Schenectady and informed them of our plans. Yesterday's picnic continues at the Roost this afternoon until the rain clouds show up to spoil it. Most people are too tired to sleep. Forecast from Danish weather does not look too encouraging for tomorrow."*

Early Wednesday morning, the weather at Sondrestrom was poor. Rain at Sondrestrom, rain and snow at DYE-2, and clear and fifteen miles visibility at DYE-3. *"Ha! Ha! Ha!"* Zicha thought cynically. At 3:25 a.m., he was airborne to assess the Central Cluster. When he arrived overhead, he descended into the weather to five hundred feet above the ground and still couldn't get below the low clouds. He called back to Sondrestrom and told Bradley's aircrew to stay put. They weren't going anywhere. Zicha continued to DYE-3.

The weather was good, but he was inside the ping-pong ball. The sky was white. The horizon was the same color of white, and so was the snow. He saw a small black dot in the distance. As he approached, the dot took on a form. It was the DYE site floating around the surrounding whiteness. Zicha eventually picked out the skiway flags. Each flag was black radar reflective material between two bamboo poles. He landed without incident. He loaded the eleven passengers and the seven thousand pounds of cargo he refused to take the day before. On his return, he took another look at the Central Cluster location. He still saw nothing. He landed at Sondrestrom at 6:35 a.m. Shortly after that, DYE-3's weather went down and didn't improve for the rest of the day.

In the mission commander book, Zicha noted:

*"Weather people say clearing after midnight. Plan a midnight takeoff for the icecap, then return to Sondy, gas up, and go to Schenectady."*

He called New York. In the mission commander book, he noted:

*"Schenectady advises us to stay one more day (Fri) if necessary to get the job done. People are getting nervous about getting home for the 4th of July weekend."*

# Central Cluster 1981

On 2 July 1981, Zicha planned for a midnight takeoff, but the weather at showtime was obscured skies, one-half mile visibility with light snow and fog at Sondrestrom, so he moved the takeoff time to 2:00 a.m. The weather was worse at 2:00 a.m., obscured skies, one-quarter mile of visibility, and snow. The forecaster said the weather would be clear by noon, so Zicha sent everyone back to bed until 10:00 a.m.

Bradley flying Raven 90 was airborne at noon, and Zicha flying Raven 93 departed Sondy ten minutes later. The weather was beautiful. Bradley had the same nine passengers and twenty thousand pounds of cargo. He arrived overhead the Central Cluster, picked out a section of snow, and landed the aircraft at 2:35 p.m.

Unlike Tousey the year before, he stopped, shut down the engines, and offloaded his passengers and cargo. It took the loadmasters an hour and ten minutes to complete the offload. Nobody face-planted. When they were finished, the aircrew got in their seats to start the engines, but the #3 engine wouldn't start. After a second attempt, Bradley's flight engineer, Frank Murray, pulled a ladder from the back of the aircraft, went out to the right wing, and took a look in the engine. The ignition relay had failed. It was a twenty-minute replacement fix on the Sondrestrom ramp, but he didn't have the part he needed, and he wasn't in Sondrestrom.

Bradley talked things over with Zicha overhead. They agreed Bradley needed to start the remaining engines and taxi to DYE-3, fifty-three miles away. Raven 90 could only get about ten knots while he taxied on three engines. It took a lot of power to plow the aircraft through the snow. Bradley pushed up the power on #1 and #4 engines, the outboard engines on each wing, to about 18,000 inch-pounds of torque. He used the #2 engine, like a tiller on a boat, to direct the aircraft where he wanted to go.

Zicha returned to Sondrestrom and 6:55 p.m. He noted in the mission commander book:

*"... return to Sondy (6.7 hours so far) for gas, food, recovery team."*

He was airborne again at 7:40 p.m., with a maintenance team including Technical Sergeant Floyd Kilmartin, Technical Sergeant Dave Graff, and four other maintenance guys. He also had aircraft repair parts and the remote fueling kit, which consisted of hoses, connectors, and nozzles.

Zicha contacted Bradley when they were about fifteen miles from DYE-3. He was able to locate their position using his radar. Bradley stopped within a mile of the skiway and remained clear of it. The weather was very poor as Zicha approached DYE-3. The clouds were covering the surface of the snow. Sob Story, DYE-3's call sign, reported the weather was three-quarters miles visibility with ice fog and blowing snow. Zicha landed at DYE-3 at 9:25 p.m. Raven 90 was very low on fuel. The aircraft had about 850 pounds of fuel remaining after the 4.3-hour taxi to the DYE site. They shut down the aircraft engines to avoid cavitating the fuel lines.

Zicha taxied Raven 93 over to Bradley. He taxied nose to nose with Raven 90 and passed it on the copilot's side. Zicha stopped soon after their wingtips passed. He had lined up the two aircraft's refueling panel.

The maintenance folks began repairs and used the remote fueling kit to move fuel from Raven 93's fuel tanks to Raven 90's wing tanks. While they did so, Bradley's aircrew walked to the DYE site to get some hot chow. The fueling and repairs took 2½ hours. The maintenance team had some difficulty installing the new ignition relay, but before long, they had the engines running. Bradley aircrew returned to the aircraft and taxied Raven 90 to the skiway. They took off, and their return to Sondrestrom was uneventful.

Zicha's aircrew started Raven 93's engines, but the aircraft wouldn't move when they tried to taxi. It was stuck in the snow. The maintenance guys got shovels from the back of the aircraft and dug the snow from around the skis until the aircraft finally broke free. Zicha taxied the aircraft over to the DYE-3 skiway and was airborne at 1:05 a.m. and landed at Sondrestrom an hour later. He had flown 9.4 hours that day.

On this final night in Greenland, the "Zicha's Zombies" celebrated at the Roost. It had been a challenging week. Zicha made a final note in the mission commander book:

> *"Schedule 1630L departure for home. Bradley in 490 to go via Niagara to drop off people and ice cores. 493 to go straight to Schenectady. So endeth this saga. So long, for now, Sondy, we'll be back."*

CHAPTER 12

# ICE FLOE'S LARGE AND SMALL CAMPS

*"An Arctic expert is one who has been to the Arctic less than three times or more than twenty times."*

—Beau Buck

In the late 1980s, the 109th Airlift Wing continued to pursue avenues to expand the Raven Gang's ski mission. Support for the Department of Defense on the frozen Arctic Ocean had new and interesting challenges. Also notable in the late 1980s, the Raven Gang was directed to create an official callsign. The Raven callsign was already taken. So, they chose "Skier." It was fitting.

## Origins of Ice Stations on the Arctic Ocean

Drifting research stations on the Arctic were proposed by a Norwegian, Fridtjof Nansen, in the late 19th Century. He believed beneath the ice, the westerly currents from Siberia flowed toward Greenland. In 1895, he took the Fram, a ship specifically designed for his voyage, on a three-year scientific journey.[82] He proved maintaining science camps on drifting ice stations was possible.

In the 1930s, the Russians were the first to use drifting ice stations to their advantage. Always pushing northward, mapping their coastline, and pursuing their desire to know more about the currents and flows of the Arctic

Ocean, one of their research ships got trapped in the ice on the Chukchi Sea north of Siberia. The ice eventually crushed the ship, but not before everyone abandoned the ship. In February 1933, 104 forsaken passengers were trapped north of Russia's distant eastern reaches, stranded on an ice floe. On 7 April 1933, Russian airplanes landed on the ice and rescued these shipwrecked people. This prevented a near-catastrophe, and aviation took on new prominence in the Arctic.

Four years later, on 21 May 1937, the Russians took the next logical step. They used aircraft to airlift supplies and equipment to build a science camp at the North Pole. They called this camp North Pole-1. Soviet scientists and researchers continued from this point forward to construct camps on the ice floes in the Arctic.

## Landing on Sea Ice

The Russians always had a significant interest in the Arctic Ocean. They viewed it through a different lens than the rest of the world. The Arctic was their frontier. They launched scientific explorations to survey their sprawling northern coastline, then pushed further and further north.

Americans didn't begin any serious operations on the Arctic Ocean until the 1970 Arctic Ice Dynamics Joint Exercise, or AIDJEX. AIDJEX was a joint United States-Soviet Union cooperative effort to determine whether the Arctic climate was changing. A climate database was created, and information from other countries was added to it.

Large science camps like AIDJEX studied multiple fields of research, including climate change, gravity, magnetics, oceanography, seismic studies, and more.[83] These large camps required a significant amount of resources to maintain them. Large fuel requirements were needed for science projects, for the camp's needs, and vehicles. Bigger aircraft with greater fuel capacity required larger runways to deliver it. Finding a suitable location to land an aircraft was the greatest challenge for a pilot. Would the ice hold the weight of the aircraft? The first C-130 wheeled landing on unprepared sea ice was during AIDJEX 72.[84]

Above the ice, there was a cooperative atmosphere among the scientists. However, below the ice, the Cold War raged. During the 1980s, the Cold War inserted itself into research on the ice floes. The Soviet Union developed submarines with long-range missiles capable of striking the United States from the Arctic Ocean. American submarines needed improved sonars to track them, and they wanted to reduce the danger of collisions while they hid beneath the ice.

The military priorities were resented in academia. A contractor at the Office of Naval Research put it this way, *"Instead of being science-driven, ONR became navy-driven."*[85]

# Beau Buck

Beaumont "Beau" Manor Buck was an early pioneer in underwater acoustics beneath the icecap. While in the US Navy in the early 1960s, Beau Buck also became an early pioneer of small Arctic ice camps, with less than ten people. Beau Buck mainly used small camps to fulfill his work on underwater acoustics beneath the icecap. Time in the day at smaller camps was divided into scientific work, camp and aircraft needs, and house cleaning among the few people at the camp. People at the camp needed to be multi-talented or learn quickly.

Beau Buck left the Navy in the mid-1960s and worked at General Motors. His acoustics interests led him, and other engineers and technicians, to Alaska's west coast and northern frontier. Out of Barrow, Alaska, Beau Buck began working on ice floes in the Arctic Ocean during the GMIS, or General Motors Ice Sheet projects. In 1973, he left General Motors, created Polar Research Laboratory, Inc., and continued his acoustic work under Navy contract. His company's main work was underwater acoustics beneath the icecap, and he developed various underwater buoys and other acoustic devices.

Much of Beau Buck's research work on the Arctic Ocean ice became autonomous. During the winter months, field operations were brutal. Manned stations were often inaccessible and unnecessary. With a "suite of sensors, unattended buoys could acquire, monitor, navigate, and relay, via satellite telemetry, environmental data sets in all seasons."[86] Buck's company became a primary production source for many of America's unmanned drifting buoys. Polar Research Laboratory, Inc. "... conceived, installed, and operated all the 'data buoys' supporting AIDJEX."[87]

AIDJEX required the use of large camps on the ice. According to Beau Buck, large camps "were hardly ideal for low-frequency acoustics research. Four KW generators going full time, road graders on the runway at all hours, uncleared personnel, electromagnetic radiations from strong HF (high frequency) radios, and aircraft beacons made an acoustician's life a hard one. Small, quiet camps were obviously needed."[88]

Beau Buck's acoustics work took on great significance in the 1980s. With the knowledge of Soviet submarines capable of going beneath the ice, the Navy's Space and Naval Warfare, or SPAWAR, Center asked Beau Buck to develop a means to track them. It was already possible to monitor the Soviets in the open ocean, but when submarines went under the icepack, there was no way of knowing where they would come out. Greenland became an important chess piece in the strategic games being played between the world powers.

Beau Buck gave his work its name, Arctic Research in Environmental Acoustics, or AREA. He retired in 1988, but his handiwork lived on. Even with the end of the Cold War in 1989, it didn't stop the Navy's interests in his work.

## "Jumper" John Bitters

Beau Buck met John Bitters in 1975. In his early years, Bitters was a member of New Zealand's Special Air Service. He did many parachute jumps in Antarctica in the early 1970s. In 1975 he was contacted by a member of the United States government to see if he was interested in helping them with projects in the Arctic.

After finishing a couple of smaller projects, he met Beau Buck. Buck wanted to use small teams of people to build temporary camps on the Arctic Ocean. Bitters was interested. His primary job was to pick locations where the scientists wanted to go and establish a camp. One of several collaborators of Jumper Bitters was Drew Dix.[89] Bitters met Dix through a mutual friend in Fairbanks, Alaska. Dix, a retired member of the U.S. Army Special Forces, had been awarded the Medal of Honor for his service during the Vietnam War. After the war, he started an air-taxi service in the small town of Manly Hot Springs. Among other things, he used his air service to guide hunters in the North Brooks Range and deliver supplies for the Iditarod Dog Sled Race waystations along the route.

Jumper Bitters: *"Anyone I needed to perform the skills required to deal with and work in such circumstances had to have a unique set of skills—a good attitude—work under cold, harsh conditions—parachute skills—medical skills—and could work well together."*

Beau Buck usually picked an ice flow in a general area of the frozen ocean based on the floe's potential drift pattern. He and Jumper would fly out and explore the location and pick a couple of floes locked together by refrozen leads. They learned to pick out leads by their variation in color from the floe, the drifting snow on the lead, and the general area where it was located. If they didn't land that day, they dropped a dye marker to identify it in the future and marked its coordinates before they left.

Early camps were close to the coastline and approachable by snowmobile. Later camps were reached by helicopter. As they pushed further north, many camps were beyond helicopter range, so Bitters and his team would fly in the back of an aircraft and search for potential locations, occasionally parachuting out when they found one.

Bitters' perspective on parachuting was, *"Everything we did on these operations was check—check—and recheck. No matter how ready you think you are, check again your equipment, your individual team members. The whole system had to be 100% on the ball, or someone was going to die!*

*I used to say to everyone that once we leave the comfort of the aircraft door, we are on our own. No mistakes can be afforded. I don't care how close to God you are. After exiting the aircraft door, it's up to you. God can no longer help. You're on your own. I lived this code a good part of my parachute career."*

Bitters typically sent two people out of the aircraft initially, at an altitude of 1500 feet. He emphasized to his people that parachutists needed to know their business. There wasn't much time after the chute opened to assess their conditions. They needed to assess the winds and what they were doing to them. They needed to drop their personal survival kit below them on a sixteen-foot line. Most importantly, they needed to prepare for contact with the surface. Their landing position was very important.

Bitters reflected on the uniqueness of their mission. *"Our drops were not pre-inspected for safety purposes. They were referred to as virgin surface conditions. Landing skills were considered extra important, and mistakes could be fatal in relation to broken limbs."*

After the first two people were on the ice, the remaining people in the aircraft prepared for their equipment to be dropped. They set up an impact point for the aircraft to the target. The aircraft approached at an altitude of 250 feet.

**Bitters:** *"The third jumper, usually myself, with the assistance of the engineer or loadmaster, through the pilot and ground control, would then start to disperse the equipment containers to the ice team on their drop commands. A deployment of equipment usually 2000 pounds would sustain three people for several days until an airstrip could be marked out to safely receive aircraft wheels or skis to start build-up of main camp operations."*

After the equipment drop, the third jumper parachuted out of the aircraft and joined the team.

**Bitters:** *"The aircraft usually circled us two or three times to conduct a well-being check of the ice team, during which quick radio HF/VHF communication was conducted making certain everyone was okay."*

The aircraft noted the camp location then departed for the mainland.

Beau Buck's dream was to take these types of camps deeper and further into the Arctic and do it safely. It raised some eyebrows at first.

**However, Bitters pointed out:** *"I have done many parachute deployments into Arctic and Antarctic conditions at locations in support of a variety of agencies. We never lost a cargo door load due to parachute failure, and we never had any individual injuries other than a few scrapes and bruises that would possibly jeopardize any of the missions. A record of 100% success and* Beau Buck *would always reply to the skeptics, 'This is working very well for what we are endeavoring to carry out.'"*

By the end of his career, Bitters was in the Guinness Book of World Records. He had over 3,000 jumps; 1,537 of them were cold-weather jumps.

Jumper Bitters shared with me some suggestions for future ice caps.

"I have been on many ice-related projects from Antarctica to the northern polar regions—U.S., Canada, Greenland —small science-related stations to large-scale projects which are usually research and development projects funded by an assortment of government agencies from NSF, ONR, ARCSUBLAB and many more. After the collapse of the Soviet Union, funding slowly went away to nothing. To my knowledge, no work on projects like that has not been done since. We had them on 'the wall' with our work, and we dropped the ball. A lot of people thought the Soviet threat would go away. It did for a while. You could say the 'Bear' took a little nap for a while, but they have rebounded bigger than ever, and it's us in the high polar regions that are up against the wall. Consider the Russian push of Arctic ice and claims about sea bottom projects. It goes on and on. We, on the other hand, have done nothing to maintain our claims. The U.S. had done nothing in the last twenty-plus years.

"The last major project I was on was the year 1996. I spent a year locked in the ice on Project Sheba, a year-long study, mostly science-related, performed off a Canadian icebreaker out of Quebec, supported by a second icebreaker from Halifax; it was a wonderful experience. I had the responsibility of flying with the Canadian ice patrol up to 87°–88° North, plotting and picking several possible ice floes to establish a station. A large floe was selected at 87° North, and we set sail north. I also had the added responsibility of selecting a safe route into the ice floe and final site to lock the ship in for the winter. A major logistical task took place to transfer thousands of gallons of fuel in bulk and drums to support the operation for a year or more. With all that done, one ship departed back to Canada, and we were alone.

"My next job was to offload the D-4 Cat and get started on developing a 3,000-foot airstrip on the floe for emergency airlift and later on crews' rotations. I would build and construct five airstrips during the next year due to movement and cracks developing in the floe surrounding the ship—a monumental task. The project was a huge, costly undertaking, as well as a huge success both science-wise, environmentally, and logistics-wise. It was extremely safe since a lot of work was done off-ship in small shelters. That way, in an emergency like ice movement, cracking, adverse weather, polar bears, etc., people made a good retreat to shipboard safely. People slept on board, ate on board, spent their off-hours, social time, on and in the safety of the ship.

"I learned from this operation points of ability to do work safely on board. The confines of the ship safety far outclassed being in buildings or tents on regular ice floes with all the many things that can and will go wrong in a storm, or movement or cracking of the ice, or polar bears, to include the massive loss of equipment, buildings, and potential movement of camp and materials. An example is the AIDJEX Project 75-76, which had a major break-up to satellite camp 'Caribou' at the start of winter that year. The project carried on but a major cutback due to loss of fuel, equipment (two bulldozers), and a variety of other expensive logistical equipment. Sheba was an experience that indicated long-term, high-polar research ice stations are going away. The Russians have been doing off-ship high Arctic science and research and development for years.

"Looking back at Arctic polar history, the Russians have years of experience on ice stations. They developed them as far back as 1938. NP-1, four guys together in a hut or tent on ice for a year. We learned a lot from them, but in the end, our technology and mechanical expertise were superior. In 1995, we gave it all away.

"Beau Buck told me a long time ago that the Navy should take over the icebreaker fleet and make them nuclear-capable to compete with the Soviets, then we can go where they go and accomplish what they do. He was exactly right. The Russians currently operate a fleet of forty breakers—heavy duty, diesel, and electric, large nuclear breakers, fully loaded with all the logistical needs. I've seen some of their ships and what they can do. The last one I saw was the largest, called the Yamal. It looks like a city at sea and is truly impressive.

"The Russians can do it. The Germans, China, the Canadians are still doing work in their Arctic communities. And the U.S is still 'trying' to service their needs in Antarctica, and with small trips to the Arctic Ocean, with the Healy, a small class breaker, already classified obsolete. The Polar Star and Polar Sea, one in dock, basically stripped of its systems to keep its sister-ship operations. It is a hard road to compete and keep up in the world of the Arctic power curve. I think in the future, we may see small offshore research camps, very short term, due to the melting and diminishment of the Arctic ice floes. I see more programs like Sheba, floating bases, for some of the reasons I previously mentioned."

# Refrozen Leads

During winter months in the Arctic, salt in the ocean lowered the freezing point of water, but it couldn't stop it from freezing.[90] As the temperature dropped, thin plates of ice granules, known as frazil ice, began to form on the surface. As the sun angle lowered upon the horizon, the water reflected the solar radiation, and the water lost heat. The blowing wind increased the loss. These thin sheets turned into sludge as the ice continued to form until they took on a pancake-like formation. As these pancake-like formations continued to grow, they came into contact with other pancake-type formations until they merged into floes of pack ice.

New sea ice eventually became freshwater ice. The ice rose from the surface of the water. Pockets of saltwater formed on its surface. This brine became more concentrated and increased in weight. The high salinity and weight enabled it to form cracks in the ice as it melted a path downward and flushed out of the ice into the water beneath. Freshwater filled the cracks. Its crystals began to become more granular, brittle, and clear. This strengthened the ice.

Dense snow covered the pack-ice, and it became a firm covering over the ice floes. Across the barren, wind-swept Arctic Ocean, the surfaces were often rough due to drifts and sastrugi, which reached two feet high. This was one of the more interesting challenges of landing an aircraft on the ice.

Through the late summer months on the Arctic Ocean, radiant heat from the sun beat upon the surface twenty-four hours a day. Gaps formed between the ice floes, and once again, open water appeared. The winds and currents caused the ice sheets to smash into each other, breaking the ice floes into smaller pieces. Ray Tousey's description for these broken floating ice sheets was, *"They were a bowl of floating ice cubes."*

When the winter arrived again, the gaps, or leads, refroze. These refrozen leads were the weaker part of the ice pack. The salt content in this new sea ice was higher than the ice floes. But the positive thing about the refrozen leads was the surface was smoother than the ice floes, with few or no sastrugi. The refrozen leads were good locations to find suitable landing surfaces.

## Manor Buck and Imants Virsnieks

In the early 1990s, Imants Virsnieks was SPAWAR's representative with overall responsibility for the Arctic camps. The Arctic was divided into two general sectors, west and east. The western sector was north of Alaska and further west across the Bering Strait. The eastern sector was north of Canada, Greenland, and further east.

Manor Buck started his own business, Polar Associates, after his father retired. Virsnieks contracted Buck's Polar Associates to be the logistics and supply chain for ice camps in the Arctic's eastern sector through the mid-1990s. Manor Buck had learned from his father about ice camps' necessities, of the people's and sciences' needs. As the ice camps became larger, with more scientists and logistics personnel, Buck was equal to the challenge.

Each year Manor Buck built a base camp and set up satellite camps, when necessary, positioned up to one hundred miles apart in locations from eighty-seven degrees north latitude to ninety degrees north, the geographic North Pole. The main camp usually had about twenty people and the satellite camps, fewer.[91] Each year regardless of the location, the main camp was named after Beau Buck's wife, "Ruby."

In the early years of his father's work, Manor Buck stored supplies and equipment at Resolute Bay, Canada, until they could be transported to the ice camps. When Beau Buck's work moved further east between Greenland and Spitzbergen Island, Manor Buck moved his operation to Thule Air Base, in northwest Greenland. From Thule, he moved his cargo to Station Nord, a Danish station in northeast Greenland.

Station Nord was much closer to Ruby Camp than Resolute Bay or Thule. The shorter distance meant aircraft could fly to Ruby with less fuel and more cargo. The smaller aircraft, helicopters, Twin Otters, and the Tri-Motor-3[92] didn't have the capacity to keep up with the increased amount of needed supplies as the research camps expanded. He needed bigger aircraft. A contractor at the Office of Naval Research told Beau Buck about the Raven Gang, located at the 109th Tactical Airlift Group, in Schenectady, New York.[93]

Initially, the Raven Gang moved large amounts of cargo from Thule Air Base to Station Nord. In later years they moved the fuel and supplies from Thule directly to Ruby.

## Every Place Has a Story

Station Nord was an interesting place. It is located at 81°43' North and 17°50' West, about five hundred miles from the geographic North Pole. The runway was 5,400 feet long and 200 feet wide. In the high northern latitude, snow and ice were always present. There was an ARA/NDB approach to Runway 22. It was published for the Raven Gang's use only, and it stated:

> *"With proper notification, Nord personnel will place flares prior to the approach end of the runway. First aircraft of the day should ensure that the ground personnel makes an abbreviated centerline to taxi to the fuel tanks…"*

On one occasion, Lt. Col. Kevin Grna was the aircraft commander flying a mission to Station Nord aboard Skier 90. His copilot was Second Lieutenant Roger Shapiro. They had been there the day prior. The snow had provided good traction for stopping due to the cold temperatures and a thick overcast sky obscuring the sun. They were back again. This time it was relatively warm, and the sun was shining. It was a beautiful day.

Grna let Shapiro fly the approach and landing. The NDB approach took the aircraft over the Arctic Ocean to line up on the 216° magnetic bearing. Shapiro descended to 2,000 feet above the surface until he was eight nautical miles from the field. He then continued lower.

When he saw the airfield, Shapiro descended further and landed. The aircraft touched down a little longer than he intended, and he was faster than he should have been. He pulled the throttles back to flight idle. He had a problem lifting the throttles over the flight idle gate, a mechanical stop in the throttle quadrant to prevent the pilot from going in the ground range while in flight. He thought Grna was blocking him from going into the ground range because his airspeed was a little fast, but Grna wasn't.

The distance to stop was diminishing rapidly. Grna took control of the aircraft. He lifted the throttles over the gate, pulled them into reverse, and stood on the brakes. The anti-skid cycled over and over. There are three things Shapiro never liked to hear from the pilot: "Watch this," "Oh, shit," and "I can't see." He now had a fourth. Grna yelled, "Hold on! We're gonna bite it!" They spun ninety degrees to the left as Grna tried in vain to slow the aircraft. The relatively warm temperatures and sun reflecting off the snow created a thin layer of meltwater on the snow-packed runway surface. Grna later described it as "slicker than owl shit." Through the aircraft's front windscreen, Shapiro saw the terror-stricken faces of the men in the fire truck parked on the side of the runway as they slid by them sideways.

Finally, the aircraft stopped. Garry Quick was sitting in the back next to the right wheel well. He didn't feel an impact. The aircraft was sitting sideways at the end of the runway. The snow had not been cleared beyond the confines of it. The propellers were inches above a large snow berm at the end. Grna directed Shapiro to shut down #3 and #4 engines. And that's when the Danish film crew came out of the building.

CHAPTER 13

# FROZEN OCEAN LANDINGS

In 1988, the United States military planned a joint exercise on the Arctic Ocean north of Alaska. Their purpose was to put sonar buoys in the ocean to monitor what was taking place below the ice. They called this exercise "White Trident." Well before this exercise began, the Army contacted Lt. Col. Karl Doll, the air operations officer for the 109th Tactical Airlift Group, to see if the LC-130 aircraft could support the exercise. It took time to develop the game plan.

Doll coordinated with the US Army to have a bulldozer and a combat control team on the frozen Beaufort Sea to groom a skiway on the frozen ice. He told them to schedule two bulldozers in case the first one was damaged from the airdrop. In 1988, two New York aircrews flew to Eielson Air Force Base, Alaska. The 109th Tactical Airlift Group Commander, Colonel Pete Terusi, and Major Giles Wagoner were the pilots on the first aircrew.

Terusi canceled the bulldozer airdrop. He was convinced he could determine the condition of the ice below simply by looking at it.[94] He overflew the frozen ocean to find a suitable landing location. In the back of the aircraft, his loadmasters combined a speedy-dry absorbent with hydraulic fluid, creating a red mixture. When Terusi found a satisfactory location, he flew low across the ice, and the loadmasters dumped out their red concoction from the paratroop doors from either side of the aircraft. This marked Terusi's landing zone.

Lt. Col. Wolfgang "Wolfie" Walther and Major Paul Bury were the pilots on the second aircraft. Wolfie came in behind Terusi and landed between the red tracks. They offloaded Navy personnel and spent a few hours on the ice. When the Navy was finished with their work, they returned to the aircraft, and Wolfie flew back to Alaska. Upon their re-entry into Alaskan airspace, Bury contacted the air traffic controllers, who were very interested in what the aircraft was doing. They were told the Soviet Union was very interested also.

The success of their mission was a proof of concept for the future. This would not remain the Raven Gang's standard procedure for landing on the Arctic Ocean. In the mission's after-action report, recommendations were made to improve their conduct of the operation.

On 2 April 1989, the Raven Gang went to Eielson Air Force Base to do it again. Skier 93 had two pallets of sonar buoys on board. The aircrews were told the buoys were for monitoring whales, but they suspected they would be used for more than that. Soviet submarines were known to operate below the ice.

Colonel Pete Terusi was the aircraft commander for Skier 93. Lt. Col. Giles Wagoner was the aircraft commander of Skier 91. The plan was for Skier 93 to land. Skier 91 would orbit overhead as a communication link in the event of a problem on the ice.

| Skier 93 Aircrew | |
|---|---|
| **Pilot:** | Colonel Pete Terusi |
| **Copilot:** | Major Paul Bury |
| **Navigator** | Captain Richard "Dick" Van Patten, Jr. |
| **Flight Engineer:** | Technical Sergeant Gregory Doriski |
| **Loadmaster:** | Chief Master Sergeant Edward Charles |
| **Loadmaster:** | Senior Master Sergeant William Divine |

A scout helicopter and a Twin Otter aircraft proceeded in advance of the LC-130s to look at the desired landing location. If the ice wasn't suitable, they needed to find an alternate location where a landing could be made. The frozen ocean was a big place. When the helicopter arrived at the initial site, the pilot determined it was not a suitable location. He went in search of another location. Meanwhile, Skier 91 and Skier 93 departed Eielson on time for the four-hour flight to their destination.

The helicopter pilot thought he found a potential location, so the Twin Otter landed. It was the roughest landing of the pilot's career.[95] The frozen pressure ridges were very firm. When Skier 93 and Skier 91 arrived overhead, they established radio contact. The Twin Otter pilot relayed the information about the poor landing conditions to the LC-130 aircrews.

Terusi chose to continue with the mission. Wagoner set up an orbit pattern while Terusi descended from altitude. Major Paul Bury was an instructor pilot in the squadron and Terusi's copilot on the flight. He listened to Terusi as he briefed his intentions. Terusi planned to do a ski drag along the surface of the ice to determine the conditions for himself. Bury knew some people within the flying squadron had done ski drags in the past, but he was unfamiliar with the technique. He deferred to Terusi's expertise and watched him do it. The maneuver was to land on the main skis but keep the aircraft's nose in the air, essentially "popping a wheelie."

Before he started the ski drag, Terusi made a couple of low passes over the Twin Otter's landing location. There was no discernable horizon. It was difficult to pick up any shadows on the surface. He was inside the ping-pong ball. The last pass was at fifty feet above the ice. Everything looked good as far as both pilots could see. On the final approach, Terusi stated, "If it looks good, I'm going to set it down."

The aircraft touched down short of where the Twin Otter pilot recommended. It was very rough. The nose of the aircraft impacted a large and very solid pressure ridge. Bury was slammed forward in his shoulder straps. His head almost impacted the edge of the front console of the instrument panel. Terusi pushed the throttles forward and pulled the aircraft off the ice. Afterward, Bury thought how suddenly you could die.

The aircraft's utility hydraulic system lost all pressure. It dumped its fluid. Bury saw multiple lights on the hydraulic panel and shut off the utility hydraulic switches associated with them. Without the utility hydraulic system, they couldn't raise the landing gear. The aircrew talked about their problem while Terusi climbed to altitude.

Terusi told Wagoner, in the other aircraft, about their problem. Wagoner thought Terusi sounded odd. Captain Dick Van Patten, Jr., Terusi's navigator, said he was feeling light-headed.[96] Technical Sergeant Greg Doriski, Terusi's flight engineer, looked at the aircraft cabin pressure indicator. It was reading zero. The aircraft wasn't pressurizing. At higher altitudes, the atmosphere thinned, and oxygen levels decreased. Without oxygen, people would begin to lose consciousness. Doriski needed to find where the aircraft was leaking air. Terusi directed everyone to put on their oxygen masks.

Wagoner flew under Skier 93 and did a visual inspection. The damage was significant. Damaged parts were hanging below Terusi's aircraft. Wagoner said to himself, *"What am I doing here?"* and immediately swept wide of the aircraft above. He didn't want any falling debris to hit him. Skier 93's nose ski was broken. The birdcage which held the hydraulic lines and electrical wires in the nose section on the aircraft was shattered. The front of the ski was hanging low. A metal bar from the birdcage, the spreader bar, had come loose and punctured the aircraft's belly.

The puncture prevented the aircraft from pressurizing. Doriski went back to the cargo compartment to try to find the damage. Eventually, he found the puncture beneath one of the two pallets of buoys, but there was little he could do to plug the hole. Wagoner advised Terusi against landing on the northern coast of Alaska. There was no support to fix the aircraft. Both agreed it might be possible for Skier 93 to make it back to Eielson. Terusi climbed to 28,000 feet to conserve fuel. The aircrew stayed on oxygen.

Their return flight to Eielson was horrible. One of the loadmasters, Chief Master Sergeant Ed Charles, had passed out due to oxygen deprivation called hypoxia. Doriski said, "I was scared shitless, buddy!" He didn't return to the flight deck. He wanted to keep an eye on Charles. There weren't enough oxygen regulators for the ten people in the back of the aircraft; aircrew, maintenance people, Navy divers, and a weather specialist. Senior Master Sergeant Billy Divine, the other loadmaster, used one of the aircraft's walkaround oxygen bottles to continue with his responsibilities in the back of the aircraft. Doriski, Charles, and two of the Navy divers were buddy-breathing off two oxygen regulators.

They made it back to Eielson. Both aircraft commanders knew Terusi wouldn't be able to taxi clear the runway after he landed, so Wagoner landed first. After landing, he exited the runway and stopped on the parallel taxiway to watch Terusi land.

At 9:35 p.m., Skier 93 touched down.[97] Terusi gingerly lowered the nose ski to the concrete. Looking down at his kick window, by his right foot,

Bury could see sparks and reflections of fire trailing behind them, under the belly of the aircraft. He said, "Crew, we have a fire." Terusi jumped on the brakes and brought the aircraft to a stop. It was a sight to behold. The nose ski dragged along the asphalt runway. Sparks flew and ignited the hydraulic fluid. The aircraft was engulfed in flame, and every window on the flight deck was "sun" orange[98]. Giles Wagoner thought they were dead.

Terusi directed his aircrew to do an emergency egress of the aircraft. Bury pulled the condition levers to the feather position to stop the engines and propellers. When Doriski opened the crew entrance door, flames were everywhere. He screamed, "No, not this way!" Bury was stunned. The flames dissipated a few moments later. The crew entrance door didn't open completely. The nose was sitting much lower because of the damage to the nose gear and ski assembly. Everyone found an exit, and they gathered three hundred feet off of the nose of the aircraft. All fourteen people escaped the aircraft unharmed. In Doriski's words, "God spared us, idiots."

Terusi had just closed a Strategic Air Command airfield at the height of The Cold War. Eielson was a major emergency response location for tanker aircraft to launch in case of a Soviet attack. Skier 93 couldn't remain on the runway. It needed to get off and get off now! If Terusi didn't get the aircraft off the runway within two hours, the Eielson base commander would plow it off.

A brilliant member of the 109th Maintenance Squadron was in the back of the aircraft throughout their ordeal. He had an idea. He commandeered a flatbed truck and railroad ties.

He used the airbags from the CDDAR[99] equipment that the maintenance team had brought along from Schenectady. He inflated airbags under the aircraft to raise the nose and put the railroad ties beneath it to the same height as the back of the truck. The railroad ties stabilized the aircraft. He then backed the truck under the aircraft and deflated the airbags. He chained the aircraft to the back of the truck, then removed the railroad ties. The truck drove away, and the aircraft followed it off of the runway.

There was an investigation into the damaged aircraft. One of the outcomes of the calamity was the creation of *109 TAG Regulation 86-1*, "Criteria for LC-130H Skiway and Ski Landing Areas." Lt. Col. Graham Pritchard, the chief of standardization and evaluation for the Raven Gang, was the driving force behind this regulation. He used information provided by the Space and Naval Warfare Systems Command, SPAWAR, and the Naval Arctic Research Laboratory to determine sea ice depth requirements and to evaluate surface requirements.

Definitions were created to delineate the difference between a skiway from a ski landing area. Different requirements were established to operate at these locations in the future. How skiways and ski landing areas would be marked were formalized. Perhaps the incident's biggest result was the creation of the ski landing area control officer, SLACO, program. *109 TAG Regulation 86-1* stated, "The SLACO will be at the site and examine results of ski landing area testing, preparation, and marking. If the area meets requirements, and with the concurrence of the officer in charge of the camp, the SLACO will advise the 109 TAG mission commander that LC-130H ski landings may commence. An authorized SLACO will remain at the ski landing area during all LC-130H ski operations."

# Math and Science

The most important answer a SLACO could provide pilots was the ice's weight-bearing capacity before they landed on it. The correct answer depended on the aircraft's weight and also, the amount of time they spent on the ice. A lightweight aircraft, heavily loaded with cargo, could break through the ice immediately after landing. However, the ice could support the same aircraft, gradually loaded with the heavy cargo, for a short time. Ice has an elastic nature.

In determining the load-bearing capacities of ice, particularly concerning airstrips and the loads imposed by aircraft, SPAWAR adopted the formulas defined by a Russian engineer. The formulas are summarized below:

| Types of Ice | Aircraft on Skis | Aircraft on Wheels |
|---|---|---|
| River ice | t = 15/4 x square root of P | t = 9/2 x square root of P |
| Lake ice | t = 27/8 x square root of P | t = 81/20 x square root of P |
| Old sea ice | t = 27/4 x square root of P | t = 81/10 x square root of P |
| Young sea ice | t = 81/8 x square root of P | t = 243/20 x square root of P |

P = the gross weight of aircraft in tons; t = the ice thickness in inches. The formulas apply only for ice formed and maintained at a temperature below 16° Fahrenheit. At high temperatures, twenty-five percent greater thickness was required. According to the formulas, twenty percent greater ice thickness was required for airplanes with wheels than those with skis.

For ski landings on old sea ice, less than five feet of ice depth was required. For wheel landings on old sea ice, just shy of six feet of ice depth was required. For ski landings on young sea ice, almost 7.5 feet of ice depth was required. For wheel landings on young sea ice, almost eleven feet of ice depth was required.

Now, with better planning and a better understanding of what the pilots needed before landing on the frozen ocean, the Raven Gang was at it again.

Beau Buck had worked on leading-edge acoustical research north of Alaska since 1963. His camps on the Arctic Ocean were used for the scientific study of acoustics beneath the Arctic Ocean's ice. Through his research, he mapped the ocean floor, watched pods of whales and other sea creatures as they swam in the frozen ocean below the ice, and listened to ice crack and break apart as the ocean currents flowed beneath the ice.

Beau Buck separated the ice cap's natural noises, whales, fish, ocean currents, cracking and grinding of the ice, and identified peripheral noises in the ocean below the ice. His central purpose was scientific, but the Cold War inserted itself into his work. He was asked to look through the background environmental data for long-range surveillance of Soviet submarines in the Arctic Ocean and the Bering Straits.

Beau Buck worked closely with SPAWAR. They contracted him to focus on different areas of the Arctic Ocean. His work shifted from smaller camps on the Arctic Ocean north of Alaska to larger camps north of Greenland. By 1977 he established the first United States ice camp in the Eastern Arctic, Greenland-Spitzbergen area. This was a pilot experiment for the East Arctic Project.[100]

## Logistics

Beaumont "Manor" Buck, Jr. became the logistical arm behind his father's work. When his father's science camps moved eastward to the Fram Strait between Greenland and the island of Spitzbergen, Manor Buck moved the intermediate location of supplies further north to Thule, Greenland.

From Thule, his supply chain went to Station Nord, a Danish base in northeast Greenland. From Station Nord, the supplies went to Ruby Camp and beyond. The distance between Thule and Nord limited the amount of cargo a C-47 aircraft could haul. In 1989 Manor Buck asked the Raven Gang for help. The much larger cargo capacity of the LC-130 allowed Manor Buck to move a lot of cargo to Station Nord, enabling smaller aircraft to move it to the ice camps. Frequently the Raven Gang moved the cargo directly to Ruby. From there, smaller aircraft moved supplies to the satellite camps.

# Ruby Camp

Lt. Col. Verle Johnston was the new air operations officer for the Raven Gang. He was looking for new opportunities for his ski mission aircraft. The DYE sites on the Greenland ice cap were closed and abandoned. The mission for which these specialized aircraft were designed was over. When Manor Buck called him, Johnston agreed to land the LC-130s at Ruby. The Raven Gang had already been flying support missions to Nord for years.

In 1989, Lt. Col. Ray Tousey agreed to go to Camp Ruby at the beginning of the science season and become the Raven Gang's first SLACO. His only guidance was *109 TAG Regulation 86-1.* Tousey climbed aboard a C-47 aircraft at Station Nord with Manor Buck and "Jumper" John Bitters to find a place to establish Ruby Camp.

In *Spring to the Ice*, a memoir written by Beaumont M. Buck:

> *"The criteria for choosing the camp location was to find a smooth refrozen lead at least three feet thick adjacent to a large, multi-year floe. The former was for aircraft landings and the latter for the ice camp, the idea being the thicker the ice, the less apt it was to break up."*[101]

Buck's desired three-feet of thickness was increased when the LC-130 aircraft were needed. Tousey's regulation helped him determine how much ice the aircraft required.

Refrozen leads tended to be linear because they were stress fractures in the ice. However, the wind and ocean currents caused them to take different shapes. As they flew over the ocean, Bitters and Manor Buck found several locations suitable to set up the camp. When they agreed on a location, the pilot landed the aircraft, and Bitters and Tousey dragged their equipment out of the aircraft. They tested the depth of the ice to ensure it was suitable. Manor Buck wanted a minimum of nine feet of ice for his camps. When they confirmed the depth of the ice, Bitters and Tousey set up their camp for the next couple of weeks, *"...a pioneer camp consisting of a tent, radio beacon, HF communications radios, food for at least two weeks, rifles, ice drills, first aid kit, and various other light camp paraphernalia."*[102]

Bitters established communications with Station Nord then Manor Buck returned to Thule aboard the C-47. Bitters and Tousey had just established Ruby Camp for the season. They continued work on their camp, and for the next week, they groomed a rudimentary skiway. They had snowmobiles and other support equipment to assist in their work.

Bitters taught Tousey a great deal about finding refrozen leads and grooming skiways. They drilled into the ice daily to verify it was thick enough to support LC-130 aircraft. Measurements were made by boring a hole through the ice with an auger. The lower part of a hole was likely to be cone-shaped, so they used a hook or L-shaped rod to measure the thickness of the ice.[103]

Aside from supporting the aircraft landing, the ice needed to be strong enough to handle the plane's static weight as it sat on the ice and snow for extended periods. The ice experienced fatigue under constant heavy use. If the ice cracked, they stopped operations until water sealed and refroze the ice.

# Landing at Ruby

Bitters and Tousey completed an initial survey, drilling for ice thickness, taking runway length and width measurements, and looking for hazards. They rode up and down on the refrozen lead on large heavy-duty Alpine snowmobiles dragging metal bars with teeth to remove some of the small brash ice ridges to prepare for the first C-130 landings. They put flags in the ice on both sides of the prepared surface and established a rudimentary skiway. Tousey used the camp's radio to call Raven Operations at Thule Air Base. He notified them he was ready for the LC-130s. The landing surface was good, not great. Major Giles Wagoner took off the next morning. Major Jim Wilbur was an hour behind him.

*Author's Note: Jim* Wilbur *had a reputation for being able to land with his knees. His legs were long enough to maneuver the ailerons while his toes were on the floor. He trimmed up the aircraft on final approach then let go of the yoke.*

*According to Nick Tredennick, after a particularly poor landing by another pilot,* Wilbur *told him he could do a better job landing with his knees. He then proved it. When the group commander heard* Wilbur *was landing with his knees, he told him to stop it. According to* Wilbur, *the agreement was he didn't have to wear his hat if he stopped landing with his knees.*

Wagoner had the D-4 Caterpillar bulldozer in the back of his aircraft. Wilbur had a large metal beam to attach to the bulldozer. By dragging this beam with the bulldozer, they would improve the condition of the skiway. A snowmobile could only do so much. It was about a two-hour flight to Camp Ruby. A lot of things needed to be in place for Wagoner to land. There was no instrument approach to guide him into the camp skiway when he arrived, so the weather had to be good. The Raven Gang placed visual weather restrictions on the airfield; the cloud ceiling needed to be a minimum of one thousand feet above the frozen ocean's surface. The visibility needed to be at least three miles.

There were unusual hazards when landing on the ice. Bare ice damaged the skis of the aircraft. Snow cover was necessary to cushion and distribute loads over the skis. Even small ice ridges, cracks, and other irregularities in bare ice created stress points along the ski that caused damage.

Lack of depth perception was a notorious problem on the ice. Snow-covered terrain on cloud-covered days made the terrain featureless, and the lack of shadows caused an illusion as if the aircraft was traveling inside a ping-pong ball. It was difficult to judge the height of the aircraft from the ground. Tousey's flags were seven feet high on either side of the skiway to help the pilots judge their height above the surface while landing.

As Wagoner approached Ruby, he contacted Tousey over the radio. Tousey had some good news and some bad news. The good news was he created a 5,000-foot ski landing area. The bad news was the first half was unusable. Overnight a windstorm blew through the area and cleared the surface of the snow. It was bare ice.

Wagoner was confident he could land halfway down the ski landing area and stop safely. Tousey warned him, "If you go beyond the runway, there is a large ice berm." He marked a location for Wagoner to set the aircraft down. Wagoner was one of the best pilots the Raven Gang had. He was aware of the hubris of some pilots. He had witnessed Terusi's landing north of Alaska years earlier.

Wagoner touched down at the precise location Tousey identified. The aircraft sent a wave through the ice ahead of the aircraft, and another wave followed in-trail. He slowed the aircraft, cleared off the skiway, and taxied it to the designated parking location. Wagoner taxied slowly to allow the skis to cool before stopping the aircraft. The faster the aircraft traveled across the snow and ice, the greater the friction between the skis and the surface. Greater friction caused greater heat. When the aircraft stopped, the heat melts the snow and ice below, and the skis welded to the surface as they cooled. The greater the friction, the greater the heat weld's depth, and the more difficult it would be to move again. So, when Wagoner stopped, he raised the skis. The aircraft rested on its landing gear. He lowered the skis back down when he was ready to leave.

Jeff King, known as the "Cat-man," drove the bulldozer off the aircraft, and shortly afterward, Wagoner taxied to the opposite end of the skiway. This put the large ice berm off the end of the skiway behind him. He had a very short snow-covered skiway ahead of him. He intended to use as little distance as necessary due to the poor condition of the landing surface. The drag from the snow surface was unpredictable. If all went well, the takeoff wouldn't be a problem, but if he needed to stop, he'd go off the snow and onto the ice. Wagoner knew if something occurred to cause him to stop, he had a bigger problem than worrying about the skis on the bare ice. His takeoff was flawless.

Wilbur came in shortly afterward. He landed, offloaded of the large metal beam, and soon was airborne without any difficulties. King went to work immediately afterward to build a high-quality skiway so the C-130s could ferry fuel, camp materials, and cargo to build up the Ruby ice camp. Over the next days and weeks, Ruby's skiway became the main support hub for several distant sea ice satellite camps. Twin Otter aircraft transported supplies, fuel, and people to those installations.

Afterward, Bitters said, "Thanks to Jeff King's skills as a master operator, the humble and hasty beginnings by Tousey and myself became 'Ruby International,' Jeff King-style, with a surface condition for the ski aircraft that any airport could be proud of."

*Author's Note: Lillian King, Jeff King's wife, was the cook at Ruby. She was the first female the Danish government allowed to work in the Arctic. It was an antiquated law that she helped change. According to Jumper Bitters, "She was a good cook. No one lost weight at Ruby when she was there."*

When the camp was ready, Manor Buck flew passengers, survival gear, and science equipment to the camp. The Raven Gang began to arrive regularly. As the science season progressed, satellite camps were set up on the frozen ocean. When the number of people expanded significantly, food and supplies needed to be flown in. Fuel from the LC-130s was critical to maintaining these camps.

The Raven Gang built a reputation. Bitters loved them, *"For a bunch of guys that were part-time warriors, what they did was pretty amazing. I have worked with and around many military units in my career. This group of individuals was incredibly unique, coming together for these missions from varying professions outside their Guard duties. To fly and man these aircraft, a specialty aircraft in the US military inventory, and perform their duties in many situations in hostile and unforgiving elements of weather and get the work completed. They were and are an amazing group of people."*

Manor Buck put it very well when he said, *"There were so many ways for people to get hurt and a variety of things that could go the wrong way. The members of the New York Air National Guard were an impressive group of people and a credit to their organization."*

The Raven Gang continued to support Ruby until 1995.

*Dick Bayly Overhead Ruby, Tousey Pic*

CHAPTER 14

# OPERATION DEEP FREEZE

The United States established three stations in Antarctica in 1957–1958; Palmer Station on the southern tip of the continent near South America; Amundsen-Scott Base at the South Pole; and McMurdo Station about 2,700 miles south of New Zealand. They are named after famous Antarctic explorers.

The first was Nathaniel Brown Palmer, a young American seal hunter, and captain of the ship Hero. In mid-November of 1820, he returned to the Shetland Islands from New England and found the seal population there was decimated, so he pushed southward and sighted land with more seals. He is reputedly to be the first person on the Antarctica continent. Palmer Land, Antarctica, Palmer Station, and the scientific research vessel, Nathaniel B. Palmer are named after him.

Two decades later, Captain James Clark Ross, a British Antarctic explorer, led an expedition that lasted from 1839 to 1843. He had two ships, the HMS Erebus and the HMS Terror. Ross intended to sail to the South Pole. He found a large landmass in his way, later known as the continent of Antarctica. During his adventure, he discovered an island in February 1841 and named it after himself, Ross Island.

The waters between the island and the continent he named after his lieutenant, Archibald McMurdo. It's called the McMurdo Sound. McMurdo Station, the National Science Foundation's primary station on Ross Island, is also named after him. Interestingly, the two large mountains on Ross Island were named after the two ships on the expedition. The large active volcanic mountain, Mount Erebus, and the smaller mountain, Mount Terror.

# Terrain

From east to west, Ross Island has three peaks, Mount Terror, Mount Terra Nova, and an active volcano named Mount Erebus. There is a fourth peak, Mount Byrd, north of Erebus. The altitude of the terrain on Ross Island goes from sea level to greater than 10,000 feet, Mount Erebus. Following the terrain down the southern face of Erebus leads to Hut Point Peninsula, and on the tip of this peninsula is McMurdo Station, operated by the National Science Foundation.

Further south of Erebus, again going east to west, is White Island, Black Island, and Mount Discovery. Minna Bluff is a peninsula leading down from Discovery to the east, behind White and Black Islands. This is the standard routing to the South Pole; from Williams Field, fly between Mount Discovery and Black Island, over Minna Bluff, and continue south. Discovery is on the mainland of the Antarctica continent. Tracking the coastline northwesterly from Discovery leads to the Royal Society Mountain Range. The coastline continues to Marble Point.

To the west of Marble Point is the Wilson-Piedmont Glacier and the Olympus Mountain Range beyond that. About fifty miles to the east of Marble Point is Mount Erebus.

Between Marble Point to the west and Ross Island to the east is a body of water called McMurdo Sound. Following the water to the north of the sound leads to the Ross Sea and open ocean. Southeast of McMurdo Sound, the water is frozen into a permanent ice shelf, appropriately named the McMurdo Ice Shelf.

The McMurdo Ice Shelf is along the eastern coastline of the Hut Point Peninsula. From the southern tip of the peninsula, the ice shelf's coastline tracks to the east, then south, for about five miles before it turns again toward a more westerly direction and contacts the continental coastline. About seven miles from the east of Hut Point Peninsula, on the ice shelf, is Williams Field Skiway. It's carved out of the ice shelf by contractors working for the National Science Foundation. The skiway is exclusively for ski-equipped aircraft to operate.

The McMurdo Ice Shelf separates Ross Island from White Island and Black Island to the south. On the ice shelf, between four and twelve miles east of Williams Field, with Mount Terror to the north and White Island to the south, is the white-out landing area. Further east beyond the white-out landing area is the Ross Ice Shelf.

As the McMurdo Ice Shelf turns westward and about seven miles beyond Williams Field was Pegasus Ice Runway. This was the only alternate location available for LC-130 aircraft to land in the McMurdo area.

## Heroic Era

The late 19th Century and the early 20th Century have been deemed the heroic era of Antarctica exploration. The science station at the South Pole is named after Roald Amundsen and Richard Falcon Scott and is called Amundsen-Scott Base. Scott, an Englishman, spent a great deal of time on the coast of the continent, preparing an exploration into the interior of the continent. He intended to be the first person to reach the South Pole.

Amundsen, a Norwegian explorer, intended to be the first person to the North Pole. When he heard an American, Robert Perry, got there before him, he reversed direction and went south. He beat Scott to the South Pole by one month.

## Age of American Exploration

Richard E. Byrd, Jr. was the most prominent person in American Antarctic exploration throughout the first half of the 20th Century. He had access to rich and powerful people in the United States, including a friendship with Franklin Delano Roosevelt. He launched privately financed expeditions to Antarctica and brought aviation and other new technologies to the continent. In 1929, he was the first to fly an aircraft over the South Pole.

After World War II, politicians demanded a more balanced budget after years of debt to support the Great Depression and the war effort. The Navy's fleet of ships was on the chopping block. Influential people were looking for ways to maintain as much of the fleet as possible. In 1946–1947 the Navy launched Operation High Jump. This venture's leader was now-retired Rear Admiral Richard E. Byrd, Jr. The military force, Task Force 68, was commanded by Admiral Richard H. Cruzen. It remains the largest-ever expedition to Antarctica. It mapped large portions of the continent's coastline, and it saved the Navy's fleet from the chopping block.

There was a lot of speculation about the true purpose of Operation High Jump. Other countries were concerned about their territorial claims on the continent. The Soviet Union was concerned Operation High Jump was a training scenario for an American attack over the Arctic ice cap. Others were concerned America was searching for uranium deposits to build more nuclear bombs. None of this was completely accurate, but it opened channels for international cooperation.

## The Antarctica Treaty and the Military

The Antarctica Treaty was completed on 1 December 1959 and entered into force on 23 June 1961. Following a preamble, the treaty listed fourteen articles. Article 1 addressed military involvement in Antarctica. It stated the following:

> *1. Antarctica shall be used for peaceful purposes only. There shall be prohibited, inter alia, any measure of a military nature, such as the establishment of military bases and fortifications, the carrying out of military maneuvers, as well as testing of any type of weapon.*
>
> *2. The present Treaty shall not prevent the use of military personnel or equipment for scientific research or for any other peaceful purpose.*

The Antarctica Treaty was designed for peaceful worldwide cooperation on the continent. The United States started building upon the existing scientific ventures in Antarctica within the bounds of the treaty.

The Navy commissioned Air Development Squadron Six, or VX-6, to support operations in Antarctica on 19 January 1955.[104] VX-6 was located at Patuxent River, Maryland. They made their first deployment for Operation Deep Freeze in November 1955. They called their deployment Task Force

43, a four-year operation, to prepare three stations for scientific ventures in Antarctica.[105] They completed long-range exploratory flights and transported people and materials for the construction of Little America Base Camp, the Naval Air Operations Facility at Hut Point on Ross Island, the South Pole station's construction, and the construction of Byrd Surface Camp.

Williams Airfield was named after Richard T. Williams[106], a young enlisted man who was driving a D-8 tractor from the USNS Wyandot onto the frozen bay near Ross Island. As he crossed an ice-bridge, his tractor fell through a crack in the ice into the bay. His body was never recovered.[107] VX-6 was relocated to NAS Quonset Point, Rhode Island, upon their return to the United States, in February 1956.[108] On 31 October 1956, "Qué Sera Sera," an R4D Dakota, became the first airplane to land at the South Pole during the following season. Later in the season, eleven Seabees and eleven dog sleds were flown there to begin construction of the first South Pole Station.

## The United States Air Force

On 26 October 1956, the US Air Force flew their first mission to support Operation Deep Freeze. They used eight C124 Globemaster aircraft to airdrop equipment at the South Pole. The aircraft belonged to the 18th Air Force's 63rd Troop Carrier Wing. Each season after that, the C-124s returned to Antarctica and resupplied outlying camps with this airdrop capability.[109]

As part of Operation Deep Freeze 1959–1960, the Air Force's 61st Troop Carrier Squadron was ordered to Antarctica. These aircrews had just returned home to Tennessee from Sondrestrom, Greenland. They had completed the first of two seasons, providing supplies for constructing the DYE sites on the Greenland ice cap.

The 61st Troop Carrier Squadron Commander noted years later:

> *"According to information available at the time, the emergency airlift was essential because the two US stations in Antarctica would be abandoned unless essential equipment and supplies could be provided for the wintering over party."*[110]

On 23 January 1960, the 61st Troop Carrier Squadron flew the first C-130D to McMurdo, Antarctica. Over the next few days, seven C-130Ds and one C-130A aircraft arrived, with ten aircrews. They called it Operation Ice Flow.[111] It was the first time the ski-equipped C-130s operated in Antarctica. Expectations were high. A key interest of the scientists was whether the aircraft could land at outlying camps without damage. They remarked:

> *"The use of C-130 aircraft, with its ability to land on snow, will minimize the danger of damage to sensitive instruments; ensure delivery of maximum payloads, including heavy, bulky items; require less cargo handling by personnel exposed to the Antarctic climate; greatly minimize the need for airdrop parachutes, and relieve the burden of recovering parachuted items by the few men stationed at these inland bases. The C-130 may make it feasible for key scientists to visit and oversee programs for short periods at the Byrd and Pole Stations throughout the Antarctic operating season."*[112]

On 28 January 1960, the 61st Troop Carrier Squadron landed the first C-130D aircraft at the South Pole.[113] Large loading platforms, sleds, had been built specifically for the aircraft to facilitate the loading and unloading of cargo. The squadron left Antarctica on 15 February 1960 and returned to Tennessee. They had provided everything the camps needed to operate throughout the year.[114] In March 1960, they were back in Sondrestrom, Greenland, moving people and construction materials to the ice cap to finish the construction of DYE-2 and DYE-3.

# Slide III

In 1959, the National Science Foundation, in coordination with the VX-6, pursued getting new aircraft for Antarctica's science activities. Representatives of the Navy outlined their operational requirements for a new cargo aircraft to support Operation Deep Freeze during discussions on 10 September 1959 at Wright-Patterson Air Force Base.[115] The operation requirements were as follows:[116]

1. The aircraft would operate from the Antarctic region with a range of 2,200 nautical miles and fuel to hold overhead for two hours.
2. The highest elevation for takeoff and landings would be 9,200 feet.
3. Prepared snow/ice runways would be provided. The aircraft would operate from relatively smooth surfaces.
4. The aircraft should be capable of performing the airdrop mission.

The National Science Foundation purchased four C-130B aircraft with skis, or C-130BL aircraft, in 1959, tail numbers 59-5922 through 59-5925. They were later designated as LC-130F models. Tail number 59-5922 rolled out of the Lockheed factory in September 1960, and it was used for flight tests in Antarctica.

There were many differences between the C-130BL aircraft and the Air Force's older C-130D aircraft. The C-130BLs had the external fuel tanks attached to the center wing section instead of outboard of the #1 and #4 engines. The center wing section also received some structural strengthening to reduce the effects of metal fatigue. The C-130BL engines were upgraded, and a four-bladed propeller was added in place of the three-bladed propellers on the C-130D models. The landing gear was strengthened. The maximum weight of the C-130D was 124,200 pounds. The strengthened C-130BL landing gear increased the maximum weight to 155,000 pounds.

Wright Air Development Center conducted the flight tests. The same test pilot for the earlier flight tests was assigned as commander of the Joint Task Force Slide III. He started the early Navy tests with an old prototype C-130D, tail number 55-0021, at Bemidji. Bemidji didn't meet the 9,200 feet field elevation as the Navy requested, so he simulated it. He determined how much power the engines would be able to produce at 9,200 feet. He then limited the engines to that power setting during the tests. Between 22 January and 3 March 1960, a total of thirty-seven takeoff runs were recorded. The weather was relatively mild. The results were limited.

The next phase of the ski tests was conducted at McMurdo, Antarctica. Poor weather and lack of proper resources to support the tests caused some operational delays. Other administrative delays were caused by a lack of a defined chain-of-command for the test aircraft, whether it was the Navy commander supporting Operation Deep Freeze or the test pilot. Eventually, the aircraft arrived at Williams Field, Antarctica, on 9 December 1960.

The Navy didn't wait for the flight test to be completed before using them operationally, but they tempered how they used them. Although the new aircraft had greater capabilities than the C-130D aircraft, the Navy limited the C-130BL aircraft's center-of-gravity and the gross weight limitations to the same limitations as the older aircraft throughout the season. They waited until the flight tests were completed and the data were evaluated before they used the aircraft's full capability.

The test flights began on 22 December 1960. The snow was much drier in Antarctica than in Minnesota. This resulted in better takeoff performance. The weather was far from ideal. Overcast skies resulted in the loss of depth perception, and the wind was a problem. Then, more delays. During a taxi-turn test on 5 January 1961, the nose ski blew a steady stream of snow into the #3 engine air intake. The engine flamed out, so the aircrew taxied back to the parking area. After the engines were shut down, the maintenance team found the #3 engine's propeller blades were unsymmetrical and needed to be replaced.

The new propeller arrived ten days later. After it was installed, the engine test runs and a visual inspection revealed that the engine's main shaft was also damaged and needed to be replaced. They couldn't do this in Antarctica, so the test-aircrew flew to Christchurch, New Zealand, on 17 January. They replaced the engine five days later.

The test aircrew returned to McMurdo on February 6th. Ski tests resumed the next day. The test pilot modified the test plan due to the time lost. The remaining tests were completed on 15 February 1961. The test data returned to the United States. Lockheed deemed the aircraft suitable to fly. Wright-Patterson issued its Air Force Flight and Engineering Test Report on November 16th. There were no surprises. The conclusions allowed the Navy to fly their aircraft with increased power and cargo capacity.

# Operation Deep Freeze Funding

With the Vietnam War raging, the Department of Defense was no longer interested in funding the Antarctica scientific research program. National Security Decision Memorandum 71, *United States Antarctica Policy and Program*, dated 10 July 1970, transferred the research program from the Navy to the National Science Foundation. The Navy remained the logistical arm of promoting science on the Antarctic continent, but the National Science Foundation was responsible for the science program's budget.

This now created a strain on the National Science Foundation's resources. Funding to maintain the United States Antarctica Program's support structure, including funding for the Navy's Operation Deep Freeze, ate up most of their budget and provided little money to conduct science. National Security Decision Memorandum 318, *U.S Policy in Antarctica*, tried to correct many of these flaws. Dated 25 February 1976, it reaffirmed National Security Decision Memorandum 71 and added the following:

> *"The President agrees that the use of logistic support by the Department of Defense—assisted by the Coast Guard—gives the U.S. an important flexibility and reach to operate in that area. The DOD and DOT are to maintain the capability to provide the logistic support requested by the National Science Foundation, and are to develop in collaboration with the Foundation, the logistic arrangements and cost structure required to ensure effective and responsive program support at minimum cost."*

These national security decisions established the foundation for the Antarctic's scientific mission. It would be civilian-run with the Navy in a supporting logistical role, but the program's funding was still burdensome.

On February 5, 1982, President Ronald Reagan signed Presidential Memorandum 6646, *United States Antarctica Policy and Programs.* It refined how the Antarctica program would function. The National Science Foundation would perform the science. The United States military would support them with a logistical program to get the scientists where they wanted to go. But it also clarified in more detail how the program would be funded:

> *"To ensure that the United States Antarctica Program is not funded at the expense of other National Science Foundation programs, the OMB will provide specific budgetary guidance for the Antarctica Program."*

The funding for the mission was now clear. For the next fifteen years, the Navy sent their VXE-6 complement to Antarctica. Over four hundred Navy personnel arrived in McMurdo annually, with additional support in Christchurch, New Zealand.

## National Science Foundation's LC-130 Aircraft History

In January of 1969, VX-6 was re-designated Antarctic Development Squadron Six or VXE-6. In 1972 they moved to Point Mugu, California.[117] The National Science Foundation was given primary responsibility for the United States Antarctica Program in 1971.[118] Scientists wanted to go to new locations. New locations meant new challenges.

The first LC-130 aircraft lost, tail number 59-5922 (Navy designation 148318), was on 15 February 1971. The pilot was taxiing the aircraft in poor weather conditions at McMurdo. As he taxied around the control tower, the aircraft's left ski went up a 5½-foot snowbank. The right wing hit the ground and broke between the two engines. A fire, fed by fuel and fanned by high winds, destroyed the aircraft.

Tail number 59-5925 (Navy designation 148321) was lost during the next Operation Deep Freeze season, on Christmas Day. A traverse team departed the French station Dumont d'Urville and were on their way to a Soviet station, Vostok.[119] The traverse party was part of a US-French glaciology project. Throughout the traverse, they needed to be resupplied.

The Navy landed at D-59 for their second of five flights. D-59 was the traverse team designation for their location. They were seven-hundred-fifty miles from McMurdo. The aircrew finished offloading their cargo and started their takeoff run. The snow was challenging. The sastrugi, rolling ridges of ice, was rough as they accelerated.

The pilot directed his flight engineer to fire the ATO bottles, which helped. The aircraft accelerated, and the pilot pulled the aircraft off of the snow. At an altitude of about fifty feet, two ATO bottles departed the aircraft's left side. One went up the #2 engine's tailpipe, and the other struck the #2 propeller. The propeller broke into pieces, and some of the debris took out the #1 engine and propeller. Other large pieces of debris flew through the side of the aircraft and into the cargo compartment.[120] The pilot wrestled the aircraft to the ground, and there were no injuries.

The weather was poor. The temperatures reached -25° Fahrenheit. Coupled with the high winds, it reached a -100° wind-chill factor. The survivors, aided by the traverse team, spent eighty hours in tents waiting for rescue. When investigators arrived, they declared the aircraft a total loss. It was stripped of useable parts and abandoned at the crash site.[121] It was left buried in the snow at D-59 for the next seventeen years.[122]

*Navy Aircraft 321 Buried in Snow*

The National Science Foundation only had two aircraft remaining. The following year a third aircraft was lost. In 1968, the Navy purchased their only LC-130R model aircraft. In 1973, they crashed it on short final at the South Pole. Ice fog was determined to be the cause. The copilot was flying the approach-to-landing at the airfield. He pushed up the throttles and raised the nose of the aircraft to go around and try another approach. The aircraft commander saw a barrel identifying the skiway, and he took the aircraft from the copilot and pulled the power back. He didn't recognize the aircraft's nose-high attitude. Looking outside, there were no visual cues to identify the aircraft's high descent rate. The aircraft impacted the snow. No one considered the landing particularly hard; however, the wings snapped off, and the tail broke off at the aircraft's back end. According to the Antarctica Journal*: "...the pilot was making a GCA approach in ice fog at -26°F when the crash occurred. All nine crewmen and two passengers escaped unharmed."*[123] The Navy left the aircraft where it landed, where it remains today.[124]

National Science Foundation purchased three new LC-130R aircraft in 1974, tail numbers 73-0839 through 73-0841. On 15 January 1975, the Navy had another bad experience with ATO bottles. Aircraft 59-5923 (Navy designation 148319) lost its right wing on takeoff when ATO bottles on the right side of the aircraft broke loose during a takeoff run at Dome Charlie, Antarctica. Fortunately, the wing remained on the aircraft until the pilot brought the aircraft back to the snow surface. No one was injured.

The maintenance team was brilliant. To repair the aircraft's wing, they dug a trench in the snow and pulled the aircraft's fuselage into it. They then built a jig across the top of the aircraft and attached a new wing atop it. By December of 1976, repairs were completed, and the aircraft was flown back to McMurdo on Christmas Day.[125]

National Science Foundation purchased two more aircraft in 1977, tail numbers 76-0491 and 76-0492. They now had a total of seven aircraft. In December of 1984, aircraft tail number 76-0491 (Navy designation 160470) taxied into a crevasse at Starshot Glacier, less than one hundred miles from McMurdo.[126] No one was hurt, but the aircraft was seriously damaged. The Navy lifted the aircraft from the crevasse by inflating large airbags beneath the aircraft's wings. They then used a bulldozer to pull it clear of the crevasse. A Navy maintenance team repaired the aircraft, and it was returned to service.

During Operation Deep Freeze 1986–1987, the National Science Foundation established a camp at D-59. They decided to recover aircraft 59-5925 (Navy designation 148321) from where it crashed in 1971. During the recovery effort in Operation Deep Freeze 1987–1988, they lost tail number 73-0841 (Navy designation 159131).

On 9 December 1987, the copilot flew the approach into the temporary recovery field. The weather conditions were poor. The wind blew him right of course. The pilot saw the landing location and took control of the aircraft. He rolled into a steep left-bank turn to get back on course. The high bank angle, coupled with the low airspeed, caused the aircraft to stall. It cartwheeled on the snow and stopped upside down. Nine of the eleven people on board lived thanks to the people's swift assistance at the camp.

In 1992, aircraft tail number 59-5924 (Navy designation 148320) suffered a serious nose ski malfunction. During the flight, the aircrew didn't notice the front of the nose ski was drooped perpendicular to the bottom of the aircraft. Upon landing, the nose ski dug into the snow, pulling the ski back until it ripped from the aircraft. It slid beneath the aircraft and hit and damaged the right main ski. It then went airborne and damaged the right wing's flap. The ski then flew back and came in contact with the right horizontal stabilizer on the aircraft's tail. No one was injured.

CHAPTER 15

# COMPETITION

In 1988, the Raven Gang began supporting the U.S. Navy in Antarctica. They had new airplanes, but the aircrews were less reserved in their military bearing. Officers and enlisted people laughed, joked, played, and stuck together. The Navy had old airplanes with strict discipline. There was no fraternization between officers and enlisted people, except in a professional nature. The different cultures immediately clashed.

The December 1997 mission report, transcribed below, was written uniquely but clearly showed the competitive nature between the U.S. Navy and the Air National Guard. The mission was planned to deliver food and fuel to the South Pole. The "chronicler" of the mission report described how the temporary or "Tempo" weather condition lasted for more than twenty-four hours and prohibited the crew from returning to McMurdo for two days.

The saga of this Navy aircrew, aircraft XD-06, began after they completed their mission to deliver pallets of cargo and 13,000 pounds of fuel to the South Pole station. On their return flight, Herc Operations told them to return to the South Pole due to poor weather conditions at McMurdo. They returned to the South Pole and spent the night as instructed, but they needed to take the fuel they had delivered there earlier in the day, and more, for their flight the following day.

The next day they tried to return to McMurdo, but after they were airborne, they were told again, the weather at McMurdo was too poor, so they diverted to Siple Dome and again took fuel from a camp in need of fuel. When they arrived at Siple Dome, they shut down three of their engines and kept the #4 engine running because their gas turbine compressor, or GTC, had failed. When they started to refuel, the #4 engine flamed out.

Now all their engines were shut down. To start C-130 engines without the GTC, the aircrew needed an external air supply, "the Huffer," to start engines. Siple Dome didn't have one, so McMurdo needed to provide one. The aircrew spent the night at Siple Dome. A Raven Gang LC-130 aircrew was scheduled the next day to bring them the maintenance personnel and the aircraft parts they needed for the aircraft repairs. The trip report was written with a uniquely entertaining style, but it also showed the resentment of being helped by the Guard.

## Crew 8 Mission Report

*In the beginning, there was Crew 8. And the Lord looked favorably on Crew 8, and provided them with a great bounty of recces, put-ins, and two-piloted Pole Tankers. But then Crew 8 sinned a great sin against the Lord, and his wrath was great upon them. Yet they stiffened their necks and repented not. Thus, the Lord decided that they must be punished so that they might sin no more.*

*And so it was, in the time when the people were led by Nicholson the Irrelevant, that Crew 8 set out once more to seek the bounty of the Pole. And they brought with them JP-8, that they might gain cookies in return. After they had finished their trading, they set out to return home. But the Lord, in his great anger, put a great storm in their path. And that they might know it was his judgment, the Lord so made that the sages and wise men foresaw it not, and spake unto Crew 8, "It is naught but a Tempo line you see, continue home to the land of your brethren, for we await you with wine, beer, and song. But the Lord took pity on them and sent an Angel who spoke to them by HF: "I am* Wilbur, *Angel of the Lord. This storm is not a Tempo line, but the Wrath of the Lord turned against you. For you have sinned a great sin, and shall not come to McMurdo, but shall return to Pole and stand by." And Crew 8 did as the Angel said.*

*Now when they returned to the Pole, they were met graciously by the people there. And Nicholson spoke to them saying, "A great storm has come to McMurdo, and we would have perished had not an angel warned us that we might return here and live. But we have nothing to trade, and will make our camp apart from you, that we might not be a burden." And the leader of the people replied, "You will not be a burden, for you are Crew 8, and well-loved at the Pole. You will have the highest ground for your camp, and tonight you will all be guests at my table. You will eat of the choicest meat, potatoes, and freshies. You will drink the freshest juice, and your dessert will be pastries and fresh ground coffee. And those who are too tired to return to your camp shalt rest with us tonight. To show that we do this out of friendship and wish nothing in return, we give you back twofold the JP-8 you brought us earlier so that your Herk might eat, too." And Crew 8 was overcome by these words and joyously went into the Dome, all except for LeClaire, the keeper of the Beast, who led the fuelies out to feed the Herk. And they ate and drank, and many slept in the camp of the people.*

*But the Lord looked down upon them and was still wrathful, for their punishment seemed light, and he feared that soon they might find husbands and wives at the Dome and live out their days contentedly there, forgetting completely their brethren in McMurdo. And the Lord sent an Angel to cast them out of the Pole. So, he spake to them by HF, saying, "I am Neck, Archangel and Mouth of the Lord. Hear his decree—'Oh, Crew 8, your sin is great and the burden of your punishment is but like a feather, for you do eat fine meats and drink fresh juice among your friends. But now you will be cast out from them to wander aimlessly the frozen wastelands, from camp to camp, always despised and accursed, because you take from them food and fuel, and bring nothing in return. And so the name "Crew 8" will become a hateful name, whispered only in the shadows and used by parents to frighten small children into eating peas, okra, and other icky things'—The Mouth of the Lord has spoken thus. Neck, out!"*

*And so it was, that Crew 8 was cast out into the frozen wasteland of Nod and became as thieves and marauders, for they could only take and could not give. Many camps tried to turn them away and were taken by force, their food seized, their fuel drained, their tents burned, and their Beakers scattered like dry leaves before the wind. For there were many valiant men and women in Crew 8, and none could stand before them. And so perished many camps, fuel caches, and refuges from the face of the GNC-26. And the Lord allowed this to happen because most of them had foolish names anyway, like "Camp Ohio II" and "Upstream Charlie." But the Lord put his protection on Downstream Bravo and covered it with a thick fog so that Crew 8 might not suck it dry also. Thus, it was that Crew 8's sin grew larger, but they stiffened their necks and repented not.*

*After many years of wandering and marauding, there remained but Siple Dome to raid, for all the others had already been destroyed, and the Tempo line was still predominant at McMurdo. And Crew 8 made well ready to attack and armed themselves with tie-down chains, fire axes, crowbars, and chart dividers, for Siple Dome was a large camp and well-armed. And the leaders at Siple Dome said to each other, "We are a large camp, and well-armed, but naught can stand before Crew 8, for they are strong and valiant. Therefore, let us stand back when they arrive and send but one fuelie to meet them. We will feed their Herk, and they will leave and spare us." Thus it was when Crew 8 arrived. And they accepted the offer of tribute, shut down three, and made ready to fuel. Then the Mouth of the Lord spoke: "I am Neck—hear the word of the Lord! 'Oh, foolish crew, how long will you stiffen your necks? I put a storm in your path, sent you back to Pole, and you repented not. I cast you out from Pole and made you wander the wasteland, hated and despised, yet you repent not. I allowed you victory at camp after camp, and you repented not. Now you will listen to me, your Lord! You will stay at Siple Dome, and you will put your Herk to sleep. And it will stay asleep until the Huffer comes to wake it, for your GTC is inop. And so you know the Wrath of the Lord is upon you, the Huffer will be carried by the Guard, so that your shame will burn with you all your days, and the name 'Crew 8' will be a laughing stock, even unto a thousand generations." And Nicholson sought to reason with the Neck, saying, "Surely this punishment is too great, for a man cannot live with the shame of rescue by the Guard, which is like unto a thousand deaths a day unto eternity." Yet as he spoke, the Lord reached out and caused #4 to flame out. And the crew was awed by the power of the Lord.*

*And so it was that Crew 8 was brought to repentance, for as they sat on the ground, they felt shame of their many sins, and they understood that the Lord was right to bring unspeakable shame on them, for they had not crew-rested. And there they formed a covenant, that they would crew rest, and read the Ops Manual, and follow his many laws and regulations, and teach them to their sons, and their sons' sons. Thus it was, as they sat around lamenting the inop GTC, LeClaire was moved to cry unto the Lord, "Lord, you are our only hope. Save us from the shame of our sin!" And the Lord gave him insight, and he flipped the switch, and the GTC did start.*

*And they did wake the Herk, and did feed it, and readied themselves to return to their brethren. And the Neck spoke to them saying, "You foolish crew! Have you learned nothing? The Tempo line still prevails. Go and crew-rest, and do not tempt the Lord's anger again!" And Crew 8 asked forgiveness of the*

*Sipoleans, that they had come to steal and plunder. And the Lord moved the hearts of the Sipoleans, and they took Crew 8 in as honored guests and gave them steaks to grill and fill their empty stomachs and took them to the drill sites and the sauna, and the hot tub. And they did bathe in the hot tub and were brought into their tents by the Sipoleans and crew-rested a full 12 hours as per the Ops manual.*

*The next day they did depart for the land of their brethren. And the Lord placed a mountain above the clouds to guide them, for he didn't trust the nav, either. And as they arrived, they wondered at the beauty of the snow that the Lord had set as a symbol of the new covenant of the Ops Manual, which had cleansed their sin. And the snow bore them up as they touched down, and they felt it not. (Deep Freeze 41:1–3)*

*Chronicler J. M. Green's Dates: 12–14 December 1997.*

CHAPTER 16

# RAVEN GANG'S NEW LIFE

During the mid-1980s, Lt. Col. Karl Doll saw the DYE site mission wasn't going to last much longer. He was the operations officer for the Raven Gang. Every year was in question because the DYE sites were antiquated.

In 1986, Dr. Simon Wheeler, the Division Director of Polar Programs for the National Science Foundation, contacted Doll. Wheeler was a key player in establishing the foundation's Arctic research programs, and in Antarctica, he set the agenda for polar science. He wanted the Raven Gang to provide a winter search-and-rescue capability for Antarctica beginning in 1990. The aging National Science Foundation LC-130 fleet was going through depot-level maintenance, and their aircraft couldn't be relied upon during the off-season.

Doll began toying with the idea of the Raven Gang taking over the Operation Deep Freeze mission from the Navy. He told Wheeler his people needed to fly in Antarctica to understand the nature of what they were being asked to do before making the decision. It was best to see the daylight operation before they were asked to support the dark months' operation. Wheeler agreed. His formal request included continental airlift support in Antarctica during the Operation Deep Freeze Season, and it was a multi-year request.

Doll coordinated with the Operation Deep Freeze squadron commander to make it happen. However, he got in trouble with the National Guard Bureau when they found out about the Raven Gang going to Antarctica. He needed proper authorization from them. So, Doll sent a written request, and it was approved.

In 1988, from January 17th through the 22[nd], months before DYE-2's rapid abandonment, the Raven Gang flew two aircraft and two aircrews in Antarctica to gain experience. In 1988, from December 4[th] through the 10[th], two more aircraft and two different aircrews flew on the continent. The rotations were fifteen-day rotations; five days to travel from New York to McMurdo, five days in Antarctica, and five days to return to New York.

Doll wanted as many aircrews as possible to get some flying time in Antarctica to prepare for future requests from the National Science Foundation. These weeks in Antarctica gave the Raven Gang a good look at a potential new mission. They also gave the National Science Foundation a good look at the Raven Gang's capabilities.

When his old friend Lt. Col. Archie Berberian heard about Doll's fracas with Guard Bureau, he called him from the Pentagon. Berberian's responsibilities included the policy and program development of the Air Guard. He represented the Air Guard at the Air Staff's Programs Review Committee and Mobility Panel.

Doll confided in him that he was interested in taking the Operation Deep Freeze mission from the Navy. Berberian was immediately on board with the plan. He told Doll, "Karl, if we're going to do this, we've got to do a feasibility study. Can you come down and do this?" Together they worked on the feasibility study to make it happen.

# Single Point Manager for the Skibirds

In the Spring of 1989, back at the National Science Foundation, Wheeler received some very positive feedback about the Raven Gang's success. On 28 June 1989, Wheeler visited General Duane H. Cassidy, the Air Force's Transportation Command commander. They discussed the Raven Gang's participation in Antarctica the previous winter. They also discussed the larger concept of combining the LC-130 fleet into a single-point manager of the skibirds. The fleet's single-point manager would be either the Navy with a long history in Antarctica or the Raven Gang from a small Air National Guard unit in Upstate New York.

Two weeks later, on 11 July 1989, Wheeler sent a letter to Cassidy, referring to the LC-130s as a unique "national resource." Wheeler wanted joint management of the LC-130 aircraft and told Cassidy it warranted serious consideration. Later in the month, Wheeler went to Greenland to watch the Raven Gang operate. The night before his departure, Doll and Wheeler went to dinner at the Rain Dancer Restaurant in Amsterdam, New York. Doll prepared him for what to expect in the week ahead. It was very different from the operation in Antarctica.

Doll had done his research. He found out the Navy was charging the National Science Foundation $50 million annually to support Operation Deep Freeze. At dinner, Doll told Wheeler the Raven Gang could fly the Operation Deep Freeze mission for half the price, $25 million. He had no data to back it up, but his arguments were sound. From 31 July through 5 August 1989, Wheeler went to Sondrestrom and watched the Raven Gang operate.

Lt. Col. Jon Adams was the mission commander. He scheduled two airplanes and two aircrews to DYE-3 three times a day. They started flying after an early breakfast, and they were done each day around 3:30 p.m. When Wheeler talked to the aircrews, he found they were confident and had an impressive knowledge of their mission. Many of them had been doing the mission since the Spring of 1976. He became a true believer in the Guard.

Although Wheeler wanted the 109th Tactical Airlift Group to become the single point manager for the LC-130 fleet, the military still needed to be convinced that the Guard could manage the Operation Deep Freeze mission.

Wheeler sent Cassidy another letter on 11 August 1989. He told Cassidy, a single-point manager for the LC-130 aircraft, had become a matter of some urgency. It would provide substantial gains for the mission. He detailed this point in a position paper for Cassidy to review. In response, Cassidy, on 19 September 1989, said, "I agree in principle, but further study is required." Cassidy was already coordinating with the National Guard Bureau. The Guard needed to do a feasibility study to determine what the 109th Airlift Group needed if they became the single-point manager for both the Arctic and Antarctic missions.

# Transition of Operation Deep Freeze to the Raven Gang

In the mid-1990s, following the end of the Cold War, the United States Congress cut funding to the Department of Defense. The National Science Foundation felt the squeeze too, but they wanted to rebuild the Amundsen-Scott Station at the South Pole. This would require a major commitment of resources and reliable airlift to move building materials, construction contractors, and machinery over many years.

*South Pole Stations Old (Dome) and New*

Rebuilding the South Pole station required a huge flying commitment, and the single-point manager for the LC-130 fleet must be able to handle those needs. The Navy's fleet of seven skibird aircraft was owned by the National Science Foundation and dated from the 1970s. The National Science Foundation wasn't interested in purchasing new aircraft for the Navy, and the Navy certainly wasn't going to do it. The Navy had no incentive to maintain their flying squadron dedicated to Operation Deep Freeze in Antarctica. They were better served by keeping more combat-related personnel.

# The Game was Afoot

Doll and Wheeler talked with each other frequently. Wheeler gave the Raven Gang all operational support they requested for the Operation Deep Freeze mission. They had free reign to change how their flying operation functioned.

Doll wanted the flying mission, but he didn't want responsibility for the support structure in Antarctica. He told Wheeler the Guard would fly the airplanes. But the National Science Foundation would need to provide weather forecasters, air traffic controllers, cargo specialists, and many other aspects of support required for a smooth flying operation. These positions would be converted into civilian contract positions when the Navy left.

In October of 1989, Doll wrote an article in the base's news magazine, *Transport Topics*. In it, he said:

> "I have just received word that DYE-3 will be closed down this fall. The remaining fifty percent of the mission we have known these past fifteen seasons is about to conclude. During the past several weeks, however, initiatives regarding a change in management of our nation's polar airlift capability have been presented, which seem to be pointing in the direction of a future increase in mission tasking for us.
>
> "Dr. Simon Wheeler, Director of the Division of Polar Programs for the National Science Foundation, has corresponded with General Duane H. Cassidy, Commander in Chief of the U.S. Transportation Command, regarding a Single Point Manager of all LC-130 assets which would support a bi-polar mission. This single unit would have the responsibility of supporting the Arctic and the Antarctic airlift requirements. It would mean a significant increase in nearly every function within our Group. Flying hours would likely double from our present 4400 hours to around 8000 hours. This would necessitate increased maintenance support. The flying squadron would double in size, which would necessitate an increase in all of the support functions, i.e., clinic, personnel, dining hall, finance, etc. New facilities would have to be built to accommodate this increase in manning, which at this time is estimated to be about five hundred additional military positions, including approximately one hundred and fifty full-time personnel. An increase of this magnitude could certainly not occur overnight, but rather should be a phased buildup over a three-to-four-year period."

Some Navy representatives in the Pentagon opposed the idea of the Guard taking over Operation Deep Freeze. The Navy's argument was based upon tradition. They had been flying in Antarctica since the days of Byrd. Berberian's counterargument was that the Antarctica mission took 787 non-combat positions from the Navy when the military was reducing its forces following the Cold War. His argument was compelling.

Over the next five years, it became obvious that the Raven Gang would be the single point manager for the ski mission. However, the feasibility study indicated there would be challenges. All these weren't worth the paper they were printed on unless they could convince the decision-makers that the Raven Gang could do the mission. The feasibility study indicated 109th Tactical Airlift Group needed to build up their manning, acquire more aircraft and more base facilities to support these increases.

On 29 September 1989, Major Don Boone prepared a point paper regarding how base facilities were impacted by adding four to six aircraft at Stratton. The projection included constructing additional hangars and facilities for the Raven Gang, the air terminal, and the services and supply building. He also included an expansion of the aircraft parking ramp. His cost estimate for the improvements was $27,280,000.

Over the next three years, there were letters, point papers, conferences, man-power studies; site surveys of buildings, the aircraft parking ramp, and resources at Stratton Air National Guard Base; that involved U.S. Air Force general officers, Navy admirals, and politicians. This would eventually lead to the building of two new aircraft hangars, a new dining facility, a modern communications center, an extension to the Raven Gang's operations building, and an expansion of the aircraft parking ramp.

## Leadership Changes

On 4 February 1989, Karl Doll was medically removed from flying status. He returned to flying for a short time, but his final flight was on 5 December 1989. He was grounded. He could no longer serve as the operations commander for the Raven Gang. On 24 October 1990, Doll transferred to the Air Force Reserves in New York's State Emergency Management

Office in Albany. Pete Terusi, the commander of the 109th Tactical Airlift Group, transferred Major Verle Johnston from the maintenance commander position to replace him. Weeks later, Pete Terusi got a job at New York Air National Guard Headquarters. In December of 1990, a new commander was appointed to replace Terusi, but he also was transferred to New York State Headquarters a few months later.

In October of 1991, Colonel Archie Berberian became the new 109th Tactical Airlift Group's commander. Berberian chose Lt. Col. Graham Pritchard to be his vice-commander. Pritchard brought years of experience with him to help Berberian understand many of the ski mission's unique challenges.

# Aircraft

How decisions are made in the United States Congress has always been a mystery. In 1991, they approved $92 million to purchase two new C-130H3 model aircraft, with skis, for the New York Air National Guard. It came with a caveat. Two of the older Guard C-130H2 aircraft, with skis, would be transferred to the Navy to support Antarctica's operations. Both the Guard and the Navy would receive newer aircraft, which gave them a mix of different aircraft models for their maintenance people to maintain and their aircrews to fly.

The Navy was considering whether to remove the technology from the newer aircraft to standardize them with the rest of their fleet or convince the National Science Foundation to provide the resources to upgrade the rest of their fleet. The newer technology in the Guard wasn't as straightforward. The newer C-130H3 model aircraft had a hybrid glass cockpit.

Eventually, their four C-130H2 model aircraft, with skis, received funding from Congress to modify them to the same standard as the C-130H3 model aircraft, but the four C-130H2 models, without skis, did not. In a different funding source, the National Science Foundation purchased a single C-130H3 model with skis. Now the National Science Foundation had a decision to make. They needed to either remove the aircraft's modifications to bring it in line with the rest of their fleet or modify their whole fleet to the Guard's standards. It was a threshold decision and a precursor for future decisions. The National Science Foundation chose to standardize their aircraft with the rest of the Guard fleet.

In another twist, the National Science Foundation owned the seven aircraft the Navy flew in Antarctica, not the Department of Defense. They didn't immediately concede turning their aircraft over to the 109th Airlift Wing. California and Alaska were also making a bid to take over the single-point management program. Both California and Alaska made the case they were closer to Antarctica than New York. However, there were more rotations to Greenland annually than Antarctica. The 109th Airlift Wing's location was only six hours from Sondrestrom. Therefore, it was more cost-effective for New York to fly to Greenland. Besides, it was hard to argue with the Raven Gang's success over the years.

In the final agreement, four National Science Foundation aircraft were transferred to the 109th Airlift Wing. Before they arrived, upgrades and modifications were made to standardize these aircraft with the rest of the 109th Airlift Wing's aircraft. Three of the National Science Foundation aircraft were tail number 73-0839, with a new tail number designation, 73-3300; tail number 76-0491, with a new tail number designation 76-3301; and tail number 76-0492, with a new tail number designation 76-3302.[127] When their new C-130H3 came off the assembly line, it was also given to the Guard to maintain.

The 109th Airlift Wing ended up with ten LC-130 aircraft and four C-130 aircraft:

| Wheel-Birds | | Skibirds | | Additions for Antarctica Mission | |
|---|---|---|---|---|---|
| Tail Number | Date | Tail Number | Date | Tail Number | Date |
| 83-0486 | 1983 | 83-0490 | 1983 | 92-1094 | 1992 |
| 83-0487 | 1983 | 83-0491 | 1983 | 92-1095 | 1992 |
| 83-0488 | 1983 | 83-0492 | 1983 | 93-1096 | 1993 |
| 83-0489 | 1983 | 83-0493 | 1983 | 73-3300 | 1973 |
| | | | | 76-3301 | 1976 |
| | | | | 76-3302 | 1976 |

# Proposed Changes to the Mission

Berberian contacted Karl Doll in Albany, New York, and told him to go to the National Science Foundation to work on the single point manager program. Little work had been done over the last few years on the 109th Airlift Wing's concept of the Operation Deep Freeze mission, including the airfield modifications, the concept of how the Guard would deploy their people, and overall personnel issues such as upgrades to dormitory and work facilities in McMurdo. Fortunately, Doll's work in the Reserves allowed him ample time to help Berberian.

Doll's purpose at the National Science Foundation was to create a liaison office between the National Science Foundation and the Department of Defense. He also worked on memorandums of understanding and memorandums of agreement between the Air National Guard and the National Science Foundation.

While working at the National Science Foundation, Mr. Dwight Fisher, the National Science Foundation Deputy Head of Polar Research Support in the Office of Polar Programs, often stopped by Doll's office. Fisher's position funded and managed the U.S. Antarctic Program and the Foundation's Arctic Research Program. He asked Doll questions to help transition the single-point management program from a dream into a reality.

On another battlefront, the Navy and Air Force had separate supply systems. When the Navy left in February of 1999, the Guard would have nothing, so Pritchard's transition team built a Guard supply system in Christchurch, New Zealand. His supply specialists assured aircraft parts and supplies would be available to sustain them.

# Out with the Old

When the Cold War ended, Congress told the Department of Defense to reduce its size. To do so required the Navy to streamline its defensive posture. By 1993, the Navy already had an exit strategy from Operations Deep Freeze. Initially, the Navy had doubts about the Raven Gang. There was a general concern the transition would be a disaster for the United States Antarctic Program.

Pritchard went to Washington D.C. and presented a briefing on his concept of operations to the Oceanographer of the Navy. When he arrived, several Navy officers wouldn't shake his hand. His briefing addressed their concerns one at a time with counter-arguments. Halfway through his brief, the Oceanographer folded his notes and pushed back from the table. He was on board with the transition.

On March 30–31, 1993, the Navy's Deputy Oceanographer opened a meeting to address a proposal for the U.S. Navy to withdraw from the Antarctica program. The following was stated for the reasons for closing VXE-6, the Navy's Puckered Penguin squadron:

> *"It was noted that as DoD support to the United States Antarctic Program is on a cost-reimbursable basis, proposals for Navy withdrawal were being forced by total end-strength reductions and not budgetary reductions. Under current directives and agreements, reductions in overall Navy-wide authorized end-strength will result in the imposition of proportionate decreases in Navy billets assigned to the USAP (United States Antarctica Program)."*

The Department of Defense had cut manning billets for the military following the end of the Cold War. The Navy had 787 non-combat billets assigned to the United States Antarctica Program. They could not rationalize maintaining these positions at the cost of their combat-related manning end strength.

On 9 January 1994, a former Navy commander in Antarctica sent a letter to the Oceanographer of the Navy. He made one last attempt to stop the Air National Guard's takeover of the mission. His objections were passed to Pritchard in New York. Pritchard provided a briefing to answer his concerns, and the Navy objections were withdrawn.

# In with the New

On 22 September 1992, the Air Force's Air Mobility Command wrote a staff summary sheet that supported the Guard takeover of the mission as long as the National Science Foundation paid for the flying time.

On 14 September 1993, the new full-time manpower study was completed. It added eighty-four new positions to the Raven Gang, ninety-four positions to the maintenance group, and sixteen additions to the support group. It was a total of one-hundred-ninety-four positions and eventually rose to two-hundred-thirty-nine positions due to increases in flying hour projections and manning for the creation of Detachment 13 in Christchurch, New Zealand.

At the forefront of Pritchard's mind during his efforts to get the approvals to take over the Operation Deep Freeze mission was his determination to keep the ski mission a Guard mission. He frequently went to Air National Guard Readiness Center at Andrews Air Force Base. In January 1995, he invited Major General Don Shepard, the Air National Guard Commander, to go to Antarctica. Shepard's firsthand experience with the mission left no doubt in his mind the bi-polar ice cap mission was a Guard mission. This sealed the deal. The 109th Airlift Wing received authorization to increase the manning necessary to support the mission. In June 1995, the United States Congress agreed on the proper language necessary to make this happen.

Finally, in 1996 the Department of Defense and Transportation designated the 109th Airlift Wing in Schenectady, New York, as the logistical arm of the United States Antarctica Program.

Through the struggles to obtain the Operation Deep Freeze mission, the friendly atmosphere between the 109th Airlift Wing and the National Science Foundation became more contentious. The friendly tone Doll and Wheeler experienced early on between their organizations was gone. The contractors who replaced many of the Navy functions of the mission added to the discord.

# Experience

McMurdo, Antarctica operations were much different than Sondrestrom, Greenland operations. In Greenland, the Raven Gang supported university science objectives funded and backed by the National Science Foundation. The operation was small in comparison to Antarctica. There were small camps in Antarctica; however, much of the research activities were at larger camps, such as Amundsen-Scott Base at the South Pole. At these camps, the researchers and scientists were more disconnected from camp activities. Instead of dealing with the researchers, the Raven Gang often dealt with the contractors running the camp.

By 1995 the Operation Deep Freeze mission was a familiar mission to the Raven Gang. Karl Doll had seen to that. They had experienced many interesting events in the Antarctic and prepared for what was to come. When Dick Bayly's aircraft broke on the Antarctica ice cap, the Raven Gang had been flying in Antarctica for seven years. They learned there needed to be additions to the standard Air Force hostile environment repair kit. They created a ski mission-specific kit that included a supply of hydraulic hoses, unions, and reducers. For Dick Bayly, it was just another mission. For the National Science Foundation, the Navy, and the contractors, it was an eye-opener.

CHAPTER 17

# BALLOON CHASING

Scientists launched the balloon on 22 December 1994. It floated to altitude and started a counter-clockwise turn around the South Pole. It made one full revolution of Antarctica at an altitude of 131,000 feet. The payload hanging below the balloon weighed 2,940 pounds, but overall it weighed 4,576 pounds. The National Science Foundation and National Aeronautics and Space Administration had developed this capability and used it to support several disciplines, including a low-cost substitute for space flight.[128]

On 8 January 1995, scientists removed the overhead escape hatch above Skier 92's flight deck, as the contractor fuel specialists put 50,000 pounds of fuel onboard the aircraft. They replaced the hatch with one that had several antennae sticking out from it. They ran cables from the hatch down the flight deck stairs and to the cargo compartment and connected them to their computers to get the telemetry they needed to locate their balloon.

Days earlier, on 3 January 1995, they tried to recover the balloon, but ground fog prohibited the aircrew from landing, so the mission was postponed. Five days later, the weather forecasters anticipated a beautiful day to recover the balloon and its gondola. Later in the evening, a snowstorm was anticipated. This would be their last opportunity before the weather set in.

The Japanese American Collaborative Emulsion Experiment was a scientific effort to measure the composition and spectra of primary cosmic rays at the top of the atmosphere. The collaboration utilized Japanese expertise in photographic materials and microscopy, American expertise in ballooning and data analysis, and Polish resources to scan and measure emulsions.

They used a gondola design attached to a balloon. It was a simple, lightweight, and rugged framework that protected the gondola in an awkward landing or parachute drag. The gondola included an onboard data-logging computer to record pressure altitude, module temperatures, and the project's control mechanisms. The balloon facility at McMurdo interfaced with the gondola's computer throughout its flight to monitor the status of the project and download data.[129]

Unique geophysical conditions above Antarctica made long-duration balloon flights that circumnavigate the continent possible during the austral summer. First, a nearly circular pattern of gentle east-to-west winds established itself in the Antarctic stratosphere lasting for a few weeks. This pattern was generated by a long-lived high-pressure area caused by the constant solar heating of the stratosphere. It allowed the launch and recovery of a balloon from roughly the same geographic location and permitted a flight path almost entirely overland.

Second, because the sun never set during the austral summer, the balloon was illuminated continuously, both directly and by reflection from the underlying clouds or snow. As a result, the balloon maintained a constant temperature and was able to maintain a stable altitude. In other areas of the world, the daily heating and cooling cycles changed the volume of gas in the balloon, causing it to rise and fall and expend ballast, severely limiting flight times. Since an international zone under the Antarctic Treaty existed, balloons could be launched, flown, and recovered anywhere on the continent without the diplomatic complications experienced in other areas of the globe.[130]

## Chasing the Balloon

Dicky Bayly took off from McMurdo with the science team in the back of his aircraft. The weather was good in McMurdo and also expected to be good in Victoria Land, their destination. They intended to locate the long-duration balloon and bring its payload back to McMurdo.

| Skier 92 Aircrew | |
|---|---|
| **Pilot:** | Major Dick Bayly |
| **Copilot:** | Major Gerard Kozic |
| **Copilot:** | First Lieutenant Steve Yandik (sat on the bunk) |
| **Navigator:** | Major Ginny Reilly |
| **Flight Engineer:** | Technical Sergeant Brian Alix |
| **Loadmaster:** | Master Sergeant Kurt Garrison |

It took an hour and a half to reach the balloon's location. Upon arrival, the scientists needed a couple of hours until they were ready to bring it down from altitude. When they arrived, no one could visually see it, but the scientists saw it on their computers. The skies were clear. Bayly flew a fifty-mile radius around its location until the balloon landed.

When they were ready, the scientist brought down the balloon by radio control, which sent a signal to release the helium inside it. As it descended, it took about thirty minutes until they could see it visually and another fifteen minutes until it impacted the snow. As it descended, Bayly chased after it. He looked at the direction of the wind. He intended to get in front of the balloon, land Skier 92, and let the balloon blow towards them. It sounded like a good plan at the time. However, when he thought about it later, he reconsidered whether he could catch a very large balloon moving with the wind at twenty knots and whether he really wanted to.

Initially, the landing was smooth, but as the aircraft slowed, it hit sastruga. Hitting the first large, hard-packed, rolling dune of ice was violent. Brian Alix, Bayly's flight engineer, took the violence in stride initially. There was nothing he could do. He stated, "Yep, there goes the nose ski." He was certain they had just ripped it off. He watched the pressure gauge on the copilot's hydraulic panel go to zero. Alix said, "Yep, there goes the hydraulic pressure." When they hit the next sastrugi, he was a little more anxious. He said, "Stop the fucking airplane, Dick!"

The aircraft stopped. They were at a pressure altitude of 8,800 feet and about five hundred miles from McMurdo.[131] Brian Alix went outside and looked at the aircraft's general condition. The ski was against the fairing of the aircraft, pushed up against the nose. He was initially happy the ski was still below the aircraft, but he was certain they snapped the nose gear cylinder. There should have been about a two-foot gap between the ski and the fairing. He reported what he saw to Bayly.

# Herc Ops

Gerard Kozic, Bayly's copilot, called McMurdo Operations (Mac Ops) and notified them of their status. Mac Ops was the communications link from McMurdo to all of the camps in Antarctica. Kozic reported their location at 73° 45' South, 152° 22' East.

Mac Ops was across the hall from Herc Ops. The radio operator went across the hall and notified Lt. Col. Bill Mathews and Major John de Graaf of the bad news. De Graaf heard smug whispers from the Navy crewmembers in the room. They seemed pleased to see the Guard, with their new aircraft, about to witness what it was like to spend some time on the ice cap; the Guard, with their new aircraft, about to be rescued by the Navy. None of it was malicious, just mischievous. Mathews said, "And yes, the Navy crews were giddy that we busted up an airplane."

Together the Navy and the Raven Gang worked on a rescue plan. The weather was expected to move in, and snow was expected to blanket the area for quite a while. If the aircrew didn't return soon, they would remain there for the next week.

Lt. Col. Elliot "Aldo" Marchegiani was returning from the South Pole and overheard Kozic's conversation over the Mac Ops frequency. He called Herc Ops. He intended to find Bayly's aircrew and bring them back to McMurdo. Mathews, the Raven Gang's deployed commander, refused to allow it and remarked, "Aldo was furious that I wouldn't let him get Dicky and company, and crew rest was the least of my worries. The possibility of having two LC-130's broken on the ice was totally unacceptable!"

While the maintenance section was trying to solve the problem, Mathews was shuffling back and forth from a congressional delegation's visit to Antarctica while keeping the commander of operation Deep Freeze abreast of updates regarding the broken aircraft.

As the hours passed, the telephones started heating up. The Navy called Point Mugu, California, for aircraft parts and a hydraulic specialist to fly to McMurdo then out to the ice cap to repair Bayly's aircraft. They would have to wait for the coming snowstorm to pass.

In the meantime, Herc Ops planned for an airdrop to provide Bayly's aircrew and the scientist with needed food and supplies to remain there for the next week.

# The Guard

Bayly was concerned about the scientists. The aircrew had survival gear to wait out the storm. The scientists did not. When the aircrew heard about the oncoming snowstorm, Bayly looked at his aircrew and said, "We're not staying here." He didn't want to hear otherwise.

Alix said, "No, we're not staying here."

Yandik followed, "No, we're not staying here."

Perhaps they repeated what Bayly said because they believed it. Maybe they said it because they didn't want to disappoint him. It didn't matter. He put them to work.

Dick Bayly joined the Guard at Schenectady, New York, in 1970. When he returned from pneumatic repair school in 1971, the airbase had transitioned from C-97 aircraft to C-130A model aircraft. He remained a pneumatic repair specialist in the hydraulic shop for six years. In 1976 he went to officer training school to become a maintenance officer. When he returned from school, the 109th Tactical Airlift Group commander, Colonel Stan Hemstreet, issued orders for him to go to pilot training.

Bayly said, "I didn't ask for this."

Hemstreet said, "That's okay, you're going."

Steve Yandik graduated from pilot training in 1993. He was on his first rotation to Antarctica. His civilian job was working on aircraft at Albany International Airport. He had a Federal Aviation Administration airframe and power plant (A&P) certification, and he also had an inspection authorization (IA). He could validate the airworthiness of aircraft.

Brian Alix started his career as a C-123 flight engineer at Westover Air Reserve Base, Massachusetts, in 1980. In 1984 his flying squadron changed to C-130 aircraft. In 1989 he joined the Raven Gang. He was not only the systems specialist on the aircraft, but he also had a Federal Aviation Administration airframe and power plant (A&P) certification. A military aircrew with this much maintenance experience could only be found in the Air National Guard.

## A Closer Look

Alix's first action inside the aircraft was to isolate the nose ski from the rest of its utility hydraulic system. LC-130 aircraft had the means to isolate each of the skis' hydraulic fluid from the rest of the system by closing a valve in the cargo compartment. Kurt Garrison and Alix filled the hydraulic system with the spare hydraulic fluid kept in the back of the aircraft. When Alix was ready, Kozic flipped the pressure switch on the flight deck hydraulic panel, and pressure returned to the rest of the hydraulic system. Alix then opened the main ski isolation valves one at a time. The pressure continued to hold.

Next, Garrison got a shovel from the back of the aircraft and started digging. He began by pulling the survival sled out of the aircraft to block the wind. It was very cold, sub-zero temperatures, with twenty knots of wind. Before long, he had shoveled the area around the nose ski clear of snow. The ski had been resting against a pressure ridge pushing against the weight of the rest of the aircraft. Their situation looked a little better, and as Garrison cleared the snow, the nose ski extended.

Alix was able to get under the aircraft's nose to understand their situation better. The ski was still attached. He couldn't see anything wrong with it until he looked up at the ski's rigger strut. It was covered in hydraulic fluid. He took the cover off of the forward panel of the ski. When he looked inside, he saw the ski control valve had blown apart. The spool of the valve was sticking out of the top of it. The plate on the top of the valve had blown off completely. It was lying in the bottom of the ski in a puddle of hydraulic fluid. The four tiny screws that attached the plate to the valve were still safety-wired together. He climbed out from beneath the aircraft and told Bayly about it. Yandik listened as Bayly and Alix discussed what to do. Aircrews didn't carry a spare ski control valve in their pocket. Their only remaining option was to try to rebuild the ski control valve.

## Repairs

Bayly took the lead on repairs. He knew the hydraulic system better than the others. Alix did most of the work. The spool was a thick cylinder with a thinner pin-type cylinder on top. They alternated beating on the spool of the ski control valve until it moved back inside its casing. It took hours. Alix couldn't get the spool completely in the sheath. Bayly took over and knocked the head, the pin-type cylinder, off of it. With the head off of the spool, Alix could now put the cover on it. He had the screws but not the nuts to reattach the plate. Bayly sent Yandik inside with the safety-wired screws and told him to look around the hydraulic systems and find similar valves with the same size nuts.

Yandik found what he needed. When he removed a screw from a valve, he safety-wired the locations from where he removed it. This ensured the affected valves remained secured. He went back to Bayly and Alix. Alix crawled back underneath and reattached the cover to the valve. He then reattached the cover panel on the ski. When he was finished, Bayly directed everyone to get back in the aircraft and sit in their seats. Alix made a detour to the cargo compartment. He opened the nose ski isolation valve, and it held pressure. He was giddy.

Kozic called back to Skier Maintenance in McMurdo. Bayly and Alix explained the work they accomplished. When they were finished, they asked the maintenance people if they were satisfied with their temporary repair work and would they allow them to fly the aircraft back to McMurdo? Maintenance left the decision to the aircrew.

# Return

The aircrew ran through their checklists and started engines. The system pressure held, and Bayly told Kozic to raise the skis. When he did so, the nose ski went down instead of up. That was a surprise.

They talked things over. Alix went to the cargo compartment and closed the nose ski isolation valve again. The pressure held, and the nose ski remained in the down position. He returned to his seat, and Kozic lowered the main skis. They came down. Amazing! They had full hydraulic system pressure, and all of the skis were down.

Garrison returned the survival sled to the back of the aircraft. He made sure the scientists were secure. Any interest in chasing the balloon was gone. Bayly taxied around on the nose ski. While doing so, he looked at snow conditions on the surface to find a good takeoff location.

After taxiing for a while, he was satisfied the pressure would hold during the takeoff slide. He pushed up the throttles, and the aircraft accelerated. The takeoff was uneventful, and Kozic called back to McMurdo to report they were airborne. Mathews and JD, in Herk Ops, were elated. The Navy people were stunned. Mathews later said, "There were a lot of long Naval aviator faces when 92 called off the snow. Some even asked if we had a maintenance team and a ski repair kit aboard." They didn't understand the many strengths of the Guard.

CHAPTER 18

# EARLY LESSONS

In 1994, the Navy had already begun transferring many of their support functions to civilian contractors. The 1995 *U.S. Antarctica Program Review*, conducted by the Independent Agencies Appropriations Committee (Report 104-140) and reviewed by the National Science and Technology Council, stated:

> *"Transition of the remaining functions of the Naval Support Force Antarctica and the helicopter functions of Antarctic Development Squadron 6 (VXE-6) may potentially save an additional $4.4M per year. Placing the ski-equipped C-130s with a single manager is estimated to have a further potential annual savings of $9.7M by 2000."* Later in the report, it continued, *"Therefore, estimated annual savings in operations from further transition of functions from the Navy to contract support and the Air National Guard sum to $14.3M annually by 2000."*

It was decided. The New York Air National Guard would be the single point manager of the LC-130 aircraft and the ski mission, both in the Arctic and the Antarctic. The Navy's command of Operation Deep Freeze and its heroic days of Antarctic exploration was over. The Navy was no longer interested in continuing its long historical mission.

Congress approved the 109th Airlift Wing taking sole responsibility for the mission in October of 1996. The Operation Deep Freeze mission's three-year transition period from the United States Navy to the New York Air National Guard had begun. The first Antarctica season of the transition period, from mid-October 1996 through early March 1997, saw little change from the previous season. The Navy continued to run the mission; however, the Raven Gang shadowed the Puckered Penguins staff personnel throughout the season to learn the job. More Raven Gang aircrews participated in the mission than in previous years. The season was a blur to many of the aircrews. The Guard aircrews that were qualified spent an extended time in Antarctica, flew most days, and they remained on the continent for as long as they were needed.

## The End of an Era

During the next Operation Deep Freeze season, from mid-October 1997 through early March 1998, the Raven Gang took on a greater role in the mission. The transition was recorded in two articles of *The Antarctica Sun*, dated 18 October 1997. The first article was a historical perspective of the Navy's mission written by Dwight Fisher, a retired Navy Captain, and the former Commander of Operation Deep Freeze. He was the current National Science Foundation representative in Antarctica. The article stated the following:

> *"The NSFA[132] will be decommissioned in April 1998, and the Air National Guard will assume the role of Commander, Operation Deep Freeze. In April 1999, VXE-6 will also be decommissioned, bringing an end to the United States Navy's long and decorated history of opening the Antarctic to exploration and science."*

In the excerpts of the second article, the transition period was broken down in a nutshell:

> *"Support roles once performed by U.S. Naval Support Force, Antarctica (NSFA) personnel have now been taken over by civilian contractors. NSFA will have a maximum of about ten people at McMurdo Station at any time during the season. Last year that number was closer to 80. VXE-6 had a total of 417 people last year, manning Point Mugu, Christchurch, New*

> *Zealand, and McMurdo Station during the summer. This year they have only 310 people. "The number of aircraft operated by VXE-6 this year has been reduced as well."*

VXE-6's last flight in Antarctica was on February 17, 1999. Their seventy-year history, beginning with Admiral Byrd in 1929, had ended.

## First Two Weeks of the 1997–1998 Season

The Raven Gang now owned the ski mission both in the Arctic and the Antarctic. The second year of the Operation Deep Freeze transition had some serious weather challenges. It was *"Plagued by the worst weather in 24 years."* [133]

The Raven Gang's approach was very different from the Navy. The Navy's history on the continent started with an age of exploration. This mindset continued through their years of flying the mission. The Raven Gang's approach was about foreseeing problems and avoiding them. Science, not exploration, was at the forefront.

Lt. Col. Bill Mathews was the Raven Gang's first deployed commander. His eleven-day deployment commander log addressed some of the unique situations of Antarctica. The Raven Gang was beginning a steep learning curve. Mathews and his aircrews were scheduled to depart Christchurch, New Zealand, at the beginning of the week but didn't leave until Friday due to poor weather in McMurdo, Antarctica. Throughout the first few days in McMurdo, they experienced an exceptional number of severe snowstorms. And finally, at the end of his commander stint, he had to recover two aircraft from the South Pole.

## Lost

The following story is from Lt. Col. Bill Mathews' deployment commander log and the supervisor of maintenance log of Chief Master Sergeant Davis Willoughby.

**Friday, 7 November 1997**

After five days of waiting, the weather finally broke at McMurdo. The aircraft headed south to Antarctica after a lot of confusion in Christchurch. Cargo loads weren't ready, the transportation was late, and distinguished visitors were ordered on the aircraft after the aircraft engines were started.

Once they were airborne, HF radio communications were the worst Mathews had seen in his many years of flying. About an hour out of Christchurch, he lost contact with Auckland. There were five aircraft in a procession going to McMurdo, so other aircraft relayed information for him. The aircraft stayed in radio contact with one another, tuned into a common frequency using both UHF and VHF radios throughout the eight-hour flight.

Mathews was the Raven Gang's first deployed commander for Operation Deep Freeze. He was the chief pilot for the Raven Gang, and he was a meticulous aviator who focused on details. When he found something that needed attention, he made a note and took care of it when there was an opportunity. *"Note: Make sure that all crews know the rules for Special Comms during HF blackout to get to McMurdo on page 10 of the Blue Book."* The Blue Book was the Raven Gang's Antarctica guide.

Upon arrival at McMurdo, the community was still digging out of one of the worst snowstorms Mathews had ever seen. The airfield was a trailer park. Each trailer had a function; maintenance, supply, air traffic control tower, dining hall, bathrooms, and anything else necessary for an airfield. Large metal sleds were beneath every trailer to move them from one location to another. In December, the ice below the ice runway on the McMurdo Sound would begin to melt, and the airfield contractors would move the trailers to Williams Skiway on the permanent ice shelf, seven miles away.

Parking on the aircraft ramp was really tight while the snow was cleared away, but everyone worked together to make room for the aircraft as they arrived. After shutdown, the radar mount on Skier 96 needed to be repaired. It was the first time one of the new planes had a hard failure of the APN-241 radar. It was a high-quality, more advanced radar system installed in the new aircraft models.

The transition representatives greeted them when they arrived and assigned them their sleeping accommodations. Mathews hadn't heard any complaints, so he assumed that everything was fine. Their rooms were spread around McMurdo. Communications with everyone would be more difficult than in the past. Most accommodations were on the second and third floor of Building 155. The first floor of 155 had the community's dining facilities, so Mathews used a bulletin board in the first-floor hallway of 155 to post-flight schedules and notes to Raven Gang members. He posted the same information in Buildings 211, 206, and 201.

**Saturday, 8 November 1997**

Mathews scheduled three Guard flights for the day. Skier 96 was scheduled to go to the South Pole at 1:00 p.m. If all went well, this would be a seven-hour round trip. Skier 91 was scheduled to go to Siple Dome at 2:00 p.m., and Skier 92 was scheduled to go to Siple Dome at 3:00 p.m. If all went well, each of these flights would be a five-hour round trip. They could be finished by 8:00 p.m. But all did not go well.

As a result of the massive amount of snow, only one pump was available at the fuel pits area. The rest of the fuel pit area still needed to be cleared of snow. A C-141 aircraft from New Zealand arrived in the morning and had priority. This made a mess of the day's launches.

Mathews spent most of his day on the ice runway. He could have sent the supervisor of flying there, but he wanted to see first-hand how the C-141s impacted his intracontinental missions. Everything grounded to a halt until that plane departed the ice. He was surprised by the unexpected negative effect on the LC-130 operations.

When the C-141 arrived from New Zealand, one of his LC-130 aircraft was already in the fuel pits; however, they got kicked out to make room for the C-141. The C-141 taxied directly to the pits and unloaded, uploaded, and refueled. With only one fuel pit operating, this meant every other aircraft had to wait until the C-141 went back to Christchurch. Once it left, the ramp got busy, and the LC-130s were able to get airborne. As usual, there was a lull in the action at the ice runway and McMurdo while the aircrews were out on their missions.

But the day was only beginning. Although everyone had a rough start to the day, they hung in there. They ended up launching the aircraft three to four hours late. It was important to get the aircraft flying. The first flight to open the South Pole station was already ten days late. Everybody busted their butts. Mathews couldn't have asked these people to work any harder than they did, for as long as they did, with absolutely no complaints. One positive thing about the day, the South Pole was opened up by the Raven Gang for the first time in history. Until then, the Navy had opened the South Pole for every Operation Deep Freeze Season since 1956.

Three out of three Guard missions got airborne, but none of them were on time because of the fiasco with the C-141. It was going to be a long day for everyone. No flying was scheduled the following day, no Sunday flying at McMurdo, so there was no concern about the day's missions affecting tomorrow's flights. An aircrew would not go back to the South Pole until Tuesday. The new people who arrived at the South Pole today needed a few days to have a proper changeover of duties with the people already there. The people leaving the South Pole on Tuesday had been there throughout the Antarctic winter.

When the aircraft was airborne, Mathews returned to town. He wanted assurances food would be served at the ice runway, and transportation was available for the aircrews to get back to town. Due to their late takeoffs, they were going to arrive back at McMurdo late. The dining facility closed at 7:00 p.m. He was assured both food and transportation would be available. Later on, he would find out differently.

In the early evening, while sitting in his office at Herc Ops, he noticed a flurry of phone calls to the Navy duty officer around 6:30 p.m. He really didn't understand the significance of the calls at the time. He overheard the duty officer tell those on the phone that he wouldn't release them until the last aircraft was on the ground at the South Pole, approximately 7:00 p.m. At approximately 8:00 p.m., the duty officer asked Mathews if he could release his maintenance personnel. He thought about it for a few seconds. He assumed the duty officer was releasing only the back-shop specialist and told him he didn't mind. Later in the evening, he would learn the flight line personnel were released, also.

Based on their original takeoff times, the weather forecast was expected to be good until all of the aircraft returned to McMurdo. However, there was a possibility of a storm after midnight. They were right.

Mathews decided to return to the ice runway. He went to Derelict Junction, McMurdo's taxi stand, but there was no van to give him a ride, so he called Movement Control Center, and they gave him a ride. The assurance he received earlier about transportation availability was now in doubt.

*Catching a Delta Ride at Derelict Junction (Joe Axe Pic)*

He arrived at the ice runway at 9:30 p.m. and went to the maintenance tower. He asked Chief Master Sergeant Davis Willoughby, the supervisor of maintenance, to double-check on the food. Sure enough, no food would be served at the ice runway, but they would make meals-to-go at the main chow hall in Building 155. Mathews sent someone to town to pick them up. It finally occurred to him that things were a little different on Saturday night after 7:00 p.m.

Mathews noticed a little burst of atmospheric energy from the direction of Black Island. The wind began to gust up to twenty-five knots for about five minutes, and the visibility went down. After that, the winds calmed down, and the visibility came back up and was unrestricted. The same thing happened about thirty minutes later, and it continued to happen infrequently. At 10:50 p.m., Skier 91 landed during one of the lulls in the winds. The aircrew was debriefed in the maintenance tower, then left for town.

The last two planes were scheduled to arrive between 12:15 a.m. and 1:15 a.m. The winds continued their periodic increases, and visibility would diminish about every half hour. They then calmed down again, and unrestricted visibility would return to the airfield. Earlier in the evening, before the Navy personnel were released and left the flight line for the town, they instructed their Guard counterparts on the use of the D-3 bulldozer. Master Sergeant Phil Cassimore, Master Sergeant Scott King, and Staff Sergeant Steve Radz were trained on the bulldozer's operation to bring power carts to the aircraft.

After the first aircraft landed, Steve Radz came into the maintenance shack and let Mathews know he had been checked out on the D-3 bulldozer. Mathews flinched a little but then thought, *"Good, our maintenance guys are working with the VXE-6 maintenance troops. They were learning the ramp and equipment operations."* Mathews was still under the assumption that Navy flight line personnel were on the ice.

The maintenance tower received an updated arrival time for Skier 96. They were going to arrive about forty-five minutes later than he thought. The aircrew had been asked to take retro-cargo. Five pallets of cargo were loaded into the aircraft. This was unexpected and delayed their takeoff from the South Pole. There had been no recent weather updates, so Mathews initially assumed things were looking good for all aircraft recoveries. Later he found the radio communications at the Guard's maintenance shack were abysmal. The Guard's maintenance tower didn't have UHF or VHF radios. They had an FM radio from which they could listen to the Navy maintenance tower frequency, but the Guard personnel could only receive information. They could not transmit. The Guard was totally out of the loop on any updated information from town and almost totally isolated as an operation.

Mathews called the Navy people sitting in the office at Herc Ops and released them from duty. They had been on duty for a very long day. He wanted them to run the operation in the morning so that he could catch up on paperwork. The Guard's supervisor of flying, Major Dan Dunbar, remained in the office for the rest of the evening.

The weather continued to improve then worsen. Skier 96 landed in another weather lull. The Navy's maintenance shack called the Guard's maintenance people to see where they wanted to park the aircraft. The only place available was at the fuel pits because of uncleared snow at the parking locations on the ramp.

Skier 96 parked without incident, and when Mathews went out to debrief the crew, the wind started to gust a little harder to about thirty to thirty-five knots, and the visibility went down. He went back to the Guard maintenance shack and called Mac Center, McMurdo's air traffic control center, to get an update on the weather.

When he returned to the maintenance shack, he heard Skier 92 as it executed a missed approach. The high winds were blowing around surface snow, which dropped the visibility down around the airfield. The aircraft was only a few hundred feet in the air, but as Mathews drove around the airfield parking area, he couldn't see it.

Things got worse. The winds picked up instead of diminishing. One of the maintenance troops rushed into the shack and said that he needed medical assistance fast for Phil Cassimore. The wind had slammed the door of the D-3 bulldozer on his hand. Cassimore came in the Guard's maintenance tower holding his left thumb. Willoughby looked at his thumb and moved it a little. The distal part of the thumb appeared to be detached from the first joint. Mathews directed one of the maintenance people to put snow in a plastic bag; then, he wrapped Cassimore's hand in the bag to control the bleeding. They called an ambulance to transport back to McMurdo to receive medical assistance.

Skier 92 landed. The flight line personnel could hear the aircraft but could not see it. Willoughby commented, *"How they landed is a credit to their airmanship."* The aircraft taxied to the parking ramp. The aircrew established radio contact with the Navy maintenance tower, and they, in turn, relayed the information to the Guard. The Guard's inability to communicate was a real problem. The aircrew needed a "Follow Me" vehicle to guide them to a parking spot due to the poor visibility.

The "Follow-Me" truck guided them in front of the Guard maintenance tower to the left and towards the fuel pits. They intended to park Skier 92 between two aircraft on the fuel pits. It was a tight taxi. This was not a good idea with the high winds blowing across the icy ramp. Both the aircrew and the guys in the "Follow Me" truck came to the same conclusion at about the same time. Again, the lack of communication caused them to stop and wait until a new plan was established.

Willoughby went to the Navy maintenance tower and cleared things up. He directed Skier 92 to make a 180-degree turn and park the aircraft into the wind. The pilot did so and shut down the aircraft engines. After a quick maintenance debrief, both aircrews of the Skier 96 and Skier 92 were put in a van and sent to town. An ambulance also arrived and took Cassimore to McMurdo. Shortly after the ambulance and van left for town, all hell broke loose. The winds began to gust well over fifty knots, and visibility was down to about ten feet. For the next twenty minutes, everyone outside remained near the aircraft. During a lull, they returned to the maintenance tower.

Mathews did a headcount to make sure everyone was accounted for. It was too crowded in the maintenance tower for the fifteen people there, so he decided to gather up all the food and go over to the chow hall, which had more room and possibly more food and water. When they moved, they tied a rope to the stairs at the maintenance tower. Mathews directed everyone to hold on to it as they made their way to the chow hall. They couldn't see anything through the blinding snow, but if they wandered off course or couldn't find the chow hall, they could always return to the maintenance tower using the rope.

They made it to the chow hall. Mathews called Dunbar, in Herc Ops, to give him a status update, and he made the same call to the firehouse in town. He asked Dunbar to find out the status of Cassimore. Before he hung up, he told Dunbar he would call him back hourly to check in with their status.

He planned to keep everyone in the galley until the weather improved. The visibility outside the galley was zero, and Mathews estimated the winds were gusting up to seventy-five knots. In one of the more surreal moments of the evening, Mathews called to receive an update on the weather. As the forecaster told him the storm was letting up and there may be a window of opportunity to get back to town, a gust of wind picked up the dining hall and slammed it back down, moving it about six inches.

Mathews' log entry, *"So much for this storm letting up and his forecasting prowess!"* Everyone settled in the chow hall and ate. As they waited, someone showed up at the door and offered them a ride back to town in their van. Mathews declined the ride. He called the fire department and gave them another status report. They told Mathews there would be a van stopping by the galley to give them a ride to town. He told them they already showed up, but he refused the ride. The fire department notified Mathews some Navy maintenance people had called, and they wanted to know if there was room in the galley for them. There was plenty of room to handle another twenty people. Mathews asked how many people he could expect?

"Two," they answered. He was stunned.

Mathews thought he still had a lot of Navy personnel on the ice. He had expected at least a dozen. He recalled allowing the duty officer in Herc Ops to release his people. It suddenly hit him the Guard was operating solo in a Condition I weather scenario.

Antarctica's weather classifications and restrictions are based on the severity of the conditions.

- Condition III. Personnel should exercise routine safety and exposure precautions.

- Condition II. One or more of the following conditions exists or are forecast with one hour: Wind velocity 48–55 knots, Wind Chill minus 75° to minus 100° Fahrenheit; Visibility between ¼ mile and 100 feet. Personnel are limited to travel within each complex (McMurdo, Scott Base, Willie Field, etc.). Travel outside the complex must be in radio-equipped vehicles, checking in/out with the Fire House, and requires Department Head/ASA Manager approval.

- Condition I. One or more of the following conditions exists or are forecast within one hour: Wind velocity greater than 55 knots, Windchill below minus 100° Fahrenheit, Visibility less than 100 feet. Personnel will remain in buildings unless approved by NSFA CDO. All travel requires a minimum of two persons in company; vehicles must check-in and out with the Fire House.

The fire department called again to notify them that another van could get his people back to McMurdo. A few minutes later, another person showed up in the galley and offered them a ride back to town. Mathews declined again.

He called Dunbar at Herc Ops to find out if Cassimore and the aircrews made it back to town. Dunbar assured him that all crewmembers were back in town and that Phil Cassimore was in the clinic. A little while later, temptation number three confronted Mathews. The fire department called and told him they had to move the crash and rescue vehicles back to town. They had room for about twenty-five people.

Ten minutes passed before the crash and rescue people arrived. They had two tracked vehicles, an ambulance, and a twelve-passenger van. The Guard had a second twelve-passenger maintenance van. They had five vehicles and twenty-three people, including the control tower operators, two Navy night watch personnel, and the firefighters.

The crash and rescue folks wanted the two track vehicles in front of the caravan, followed by the ambulance, with the two vans bringing up the rear. Mathews told them he would send his people back if one tracked vehicle led the procession, followed by the ambulance, the two vans, and the other tracked vehicle brought up the rear. They agreed.

Mathews announced the plan to everyone. They got into the vehicles and ensured they were all on the same radio frequency. He did a headcount one last time before they drove to town. He didn't want to lose anyone going from the galley to the "lifeboat." Mathews rode in the last tracked vehicle. The wind was still blowing fifty to sixty knots, and the visibility was only twenty-five feet. When the caravan started, each vehicle was fifteen to twenty feet behind the preceding vehicle.

About one hundred yards from the chow hall, one of the vans, vehicle #4, got stuck in a drift near a little depression. All the vehicles stopped. The only vehicle Mathews could see was the stuck van fifteen feet ahead of him. His tracked vehicle driver positioned himself to pull the van out. After the van was free, it passed by Mathew's window about six feet away and disappeared in the blinding snow when it was about ten feet away. His tracked vehicle maneuvered to get back into line, but the driver didn't know where to go, and the other three occupants thought the caravan was in three different directions. Mathew thought, *"We were lost and separated from the group!"* Visibility was zero. No landmarks could be seen when the visibility improved slightly.

The other vehicles slowly started backing towards his stranded vehicle to locate them. So far, their progress was one hundred yards in about one hour, one stuck vehicle, one lost vehicle, and a lot of concerned people. It took another twenty minutes to get everyone back into formation. The two-mile ride back to town took over two and one-half hours. Willoughby noted some of his people were dehydrated and lacked personal water bottles. The situation needed to be remedied. This event opened the Guard's eyes to what Antarctica was capable of doing.

They arrived in McMurdo at 5:30 a.m., Sunday morning. Mathews went to Herc Ops in Building 165. He learned Phil Cassimore was doing well, but he needed to go to Christchurch for further medical attention. The maintenance people seemed to be in pretty good shape despite the evening's ordeal.

**Sunday, 9 November 1997**

No flying was scheduled on Sunday. Mathews met with the entire Guard contingent on Sunday afternoon and brought everyone up to date on current events. The meeting went well.

**Monday, 10 November 1997**

Another Condition I snowstorm blew into town Sunday night until 7:00 a.m. Monday, with another sixteen inches of snow. Maintenance people spent the day clearing the snow. They went down to the flight line at 10:00 a.m. and dug out the aircraft. The propeller spinners were full of snow. The engine intakes were full of snow. The air condition ducts were packed with snow. And the auxiliary power unit intakes were full of snow. When the ramp was clear, they taxied Skier 96 and Skier 92 back to parking spots.

Ice Runway 25 would not be ready until 2:00 p.m. on Tuesday. Ice Runway 33 wouldn't be ready until 8:00 p.m. that evening. Two Siple Dome missions and one South Pole mission were planned for Tuesday. Mathews emphasized he wanted to fly the times agreed to in the Air Movement Table.

The Guard's loadmasters introduced themselves to the Kiwi Cargo personnel at Ice Runway. Back in town, the new supervisor of flying, Captain Tom Esposito, was the main contact with the New Zealand cargo handlers to minimize confusion.

**Tuesday, 11 November 1997**

Mathews' log entry: *"Talked to Sixers*[134] *yesterday to see if we could try to start scheduling according to the Air Movement Table we agreed to in Denver."*

He was happy to see the flying schedule came out with the proper takeoff times, 9:45 a.m., 10:15 a.m., and 11:00 a.m. The weather looked pretty good at the South Pole, Siple Dome, and McMurdo.

Mathews talked to an airfield contractor who said that the fuel pits were pretty well dug out, both pumps were in operation, and four aircraft could be fueled simultaneously. As the morning progressed, Kiwi Cargo's loading of Skier 96 was delayed due to digging cargo out from the snow. This resulted in a one-hour late takeoff to Siple Dome.

Skier 91 was scheduled to go to the South Pole. Mathews was going to fly on it, but it didn't work out. While starting the #2 engine, the propeller low oil light remained on. Both spare propellers were still in Christchurch. It would take some time to repair, so their mission to the South Pole was canceled.

The propellers were supposed to be on the ice, but the C-141 had been canceled every day since Saturday because of the poor weather conditions and the excessive snow on the ice runway. Skier 92 was delayed in loading and took off one hour twenty-five minutes late. Later in the day, both Skier 96 and Skier 92 made it to Siple Dome and back in good shape. They moved about fifty thousand pounds of cargo to the camp. Maintenance worked on Skier 91 all afternoon and finally warmed the propeller seals enough to stop the leak. They checked it out and declared it a good aircraft to fly. The Raven Gang now had three aircraft on the flight line ready to go.

Over the last couple of days, the Guard installed an FM base station in the Guard maintenance tower. Now the Guard was in the same information loop as everyone else. Mathews also tried to get a loaner VHF/UHF radio installed in the maintenance tower. Mathews tongue-in-cheek log comment, *"Believe it or not, some folks are looking forward to going home tomorrow."*

For the week, they had scheduled nine on-continent missions and completed five of them. The weather conditions canceled three, and maintenance canceled one, for a fifty-six percent sortie reliability rate. Mathews' log entry, *"Not great, but we took what Mother Nature let us have on her turf."* Mathews made another note, *"Considerations for Next Season: Consider stacking the first few rotations with some of the more experienced people and limit the number of Guardsmen who need training due to unreliable weather and the growing pains of spinning up operations. There should be no problem with sending a fully qualified Guardsman the first few weeks, but he may not get a lot accomplished."* He also noted they must develop a better procedure for handling the C-141 arrivals, downloading, uploading, fueling, and departure. Mathews' log entry, *"Everything grinds to a halt when the "Queen of the Prom" rolls into town."*

**Wednesday, 12 November 1997**

A southbound flight from New Zealand, Skier 94, was delayed because of high winds in the Christchurch area. They took off an hour and one half late and were due to arrive at McMurdo at 6:30 p.m. The high wind conditions would be over before they arrived. Skier 96 had an on-time takeoff from the ice runway going to Christchurch.

Colonel Jon Adams, the 109th Airlift Wing's commander, was scheduled to depart Christchurch on a C-141, but the flight was canceled. So, he jumped on a Navy LC-130 aircraft coming southbound. It took off from Christchurch but returned with a fuel leak. The weather looked good for the day's Siple Dome mission. Skier 92's takeoff was on time. They landed back in McMurdo at 4:00 p.m. from Siple Dome. Communications people continued to work on a VHF radio problem in Skier/Herc Ops, Building 165.[135]

When the passengers on Skier 94 arrived in McMurdo, they were greeted with an emergency response exercise simulating an aircraft accident on the ice runway. Mathews' log entry: *"Everyone took it in stride and finally got chow and their rooms about an hour later than normal. All in all, a good day flying."*

*McMurdo (credit NSF)*

**Thursday, 13 November 1997**

Mathews' log entry: *"Weather is supposed to be pretty nice here at McMurdo all day, with marginal to improving conditions at Siple and Pole. Last night when I recovered the Southbound Skier, the pits and the ramp looked like they were in good shape, and with more time, they will remove more snow from the ramp. All aircraft are in the green, and all of the crews cycled through Herc Ops right on time to just a little early. This is a real good sign for on-time takeoffs today."*

Esposito ensured everything ran smoothly on the ramp with loading and fueling in the pits until a *"SNAFU with the priority cargo."* Skier 92 took off five minutes earlier than scheduled to Siple Dome. Skier 91 took off sixteen minutes later than scheduled to the South Pole. Skier 94 was delayed by the cargo yard. Priority cargo had to get to Siple Dome. They ended up taking off sixty-six minutes later than scheduled.

The aircraft returned to McMurdo on time. Skier 91 had a problem with a brake accumulator. This was noticed while landing on an ice runway. There were no accumulators in Christchurch, nor Schenectady, New York. The supply office needed to MICAP (Mission Impaired Capability Awaiting Parts.)[136] Mathews further commented, *"All in all, a really good flying day, and we're getting closer and closer to those scheduled takeoff times."*

**Friday, 14 November 1997**

Mathews got a call from the McMurdo weather shop at 4:00 a.m. Friday morning. The South Pole weather was down and scheduled to be that way for the next twenty-four hours. Mathews' log entry, *"We changed our destination to Siple Dome, and guess what, the weather rock lied!"* The weather rock was Mathews' reference to the weather forecaster.

His team made a new plan for the day. They sent one plane to Siple Dome and two to the South Pole. With the last-minute changes, things moved a little slower on the ramp. There were delays with loading and fueling the aircraft, but overall, he noted things were improving. Skier 92 took off twenty-eight minutes late. Skier 91 was almost one and a half hours late. Skier 94 was about an hour late.

An unexpected weather system moved into McMurdo about 6:00 p.m. It was forecast to remain in the area until 3:00 a.m. the following morning. Both Skier 91 and Skier 94 were returning to McMurdo from the South Pole. Mathews contacted the aircrews and directed them to turn around and go back to the South Pole due to his bad experience with the weather earlier in the week.

The aircrew landed again at the South Pole and shut down the aircraft engines. The flight engineers on the aircraft pulled the aircraft batteries and took them inside the station to keep them warm. They stayed the night. Mathews alerted his team in McMurdo that they needed to put together a package on the South Pole flight in the morning to try to help the two stranded aircraft.

At both of Earth's poles, the longitudinal lines of navigation converged. It was quite likely the aircraft navigation systems would not be able to identify where they were and have difficulty realigning at the South Pole. The temperatures were still hovering around -40 degrees Fahrenheit. Skier 94 was one of the newest aircraft models in the inventory. Most of the instrumentation was glass and LED lights. It was going to be interesting to find out how well they survived the cold. He noted, *"After this exercise is over, we will sit down and see if we can develop a list of things to consider when and if this happens again."* Mathews summarized, *"I waited and waited for the much-feared storm, and it never materialized. The weather rocks lied for a second time today. It looks like I turned two airplanes around for no good reason. God, what a week so far!"*

**Saturday, 15 November 1997**

Mathews called the South Pole in the morning and got a status check. There were going to be challenges. The elevation of the South Pole was 9,300 feet. The thin air and cold temperatures would affect the people and the machines. Facetiously he noted, *"More good news, another weather system is headed our way, so it's "iffy" on whether or not we'll get our Pole birds back today."*

The South Pole only had four Herman Nelson heaters. The maintenance team used them to warm the engines, the propeller seals, and the aircraft in general. In mid-November at the South Pole, a warm day was -30 degrees Celsius, so it would take some time to heat the airplanes. This would delay aircraft preflight inspections, so it would take quite a while to get everything ready to fly.

As if things weren't bad enough, Mathews got a call from Lt. Col. Tom Noel, one of the pilots stuck at the Pole. He was the pilot on Skier 91. He reported his aircraft had a bad prop leak on the #2 engine. This was the same propeller that had problems earlier in the week.

The bad weather was supposed to move into McMurdo. There was a narrow window to get the aircrews back, so Mathews decided to put all his efforts into getting Skier 94 airborne. He'd work with his maintenance team to fix Skier 91 later.

Mathews' log entry, *"Everyone came back home healthy, some were a little cranky, but all were ready to fly back to get 91 tomorrow."*

**Sunday, 16 November 1997**

Everyone got Sunday morning off to give the town a little more time to recover from Saturday night. The plan was to send the maintenance team to the ice runway at 11:00 a.m. That didn't work out. The maintenance van couldn't get much beyond "the transition" due to blowing and drifting snow. The transition was where the dirt road of Ross Island changed at the coastline of Ross Island to an ice road on the McMurdo Sound.

Eventually, the Movement Control Center got the Terra Bus to take the maintenance team and the two aircrews to the ice runway. They got the aircraft airborne at 2:30 p.m., only a half-hour later than planned.

It took the maintenance people hours of work in the thin air and extremely cold temperatures to nurse Skier 91 back to health and get it back to McMurdo. It was a long day.

Mathews knew it was going to impact the next day's schedule and thought, "*Everyone's crew rest cycle is out of whack.*" He made a note regarding the navigation systems: *"If anyone does shut down at the South Pole and they have to do a High Latitude Alignment, they must have the gun box*[137] *key to get the GPS codes."*

**Monday, 17 November 1997**

Today was Bill Mathews' final day as the Raven Gang's commander for the season. He would become a crew dog and fly missions until he returned to New York. His log noted, *"After a little juggling of takeoff times today because of previous night's late landings; things seem to proceed fairly well."*

Skier 92 took off on time to the South Pole with dynamite on board. The Sixers had a Vostok mission. They had priority on the aircraft parking ramp, and they took off very late. This delayed Guard's aircraft loading and fueling. Missions were also swapped at the request of the Movement Control Center, which caused further delays.

Both Skier 91 and Skier 94 took off an hour and a half late, and both returned to McMurdo around midnight with no problems.

Mathews' final comment: *"Still trying to get crews back on a normal schedule. It's almost impossible to do that, especially with the loading problems we've seen so far this year."* It was time for someone else to take the helm. His next Antarctica season would be more interesting.

CHAPTER 19

# SKI DRAGS

It was the last season the Navy would be flying Operation Deep Freeze missions. The National Science Foundation wanted the Raven Gang to demonstrate they were capable of handling difficult missions. Scientists wanted to go to mountain valleys and glacier fields around the continent. On 16 November 1998, the National Science Foundation wanted to get the foremost glaciologist in the world to Upstream Delta.

Upstream Delta was not an approved mission in the preseason's Antarctica Planning Conference. There was no prior knowledge of the area. Since it was not part of the original plan, the Raven Gang didn't have a ski landing area control officer, or SLACO, in Antarctica to review the site before landing an aircraft there.

Despite the lack of critical information, the National Science Foundation contractors insisted the Raven Gang was more than a week behind schedule. According to the contractors, up to ten flights in the last eight days should have been accomplished. For weeks, pressure continued to build to get the Guard to fly the mission. The Raven Gang was about to learn what happens when they allow pressure from the National Science Foundation contractors to dictate which missions to accept. Another obvious lesson was the Twin Otter with the ground-penetrating radar would have been more useful if it surveyed the snow before Skier 95 went to a new location instead of afterward.

Lt. Col. Bill Mathews was reasonably certain he'd get the mission if it showed up on the schedule. To determine whether the surface landing conditions at new locations were suitable, the Navy did ski drags. Ski drags were two parallel landings on the main skis only, without stopping the aircraft. If there were no problems found during the drags, the Navy aircrews landed between them and stop. They would then complete their mission and return to McMurdo.

Many of the older pilots in the Raven Gang were familiar with ski drags. Some had done them in the past. In 1989, they had used ski drags on the Arctic Ocean, north of Alaska. Things went poorly. From this experience, they created the 109 TAG Regulation 86-1. This was a civil engineering planning and programming regulation titled *"Criteria for Skiways and Ski Landing Areas."* It was designed for landing on ice, not snow. Within it was the ski landing area control officer, or SLACO, program.

Some people in the 109th Airlift Wing were pro-ski drags, and some were anti-ski drags. Ski drags weren't reliable. Aircrews could not get a positive account of the surface conditions without putting the aircraft's full weight on the snow. Ski drags simply dragged the skis over the surface.

Skier 95 didn't uncover a crevasse on their second drag. If Mathews had decided to land after just two ski drags, it's quite possible he would have taxied into it, and it was large enough to swallow Skier 95. Mathews' aircrew did uncover a crevasse later in the day when they taxied into it. An eight-foot snow bridge was hiding it. Following the incident, the Raven Gang was restricted from opening new camps in Antarctica until they developed their own procedures for avoiding crevasses.

The concept of the ski drags didn't die easily. The Raven Gang needed some way to find the condition of the surface of a new location. During the Greenland Season following this crevasse incident, three Raven Gang aircrews got certified by two of the last Puckered Penguin Navy pilots, but operationally, ski drags were never used again.

The Raven Gang's answer to this failure was to limit landings at a new location to those approved in the preseason plan. This would provide time to get the most recent satellite imagery of the location and get it analyzed by experts to determine the conditions beneath the snow. On most missions, they decided a SLACO needed to be on-site before an aircraft landed at a new location, but they allowed themselves the flexibility to reconsider things as new situations arose. Every location was different.

# The Treachery of Antarctica

After weeks of debate, the 109th Airlift Wing agreed to fly the foremost glaciologist in the world to Upstream Delta, but the Raven Gang had a lot of misgivings. There was no information about the location. There was no ski landing area control officer, or SLACO, to look at the site beforehand.[138]

Lt. Col. Bill Mathews was the most experienced Raven Gang pilot on the continent. He agreed to command the mission. Mathews was tall and lean. He joined the Air Force in the late 1960s with the intent of becoming a medical doctor. He ended up going to pilot training. He was the most methodical pilot in the squadron. His demeanor was always professional and logical.

Upstream Delta would be a small camp, so the lead scientist would know more about the area than anyone else. Mathews told the National Science Foundation's contractors, who were pushing the mission, he wanted a conversation with the glaciologist and the Twin Otter pilots who had been operating in the area to get the most current information about the site.

Mathews was told the scientist wasn't available. He was already at Siple Dome Camp awaiting transportation to Upstream Delta. None of the Twin Otter pilots Mathews contacted at McMurdo had been to Upstream Delta. After searching for more than a week, he ended up with four sheets of paper:

1. A fair copy of a satellite image with coordinates provided by the foremost glaciologist in the world. The image had a triangle, which Mathews understood to be the ideal campsite. The date and source of the image were unknown.

2. A poor copy of a satellite image of an unknown area in the Upstream Delta region with no coordinates, date, and source unknown.

3. A page from the Ohio State website dated 21 September 1998, presumably Upstream Delta. It came with a statement, "good for landing anywhere." Coordinates were 81° 00' South and 140° 00' West.

4. A page entitled UPSTREAM "D" with three bullet statements of no significance.

Without a SLACO and adequate information, Mathews decided to use the Navy's ski drag technique to determine if Upstream Delta was suitable for landing. It was the only way available to get any information about the landing conditions. None of the Raven Gang had done ski drags, so he called New York and talked with the leadership at the 109th Airlift Wing. They gave Mathews the leeway he felt was necessary to complete the mission.

Since Mathews had never done ski drags, he flew an aircraft to the white-out landing area the week before to practice the Navy's technique. He wanted to be certain he understood how to accomplish ski drags and be proficient enough to do them properly.

| **Skier 95 Aircrew** | |
|---|---|
| **Pilot:** | Lt. Col. Bill Mathews |
| **Copilot:** | Lt. Col. Charlotte Kenney |
| **Navigator:** | Lt. Col. Karen Riley |
| **Flight Engineer:** | Master Sergeant Kevin Hubbley |
| **Loadmaster:** | Chief Master Sergeant Dennis Morgan |
| **Loadmaster:** | Chief Master Sergeant Garry Quick |
| **Loadmaster:** | Technical Sergeant Kevin Gifford |

Lt. Col. Charlotte Kenney was the copilot on the mission. She was also the deployed commander for the Raven Gang. The questionable nature of the mission prompted her to put herself on the aircrew. Kenney's demeanor was serious, but she had a ready smile and was one of the most caring people among the Raven Gang. She was an instructor pilot in the ski mission.

Lt. Col. Karen Riley was the navigator. Before joining the Raven Gang in September of 1993, she was a Navy C-130 flight officer with VQ-4, a communications mission supporting the Joint Chief Staff. Her demeanor was more serious than most. She was average-sized and had shoulder-length, dirty blond hair. She was more than qualified for the mission ahead.

Master Sergeant Kevin Hubbley was one of the best flight engineers in the Raven Gang. He distinguished himself with his above-average intelligence, a great memory for the mundane, and a quick wit. He liked to make people laugh.

Chief Master Sergeant Dennis Morgan enlisted in the Air Force on 18 July 1974 and left active duty exactly four years later, on 18 July 1978. The following day he joined the Raven Gang and was now the chief loadmaster in the squadron. He was a tall, thin, dark-haired man. He had a stern personality in the office, but he liked to laugh and tell stories with the more senior members of the Raven Gang.

Chief Master Sergeant Garry Quick joined the Raven Gang in 1970. He was a big, burly man. He had thinning blond hair and a thick red mustache with a ready smile under it. He had a big voice. He was highly experienced and the second most senior loadmaster in the squadron. Morgan was giving Quick a flight evaluation, a check-ride, on this flight.

It was Technical Sergeant Kevin Gifford's first week in Antarctica. He came to the Raven Gang as a fully qualified loadmaster from the Rhode Island Air National Guard. He was another big man. He had dark hair and a mustache. He was a prankster, and he loved to tell stories and laugh.

## Plan A

Mathews needed to pick up the glaciologist at Siple Dome Camp on the way to Upstream Delta. Siple Dome was a small camp east of the Ross Ice Shelf. Its location was perfect to use as a hub for more distant camps in western Antarctica, and it was a familiar location. The Raven Gang frequently went there to provide fuel and supplies to the camp. The fuel allowed the smaller Twin Otter aircraft to accomplish missions into more remote locations in the area.

The Raven Gang had a 118,000-pound aircraft-weight limitation for landings in open snowfields. The lighter the aircraft, the less potential for damage to the aircraft. Mathews intended to take extra fuel to Siple Dome and leave it there until he completed the mission, then use this fuel for his return to McMurdo. This would prevent him from taking fuel from the camp that was needed for the Twin Otters.

When he arrived at Siple Dome, Mathews intended to talk things over with the glaciologist and get the much-needed information he lacked.

Next, he planned to go to Upstream Delta, overfly the area several times, pick a location to land, do the ski drags, and return to Siple Dome.

He then would load the glaciologist's equipment in the aircraft, fly back to Upstream Delta, and land between the ski drags. When the mission was complete, he would return to Siple Dome a third time, upload the fuel he left behind, and return to McMurdo. It was going to be a long day, but Mathews' plan would allow him to gain the information he needed, and it would allow him to remain within the weight limitations for landing.

## Plan B

On Monday, 16 November 1998, at 6:00 a.m., Mathews, Kenney, and Riley arrived in Building 165 to complete their pre-mission planning. The rest of the aircrew showed up at Derelict Junction to catch the shuttle to the ice runway to preflight and load the aircraft. Their scheduled takeoff time was at 8:30 a.m. The aircraft designated for the mission was Skier 95. It still smelled new. It had come off of the Lockheed assembly line about two years prior.

Three pallets of cargo and ATO bottles were loaded inside the aircraft. Mathews intended to mount the ATO on the outside of the aircraft at Siple Dome. The first unexpected issue of the day occurred when Mathews found out he was taking passengers to Siple Dome. The passengers were the survival experts for the future Upstream Delta Camp. Their purpose was to help the glaciologist achieve a successful science expedition by setting up and managing the camp. The three pallets of cargo were the science equipment, survival gear, and food for the duration of the project.

ATO bottles and their ignitors were hazardous cargo, and Mathews didn't have the special permissions required to fly with the ATO inside the aircraft, with passengers. Therefore, the bottles were mounted on the outside of the aircraft. This hour delay would have been okay, but the weather was expected to worsen throughout the day at Upstream Delta.

During his pre-mission planning, Mathews modified his plan. He already had the science equipment he expected to pick up at Siple Dome. When he arrived at Siple Dome, he intended to offload the extra fuel and pick up the glaciologist. He would fly the reconnaissance flight, complete the ski drags, and if things looked good, he would land at Upstream Delta, all on the same flight.

At any time throughout the flight, if the area didn't look good, he planned to return to Siple Dome and drop off the passengers and cargo and return to McMurdo. He needed to watch his fuel closely throughout the day to ensure the increased weight of the aircraft would be within limitations for landing.

## Siple Dome

When he arrived at the ice runway in McMurdo, Mathews gathered his aircrew and briefed them on his plan. The aircrew started the aircraft engines and taxied to the fuel pits. When the fueling was completed, they started engines again and taxied to the ATO loading area. When they were finished, they started engines again and taxied to the ice runway. Skier 95 was airborne an hour late. On the way to his destination, Mathews tried to contact Siple Dome on the HF radio, but radio communications were poor.

A Twin Otter was flying around the area. Mathews asked the pilot on the VHF radio if he knew anything about Upstream Delta. He wanted to know if there was a safe location to land, and he wanted to know the snow conditions of the area. The Twin Otter pilot had very little useful information for Mathews, but he knew there were crevasses in the area.

The approach and landing at Siple Dome were uneventful. Hubbley offloaded the extra fuel. The foremost glaciologist in the world came onto the aircraft. He had the same satellite photo of the area that Mathews had, and he had plotted six points on the photo with associated coordinates on a 3"x5" card. His information was useless. It didn't tell Mathews what he needed to know. When the glaciologist and the rest of the passengers were seated and buckled in the aircraft, Mathews briefed the reconnaissance profile for Upstream Delta. The glaciologist was wearing a headset but didn't have anything to add to Mathews' plan.

# Upstream Delta

Skier 95 left Siple Dome with four passengers, 11,000 pounds of cargo, and 22,000 pounds of fuel. The basic weight of the aircraft was 90,700 pounds. The total weight was 123,700 pounds. The additional 5,700 pounds of fuel allowed him to take the necessary time to do a thorough reconnaissance of the area.

The flight from Siple Dome to Upstream Delta took about twenty-five minutes. Mathews flew to the coordinates the glaciologist gave him. The aircrew completed their required checklist items and descended into the Upstream Delta area. Mathews leveled off his descent and directed Kenney to set the flaps to fifty percent while he slowed the aircraft to one hundred and fifty knots.

The weather upon their arrival was a 20,000-foot thin overcast cloud ceiling. The visibility was unrestricted. The horizon was discernable but was beginning to blend with the snow surface. There were no shadows on the ground. The winds were mild. It was a beautiful day at Upstream Delta. Mathews spent two hours flying over Upstream Delta from different perspectives. It looked benign.

Some of the things they noted on the area's reconnaissance were the wind direction and its speed and terrain features, such as general rises of the terrain. Mathews hoped his ski drags would uncover any hazards below the surface.

After the reconnaissance, Mathews flew a fourth pattern, and the crew completed the before landing checklist. He worked with Riley to develop the best direction for the approach based on the winds. He set up a box pattern at 1,000 feet above the snow. The winds were from a 300° grid-heading at five to eight knots. He flew into the headwind for their ski drags.

He lined up on his final approach and started a long gradual descent to fifty feet off the snow for a close-up view of the surface. Again, the aircrew noted the surface conditions. On the next pass, Mathews began his first ski drag. The aircraft touched down. The snow was smooth. He kept the nose of the aircraft off of the snow, popped a wheelie while the main skis slid through the snow. Riley timed for ninety seconds. Mathews maintained eighty-five to ninety-five knots of speed throughout the slide. At the end of ninety seconds, Riley called: *"Time."*

Mathews added power, and the aircraft became airborne. He flew the box pattern again at 1,000 feet above the snow to review his slide marks. The snow from the drag was a lighter color than the snow around it. There were no obvious brakes in the drag. It was somewhat curved in the beginning and straightened out at the end.

On the next pass, he aligned the aircraft on the right side of the first drag to set up for the second drag. Again, they descended, and the aircraft touched down. Riley started timing. Mathews was where he wanted to be, perhaps a little too far to the right, but he was parallel to the previous ski drag. Bump. The aircraft popped up in the air. No one saw that coming. The aircraft hit a berm of snow, and due to the aircraft's momentum, it popped up. Mathews maintained control of the situation and gently touched down into the snow again, and continued his ski drag. When the time was up, he added power and went airborne. He reviewed the second drag.

There was a noticeable skip at the beginning and possibly at the end of the drag, but there was no evidence of a crevasse. Mathews was concerned by the skip. He wanted to know what was beneath that area. In the days that followed, this bump was identified as a crevasse large enough to swallow the aircraft.

The glaciologist was on a headset throughout the flight to Upstream Delta. He was listening on a headset throughout the reconnaissance of the area and throughout the ski drags. Again and again, Mathews asked him for input. He was surprised and concerned that throughout the flight, the leading glaciologist in the world gave him no significant information about the location.

A third time Mathews lined up for a ski drag. This time he allowed Kenney an opportunity to learn how to do ski drags. Sitting in the copilot seat put Kenney in a challenging position to do a ski drag. The throttles were nearer to Mathews on the center column. Kenney needed to reach around the condition levers to maneuver the throttles. She was not tall in stature, and the reach was a challenge. This made rapid movements difficult, but Kenney was an instructor pilot and very familiar with these challenges. She agreed to do it.

Mathews kept his right hand below hers as she started down the final approach. He wanted to be ready for anything. It was a typical instructor pilot technique. Her approach was to the right side of the second ski drag. This created a further challenge. She needed to look cross-cockpit, out Mathews' side window, to line up parallel to the previous ski drags. The lower she descended the more difficult it became to keep the other two ski drags in view. She lined up parallel to the other ski drags, but the aircraft touched down further right than she planned.

Kenney kept the nose of the aircraft in the air. The snow was smooth but soft. The airspeed stabilized at eighty-five to ninety-five knots, but then the aircraft bogged down in the soft snow, and the speed decayed rapidly to eighty knots. She pushed up the throttles. The speed started to increase, then the aircraft bogged down again, and the speed rapidly decreased below stall speed. The nose ski dropped in the snow.

Mathews took over the controls and immediately pushed up the throttles. He over-torqued all of the engines in an effort to increase the speed, but the aircraft refused to accelerate. With the nose ski in the air, there was hope of getting airborne, but the speed continued to decay below seventy knots. It was too late. Skier 95 wasn't going airborne.

## The Crevasse

Mathews slowed to taxi speed, and the aircrew discussed what they would do next. They were in a predicament. Mathews thought through his options; should he stop the aircraft, or should he turn back on the last drag; or should he attempt to taxi to where he thought they would find better snow conditions near the first two drags. He decided on the latter option. When he reached the first two ski drags, he intended to do a ski takeoff between them. This seemed to be the safest option available.

He wanted to get rid of the extraneous weight in the back of the aircraft. Morgan, Quick, and Gifford opened the ramp and door in the back of the aircraft. They released the locks that were holding the pallets to the floor. Mathews added power. The pallets rolled out of the aircraft without a hitch. He then slowed the aircraft, and the loadmasters closed up the back of the aircraft.

Mathews made a left 180-degree turn to parallel the previous ski drag tracks. His intent was to get the favorable wind, so he needed to back-track. After making a left turn, Skier 95 traveled about five hundred yards with no visual signs of crevasses. The plane suddenly lunged to the right, and the right wingtip and the #4 propeller hit the snow. Mathews directed Kenney to do an emergency engine shutdown of the #4 engine. Kenney pulled the condition lever all the way aft to the feather position and the engine shutdown.

As the aircraft continued forward, the nose of the aircraft rose higher. The right wing corrected itself, and the left wing began to dip. The left wing touched down gently into the snow as the aircraft came to a stop. The plane was now listing to the left, with the back end of the aircraft much lower than the front. The left ski was in a crevasse, and the left wing was straddling it.

Smoke was billowing from the engines. Hubbley said it was probably steam from leaking fluids coming in contact with the hot engines. Morgan didn't want anyone leaving the aircraft.

Hubbley didn't want to feather the #1 propeller, positioned on the outside of the left wing, while it was in the snow. He was concerned it would cause greater damage to the propeller because the pitch change would be dramatic. Mathews directed Kenney to shut the remaining three engines down by going to the ground-stop position, limiting the pitch change. Everything went dark and quiet.

In the back of the aircraft, Gifford turned to Morgan and asked him, "Did Chief Quick pass his check ride?" It was a joke to break the tension. Morgan returned a look that only he could give. He wasn't laughing.

Assessing their situation, it was obvious the #4 propeller was trashed. The blades of the propeller were no longer aligned. It needed to be replaced before the aircraft got airborne again. They needed help. They found themselves in a very remote location in the middle of a crevasse field, far from any support. Their location was 81° 04' 53.37" South, 140° 03' 01.40" West.

# The Wait

Mathews needed to make some radio calls to let people know where they were. The auxiliary power unit or APU, located on the left exterior of the aircraft, was near to the edge of the crevasse. After talking things over with Mathews, Hubbley started it. It ran fine, so he turned on the power to the aircraft electrical systems, which provided lights, and Mathews could use the radios. He contacted Siple Dome and let them know he needed assistance. Siple Dome contacted the Twin Otter pilots to see if they would help out, and they agreed.

While waiting, the crew had time to think about their circumstances. They realized there was a possibility the aircraft could still fall into the crevasse. If it did, it wouldn't be recoverable. Hundreds of years from now, it would come out in an ice flow. This concept was intriguing, so each crew member put their name and signature on an approach plate, and they left it on the bunk of the aircraft as a potential memorial to the events that transpired.

Mathews took charge of everyone's exit from the aircraft. He had a total of eleven people to keep safe until the Twin Otter arrived. One by one, he had the crew members and passengers put on a loadmaster restraint harness. The purpose of the harness was to secure the loadmasters during airdrop missions while the doors were open in the back of the aircraft. Mathews borrowed a rope from one of the survival experts and tied it to the restraint harness, and one-by-one, he had the passengers and the aircrew exit the aircraft, with their gear, from the overhead escape hatch on the flight deck. Once they were outside the aircraft, they walked down the left wing, over the crevasse, into the snow on the other side. They took off the harness, and Mathews pulled it back to the aircraft for the next person.

The Twin Otter arrived, and the pilots flew over Upstream Delta to do their own reconnaissance. Mathews' first ski drag location looked like the best place to land. After the pilot set the aircraft down, he stopped and let the castaways walk to his aircraft. Once outside Skier 95, one of the survival experts took over. Slowly she staked and flagged a safe path to the Twin Otter. The rest followed.

Mathews, Hubbley, and Morgan were the last to exit the aircraft. Before he left, Morgan opened the right paratroop door, located in the aft portion of the cargo compartment, and looked down into the crevasse. What he saw awed him. He was looking down a massive "bottomless" blue ice trench. It would later be measured to a depth of one hundred thirty-four feet deep.

Morgan convinced Mathews to look. When Mathews peered down into the gapping depth below, he was repulsed by what he saw. The impact of what had just happened swept over him. He became angry. He was pushed into this mission. He searched for as much information as he could find on Upstream Delta. His ski drags were successful. The only questionable event was the third ski drag, but the third ski drag didn't explain the crevasses in the area. Now he was leaving an aircraft seven hundred miles from McMurdo, Antarctica. His crew, his friends, had nearly died with him. He felt he was set up for failure.

It took the Twin Otter three round-trips to get everyone out of Upstream Delta, and each time it was an hour and a half round trip; twenty-five to thirty minutes of flight-time each way, plus time on the ground at Siple Dome and Upstream Delta. Mathews, Hubbley, and Morgan were the last to leave the crevasse field.

# Return of the Aircrew

I walked down the dirt road to Building 165, entered the building, and walked up the stairs to the second floor at about 3:30 in the afternoon. When I entered Raven Operations, I was given a briefing from the supervisor of flying on the day's events so far. I was the deputy deployed commander.

Being second-in-charge of the Raven Gang's deployment relegated me to run the night shift operation. Night is a relative term in Antarctica during November. The sun never sets at this time of year. I liked the night shift. It was quiet. Typically, my job was to recover the day-shift missions, launch and recover the night missions, and close out the day's paperwork.

It wasn't long after I showed up at work that I got word Skier 95 was in a crevasse—so much for quiet. "How did that happen?" was my first question. "Is everybody alright?" was my next question. News about the fate of Skier 95 came in slowly. The HF radio communications were poor due to solar flare activity.

I went downstairs to the Operation Deep Freeze deputy commander's office. He knew Bill Mathews' concerns before they left to fly the mission. He knew the contractors pushed to complete this mission day after day. He didn't seem surprised when I filled him in on recent events. When I was finished, he said he wanted periodic updates. I went back upstairs. My job now was to manage the rescue of the crew.

It was an interesting day so far. I asked myself, *"How big is that crevasse? Is the whole plane in the crevasse? Can anyone escape from it?"* I was stationed in Alaska for four years. Crevasses are found in glaciers. *"Are these guys on a glacier? Where is Upstream Delta?"*

I began to research what had happened. The HF radios were the biggest challenge throughout the day. I walked across the hall into McMurdo Operations, Mac Ops, to see what they knew. They always kept the lines of communication open to all out-camps in Antarctica.

I wanted to be in direct communication with the Skier 95 aircrew, but instead, everything was relayed through Siple Dome. Siple Dome told me a Twin Otter aircraft was flying shuttles from Upstream Delta back to Siple Dome. There was no word on injuries or damage to the aircraft. I walked out of Mac Ops, made a right-hand turn, and walked down the hall to Mr. Steve Dunbar's office. He was the lead mountaineer and survival expert on the continent. We talked at length. I told him I would send an aircraft to Siple Dome and pick up the Skier 95 aircrew. He told me, "I don't think you should do that yet." I told him, "We need to pick up the crew." He responded, "We don't know if anyone is stranded at the aircraft. We don't know if anyone is injured and needs medical support. We don't know what equipment we may need to help the crew. We should delay to find out what they need before we rush out there." The man knew his job. So, I waited for more information.

Emotions ran high. Captain Steve Yandik arrived to plan for his flight to the South Pole. I filled him in on the day's events. Yandik wanted to go to Siple Dome to get the aircrew. He was a stubborn cuss. I told him what Dunbar told me. He didn't like it. He was understandably upset. There's a bond among the Raven Gang aircrews. Many of us grew up together, faced the same challenges, and lived together for weeks and months on the ice. I wanted Yandik to go to the South Pole, and he did.

As the hours passed, we received more information from Siple Dome. Everyone from Skier 95 was alive and well. They were at Siple Dome awaiting transportation back to McMurdo. Yandik, by now, was on his descent into the South Pole. I went to Mac Ops and called him. I told him to keep enough fuel aboard the aircraft so he could fly to Siple Dome and pick up the aircrew of Skier 95. I could hear it in his voice that he was elated. He told his crew, "It's about time they got their head out of their ass." Five hours later, Yandik returned from Siple Dome with the aircrew of Skier 95. Now the aircrew was safely back in McMurdo; the concern turned to getting the aircraft back.

## Return of the Aircraft

The next day a Navy aircrew went to Upstream Delta to get pictures of Skier 95. Everything had changed. The thin overcast sky was gone, and it was a bright sunny day. The direct sunlight clearly reflected the shadows in the snow. There were crevasses everywhere, and Skier 95 was in the middle of it. It was the treachery of Antarctica. People looking at the pictures in McMurdo couldn't believe Mathews had landed there. The foremost glaciologist in the world was trying to get back there.

A week later, 22 November 1998, the McMurdo community's newspaper, *The Antarctica Sun*, stated, *"The area is laden with crevasses, and a team of investigators and mountaineers are searching for a safe landing site. Due to the varied movement of the ice stream, which can be 10 to 100 times faster than the surrounding ice, enormous crevasse areas, called shear margins, form in the middle of these big stream zones.*[139]

The National Science Foundation considered the retrieval of the aircraft secondary to completing science because the science season in Antarctica was short. They talked of leaving the aircraft in the crevasse instead of recovering it. In 1971, they lost one of their aircraft, tail number

59-5925, when it crashed. They left it buried in the snow for seventeen years until they recovered it in 1988.

*Skier 95 in a Crevasse Field*

# Joe Butler

The Guard thought their aircraft was the immediate concern, not the science. They started making plans to bring the aircraft home. This became the pivotal event to ensure the LC-130 maintenance recovery team became a reality. Master Sergeant Joe Butler was the most experienced line chief at the 109th Airlift Wing, and he led the team to bring the aircraft home.

On 6 December 1998, another article in *The Antarctica Sun* stated:

> *"For the last few weeks mountaineers and plane-recovery experts have visited the site to find a safe landing spot for subsequent LC-130 missions, assess the damage to the plane, and draft a recovery plan."*[140]

Butler spent weeks in New York, assembling his maintenance team to recover the aircraft.

| Maintenance Team | |
|---|---|
| **Chief Master Sergeant** | Charlie Lucia remained in McMurdo |
| **Master Sergeant** | Joe Butler, crew chief |
| **Master Sergeant** | Bob Thivierge, crew chief |
| **Technical Sergeant** | Chuck Shannon, engine specialist |
| **Technical Sergeant** | Mike Craig, engine specialist |

Butler contacted the 653rd Combat Logistics Support Squadron, located at Warner-Robbins, Georgia. They specialized in aircraft recovery operations. Initially, they saw no way forward. They could not conceive a way to recover an aircraft from a crevasse field in the middle of Antarctica, seven hundred miles from any sort of civilization. They told Butler it was impossible. They didn't understand.

Butler explained to them the capabilities of the LC-130 maintenance recovery team. He told them of their resources and the equipment available. He told them he had a plan, and the 653rd Combat Logistics Support Squadron believed in his plan. On 8 December 1998, they sent a twelve-member team to Antarctica. Everyone likes a good challenge.

# Recovery of Skier 95

While the maintenance recovery team was being assembled, the National Science Foundation sent a Twin Otter aircraft to Upstream Delta with a ground-penetrating radar attached to it. The Twin Otter scoped out the snow around Skier 95's first ski drag and determined it was a safe location to conduct operations.

Survival experts also went there. They put flagging around hazardous areas to easily identify them later. They marked a safe trail from the Twin Otter to Skier 95, in case blowing and drifting snow covered their tracks. Snowmobiles arrived to groom a location for an LC-130 to land. Antarctica is a unique place. No individual country owns the land. It is international territory due to the Antarctica Treaty. Therefore, no country can lay claim to anything left there. Although there is no other large aircraft with the LC-130 capability, anyone with the gumption to land at Upstream Delta would have rights to anything on the aircraft.

*Crevasse, Saburro Pic*

Skier 95 remained at Upstream Delta for thirty days before the recovery began, but then things happened fast. Master Sergeant Bob Thivierge said, "We were given two weeks to prepare to go recover the plane, but then rumors started to spread that the Italians were going to scavenge it. So, we left three days later."

Lt. Col. Dave Fountain, with his cargo compartment full of heavy equipment, was the first LC-130 to land. Before long, bulldozers were dragging heavy metal bars of steel and groomed a skiway and an aircraft parking ramp in the snow. Once the skiway was built, it was left alone for several hours to allow the snow to sinter. This gave a firm platform for more LC-130 arrivals. The LC-130s landed with more frequency. Some aircraft supported Butler's recovery team, and some provided supplies for the glaciologist's science camp. Both Butler and the glaciologist shared the camp.

Butler's initially needed to create a safe work environment for his team. This was the reason Butler called upon the 653rd Combat Logistics Support Squadron. They used bulldozers to push snow into crevasses and build a snow road from the skiway to Skier 95. The next challenge he faced was how to get a 118,000-pound aircraft out of a crevasse. Butler and his team put balloons under the left wing and inflated them. These balloons were modular lift devices attached to a compressor. They were part of the CDDAR[141] equipment. The 109th Airlift Wing stored a set of these balloons at McMurdo.

When the balloons inflated, the aircraft rose out of the crevasse. Butler had a bulldozer with the bridle assembly attached to the main skis. He pulled the aircraft forward until it was away from the crevasse. The maintenance team then completed a thorough damage assessment of the aircraft. Their next challenge was to repair it.

The 653rd Combat Logistics Support Squadron used the bulldozer to build mounds around the wings of the aircraft. This allowed the maintenance people to walk up to the wing and work on the aircraft engines and propellers. Technical Sergeant Mike Craig took the lead on repairs, and he used the over-the-wing sling to replace the #4 engine and propeller with the help of Chuck Shannon and Bob Thivierge. The over-the-wing-sling looked like an erector set when assembled and allowed Craig to remove and replace the engine on the uneven surface of the snow. It used attachment points on top of the wing and in the flap-well to secure it.

The #4 propeller didn't cooperate initially. Craig couldn't get it off of the engine shaft. The shaft was bent. So, he chained the propeller to a bulldozer and pulled it off. Once the engine installation and rigging were completed, Craig and Thivierge installed the propeller.

Meanwhile, Shannon shifted his focus to the other wing and removed and replaced the #1 propeller assembly. The mound of snow in front of the engine gave him easy access to the wing. He used a bulldozer to lift the propeller from the engine and a new one to the engine. The right aileron was also damaged, and it was replaced. When the repairs were completed, Butler used a bulldozer to pull the aircraft to the parking ramp near the skiway.

The maintenance team had been at Upstream Delta for nineteen days. They were now ready to go home. On 4 January 1999, forty-nine days after taxiing into a crevasse, Lt. Col. Bill Mathews strapped into Skier 95 and did a ski takeoff out of Upstream Delta and returned to McMurdo. He said, "I have never borrowed an aircraft entrusted to me by Uncle Sam and not returned it when I was finished."

CHAPTER 20

# WHAT YOU DON'T KNOW

Sondrestrom commander, "Where's your hat?" Guard Lieutenant Colonel, "It's in my pocket." Sondrestrom commander, "Why isn't it on your head?" Guard Lieutenant Colonel, "I can't get my head in my pocket."

In the 1980s, Sondrestrom, Greenland, was the Raven Gang's playground. The Sondrestrom Air Base was an active-duty base. The Raven Gang aircrews were civilians on active-duty orders for a week. That was how the Guard operated. Sondrestrom had a military support structure for a mostly civilian flying organization.

In the late 1990s, when the Guard took over the Operation Deep Freeze mission, the civilian community took on more responsibility. About one hundred and twenty-five Guard people deployed when they came to town. All Raven Gang aircrews were on active-duty orders, but their support structure was civilian contractors. McMurdo was a civilian support structure for a military flying organization.

In both cases, the civilians were not up to the standards the military expected.

## The Old Guard

The original Raven Gang, who had resupplied the DYE sites since 1975, had grown old by the late 1990s. Most of them were already retired. The new people who replaced them were trained in the old ways, but the unit's experience level dropped dramatically.

Before the transition of the Operation Deep Freeze mission to the Guard, the Raven Gang had twelve aircrews of drill-status guardsmen, traditional guardsmen, that is, part-time guardsmen. The part-time Guard pilots ruled the roost, or the "unkindness," for they were ravens. There were also federal civil servants, technicians whose job was to manage the airbase. The technicians accounted for three additional part-time aircrews in the squadron. This structure was much like every other Air National Guard unit at the time.

The build-up of twelve more aircrews was rapid. Many new crewmembers arrived from the active-duty Air Force, and we had a chip on our shoulders upon arrival. Some of us learned rapidly that there were many facets to the Guard we didn't understand.

I flew a training mission one night with the 109$^{th}$ Operations Group Commander in the summer of 1996. I didn't understand why everyone in the squadron flew assault landings and stopped the aircraft so gently. My philosophy was, get the aircraft in the zone and stopped, now! And this is what I did. I landed in the zone and got on the brakes. I had everyone hanging forward in their seat belts and shoulder harness when we came to a full stop.

From ear to ear and from hairline to chin, my commander's, Lt. Col. Verle Johnston's, face turned red. While we were stopped on the runway, he looked over at me and asked firmly, "What was that?!" With the same emphasis, I said, "That was an assault!"

He cooled down a bit and said, "Joe, we don't do those here. These aren't a rent-a-plane on the Little Rock ramp. These are our airplanes, and they have to last another twenty years."

Johnston was previously a maintenance officer. He explained later how an unnecessary brake change put a burden on maintenance. In a C-130, a brake change took a few hours. A brake change in an LC-130 took at least a day. The aircraft needed to be jacked up off the ground, and the skis needed to be removed before it could be done. Also, an aggressive landing in an LC-130 could damage the bottom surface of the skis. The bottom surfaces were critical to how the aircraft performed on the snow. This was one of many lessons I would learn about the Guard.

# Efficiency Versus Quality

When the 109th Airlift Wing took over the Operation Deep Freeze mission, the agreement they made with the National Science Foundation was to have twelve Title 32 active duty aircrews, that is, active duty guard-reserve aircrews, AGR aircrews, trained to fly the ski mission in three years by the 1999–2000 season.

It required an act of Congress to authorize the increase in manning positions within the National Guard to make this happen. Twelve additional full-time aircrews came to the flying squadron, as well as additional maintenance and support personnel. The National Science Foundation reimbursed the National Guard for the use of these additional people.

Nothing could prepare the squadron for the influx of twelve additional full-time aircrews, seventy-two aircrew members, plus support staff. The twelve additional full-time aircrews, two pilots, one navigator, one flight engineer, and two loadmasters per crew would be the backbone of the Operation Deep Freeze mission.

To have enough pilots qualified in three years, the Raven Gang training office needed to streamline how pilots upgraded. I was the first pilot upgraded in a more streamlined manner, but there was no formal program on how it was to be accomplished. Within a year, I was in charge of the pilot training program, and I standardized and streamlined the process.

Initially, every pilot came into the Raven Gang as a copilot, sitting in the right seat. The new training process was to upgrade pilots to basic aircraft commanders before they were ready to upgrade to ski mission aircraft commanders. For many, this happened quickly. As George Rob used to say, "The cream rises to the top."

Instructor pilots monitored the new basic aircraft commanders until they were ready to become ski aircraft commanders. The instructor pilot meetings became more contentious, but pilots upgraded faster to meet the mission's requirements. It created a great deal of conflict in the flying squadron, but the conflicts were local. They didn't spread out of the squadron. The pilots that upgraded were good. They knew the airplane, they understood the mission, and they could manage an aircrew. But this wasn't enough. You don't know what you don't know.

# Introduction to Jungle Rules (Author's Story)

I learned two very big lessons during the 1998–1999 season. The first lesson I learned was I was naive. I thought the Operation Deep Freeze mission ran like an active-duty mission. I placed too much trust in the civilian contractors who supported the flying mission. The second lesson I learned was "jungle rules." I learned how things operate on the ice cap. It had a different set of rules.

It was mid-February 1999, and the South Pole was getting colder. The sun was about to set for the first time since October 1998. The winter-over people, the people who would remain in Antarctica throughout the frigid Antarctic winter, were already on-station. The summer people had returned to McMurdo from the out-camps in anticipation of their flight to New Zealand. At McMurdo, four ships had come and gone since the beginning of the month. The first was the Coast Guard ice breaker. It smashed a passage through the ice in McMurdo Sound for the other ships to follow. The other three vessels were a science vessel, a fuel ship that refueled McMurdo, and a cargo ship.

*Cargo Ship at Pier (John Stiles)*

The cargo ship arrived on time, but it was scheduled very late in the season. Onboard were two large helium dewars that needed to get to the South Pole. The helium was for the South Pole telescopes. Without the helium, the science throughout the winter would be wasted. The aircrew's first reaction was, "Why did they wait until the last moment to get this to the South Pole?" It was late in the season. If an aircraft broke at the South Pole, quite likely, it would remain there over the winter. It was a mistake the National Science Foundation would not repeat.

My crew flew the first dewar. We planned the mission, pre-flighted the aircraft, and loaded the dewar. It was huge. It filled most of the cargo compartment. The flight to the South Pole was routine. It was a typical 2.9-hour flight. When we taxied on the ramp to offload the dewar, the temperature was -48 degrees Celsius.

We kept the engines running when we operated at camps in Antarctica. This lessened the potential for engine malfunctions and propeller leaks. When the loadmasters opened the ramp and door of the aircraft, it was foggy outside. It wasn't your typical fog. It was ice fog. But, looking out the windows in the front of the aircraft, I saw a beautiful sunny day outside. The fog was caused by the extreme cold temperature sublimating the moisture in the engine exhaust, and it created a cloud behind the aircraft.

*Lining Up a Sled Behind Aircraft*

The dewar needed to be offloaded onto a large sled platform mounted on skis and maneuvered by a forklift. Loadmasters used hand signals to direct the forklift driver to align this large sled behind the aircraft. Frequently the sled got stuck in the snow and required the forklift driver to give the sled a nudge. On a good day, there was potential for pushing the sled too aggressively and running it into the ramp of the aircraft, so rubber tires were attached to the leading edge of the sled to limit any potential damage to the ramp. It was a challenging, cooperative effort.

This was not a good day. The ice fog hindered the loadmasters' ability to see beyond the ramp and door of the aircraft. It was impossible to see the sled. It was impossible to line the sled up behind the aircraft. The forklift driver couldn't see the loadmaster. It was the first time I knew this was possible. I had never seen engine exhaust crystallize and create ice fog behind the aircraft, so I walked to the back of the aircraft to take a look. It was amazing to see. The frozen contrails from the engines lingered in the back of the aircraft and created a fog bank. I thought it was pointless to continue to offload the dewar.

Mr. Dwight Fisher came up onto the flight deck of the aircraft. His salt and pepper head of hair matched his beard and mustache, and he wore a red parka.[142] I had no idea who this man was. He asked me about the situation. I was angry and frustrated with my problem and told him, "I'm going back to McMurdo" He suggested, "Down speed the engines and apply a little reverse power. This may clear the contrails." When the throttles were in the low-speed ground idle position, it lowered the engines' speed from one-hundred percent to a range of 69 to 75.5 percent. This was called down-speeding the engines. But I didn't want him butting in my business. Who did this red coat think he was?

I would later find out Mr. Dwight Fisher knew a lot more about the mission than I did. He was previously the commander of VXE-6, the Navy's flying squadron in Antarctica, from 1982–1985. He returned in 1987 as the Commander of the Naval Support Force Antarctica. Following that assignment, he became the Department of Defense liaison officer to the National Science Foundation until he retired in 1992. Fisher was currently the National Science Foundation Deputy Head of Polar Research Support in the Office of Polar Programs, which funded and managed the U.S. Antarctic Program and the Foundation's Arctic Research Program.[143]

The months away from home, flying risky missions, for an organization that always seemed concerned about the price tag and cutting costs, an organization whose contractors frequently displayed incompetence had taken its toll on me. Why did they wait so long to get the dewars to Antarctica?

I was faced with an unfamiliar situation. I believed if it didn't look right or feel right, don't do it. Go home, ask questions, and try again later. And that's what I did. I told the loadmaster to close up the back of the aircraft, and I flew the dewar back to McMurdo.

## Fallout

When I returned, there were a lot of questions I needed to answer, but there was no open criticism. I felt vindicated; however, the National Science Foundation was not happy. I created a lot of friction between the military's Commander of Operation Deep Freeze, Colonel Richard Saburro, and the National Science Foundation leadership. It was the first year the Raven Gang was in charge of Operation Deep Freeze, and now, one of the premiere science projects was in jeopardy. It was a very high visibility issue, and there were some very high-level conversations.

The lead scientist for the South Pole telescope entered Saburro's office and pleaded with him to get the dewars to the South Pole. Saburro agreed to do it if it could be done safely. In New York, the Raven Gang's operations group commander, Colonel Verle Johnston, and the chief of standardization and evaluation, Lt. Col. Brian Gomula, called the National Guard Bureau Commander's office to try to put a halt to the mission. The National Science Foundation shouldn't have waited to the end of the season to get the dewars to the South Pole.

The Guard Bureau couldn't do anything to stop it. The Raven Gang was under the command of Saburro while they were deployed to Antarctica. His chain of command reported to Transportation Command, at Scott Air Force Base, in Illinois, not the Guard Bureau. In the end, the aircrews settled the issue on their own.

Over dinner, I talked to Lt. Col. Aldo Marchegiani. Aldo was a Vietnam-era pilot and a ski mission instructor pilot. I loved old pilots like Aldo. They were gods. He wanted to know what happened. I described the problem. He looked disappointed and said, "Joe, our job is to figure out how to complete the mission, not to refuse to do it." That was when I understood I had failed. He asked me, "Did you turn the aircraft ninety degrees? The wind may have blown the contrails away." I shook my head and said, "No."

After dinner, Aldo walked up to Saburro's office and agreed to give it a shot. The next day he flew the helium dewar to the South Pole and had the ice fog develop behind his aircraft. He down-sped his aircraft engines and applied a little reverse power. It cleared the fog.

There was a second helium dewar to get to the South Pole, and it was put on my aircraft, Skier 96. Raven Operations gave me my shot at redemption. And there was a backup plan. Another aircraft was going to land after me. It was the last mission of the season. I was told to shut down my aircraft engines to offload the dewar if it was necessary. If the aircraft engines didn't restart, my aircrew would jump on the last aircraft back to McMurdo and leave Skier 96 at the South Pole for the winter.

But, there were no hiccups this time. No contrails were billowing behind my aircraft. There was no reason to turn the aircraft ninety degrees to attempt the offload. There was no reason to shut down the engines. Antarctica didn't allow me my chance at redemption, but it gave me a lesson in maturity.

CHAPTER 21

# NAIVETE

I compare my rapid upgrade in the ski mission with baking a cake. When you bake a cake, and you're in a hurry, turning up the heat won't help. The cake ends up burned on the outside and gooey on the inside. The best way to bake a cake is at moderate heat over time. The same thing goes for the upgrade to ski aircraft commander.

The new Raven Gang members lacked experience. Intelligence and capability weren't enough. The faster upgrade to ski mission aircraft commander gave me confidence without a true understanding of where I was flying. I underestimated my environment and lacked the instincts to know when to do something or not to do something. It was as simple as that. I needed more time.

On 1 December 1998, two and a half months before the dewar incident, I had an interesting flight. By the end of the day, I felt as if I was burned by the cargo yard and the weather forecasters, and I felt gooey inside. Two weeks after Skier 95 went into the crevasse, I would learn some serious lessons of my own. The first lesson, there was no authorized cargo specialist at any location in Antarctica other than in McMurdo. The South Pole cargo yard personnel were not certified to approve cargo manifests and hazardous cargo paperwork. This changed rapidly.

Another lesson was the weather in Antarctica could change at an incredibly rapid rate. It had to be respected. Many years later, the weather contractors would disclose their inability to accurately forecast the weather due to the limited tools they had available. But in 1998, the aircrews didn't know, and we would continue to struggle with the rapidly changing Antarctic weather patterns.

Skier 92 was my designated aircraft. We were scheduled for the first line of the day. Our mission was to deliver cargo to the South Pole.

| Skier 92 Aircrew | |
|---|---|
| **Pilot:** | Major Joseph Hathaway |
| **Copilot:** | First Lieutenant Carlyle Norman |
| **Navigator:** | Major Marc "Sipowitz" LeCours |
| **Flight Engineer:** | Technical Sergeant Ugo Mascolo |
| **Loadmaster:** | Technical Sergeant Carmelo Modesto |
| **Loadmaster:** | Technical Sergeant Francis "Snowdog" Czwakiel |

I was the aircraft commander for the day's flight. Before joining the Raven Gang, I was a C-130 instructor pilot with eleven years of active-duty experience. My first assignment following pilot training was to fly C-130s with the Firebirds at Elmendorf Air Force Base, Anchorage, Alaska. One particular landing with the Firebirds sticks out among thousands through my career. I was the copilot when the pilot made the landing on an icy runway at Elmendorf. It was a beautiful day, but I'll give the pilot the benefit of the doubt and say there was a ten-knot crosswind.

Upon landing, the aircraft began to drift to the right. The aircraft was almost off the runway when it hit a patch of asphalt, and the pilot was able to correct back to the icy centerline and stop. After doing so, his evaluation of the job he did was outrageous. He said, "No one else could have done what I did." My evaluation of him didn't change; he was an ass. However, were he not so outrageous, I may not have remembered that landing. Through the years, I thought about what I would have done differently, and this experience probably saved us on our flight in the day ahead. Lieutenant Carlyle Norman was my copilot. He was a Citadel graduate and went to pilot training soon after that. He was an excellent pilot, a troublemaker, and a pleasure to work with.

Major Marc LeCours was my navigator. He was a former active duty KC-135 pilot who joined the Raven Gang in the hopes of getting a full-time position. His nickname was Sipowitz. It came from a television character. Both Marc and the character had the same build, the same mustache, and the same wise-guy attitude and voice. Marc had more hair. He was quick with one-liners and liked to make people laugh. The three of us walked down the dirt roads of McMurdo to Raven Operations and planned the day's mission.

Taking over the mission from the Navy required the Raven Gang to hire a lot of new crewmembers. Since many of these aircrews were new to Antarctica, they were expected to become familiar with the local area. I was one of them. This was my third Antarctica Season, but it was my first one as a ski aircraft commander.

It was common for aircrews to do some local orientation around the McMurdo area after the mission if they had any remaining fuel and the weather was good. I had flown with the same crew all week, so I wanted to show them the area and was told many scientific activities were taking place in the Dry Valleys due to its unique environment. The valleys were so arid the glaciers rolled over the mountain tops and sublimated into the atmosphere before they could descend into the mountain valleys below.

I had never seen the Dry Valleys but was told it was breathtaking scenery. I wanted to fly down them on the return flight to McMurdo if the rest of the crew was willing, so I included this into the mission. I coordinated to see if there was any helicopter traffic scheduled in the valleys. McMurdo Center, the air traffic control facility, told me there was none scheduled throughout the day.

The weather forecaster expected a 7,000-foot broken cloud ceiling with unrestricted visibility later in the afternoon. West of McMurdo, in the Dry Valleys, the cloud ceiling and visibility were forecast to be clear and beautiful. I was told the weather there was always better than the McMurdo weather. With the plan in place, I briefed the supervisor of flying and went to Derelict Junction with Carlyle and Sipowitz to catch the shuttle to the ice runway. Upon our arrival at the aircraft, we joined the rest of our crew.

The loadmasters were Technical Sergeant Francis Czwakiel, affectionately called Snowdog, and Technical Sergeant Carmelo Modesto. Both Snowdog and Carm were very competent loadmasters. Snowdog came from the Marine Corps. Not too tall and very skinny, but his size was not to be underestimated. He was lithe and powerful. He was quiet and had a ready smile, and for some reason, he'd dye his hair different colors, more as a distraction.

Carmelo came from the Maryland Air National Guard for a full-time job. He was a perfectionist, never satisfied with the status quo. When he flew, he cooked incredible meals in the aircraft microwave.

Snowdog and Carm had a T-4 pallet loaded on the aircraft, material for constructing the new South Pole Station. The T-4 designation was based on the number of pallets linked together to on-load or offload cargo of significant size. In our case, there were four pallets linked together; thus, it was given the T-4 designation. The cargo on these pallets weighed about 26,000 pounds, so the South Pole would not be receiving any fuel from us on this particular mission.

Technical Sergeant Ugo Mascolo, our flight engineer, started his career at Stewart Air National Guard Base in Newburgh, New York. He worked in the R&R, repair and replace, shop until he found a full-time position in Schenectady as a crew chief. He also worked in the ISO, or isochronal inspection, shop until he got a flight engineer position. Our aircraft was parked at the airfield fuel pit area, and Ugo already had the aircraft loaded with fuel. Things were running perfectly. We were an hour ahead of schedule. I briefed the crew on my plan to go to the Dry Valleys upon our return. We strapped into our seats, ran our checklists, and started the aircraft engines.

*Dry Valleys (photolibrary.usap.gov)*

# Small Hiccups

While I was taxiing the aircraft to the ice runway, Ugo noticed pressure in the bleed air manifold with all the engine's bleed air valves closed. Bleed air leaks were a serious issue. I understood Ugo's concerns, so we returned to the parking ramp to have maintenance check it out.

Staff Sergeant James Czwakiel, Snowdog's brother, was the maintenance guy tasked with addressing our bleed air leak. He looked and said the pressure in the manifold was within the three pounds-per-square-inch limitation. The aircraft was good to go. Ugo didn't like the explanation. I wasn't convinced myself, so I walked to the back of the aircraft and asked Snowdog if he got along with his little brother. Snowdog said, "I love my brother." It was good to know this, and it gave me the confidence I needed. I returned to the flight deck of the aircraft and told the crew to strap back in, "We're good to go."

We departed McMurdo ice runway at the scheduled takeoff time. This minor bleed air hiccup was the beginning of a very interesting day. Once airborne, I climbed the aircraft to cruise altitude and turned on the autopilot. Ugo went through the charts and determined 270 knots true airspeed to get the best fuel efficiency was the best cruise speed to fly.

The aircraft became lighter as the aircraft burned its fuel throughout the flight. As the aircraft got lighter, our true airspeed increased. There were two ways for us to maintain our 270 knots as the aircraft lightened. If we maintained a specific altitude and the true airspeed is too high, I could pull back on the throttles to slow the aircraft and conserve fuel. Another method that most pilots used was selecting a specific power setting, in our case 970° TIT or turbine inlet temperature. As the true airspeed increased, the pilot climbed the aircraft to a higher altitude to maintain 270 knots.

The big propellers of the C-130 jet engines spun at a constant speed. As the aircraft climbed into the less dense air, its propellers decreased pitch. The decreased pitch added drag. Therefore, climbing the aircraft reduced the true airspeed of the aircraft by adding drag. The atmosphere is thinner the higher the aircraft climbed. While maintaining the same speed, an aircraft at a higher altitude requires less fuel. Jet engines are more efficient at altitude. Although we slowed down and added drag, we were burning less fuel. Regardless, whether we pulled back throttles or climbed to a higher altitude, the results were the same, we maintained a constant speed with a lower fuel burn rate. But most pilots would rather climb than pull the throttles back. Climbing to altitude had an added benefit. By leaving the throttles at the same position and keeping the same power setting, 970° TIT, (Turbine Inlet Temperature), it was easier to monitor the engines.

About halfway into the three-hour flight to the South Pole, I noticed the #4 engine reading 830° TIT. The fuel flow and torque were reading lower also. The throttles were still aligned. Ugo, Carlyle, and I discussed the issue. This was either a big problem or a small problem. Carlyle said, "Go null." Null is a selection on the temperature datum system. Null removed the temperature datum system from the fuel-delivery process in the aircraft engines. If the temperature datum system was the problem, removing it from the process made it a possible quick-fix.

Ugo agreed, and being the systems expert; he selected null for the #4 engine. The power was restored. The #4 engine was reading 970° TIT again, and the fuel flow and torque also responded in line with expectations. This was a second minor hiccup in the mission. I always felt I had a sixth sense about flying. I was getting edgy. In the back of my mind, I was almost ready to turn back to McMurdo. Little things were beginning to add up. I felt uneasy. But I had no reason to turn back.

# Propane Tanks

As we approached Amundsen-Scott Base at the South Pole, Carlyle contacted the station to let them know we were starting our descent. South Pole station was a large camp with many research activities going on. The weather was beautiful, and the winds were light. Sipowitz let the station know the details of the cargo we were delivering.

South Pole station responded with a request. There were two pallets of empty propane tanks from one of the AGO, or automated geophysical observatory, sites sitting in the South Pole cargo yard. The station wanted to know if we would return these pallets to McMurdo. After verifying for a second time that the propane tanks were empty, I agreed to return the pallets to McMurdo. Later, I would regret this decision.

The landing on the skiway at the South Pole was smooth. I taxied the aircraft onto the ramp and stopped at our standard parking location. I cleared the loadmasters to open the cargo ramp and door, and a sled met them as the door opened. The T-4 disappeared from the back of the aircraft, and the two empty pallets of propane tanks were loaded into the aircraft within minutes. Things happened fast. Carm and Snowdog were on their A-game. They loaded the pallets in the last two pallet positions of the cargo compartment to get an aft center-of-gravity. The ramp and door closed, and I began to taxi the aircraft to the skiway while I briefed the ski takeoff. "BOOM!" Everything went quiet except the aircraft engines.

I asked, "What was that?" There was no response. After a few moments, I repeated, "Loadmaster, what was that?" Still, no response. "Nav, get back there and tell me what's going on." Sipowitz went down the stairs of the flight deck to the back of the aircraft. Silence. "Nav, what's going on." No response. I was losing patience. After a few moments, I demanded, "Somebody tell me what the hell is going on!" After a few moments, Sipowitz came back up the stairs to the flight deck.

The moment he had gone down to the cargo compartment, he saw liquid propane dripping from the aircraft's ceiling. Snowdog and Carmelo were running along either side of the propane pallets to the back. The manual handle to open the cargo ramp and door was there. Sipowitz told me, "One of the propane tanks blew its top and liquid propane is all over the cargo compartment ceiling. Snowdog's in the back, hand-cranking the ramp and door open instead of using the hydraulic switch, and the loadmasters don't want to key their mics to prevent a stray electrical spark from igniting the propane." Geniuses. Quick thinking. Things often happen too fast in the aviation game for the aircrew to get excited. Rapid smart reactions overcame panic due to their experiences and the training they received.

Six large bottles, about five feet high, were loaded on each pallet. Five bottles were propane, and the sixth was nitrogen. All the bottles were connected in series. The last bottle, the nitrogen, pushed propane from one bottle to the next. The first bottle was designed to connect to the AGO site. Therefore, any remaining propane was in the first bottle.

We would find out later the bottles had been vented, not purged. Venting the bottles equalized the pressure in the bottles with the outside atmosphere. Venting did not remove all the propane from the bottles. The two pallets of propane bottles had been in the South Pole cargo yard for several days. The temperature was -40 degrees in the cargo yard. When the pallets were loaded into the aircraft, the inside of the aircraft was seventy degrees. Boyle's Law: The immediate temperature change of one hundred and ten degrees caused a significant and rapid pressure increase in the propane bottles. The first bottle blew open its pressure relief safety valve and sprayed liquid propane throughout the cargo compartment.

By the time Snowdog got the ramp and door fully opened, the propane had dissipated. I taxied the aircraft back to the South Pole ramp, and we got rid of the pallets. Carlyle let the station know what happened. Snowdog and Carm had saved our lives. The crew was not happy. I taxied the aircraft to the skiway, and once we were airborne, I let Carlyle fly the leg back to McMurdo. We discussed what had happened, but other than that, it was a quiet return flight.

## Dry Valleys

Hours later, upon reaching Pole-1, the final reporting point, I contacted McMurdo and asked for a weather update. The weather was seven-thousand-foot ceiling and unrestricted visibility. It was just as forecasted, and I was impressed. *"Wow,"* I thought, *"These guys know what they're doing."* If I only knew then what I know now. Snowdog was on the flight deck bunk. He asked, "We're still going to the Dry Valleys, aren't we?" If someone other than one of the loadmasters had asked the question, I would have said, "No." The unexpected events at the South Pole had sapped my energy. So, I asked the crew if they were up to it. There was some discussion, and in the end, I decided we would go to the Dry Valleys. I can't say it was a smart decision.

I let McMurdo Center, our air traffic control, know our intentions. Sipowitz programmed the navigation systems to show us the way. Carlyle turned the aircraft to the new heading. The first indication something was wrong was after ten minutes had passed. McMurdo Center reported the weather had decreased to a six thousand foot ceiling and unrestricted visibility. No big deal.

I recalled what the weather forecaster said before the flight. In contrast to the McMurdo weather, he said in the Dry Valleys, "The weather is always better." I asked McMurdo Center how the weather was over the Dry Valleys. The controller said no one was there, so the forecaster couldn't give me an update. I clarified what I wanted to know. I asked if we could descend below six thousand feet. McMurdo Center asked the weather forecasters. In reply, he told us the clouds had descended into the mountain valleys.

The lowest the air traffic controller could allow us to descend was sixteen thousand feet. I let the crew know it was unlikely we would be able to descend any further until the weather cleared. We were about twenty miles from the Dry Valleys, and we were in the clouds. The next indication things were going from bad to worse was when McMurdo Center announced an unforecasted wind event. McMurdo weather was now reporting zero ceiling and zero visibility.

There was that silence again; nothing but the sound of the engines.

I decided we needed to continue flying toward the Dry Valleys to give me time to work out a game plan. Once we arrived, Sipowitz directed the navigation systems along the Dry Valleys. We were still at sixteen thousand feet, well above the valleys and no chance of seeing them. Carlyle made the turn.

Ugo let us know we were running low on fuel. In my mind, panic happens when there are too many options, and you can't choose what to do. We didn't have to worry about that. We had few options. There was a lot of stress but no panic. Actions relieved any potential panic but increased the stress because they limited our options further. The closer we came to our final destination, whether it was going to be the runway or the crash site, the less the potential for panic and the greater the stress.

## Approach to Landing

The winds were coming from Herbie Alley. Herbie was the name given to the wind events coming from the direction of the South Pole. I wanted Carlyle to fly the TACAN, "tactical air navigation system," approach to Ice Runway 33, facing grid north, so that the wind would be in our face. This allowed a slower ground speed, thus more time to react to any unexpected events. Flying slower made it easier to land because it would give me more time to correct minor deviations in the aircraft's direction or altitude.

I told the loadmasters to lay at the pilot's and copilot's feet and look out our kick-windows to help find the runway. There was no backup plan. The alternate runway, Pegasus Airfield, was seven miles south from McMurdo, and it had the same poor weather conditions, but there were no rescue services available there. I requested a further descent. We were now over McMurdo Sound. McMurdo Center cleared us to eight thousand feet. By starting our descent, we increased our fuel burn rate. We were committed to land in the McMurdo area, and that limited our options.

During the descent to eight thousand feet, I briefly took control of the aircraft to give Carlyle time to review and brief the TACAN approach. When he was finished, he took control again. We were cleared to descend to five thousand feet, and eventually, we were cleared to line up for the approach. We ran the appropriate checklists for landing.

I planned to take control of the aircraft and continue to descend on the approach course when Carlyle descended to the minimum allowable altitude on the approach-to-landing, and the aircraft didn't break out of the clouds. It was a violation of procedures, but we didn't have any remaining options available.

The landing gear was down, and the skis were up. We configured the aircraft to land with one-hundred-percent flaps. Most C-130 units flew the approach with fifty-percent flaps selected. The LC-130 aircrews flew instrument approaches with one-hundred-percent flaps selected while in Greenland or Antarctica. Most approaches we flew were very shallow. The idea was if a camp's barometric altimeter setting were wrong, the approach would be slow and shallow enough; no damage would occur if the aircraft impacted the snow unintentionally.

Carlyle intercepted the final approach and began his descent to land. It was then; the air traffic controller told us the winds were favoring an approach to the perpendicular runway. Ice Runway 25 had the advantage of a more precise approach with lower approach minimums.

This was good news. The PAR, precision approach radar, was designed for a radar controller in McMurdo to direct the pilot down the final approach course. Sipowitz would back up the air traffic controller's directions using the aircraft radar to verify the approach's accuracy.

We now had a better chance of getting below the weather and seeing the runway. I told Carlyle to abort the TACAN approach and prepare for the PAR. In turn, Carlyle directed me to bring the flaps from one hundred percent to fifty percent as he climbed back to altitude and banked the aircraft to the right to maneuver for the next approach. We remained with gear and flaps extended.

Sipowitz momentarily lost situational awareness. He said, "Help me out here. Where are we?" He had expected us to fly beyond the runway and make a right turn. This would have put the aircraft on a right downwind. We instead turned before reaching the runway. I replied, "We're on a left downwind." This reset Sipowitz.

He replied, "Okay, I'm back with you."

Everyone was calm. This was our profession, and we were good at it. It hadn't escaped me that if I had decided to return to McMurdo directly from Pole-1, we might have landed by now and missed this unforecasted wind event.

These were fleeting thoughts. There was no time to dwell on the past. There was no future to consider. My only focus was on the moment. My senses were heightened. My awareness was acute. Everyone else was also extremely focused. I've treated every challenge in life as a game. I was locked in a game that could cost my crew their lives. It wasn't fair. It wasn't their fault. But I was ready to play.

We were already configured for the approach, but we reviewed the checklists once again. Carlyle flew the approach, and when he banked the aircraft to align it with the final approach course, he directed me to lower the flaps back to one hundred percent. The flaps extended from the inboard side of both wings. Flaps created an extension of the wing and allowed the aircraft to fly at slower speeds, and the aircraft became a more stable platform at slower speeds.

Most pilots selected a lower flap setting in high crosswind conditions and flew higher speeds for more maneuverability. However, the air traffic controller had told us the winds favored this runway, so I expected a direct headwind. I assumed the crosswinds we were seeing would decrease as we descended on approach, and they would turn into a headwind to allow for a slower touchdown onto the runway.

Carlyle flew a perfect approach. He had eighteen degrees of right drift. The tail of the aircraft, the vertical stabilizer, sat high above the aircraft. When the wind hit the tail, it turned the aircraft on its center axis point like a weathervane. In other words, the aircraft was tracking along the ground in a different direction from where the nose was pointing. In Carlyle's situation, the aircraft was tracking eighteen degrees left from where the nose was pointing. It was much like tacking a sailboat across the water with a strong crosswind. If Carlyle aligned the aircraft with the runway's direction, the wind would blow him off course. It was a very challenging approach, and he flew it flawlessly. His life and everybody's else depended on it.

The loadmasters were still on the aircraft floor, looking for the runway through the kick windows at our feet. They didn't understand the drift and the impact of the wind hitting the aircraft's tail. Therefore, the runway was eighteen degrees left of where they were looking. I had no time to explain it to them.

What happened next, many would consider Divine Providence. Others would call it just plain luck. As for me? I was more anthropomorphic. It was easier for me to understand. I viewed Antarctica as a majestic female. She was cold-hearted, and she was hot-tempered. She caught me when I wasn't expecting it, and she intended to hurt me. She had killed many others in the past. I thought she cut me some slack, but in the end, she was toying with me.

For a brief moment, as we descended on the approach, the visibility cleared. I could see the runway. I took control of the aircraft from Carlyle and directed the loadmasters to get off the floor and go back and strap in. The C-130 aircraft was not designed to land in a crab. In other words, I would damage the aircraft landing gear if I landed the aircraft in an eighteen-degree side slip. So, I put in my crosswind controls. I stepped on the left rudder pedal. The rudder is a flap attached to the back of the vertical stabilizer, the aircraft's tail. By stepping on the rudder pedal, I aligned the aircraft with the runway. Now I had to stop the aircraft from drifting off course.

I turned the yoke of the aircraft to the right. This caused the left aileron, a flap on the aircraft's outer wing, to lower below the wing and into the airstream, pitching the left wing up. It also caused the right aileron to rise into the airstream, pitching the right wing down. Turning the yoke to the right typically caused the aircraft to turn to the right; however, I was stepping on the left rudder pedal. I had manipulated the aircraft's control surfaces to lower the right wing and track straight down the runway's centerline. These flight control inputs were considered uncoordinated flight conditions. It was uncomfortable. Flying at altitude, the aircraft was allowed to crab into the wind. But upon landing, the crosswind controls were necessary to prevent the pilot from damaging the aircraft.

There was no maximum bank angle restriction for one hundred percent flaps written in the books; however, the fifty percent limit was forty-five degrees of bank or less. I assumed it was the same. I kept my focus outside the aircraft, momentarily glancing inside at my airspeed. I had the runway in sight, and I was going to keep it in sight.

Lt. Col. Ron Smith, the deployed commander, told me afterward we had a forty-knot quartering tailwind. This explained the eighteen degrees of drift. It also explained why the aircraft's warning system barked, "Bank Angle" when I put the crosswind controls in. This meant I had too much bank angle, probably exceeding forty-five degrees of bank for the aircraft's configuration, but I wasn't looking. I was aligned with the runway, and I didn't care about the barking. When the aircraft barked, Carlyle said, "Holy Shit!" I was focused on what I was doing and absentmindedly reprimanded him, "Don't say that." In his defense, it truly was a holy shit moment.

## The Dance

As I was about to pitch the nose up slightly to start the landing process, the wind died briefly, and I could land straight ahead without any crosswind controls. I lowered the aircraft gently on the icy runway. We were down, but Antarctica wasn't finished. Upon landing, I pulled the throttles to flight idle. There's a stop in the C-130 throttle quadrant called the flight idle stop. It prevented pilots from unintentionally pulling the throttles too far back into the ground range. The flight idle stop kept the pitch of the blades on the propellers at twenty-three degrees. The throttles needed to be lifted over the flight idle gate and pulled back further to move the propellers into the ground range. Ground idle was eighteen degrees of blade pitch.

I gave Carlyle control of the yoke in flight idle. This allowed me to move my left hand to the nosewheel steering to monitor the nosewheel. I lightly rested my hand there to feel what the aircraft's nosewheel was doing as I raised the throttles over the flight idle gate and brought them into the ground idle momentarily, then further into reverse, and I applied the brakes.

The aircraft began to slide to the right. It drifted off the centerline of the ice runway. I've heard people talk about how time slows down when they're under a great deal of pressure. It certainly slowed down for me. One at a time, I considered options and tried them. The rudder was still effective at higher speeds, so first, I stepped on the left rudder to correct back to the centerline, but it had no effect. Next, I relieved pressure on the right brake and kept the pressure on the left brake. It still had no effect. I tried manipulating the nosewheel, but it did not affect our course on the icy runway.

There was only one remaining option. It seemed like seconds passed, but it could only have been a moment, or the aircraft would have been off the runway. I began to manipulate the throttles. I left the throttles for #1 and #2 engines on the left wing in reverse and brought #3 and #4 throttles back to the ground idle position. This differential power provided more forward power to the right side than the left. But it didn't have any effect.

I pushed #3 and #4 engines over the flight idle gate into the flight idle position. The aircraft began to correct back to the centerline, but it wasn't enough. I was running out of room.

I pushed #3 and #4 throttles forward to about 10,000 inch-pounds of torque. The aircraft turned, and I was able to make the necessary correction back to the centerline. I couldn't leave the throttles that way. I didn't want to go off the runway's left side any more than I wanted to go off the right side of the runway. When I got back to the centerline, I brought all of the throttles to the ground idle position again, and for a moment, I thought I was in the clear. I needed to stop, so I brought the throttles back to reverse, but the aircraft began to turn and drift right again. I knew how to handle it now.

I heard Sipowitz in the background coaching me, "You got it. You can do it. Come on. You got it." He sounded like my father, running behind me when he taught me to ride a bicycle.

I had quickly drifted further right, so I made a more aggressive correction than the first time. We passed the maintenance tower as we traveled down the runway. The visibility was low, so the tower's maintenance people were convinced we were spinning in 360-degree turns. The ramp and door of the aircraft struck one of the runway flags on the right side of the runway and knocked it over.

By the time I corrected to centerline the second time, I was well past halfway down the runway. I need to add power each time I made a correction to maintain the centerline. When the aircraft began going right the third time, I knew I was out of room. The end of the runway was come up fast. I estimated I had about one thousand feet remaining and had seconds to stop the aircraft. I wouldn't be able to correct back a third time to centerline and stop the aircraft before going off the end.

I had no time to brief the crew about what I was going to do next. I pulled the throttles into reverse once again, and instead of correcting the turn, I stepped on the right rudder and the right brake to increase the turn rate. I hoped to spin the aircraft around without going off the side of the runway and before I went off the end of the runway. It had an immediate effect.

The aircraft spun to the right. When the aircraft's nose spun 180 degrees, I released the right brake and rudder pedal and stepped on the left rudder pedal to stop the turn. Now the nose of the aircraft was pointing in the opposite direction. We were still moving down the runway, but now we were moving backward, so I added power with the throttles to stop the backward momentum. It worked. When I began to move forward again, I brought the throttles back to the ground idle position and taxied at a crawling pace. Snowdog was sitting on the bunk of the flight deck. He witnessed the whole event, and when it was over, he said, "That was great, sir! I'll fly with you any day." He had a good time. A typical Marine.

I was already questioning what I would do next. I never considered stopping and leaving the aircraft where it was. I taxied the aircraft toward the parking ramp, but I knew it was as slick as the runway. With the high winds, it would be a mistake to park next to the other aircraft on the icy ramp. I thought about my options. The crew was quiet, perhaps in shock. As I taxied, the aircraft wanted to pitch to the right. Something in the back of my mind wanted to address it, but I decided to wait until we parked. I attributed it to the wind, but I knew something wasn't right. It could wait until later; I had everything under control.

## Engine Shutdown

Before I reached the parking ramp, I stopped the aircraft on the runway. I decided to park in the snow off the runway's right side before reaching the parking ramp. I directed Carlyle to lower the skis. I briefed the crew on my intentions, then added power and made a right turn into the snow. I knew I didn't want to shut down the engines with the wind blowing up the tailpipe. The snow would compact inside the turbine and make it very difficult for maintenance to clear it out.

I wanted to turn left 180 degrees and point the nose of the aircraft into the wind. I chose the left because I was in the pilot seat, and I wanted to see where I was going. The wind was causing the aircraft to accelerate. As I prepared my left turn, I brought the throttles into reverse to slow my speed. The aircraft pitched right, so I turned right instead. I didn't think about why this occurred, but I was about to stop, and then I'd have more time to think about it.

I stopped the aircraft where it would stay for the night. The wind was howling, and the visibility was still very low. I paused for a few moments. It was quiet except for the sound of the engines. I took a deep breath, then asked for the engine shutdown checklist. Carlyle pulled the condition levers for all four engines to the ground stop position. This cut off fuel to the engines mechanically and electrically. The fuel flow gages should have dropped to zero; however, the #1 engine fuel flow indication didn't drop. I thought it was a broken gauge. Then, I looked at the RPM gauge. It was still reading one hundred percent. Looking out the window at the left wing, I said, "The #1 prop is still spinning. Feather the #1 engine." It was always a good idea to be very specific, giving instruction in the aircraft.

With confirmation from Ugo, Carlyle pulled the #1 condition lever all the way aft to the feather position. Feathering hydraulically aligned the propeller blades into the airstream and mechanically cut off fuel to the engine. It didn't work. The blades didn't move, and the propeller was still turning. I turned to look at Ugo, and he confirmed I had my hand on the #1 fire handle. The fire handle shut off fuel to the engine electrically through a different set of circuits from the condition lever. I pulled the fire handle, and the engine finally shut down.

Two days later, an engine shop mechanic showed me pictures of what he found in the #1 engine. The C-130 was designed in the late 1940s and early 1950s. The throttles and condition levers were connected to the engine through cables and pulleys. The #1 throttle cable or the #1 condition lever cable had slipped off its coordinator, a pulley system, and intertwined with the other cable. Both cables were stuck between the engine and the coordinator and couldn't move.

After we shut down the engines, Carlyle called the maintenance tower to get someone out to the aircraft and pick us up. A maintenance van arrived a few minutes later. They were convinced we had spun out of control, off the side of the runway. We couldn't convince them otherwise. The van driver said he almost hit the aircraft because the visibility was so poor. They were happy we were alright, and the aircraft was upright.

We caught a shuttle van to Mac Town. I went up to the second floor of Building 165 and debriefed the deployed commander and flying supervisor. They thought we had spun out of control, off of the side of the runway, also. We were on the schedule to fly back to the South Pole again the next day.

The people at the Pole were apologetic. I never confirmed it, but I was told Carlyle had called them and wanted compensation for their mistake. When we arrived, each of my crewmembers received a lunch with two lobster tails on a paper plate. How bizarre? Lobster tails at the South Pole.

I decided to get airborne before eating our meal. The South Pole is at a 9,300-foot field elevation. The takeoff was uneventful, but as we climbed, Ugo couldn't control the aircraft's pressurization. Something was wrong. The aircraft's cabin pressure exceeded 10,000 feet, so I directed everyone to put on their oxygen masks to protect against hypoxia.

One of the loadmasters notified Ugo he could see the safety valve was stuck open. This was why the aircraft wouldn't pressurize. We were wearing oxygen masks up to our level off altitude. I connected the autopilot while we worked on the problem. We wore oxygen masks on our faces with lobster tails on our lap. Antarctica was still wrathful.

CHAPTER 22

# THE NEED FOR AIRDROP

Many of the legendary Raven Gang pilots had retired or were within a few years of doing so when the squadron took over the Operation Deep Freeze mission. Twelve full-time aircrews were being hired and trained, and the focus was ski mission training. The Raven Gang needed to focus on building a competent ski mission squadron to support Operation Deep Freeze's mission.

But following the AGO-5 (automatic geophysical observatory) mission, they needed to adjust their training. Prior to this mission, only ten percent of the aircrews were combat airdrop qualified. After AGO-5, they recognized they needed more airdrop aircrews, but they didn't have training hours to keep everyone qualified. So, they modified their airdrop program.

The Raven Gang took specific combat airdrop requirements and adopted them for the Antarctic mission. Combat requirements they didn't need were eliminated. What remained was a descent from cruising altitude to the airdrop altitude before arriving at an initial point. At the initial point, they started a straight-ahead run to the airdrop sequence. The airdrop was limited to container delivery bundles.

This was a very basic airdrop requirement intended to airdrop fuel barrels. It could be used as a fuel cache for other aircraft, Twin Otters, and helicopters, or it could be used in case of an emergency fuel supply for other LC-130 aircraft. This was the birth of the polar airdrop program. There were unique features and challenges to flying airdrop missions on the ice cap. Both the arid climate and the cold temperature increased the aircraft engine performance, aerodynamic lift, and drag.

Antarctica, although snow-covered, is a desert. Decreased moisture in the air increased air density. A molecule of water weighs less than a molecule of nitrogen in the atmosphere. In a desert where air, nitrogen molecules, replaced water molecules in the atmosphere, the air pressure increased and increased engine performance.

Cold temperature also increased air density. The average temperature for a flight over the ice cap was -30 degrees Fahrenheit. The atmosphere is not an enclosed system. The greater movement of molecules in warmer temperatures tends to spread the molecules further apart, decreasing the molecules' density and decreasing engine performance.

As the aircraft climbed, the atmosphere became thinner, with fewer molecules in the air. This less dense air reduced engine horsepower, aerodynamic lift, and drag. The Antarctica ice cap exceeded 10,000 feet above sea level. An airdrop 1,000 feet above the snow meant the aircraft was flying at a minimum of 11,000 feet above sea level.

Due to the high elevation, the engines could not attain maximum power of 19,600 inch-pounds of torque. It became possible to push the throttles further forward to the maximum range of the throttle quadrant's mechanical stop to achieve more torque; however, the increased propeller blade angles reduced engine performance. Increasing blade angle decreased the effectiveness of the propeller. It increased drag and reduced acceleration.

The less dense air meant the aircrew would breathe less oxygen when the cargo door opened for the airdrop, so they needed to wear their oxygen masks. This was especially challenging for the loadmasters because they needed to move around in the back of the aircraft and have an oxygen source whenever the aircraft's ramp and door were open.

Although the cold and dry climate were positive features to flying airdrops on Antarctica's ice cap, the altitude presented an overall negative challenge. The final question of airdrops on the ice cap was no one understood how the inflation of the parachutes would be impacted by the thinner air.

The biggest lesson of the AGO-5 mission was everyone had to be mentally prepared to spend the night where they landed if the aircraft broke or the snow conditions didn't allow the aircraft to get airborne. Before flying, they needed to pack a personal bag with necessities they would need on the ice cap for as long as it took to get rescued. Failure to do so affected the rest of the crew.

# AGO-5

The National Science Foundation was rebuilding the Amundsen-Scott Station. It was a huge $265 million undertaking that required an immense amount of airlift. There were weeks when the only destination for the Raven Gang aircrews was the South Pole. It wasn't a surprise that after weeks of the monotony of doing the same mission day after day, Lt. Col. Charlotte Kenney's aircrew jumped at the opportunity to do something else. Chief Master Sergeant Mike Pingitore noted more than twenty years later, "We all jumped at the challenge versus just another fuel run to the Pole."

On 7 December 1998, Pingitore was a new loadmaster in the Raven Gang. Prior to coming to the squadron, he was a forward arming and refueling point team member at Charleston Air Force Base. His specialized training would prove useful in the day ahead.

| Skier 91 Aircrew | |
|---|---|
| **Pilot:** | Lt. Col. Charlotte Kenney |
| **Copilot:** | Major Gary James |
| **Navigator:** | Lt. Col. Ed "Gator" Gadarowski |
| **Flight Engineer:** | Master Sergeant Carl "Bogie" Bogart |
| **Loadmaster:** | Staff Sergeant Dave Vesper |
| **Loadmaster:** | Staff Sergeant Mike Pingitore |

Kenney and her aircrew were destined for AGO-5. She was the aircraft commander of Skier 91. Her mission was to drop off 5,995 pounds of cargo, two pallets of propane bottles, to refuel the AGO site. There was a pallet of empty propane bottles to pick up at AGO-5 and return to McMurdo.

Major Gary James was her copilot. James was still attached to active duty as the 109$^{th}$ Airlift Wing Active Duty Advisor. He had been flying C-130s for many years before coming to the Guard. He was trained and qualified in the ski mission during the previous Greenland Season. But this was his first season in Antarctica.

Lt. Col. Ed "Gator" Gadarowski was a former KC-135 navigator. He was a tall skinny redhead with a big smile. He worked at his local post office and flew for the Raven Gang part-time. He was very experienced and would be very helpful in the days ahead.

Master Sergeant Carl "Bogie" Bogart was Skier 91's flight engineer. He had been in the military for a long time and was approaching his 60th birthday. Bogie was the aircraft's systems expert and knew his job well, although he was new to the ski mission.

Staff Sergeant Michael Pingitore and Staff Sergeant Dave Vesper were the loadmasters in the back of the aircraft. Both of them were new to the ski mission but were very competent. Vesper's career started in the Mansfield, Ohio Air National Guard, working in the aerial port. He joined the Reserve Forces in Youngstown, Ohio, as a loadmaster, then came to the Raven Gang for a full-time job.

AGO-5 was one of six automatic geophysical observatory sites on the Antarctica ice cap. Servicing these sites was one of the technical projects the National Science Foundation had lined up for the 1998–1999 Antarctica Season. In his award abstract for the National Science Foundation, the primary researcher from the University of Maryland at College Park stated the purpose of the AGO sites as follows:[144]

> *"The data obtained from AGOs help researchers understand the Sun's influence on the structure and dynamics of the Earth's upper atmosphere. The ultimate objective of this research into how the solar wind couples with the Earth's magnetosphere, ionosphere, and the thermosphere is to be able to predict solar-terrestrial interactions that can interfere with long-distance phone lines, power grids, and satellite communications (AO-112-O)."*

The primary person responsible for the servicing of the AGO sites stated, *"Team members will refuel, repair, modify, upgrade the AGO and science systems and download previous season's data."*[145] AGO-5 was one of the more challenging of the AGO sites. It was located at 77.25º South, 123.50º East. The field elevation exceeded 10,000 feet. There was a skiway of sorts groomed with snowmobiles. The Raven Gang had a system to check out old skiways before sending one of their aircraft to a specific location. Before the first mission to any location, they sent one of their people via Twin Otter to see if the skiway was serviceable. The program was called the ski landing area control officer, SLACO, and it required specific training.

Lt. Col. Bob Sittinger was a SLACO. Earlier in the season, he had gone to AGO-5 skiway and found it completely unusable. It was full of huge amounts of drifting snow and massive sastrugi that were icy and hard. Hitting sastrugi felt like hitting pothole after pothole at high speed. He was convinced anyone who used it would break the aircraft nose ski.

Snowmobiles could not supply the proper grooming, which was usually done by a bulldozer on tracks, pulling a heavy metal beam behind it. However, in most cases, snowmobile grooming was considered better than no grooming at all. In the case of AGO-5, Sittinger highly recommended pilots land in the open snow instead of the skiway, which the snowmobiles had groomed.

The Lockheed C-130 technical manual recommended limiting the landing weight on unimproved airfields to 118,000 pounds. The aircraft technical manual wasn't written for the ski mission; it was written for the combat mission. However, it wasn't a far stretch to see the similarities of landing in a sastrugi-laden area to landing on a bomb-cratered runway. Therefore, when the Raven Gang wrote their supplemental technical manual, they added specific ski mission landing weights that complimented the combat mission. They used the 118,000-pound weight limitation for LC-130 open snow landings.

After the first landings and subsequent ones at any location, the aircrews were expected to evaluate the surface conditions and increase the landing weight for future operations if appropriate. Landings and takeoffs in an open snowfield had significant risks. Exceedingly high-stress factors on the aircraft, as it plowed through the snow, could cause damage to any portion of the aircraft. There was never a guarantee the open snow would be free of sastrugi, but Kenney knew the AGO-5's skiway was a problem. She knew she needed to land, then take off, in a giant open snowfield known as the Antarctica ice cap.

## The Morning of the Mission

Bogie, Pingitore, and Vesper went to Derelict Junction and caught a ride to the aircraft in the morning. Kenney, James, and Gadarowski went to Building 165 to plan for the mission ahead. The Raven Gang's "Blue Book," their Antarctica guide, had data for much of the mission's flight planning.

AGO-5 was 555 miles from McMurdo. The flight time would be two hours. To land at 118,000 pounds, the minimum fuel required to fly to AGO-5, complete the offload and on-load of cargo, and return to McMurdo was 30,300 pounds. According to the Blue Book, the maximum cargo weight they could carry was 6,100 pounds. The two pallets of propane and the three passengers with their baggage weighed 5,995 pounds. The cargo load was within the limitations of the flight.

If they were delayed on the snow at AGO-5, Kenney had a backup plan. She could go to the South Pole or Vostok to refuel on their return flight. The South Pole was never a serious consideration unless the weather was a factor at McMurdo. The distance from AGO-5 to McMurdo was 555 nautical miles, and the distance from AGO-5 to the South Pole was 540 miles. The fifteen-mile difference was insignificant. Vostok was the only other option if they didn't have enough fuel to get back to McMurdo. It was a Russian camp 275 miles or about an hour away.

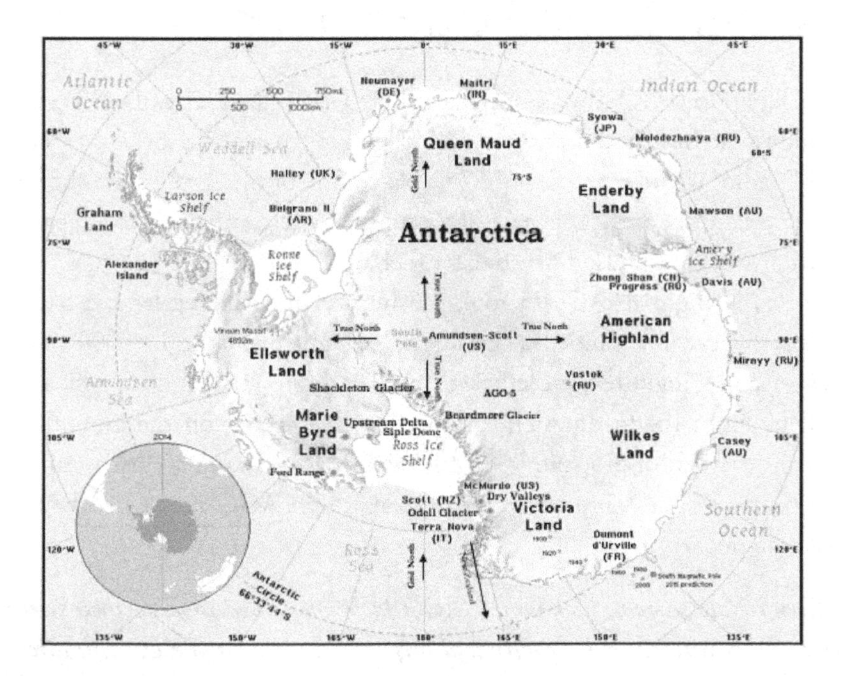


*Antarctica Map (approximate locations)*

The weather was good, and the mission was straightforward. Everything checked out. They left Building 165. Kenney, James, and Gator walked down the dirt road to Derelict Junction to catch a ride to the ice runway. When they arrived at the aircraft, Bogie had the aircraft pre-flighted, and Pingitore and Vesper had the propane bottles loaded in the back of the aircraft. The aircrew got in their seats, started engines, and taxied to the fuel pits to on-load fuel. After fueling, they started the engines again and taxied to the ATO bottles loading area.

At 10:10 a.m., Kenney and the rest of her aircrew departed McMurdo. Skier 91 was in good shape, but it had a history of taking much longer slides to get airborne. The aircraft's nickname was Skier 9-1-1. Later in the Antarctica Season, maintenance personnel would find the skis were not aligned precisely. This would be a factor later in the day.

## AGO-5 Ground Operations

The flight to AGO-5 was unremarkable. Upon their arrival, Gary James couldn't establish radio contact with the camp personnel on either HF or VHF radio. Kenney overflew the camp a couple of times to ensure she could select a landing area. This gave the people at the camp time to prepare for their arrival. But it also burned extra fuel.

The flight to AGO-5 took 2.6 hours, and Kenney landed Skier 91 at 12:45 p.m. She landed at an aircraft weight of about 115,000 pounds. Vesper and Pingitore were efficient, and it didn't take long to offload the pallets. From the loadmasters' perspective, everything on the ground went fine. The pallets of propane were offloaded. It took about twenty minutes for the people at AGO-5 to attach the propane to the AGO site before they were ready to depart.

*Author's Note: A man nicknamed "AGO Jack" was hired to go to these sites via Twin Otter aircraft or helicopter and prepare each site for the LC-130 aircraft's arrival. Once the propane was offloaded from the aircraft, he connected the propane to the AGO equipment. AGO Jack spent too much time alone. When he returned to McMurdo, he said he had been communicating with the Martians, and they were coming to McMurdo to pick him up and take him with them. He even specified a date and time. Jack was severely disappointed when the Martians failed to come. Almost everyone stopped work in McMurdo to see the spacecraft. They were disappointed too. Jack had to be escorted back to Christchurch, New Zealand, for evaluation. While in Christchurch AGO Jack disappeared. Some people claim the Martians took him.*

When the loadmasters were finished in the back of the aircraft, Bogie put the ignitors in the ATO bottles and armed the system. Everyone got back in their seats, and Kenney briefed how she was going to conduct the takeoff. She lined the aircraft up at the same location she had landed shortly before. She pushed the throttles forward and told James to adjust the throttles to maximum power while keeping her focus outside to keep the aircraft accelerating in a straight line.

The snow was soft. The aircraft didn't accelerate. With maximum power set, the aircraft speed would not exceed forty knots. After a couple of attempts, Kenney pulled into the parking location. There was an empty pallet in the back of the aircraft. It was in the #5 pallet position, which provided an aft center-of-gravity for Kenney. This was a positive. To increase the aft center-of-gravity further, Pingitore and Vesper moved the passengers onto the ramp of the aircraft and strapped them to the floor.

Again, Kenney taxied into the open snow and tried again. With each attempt, the aircraft gained a few more knots of speed, but it also reduced the amount of fuel available to get to their destination. They hit "bingo" for Camp Vostok after about nine slides. Kenney decided to try one more attempt, and on her tenth slide, she decided to blow the ATO bottles. As the aircraft accelerated, she called: "ATO—now!"

Bogie fired the bottles. They ignited. From the paratroop doors on either side of the aircraft, the passengers could see the smoke and flames shoot out of the bottles and hear the rockets' loud noise. Kenney pulled the nose off of the snow. The aircraft accelerated to sixty-eight knots, but she couldn't keep the nose off the ground. When the nose lowered back in the snow, the acceleration slowed. They were stuck. Everyone had a sinking feeling in their stomachs. They weren't going back to McMurdo. They needed to survive on the ice cap until a rescue could be generated.

James recalled twenty years later, going through their options:

> *"I remember as we tried to take off, we hit bingos for McMurdo, then South Pole, then Vostok. Then on our last attempt, before we had no gas to go anywhere, Charlotte blew ATO, and we were done. We blew ATO at fifty-six knots, and when the rocket noise stopped, and we were still on the ground, let's just say I'll never forget that particular feeling of helplessness."*

Kenney was exhausted but still thinking of options to improve their condition. She knew they would be spending the night at AGO-5, so she parked the aircraft with the flight deck pointing into the sun, the polar south. The radiant sunlight shining through the aircraft's windscreen kept them warm through the night and the following day. Antarctica, at this time of year, had twenty-four hours of sunlight.

Nothing was going to happen until the following morning, so the crew assessed their situation. Some of them were concerned about Bogie because of his age, coupled with their elevation. Their concerns were warrantless. He proved to be one of the workhorses over the next couple of days.

## Planning the Rescue

James got on the HF radio and called Mac Ops, McMurdo Operations. He asked to talk to Lt. Col. Verle Johnston, the deployed commander. Mac Ops was located across the hall from Raven Ops in Building 165. James gave Johnston an update of their status and let him know everyone was safe. They talked about a rescue mission. They considered their options. Skier 91 couldn't be left on the ice cap, and obviously, the aircrew couldn't be left there either. The only available answers were an aircraft-to-aircraft remote fueling or an airdrop of bundles containing fifty-five-gallon barrels of fuel.

The aircraft-to-aircraft remote fueling procedure was unique to the LC-130. This was where two aircraft were placed next to each other and offload fuel from one aircraft to the other. However, there were two big problems doing this. First, landing another aircraft at AGO-5 risked leaving two aircraft there. If one aircraft couldn't get airborne, the other one may not have any greater success. The other problem was the aircraft weight limitation for landing at AGO-5. The 118,000-pound aircraft weight limitation on landing posed a problem. Offloading a significant amount of fuel to another aircraft would not leave either aircraft enough fuel for a direct flight back to McMurdo. Both aircraft would need a fuel stop at Vostok.

An airdrop of fuel barrels seemed less risky. The airdrop could deliver the fuel without risking another aircraft on the snow. The problem with this plan was Johnston didn't have an airdrop-qualified aircrew. Only ten percent of the Raven Gang were airdrop qualified. There was never any reason for more. The National Science Foundation determined when airdrops were scheduled throughout the season, and the Raven Gang provided an airdrop aircrew on the weeks when they were scheduled. No one anticipated a scenario like this one.

Johnston told James to expect an airdrop as soon as it could be arranged. He asked James how much fuel hose they would need. Frustrated and tired, James responded, "I don't know, but you have airplanes there. You tell me." Johnston replied, "Good point. We can do that." Communications continued with Skier 91 throughout the day. Johnston reminded Kenney that Pingitore was previously a fuels specialist in the active duty and may be of assistance after the airdrop.

After spending a night at AGO-5, in extremely low temperatures and the high altitude, Johnston knew he couldn't allow Kenney's aircrew to fly the aircraft back to McMurdo. He didn't know what shape they'd be in, but he knew their capabilities would be diminished. Kenney suggested the replacement aircrew should take advantage of the cooler evening hours.

Lt. Col. Bob Sittinger was still in town. He was acting as a safety representative for a previous aircraft mishap. Skier 95 was in a crevasse at Upstream Delta.

Johnston asked him, "Did you bring your flight gear with you?" Sittinger replied, "Yes, I did. I always bring it down here." Johnston then asked him if he would fly to AGO-5 to recover the aircraft. Sittinger replied, "Yes, if I get to pick my own crew." Johnston was reluctant. Then he told Sittinger, "I'm only sending three of you. Can you bring the plane back with just three?" Sittinger was confident he could. Gator, Kenney's navigator, could load up the navigation systems' flight plan, and Sittinger knew how to

port guys, he moved the parachutes to the bundles, lifted them on top of the bundles, and rigged them for the airdrop.

McGuigan found a manual gurney pump that could empty the fuel from the barrels to the aircraft, but he didn't like it. A gurney pump would require a significant amount of labor to continuously hand-crank it, and someone needed to be on the wing of the aircraft to put the fuel nozzle in the aircraft fuel tanks. It was risky for someone to climb on top of the wing. Aside from the height of the wing above the snow and the danger of falling off it, the altitude was higher than 10,000 feet, and it was very cold. Both of these circumstances would decrease the aircrew's performance and judgment.

McGuigan talked to the fuel specialists on the ice runway parking ramp to see if there was a gas-powered pump available. They had a Briggs and Stratton pump, and they assured McGuigan it would work at high altitude. They gave him additional fuel jets designed for different altitudes to run the pump. The most significant benefit of the gas-powered pump was it could be hooked up directly to the aircraft's single-point refueling panel on the backside of the aircraft. As an aid to the aircrew, they wrote down instructions on the system set-up and gave them to McGuigan.

The pump and the instructions were put in the 14$^{th}$ bundle. The weight of each airdrop bundle needed to be a minimum of five hundred pounds for it to depart the aircraft successfully, so McGuigan continued to search for other items to help the aircrew at AGO-5. Any personal items the aircrew requested were put in the bundle. Lengths of fuel hose were added, but it still didn't add enough weight. In the end, McGuigan found scraps of lumber to put in it. He ended up with a seven hundred fifty pound airdrop bundle. The total weight of all fourteen bundles was 22,655 pounds, which included the weight of the parachutes.

When McGuigan was finished building and rigging the parachutes on the bundles, he had them transported to the airfield ramp. He loaded them in the aircraft and rigged the bundles to the aircraft. Whenever airdrop bundles were rigged in an aircraft, there needed to be an independent joint inspection done. There was no one in McMurdo to complete the joint inspection, so McGuigan did his own. It wasn't legal, but these were desperate times.

# Airdrop

At AGO-5, James, Gator, and Pingitore set up a drop zone and a target using the skiway flagging material, two hundred yards off the left wing of Skier 91. As the airdrop aircraft approached, Gator found gyro jet flares from the survival equipment in the aircraft. He shot one in the air as the aircraft neared their location. He also opened a smoke canister to give Captain Kimberly Dingman, Kozic's navigator, a visual expectation of the ground winds where they wanted her to drop the bundles.

| Airdrop Aircrew | |
|---|---|
| **Pilot:** | Lt. Col. Gerard Kozic |
| **Copilot:** | Captain Dave Panzera |
| **Navigator:** | Captain Kim Dingman |
| **Flight Engineer:** | Master Sergeant Shad Gray |
| **Loadmaster:** | Master Sergeant Kurt Garrison |
| **Loadmaster:** | Staff Sergeant Brian Wieser |

Perhaps the biggest concern Kozic had was he knew he wasn't qualified to do what he was doing. All of his aircrew members had been qualified in the past, but their qualifications had expired. He was concerned about hitting the aircraft with the airdrop bundles. He could ensure he flew well clear of the aircraft below, but once the bundles left the aircraft, he had no more control of them.

The winds were blowing at ten knots. Not a big deal. They considered the possibility that the high altitude could affect the bundles as they left the aircraft and blow them toward the aircraft below. It was also possible the parachutes could be affected by the altitude and open late. If so, it would bury the fuel barrels deep in the snow.

They talked things over and decided to drop just the care-package bundle first to see if the parachutes would open at the higher altitude. On the next pass, Garrison released it out the back. The parachute functioned just fine, so on their final pass, Kozic's aircrew ran the appropriate airdrop checklists and dropped the remaining bundles from the aircraft.

The sudden shift of the center-of-gravity in the aircraft, as 22,000 pounds of fuel barrels slid out of the back, surprised Kozic. The nose of the aircraft pitched up. To counteract it, Kozic needed to push the yoke forward, which moved the elevator on the horizontal stabilizers, the flaps on the tail of the aircraft, downward. The wind hit the elevator and helped alleviate the pitching-up movement. Afterward, Gray said, "He was pushing on the yoke like a son-of-a-gun."

After the bundles left the aircraft, things settled down. Kozic relaxed forward pressure on the yoke.

Kenney's aircrew watched as the bundles exited the aircraft. It was a welcome sight. Two of the parachutes failed to open. One bundle was a streamer, and the only thing showing after impact was the parachute above the snow. Pingitore thought it resembled a carrot top on the surface. They were able to recover the fuel barrels from this bundle. The other parachute failed to open at all. The bundle was buried deep in the snow and went deep into the ice cap. The smell of fuel rose from the hole it made. The barrels broke open from the impact, and they were unrecoverable.

The bundles landed further from the aircraft than James and Gator expected. They ended up about four hundred yards from the Skier 91. Digging the bundles out of the snow was a lot of work. The AGO passengers helped. They had as much incentive as the aircrew to get out of AGO-5. They dug each bundle out of the snow with shovels and attached 5,000-pound tie-down straps from the back of the aircraft. There were snowmobiles from the AGO site. One by one, the barrels were strapped to the snowmobiles and delivered to Bogie at the aircraft.

McGuigan had delivered. While working through the airdrop rigging process, he had thought through all of the Skier 91 aircrew challenges after the fuel was delivered. The fueling system arrived intact. It contained the Briggs and Stratton pump with a filter, an inch-and-a-half wide hose attached to two donkey nozzles. It also came with a single-point attachment for Bogie to connect to the aircraft. Pingitore was given the hand-written instructions to put the system together.

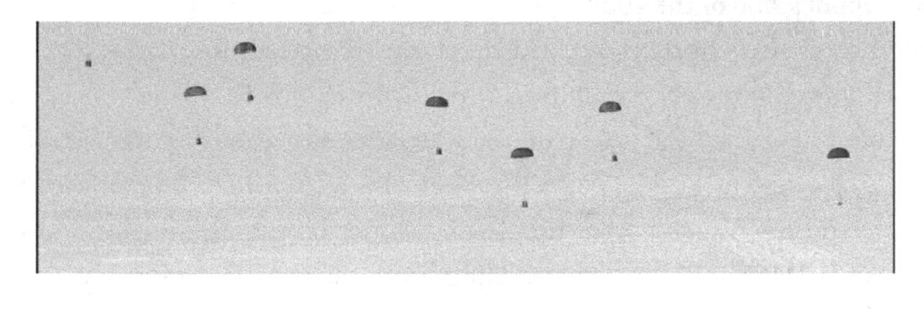

*Airdrop*

# Refueling the Aircraft

The temperature was -38 degrees Fahrenheit, and there was a ten-knot wind blowing. The wind brought the wind chill temperatures even lower. Each aircrew member was required to carry cold-weather gear. They were bundled up with everything they had. It helped a little. Beyond twenty-below zero, the cold weather gear just made things less cold. The wind was biting.

Throughout the day, everybody had a job to do, but frequently they replaced one another to give each other a break. As they rested on the flight deck, they watched the shadows go around the aircraft with the sun's movement. The back of the aircraft remained cold, but the flight deck stayed warm. When the fueling system was assembled, it was time to start fueling the aircraft. Pingitore tried to start the pump. It didn't work. He tried again to no avail. Vesper gave it several tries also. They weren't going anywhere if they didn't get the pump running. Pingitore looked around the aircraft to find anything that could help. He spotted a can of ether by the toolbox in the front of the cargo compartment. There was no reason why it was there. The only possibility was the AGO guys put it there. Pingitore thought it was a miracle. He took the can and shot some ether in the carburetor, and the pump started.

Kenney manipulated the switches of the fuel panel on the flight deck to ensure a fuel imbalance didn't occur in either wing. Vesper was in front of the aircraft to act as a safety observer. As they arrived at the aircraft via snowmobile, James and Gator dropped the barrels off behind the wing, on the copilot's side of the aircraft, next to the single point refueling panel. They stood the barrels upright, opened them, and Pingitore inserted the donkey nozzles, one nozzle per barrel. Bogie attached the inch-and-a-half hose to the aircraft. He opened the nozzle on the hose and started fueling the aircraft.

The system worked perfectly. As one barrel emptied, Bogie closed that nozzle and opened the other nozzle in another barrel. The fueling was continuous. Usually, a three-inch refueling hose was used to service the aircraft. A fuel truck on the parking ramp in New York could deliver five thousand gallons of fuel in about fifteen minutes. These guys weren't so fortunate. They needed to on-load three thousand gallons of fuel, and they were using a lawnmower-type engine with an inch-and-a-half hose hooked up to two fifty-five-gallon drums. Not the same speed or volume, but the alternative was to use a manual gurney pump, which would have taken a great deal more time.

It was grueling work. They often needed to take time to suck on the oxygen hose in the back of the aircraft to prevent hypoxia. From start to finish, the fueling process took about thirteen hours to get all of the fuel in the aircraft tanks while at the same time burning fuel as the APU continued to run. Occasionally the filter of the Briggs and Stratton motor would freeze up and shut down the pump, and Bogie would grab the ether can and spray the carburetor to clear it, then started it again.

## Kenney's Aircrew Returns

Johnston had managed to get fuel to Skier 91 without any incidents. If he had followed the rule books scrupulously, he would still be at square one. He made every effort to manage the risk for as many people as possible, but he understood the law of averages. If he kept adding risks, someone would eventually get hurt.

Sittinger, Sander, and Ardrey ate an early dinner at the dining hall. Shortly after 4:00 p.m., they walked the dirt road from the dining hall to Derelict Junction and caught a shuttle to the flight line. They boarded a cargo-modified Twin Otter aircraft, and Sittinger reviewed the cargo on board.

He brought along another eight ATO bottles and the ignitors and several fifty-five-gallon barrels of fuel. He knew the fuel situation was still very tight. Only twelve airdrop bundles of fuel were delivered to AGO-5 successfully. One bundle McGuigan dedicated to the gas-powered fuel pump and a care package, and another was buried deep in the ice cap when the parachute failed. He needed the extra fuel if he was going to fly Skier 91 directly back to McMurdo without refueling at Vostok.

He still hadn't decided what he was going to do when he got to AGO-5. He would take stock of the situation when he arrived, and the circumstances would dictate what to do next. He had plenty of time to think things over. It was a three-hour flight via Twin Otter, and it was uncomfortable. It was the coldest flight Ardrey had ever been on. The aircraft was unpressurized, and the pilots needed to fly at an altitude of 13,000 feet to clear the terrain. Sander's stomach was feeling a bit unsettled from the very beginning of the flight due to the fuel barrels' fumes. Also, he was feeling a little light-headed due to the altitude.

It was about 7:00 p.m. when the Twin Otter arrived at AGO-5. Earlier in the day, there was a lot of discussion about the high-altitude sickness drug called Diamox. The McMurdo flight doctor had recommended it. He was worried about three potential illnesses: acute mountain sickness, high-altitude pulmonary edema, and high-altitude cerebral edema. All three were deadly, but the Diamox could help with the first two.

During this same period, the military was pushing their members to get anthrax shots. There were protests nationwide and hearings in Congress. Now Johnston was pushing Kenney's aircrew to take the Diamox pills, another drug no one knew anything about. Several of Kenney's aircrew were apprehensive and Kenney, herself, was not fully on board.

Johnston got the flight surgeon on the HF radio to explain the dangers of high-altitude sickness to alleviate their concerns. It took up a lot of time throughout the day, and it could have been handled in New York before the season had he thought of it. Johnston made a note to ensure the aircrews were made more aware of altitude sickness in the future. This time could have been put to more useful purposes.

Sittinger brought pills on the Twin Otter, but he was also reluctant to take them. No one was aware of the drug's effectiveness or side effects. He was concerned his aircrew would become nauseous, thinking, *"That's the last thing I want. Nothing worse than feeling like you want to give up your cookies when you have a stressful mission you're trying to complete."*

Johnston realized he was wasting a lot of time trying to ease everyone's fears about the drug, so he ordered all of them to take the pills. Sander and Ardrey, already feeling poorly, started feeling better, but Sittinger started feeling queasy. In his words, *"Most likely, I talked myself into the side effect. Ha."* When he got out of the aircraft, Sittinger looked over the situation. Kenney's crew looked ragged. They had departed McMurdo thirty-three hours earlier. They had spent the last thirty-one hours at an altitude of greater than 10,000 feet.

Over the last thirteen hours, they dug forty-eight fifty-five-gallon fuel barrels out of the snow, transported them to the aircraft, and refueled it. They were exhausted, but they couldn't rest yet. Sittinger wanted to get the fuel barrels out of the Twin Otter and get the fuel in Skier 91. James, Gator, Pingitore, and Bogie went to work. Once they were finished fueling, Sittinger directed them to load the fresh ATO bottles on the aircraft.

Kenney and Sittinger spent time talking over the events of the last couple of days. Kenney debriefed him on her takeoff attempts, what seemed to work and what didn't work before she climbed aboard the Twin Otter. Based on her information Sittinger knew he needed another five knots somewhere to fire the ATO bottles at the proper time.

He then grabbed Sander, and the two of them took a walk. Sittinger was an old-school ski pilot. He had been flying the ski mission for thirteen years. He wanted to see the condition of the old skiway. He was searching for a section of the skiway that would be smooth enough, hard enough, and long enough to get him an extra five knots of airspeed and not damage the aircraft nose ski.

Their walk went the full distance of the skiway down and back. The first thing Sittinger noticed was Kenney had followed his recommendation. She hadn't attempted a takeoff there.

Additionally, he saw the snowmobiles had not made any effort to groom this area. He found patches of icy snow in some parts of the skiway, which would provide faster acceleration, and he found deep powdery snow in other areas, which could bog down aircraft acceleration. It had deep sastrugi and ruts on the latter part of the skiway. Overall, the latter part of the skiway wasn't any good, but the first part looked somewhat useable.

It was cold, almost too cold. The friction of the skis created a layer of water between the skis and the snow when ski conditions were good. At -38° Fahrenheit, the snow was too cold to create this layer of water. The snow crystals started to separate, and it was more like skiing on sand. The direction of the old skiway was about thirty degrees different from Kenney's tracks. Her tracks were directly into the wind. Sittinger didn't think the thirty-degree offset of wind would be an issue for him.

He found a length of skiway he was looking for, a hard patch of ice that wouldn't damage the aircraft. By the time he arrived back at Skier 91, Sittinger had formulated his plan. Instead of trying to take off in the open snow, he decided to use the first part of the old skiway. He needed to hit that hard section of the skiway at just the right time during the takeoff slide, gain the extra knots, fire the ATO, gain the airspeed he needed to get the nose up, and get the lift he needed before he ran out of hard snow.

Gator programmed the navigation systems and volunteered to fly back with Sittinger's aircrew. Sittinger refused to allow it. After Gator set up the navigation systems, he had Sander recheck everything before they departed for McMurdo. Pingitore volunteered to fly Skier 91 back also, but again Sittinger sent him to the Twin Otter. Sittinger wasn't convinced he would succeed, and after all of the work Kenney's aircrew had done over the last day and a half, he felt the risk to them was less if they flew back in the Twin Otter.

He would attempt to fly back to McMurdo with just Sander and Ardery, as planned. It was a calculated risk, but he already had the navigation systems programmed, and the back of the aircraft was loaded. The Twin Otter was already packed full, so Sittinger kept Kenney's passengers with him. Some of these guys had been at AGO-5 for days and had already acclimated to the altitude. They would be useful if he had problems.

Sittinger, Sander, and Ardrey got in their seats, strapped in, and ran the checklists to start the engines. The #3 engine wouldn't start. They tried a second time, and it still wouldn't start.

*"Damn it!"* The Twin Otter had already departed AGO-5. It had already climbed to altitude and was on its way to McMurdo when the pilots

received a radio call from Sander. Bogie needed to return to AGO-5 to help Ardrey work on their problem. Ardrey was a new C-130 engineer, and Bogie had a lot of C-130 experience.

After the Twin Otter returned, they went through the engine start malfunction checklists for the next two hours before they finally settled on the ignition relay. They took the ladder from the back of the aircraft and set it next to the #3 engine. They climbed up it and removed the engine panel located behind the propeller. Ardrey had a spare ignition relay, and the two of them changed out the failed one with the new one.

When Sittinger tried to start the engine again, it didn't work. The new ignition relay worked as well as the old one. It was a failed part also. In the end, Bogie couldn't help. He was sent back to the Twin Otter, and it took off and returned to McMurdo. Meanwhile, Sittinger, Sander, and Ardrey worked on their problem.

Sittinger was stuck. He called back to McMurdo and gave Raven Operations an update.

# Aircraft Recovery

Johnston was at dinner when he got the news. He was with Kozic. They talked about the potential of another airdrop to get Ardrey an ignition control relay. Master Sergeant Shad Gray and Senior Master Sergeant Mike "Spike" Delgiacco overheard the conversation. Both of them were highly experienced experts in their field. The flight engineers trained annually to use the equipment in the hostile repair kit. They added items to this kit for unique ski mission difficulties through the years to help stranded aircrews with this type and other similar situations. Gray said, "You don't have to do that, just jumper it." Johnston asked, "What are you talking about?" Gray said, "Keith could jump the starter. The cables are in the hostile environment kit. I can show you." Johnston, Gray, and Delgiacco walked back to Gray's room. Gray and Delgiacco opened the flight manual and explained to Johnston what Ardrey needed to do.

When Johnston was satisfied, the three walked down the dirt road to Building 165 and into Mac Ops. Johnston asked the contractors in Mac Ops to contact AGO-5, specifically Ardrey. Delgiacco and Gray talked Ardrey through how to jump the ignition relay.

Ardrey was humble and self-deprecating. This was in stark contrast to the rest of the flight engineer section and most of the Raven Gang. However, those who flew with him knew Ardrey was one of the Raven Gang's best, but while talking to McMurdo, he doubted his ability to fix the aircraft. Johnston knew everything hinged on Ardrey getting the engine started; all of the building up of the bundles, the airdrop, the hauling of the fuel and pumping it in the aircraft, the Twin Otter flight to AGO-5—everything depended on Keith. Johnston was frustrated with the pessimism he was hearing and jumped on the radio and, with assertiveness, stated, "Keith, you have to fix it!" It was an order!

Ardrey was stressed, but he listened closely. The first thing he needed to do was locate the jumper wire. The Raven Gang had a flight engineer tool kit stored under the bunk of the flight deck. Ardrey found the jumper wire. He was exhausted. The high altitude was taking its toll. He went back out in the cold and wind, and stood precariously on the ladder, and leaned over the engine. He removed the ignition relay. He then took off his gloves in the frigid weather and hotwired the ignition relay canon plug pins with the jumper wire. He recalled what Delgiacco told him, "Put a wire from C to D, then another from D to E."

He was feeling hypoxic. When he was finished, he climbed down the ladder, got the engine cover, and reinstalled it. He climbed down the ladder again, lowered it, and returned it to the cargo compartment. When he returned to the flight deck, he took a breath of oxygen from his mask to clear his head, and together with Sittinger and Sander, started the engine. It worked. Ardrey let the engine warm up, then applied bleed air to the manifold. When everything checked out, he pulled the ignition relay circuit breaker to close the circuit, to prevent the ignition sequence from continually firing throughout the flight back to McMurdo.

Sittinger then started the remaining engines without further incidents. He wasted no time running the remaining checklists and closing up the aircraft. When he tried to taxi, he couldn't move. The aircraft was stuck in the snow. He thought, *"I hope we don't have to divert to Vostok to refuel. Vostok is really a God-forsaken place."* He had been to Vostok a few times before, and the thought really nauseated him—or perhaps it was the Diamox. He remembered dealing with the people there and found it most stressful.

He knew he was wasting fuel, so he tried the simplest thing first. He decided to lighten the aircraft's weight by getting rid of the pallet of empty propane bottles. Ardrey went to the back of the aircraft and opened the ramp and door, and together with the passengers, they pushed the pallet out into the snow. Ardrey closed up the back of the aircraft again and returned to the flight deck.

When Ardrey returned to his seat, Sittinger directed Sander to cycle the skis up and down. As soon as the nose ski indicated down, Sittinger pushed the throttles forward. The aircraft began to move. He waited for the remaining skis to indicated down, then taxied into the open snow. When he was about a mile away, he turned the aircraft to align with the old skiway. He briefed Sander to drop the flaps to one hundred percent, a common ski mission technique.

He pushed up the throttles. As the aircraft accelerated, the additional flaps provided more lift under the wings, which prevented the skis from sinking deeper in the snow. By the time he hit the beginning of the skiway, he had good acceleration. The firmer surface increased acceleration. He hit the icy patch of skiway at just the right time. The aircraft continued to accelerate. Sittinger thought, *"Yeah, I'd rather be lucky than good!"* A humble thought.

When he was ready to pull the aircraft off of the snow, Sittinger directed Sander to move the flaps to fifty percent, the normal takeoff setting, and he directed Ardrey to fire the ATO bottles and said, "ATO—now!" These simultaneous actions gave him a normal takeoff configuration while ensuring the aircraft continued to accelerate with the ATO.

The aircraft was at stall speed, about eighty-five knots when Sittinger pulled the aircraft off the snow. The aircrew felt the aircraft shuddering at stall speed. Sittinger lowered the nose when the aircraft was about ten feet off the snow. Initially, the aircraft's nose drifted to the left. The aircraft hadn't achieved minimum control speed, but as it accelerated, Sittinger gained rudder effectiveness. He stepped on the right rudder and brought the nose back around.

On 9 December 1998, at 1:25 a.m., Skier 91 was off the snow and climbing out of AGO-5. Before Sander raised the landing gear, Sittinger directed Ardrey to go below the flight deck and look at the skis to ensure everything looked okay. Ardrey was still feeling hypoxic. He went below and realized he had never looked through the inspection window while the landing gear was down. He couldn't see the skis. He said, "There is no nose ski." Sittinger was surprised. He gave the flight controls to Sander, got out of his seat, and went below to look for himself. When he looked out the inspection window, he laughed and said, "Yes, there's a nose ski." He then instructed Ardrey on what to look for. They went back to the flight deck, and Sander raised the skis. Ardrey took another breath of oxygen from his mask.

They didn't have much fuel, and it was out of balance. The APU had been running since Kenney landed the aircraft about thirty-six hours before Ardrey had been supplying fuel to it out of the #2 fuel tank. As he worked to get the fuel in balance, the quantity gage began to spin. He knew the tank still had fuel, but he couldn't verify the tank's quantity. Again, he called back to McMurdo, but the problem resolved itself. The gage began to function correctly.

They had a headwind. This slowed them down and required more fuel. Ardrey opened his books, found the maximum range chart, and worked his way through it. Throughout the flight, they closely monitored their fuel status.

When Sander called McMurdo about the fuel imbalance, it prompted Johnston to contact Major Tom Esposito. Esposito's aircrew was coming back from the South Pole. Johnston told him to divert from his present course to find Sittinger and guide him back. Sander was relieved. He was concerned about the accuracy of the navigation systems. The flight back to McMurdo took 2.3 hours. They arrived back at McMurdo before the Twin Otter landed.

There was no time to rest. Now Johnston and Sittinger focused on how to get their aircraft out of the crevasse at Upstream Delta.

CHAPTER 23

# POOR WEATHER FORECASTS

The Raven Gang had built a crew force large enough to meet the National Science Foundation's needs by the beginning of the Operation Deep Freeze 1999–2000 Season. It was the first season without the Navy in Operation Deep Freeze's forty-year history. The Raven Gang aircrews would fly the Antarctic mission for the remainder of their careers.

With the new Antarctica season came milder weather than previous Operation Deep Freeze seasons and the aircrews were suspicious. By now, they were aware of the rapid weather changes on the continent. Over time, the milder weather proved to be the normal weather patterns, and the previous three years were the exception. This relieved a lot of stress on the people flying the aircraft, but it didn't improve the weather forecasting.

The National Science Foundation flight line contractors became more familiar with the operation in McMurdo, and their relationship with aircrews improved through the years. Contractors in the remote camps throughout Antarctica became more familiar with aircrew operations and limitations, and their relationship with the aircrews also improved. However, the relationship between the weather contractors and the aircrews continued to remain edgy.

## Weather Phenomena

The terrain around Williams Field Skiway has already been noted as a great place for ships but a poor place for airplanes. McMurdo Station sits at the tip of a peninsula on the south side of Ross Island. The waters of McMurdo

Sound begin northwest of the island and south of the Ross Sea. They flow between the island to the east and the continent of Antarctica to the west. As the continent's coastline curves to the east, the waters tuck in south of the island. The McMurdo Sound ends southeast of Ross Island, at the Ross Ice Shelf.

Williams Field Skiway sat on this permanent ice shelf about seven miles east of the McMurdo Station. The size of the Ross Ice Shelf is equivalent to the country of France. It's a cold basin of glacial ice hundreds of feet thick, which creates one of the many challenges to the weather forecasters and greater challenges to the aircrews.

The McMurdo Sound freezes during the Antarctica winter. As the summer thaw begins, the northeastern areas of it melt. Low stratus clouds and fog develop, and gentle winds from the maritime Ross Sea push the low clouds and fog around the island toward Williams Field. Throughout the summer, the fog becomes more frequent as the McMurdo Sound melts further south, especially when condensation comes in contact with the Ross Ice Shelf.

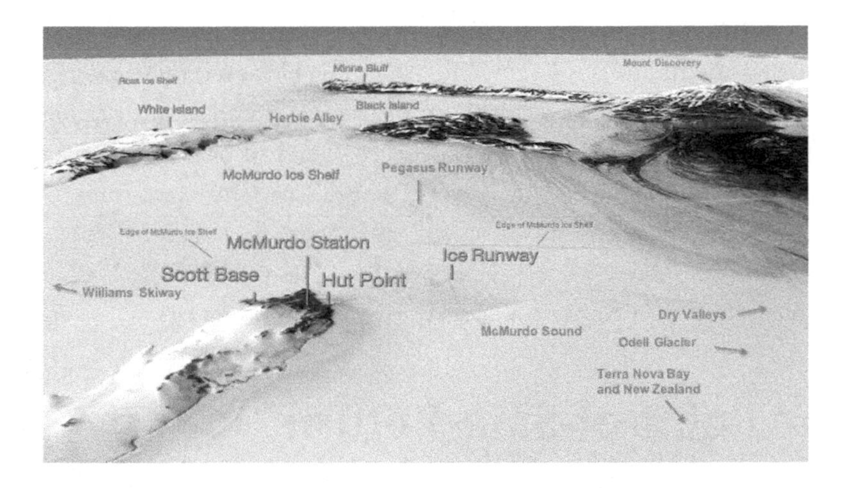


*Points of Interest Around McMurdo*

South of Williams Field Skiway is White Island, a 2,500-foot mountain rising from the Ross Ice Shelf. Further south and west is Black Island, rising to 3,415 feet. West of Black Island is the continent, and Mount

Discovery is on the coastline. This domed mountain is across the Sound from McMurdo Station and rises to 8,800 feet. Beyond Mount Discovery, the continent's ice cap rises higher than 10,000 feet.

The ice cap's plateau of snow and ice form river glaciers as they force their way down through the mountain valleys to McMurdo Sound's coastline. Dense, cold, and dry winds, katabatic winds, blow down these glaciers. These are hellacious winds and most treacherous when they blow between White and Black Island. The aircrews nicknamed these winds "Herbie," and they called the pathway between White and Black Island "Herbie" Alley.

# The Weather Forecaster

The Navy's SPAWAR, or Space and Naval Warfare Center, had a contract with the National Science Foundation to provide *"Timely and accurate local and regional weather forecasts, warnings, flight forecasts, and Terminal Aerodrome Forecasts for all stations in Antarctica that operate aircraft and support ship operations."*[146]

SPAWAR contracted civilian weather forecasters to do the actual forecasting, with SPAWAR providing oversight. However, these civilian contractors had limited tools available to provide an accurate weather forecast. They didn't have 24-hour satellite coverage, they had only a few sensors in the McMurdo region, and the diverse weather patterns were some of the most challenging on Earth. Still, year after year, they reported they were ninety-three to ninety-seven percent accurate. Despite SPAWAR's reports of accuracy, the Raven aircrews didn't trust the weather forecasters.

# The Point-of-Safe-Return

The Air Force didn't use a point-of-safe return when planning a flight. Instead, they used an equal-time-point, the half-time of their flight. Therefore, once airborne, when an Air Force aircrew experienced a problem, they were expected to continue to their destination if they were beyond their equal-time-point. If they were not beyond the equal-time-point, they were expected to turn back to their point of departure. It assumed both locations had equal resources.

The advantage of the point-of-safe-return was its calculation was based on the fuel available, not time. This made it possible for aircrews to go beyond the equal-time-point, to their point-of-safe-return fuel estimate, and still return to Christchurch if their aircraft had a problem, an onboard medical issue arose, or the weather at McMurdo turned bad. Limited maintenance and medical facilities, an unreliable alternate destination, and accurate weather forecasting were all big challenges in Antarctica. Both locations were not equal.

## 50° Below Zero

Why did the Raven Gang limit operations at 50° below zero? Because there needed to be a limit. Operation Deep Freeze began in October when temperatures warmed to 50° below zero Fahrenheit, and it ended when temperatures cooled to 50° below. Mission decisions were significantly different when the temperature was 50° below in October than 50° below in February.

In the southern hemisphere, when a plane needed repairs in October, the temperatures got warmer throughout the coming days and weeks while the maintainers worked on it. In February, when a plane needed to be repaired, the temperatures get colder. There were no aircraft hangars in Antarctica. Aircraft maintenance and repairs must be done out in the elements. There came the point when a routine engine change or other potential repairs could not be completed in time to bring the aircraft back to New York at the end of the season. If it couldn't be fixed, it had to be left behind. The beginning and the end of the Operation Deep Freeze season were the most challenging times. The next two chapters address the problems during these times.

CHAPTER 24

# THE WISDOM OF THE OLD GUARD

During the typical weekend rotations, on Saturday morning, military personnel leaving Antarctica piled into the cargo compartment of an LC-130 and flew to Christchurch, New Zealand. On Sunday morning in Christchurch, fresh personnel from New York piled into the cargo compartment of an LC-130 and were flown to McMurdo.

It was Monday morning, 1 November 1999, in Christchurch. The 109th Airlift Wing's fresh personnel were delayed from going south on Sunday due to poor weather conditions. Many of these people were going to Antarctica for the first time. Lt. Col. Bob Sittinger was scheduled to be the deployed commander for the week, but he was having difficulty getting to the ice.

He was skeptical of the weather forecast on Sunday morning, and he had a right to be. Eventually, his flight was canceled. He knew the weather had been up and down for the last three days in McMurdo and the accuracy of the weather forecasters was always in question. The forecast for his time of arrival in McMurdo today was the following:

- Grid winds from 320° heading at 12 knots
- The visibility was expected to be 4,800 meters, or 3 miles, with light snow
- The clouds were scattered at 1,000 feet and overcast at 1,500 feet
- The barometric pressure was reading 28.64
- The temperature was -14°

There was also a temporary line on the forecast:

- Grid winds were expected to gust up to 20 knots
- The visibility could go as low as 800 meters, or ½ mile, with light snow
- Overcast cloud ceilings could go as low as 1,000 feet

It was the worst kind of forecast—nothing all that positive and a whole lot of negative. But nothing prevented Sittinger from going. He called Raven Operations in McMurdo to talk to the deployed commander, but she was in a meeting. Sittinger was tall and lean and had been with the Raven Gang since 1985. He started his career flying refueling tankers out of pilot training in 1973. He flew a few combat missions before the Vietnam War ended. After seven years, he left active duty. In 1985 while driving in Albany, New York, he spotted a C-130 flying low over the area. He followed it to the gates of the 109th Tactical Airlift Group. He eventually ended up as the Raven Gang's operations support flight commander and chief of training. He had been flying to Antarctica since 1988.

| **Skier 94 Aircrew** | |
|---|---|
| **Pilot:** | Lt. Col. Robert Sittinger |
| **Copilot:** | Major Mark Doll |
| **Navigator:** | Lt. Col. Ted Bell |
| **Navigator:** | Captain Kimberly Dingman |
| **Navigator:** | Major Michael Spina |
| **Navigator:** | Captain Bill Smith |
| **Navigator:** | Major Jim Powell |
| **Flight Engineer:** | Technical Sergeant Steve Cousineau |
| **Flight Engineer:** | Master Sergeant Don Morrell |
| **Flight Engineer:** | Staff Sergeant Michael Spiak |
| **Loadmaster:** | Technical Sergeant Kevin Gifford |
| **Loadmaster:** | Technical Sergeant Tim Putman |

Sittinger had seen a lot over the years. During the transition of the Operation Deep Freeze mission, the Navy withdrew their weather forecasters, and the National Science Foundation contracted SPAWAR, the Navy's Space and Naval Warfare Systems Command, to replace them. The Navy weather forecasters were young people doing their best, but their accuracy wasn't good. The civilian weather forecasters' accuracy wasn't any better. The difference was politics. Navy weather forecasters could give a flawed forecast to the aircrews and state they did their best, but contractors were more hesitant to do so.

Sittinger was now faced with a dilemma as he looked at the forecast. He knew the weather was bad, but he also knew he had no reason to cancel the mission. So, he went to his aircraft, Skier 94, and briefed his aircrew on his expectations of the day ahead. They were airborne at 9:30 a.m. with a total of thirty-three people on board, mostly 109th Airlift Wing aircrew members and maintenance people. With the predicted tailwinds, they were due to arrive at McMurdo at 4:45 p.m.

Throughout their scheduled seven-hour-and-fifteen-minute flight, the weather was up and down at McMurdo. Sittinger kept requesting his navigator, Captain Kimberly Dingman, and his copilot, Major Mark Doll, to get constant weather updates throughout the flight. Their initial point-of-safe return was at 1:25 p.m. and was the last opportunity Sittinger had to return to Christchurch. Beyond this point, the aircraft wouldn't have enough fuel to turn back and, he would be committed to continuing southbound.

Auckland Radio was their air traffic controlling agency until they reached 60° South latitude. Auckland initially gave them a block altitude between 18,000 feet and 24,000 feet. Mark Doll later requested and received an increased block altitude up to 28,000 feet, as the fuel burned from their tanks and the aircraft got lighter. The aircraft engines were more efficient at higher altitudes and burned less fuel. If things worsened, this would give Sittinger more fuel, thus more time, for conditions to improve before going to a backup plan.

There was an added benefit to climbing higher; the tailwinds increased. The weather forecast estimated they would have a ninety-five-knot quartering tailwind along their route of flight. They had a one hundred-fifty-five-knot quartering tailwind, sixty knots faster than expected, after leveling off at altitude.[147] The aircraft's ground speed was faster due to the tailwind, so Skier 94's point-of-safe-return time needed to be recomputed. They had flown faster and were further along the planned route. If they decided to turn back, they'd be facing a greater headwind. Both the greater distance traveled, and the increased headwind meant they needed additional fuel in their tanks to make a potential return to Christchurch. Dingman called Auckland Radio and gave them their new point-of-safe-return time of 1:00 p.m. If they turned back, they needed to descend to take advantage of the lesser headwind.

Sittinger heard Skier 96, commanded by Major John "JD" de Graaf, depart McMurdo for the South Pole. JD's expected arrival time back at McMurdo would be two hours after his arrival time.

The 12:00 p.m. current observation was as follows:

- The grid wind was 320° at 11 knots
- The visibility was 6,000 meters, or 5 miles, with light snow
- There was an overcast cloud ceiling at 1,500 feet

At 12:05 p.m., Mark Doll contacted McMurdo Operations, Mac Ops, and got patched in to Mac Weather. He gave them Skier 94's new point-of-safe-return time and new arrival time. He wanted an updated weather forecast for their new arrival time. When he got it, Sittinger was not pleased. It was the same forecast he got for their departure from Christchurch hours prior.

The point-of-safe-return forecast for the time was the following:

- Grid winds were from 320º heading at 12 knots
- The visibility was expected to be 4,800 meters, or 3 miles, with light snow
- The clouds were scattered at 1,000 feet above the ground and overcast at 1,500 feet
- The barometric altimeter reading was 28.64
- The temperature was -14º
- There was a temporary forecast indicating what they anticipated:
- Grid winds were expected to gust up to 20 knots
- The visibility could go as low as to 800 meters, or ½ mile, with light snow
- Overcast skies could go as low as 1,000 feet

Although Sittinger thought the weather was marginal, John de Graaf was on his way to the South Pole. Everything seemed to add up. At 1:00 p.m., he flew past his point-of-safe return. It didn't take long before the weather began to worsen at McMurdo. Sittinger was livid. "Those sons of bitches!" He said with a chuckle. He often chuckled when he was stressed, angry, or disappointed. It didn't require a look in his eyes to know he wasn't chuckling because he was happy.

## Terra Nova Bay

Sittinger tried to call the deployed commander again, but she was in another meeting and unable to talk to him. He had additional fuel now. Thank God for the tailwind. This gave him more options than he usually had after passing the point-of-safe return.

1. The white-out landing area was always an option, his last option.
2. The Italian Camp in Terra Nova Bay was an option. It was still early in the season, so the Italians hadn't closed the camp. It was along the Ross Sea before reaching McMurdo. The Navy had gone there several times through the years, but no one from the Raven Gang had ever been there.
3. With the additional fuel, he could make it to Siple Dome. Siple Dome was a two-hour flight from McMurdo. Instead of flying to McMurdo then going to Siple Dome, he could cut off the angle to get there. Siple Dome wasn't open, but it was a place to set the airplane down.

He thought, *"If I go to Siple, I'll have to babysit all these newbies. I'm not going to do that. We'll try the Italian camp."* With his decision made, he began searching for all the information he could find on the Mario Zucchelli Runway. Some of the information he found was good, and some of it gave him pause.

Mark Doll had the radio frequencies and some detailed information about the camp. The orientation of the ice runway was 042°–222° true direction. The coordinates for the threshold of Runway 22 were 74º39'54.84" South, 164º09'13.20" East. It was 10,000 feet long and 210 feet wide and had a 155,000-pound weight capacity.

The terrain in the area was an issue, especially in poor weather conditions. High terrain was two miles southwest of the runway. It was Mount Abbott, 3,353 feet in height. Due to its location, the landing runway was Runway 22, and the takeoff runway was Runway 04. Sittinger knew if he couldn't make a safe landing, he needed to make his missed approach decision early, or he'd hit the terrain.

The Raven Gang created values for the surface and horizon conditions. These values have had minor changes through the years. The definitions were as follows:

| Surface Values | |
|---|---|
| *Good:* | Snow features such as sastrugi, drifts, and gullies are easily identified by shadow. The sun is usually unobscured. |
| *Fair:* | Snow surface features can be identified by contrast. No definite shadow exists. The sun is usually partially to nearly totally obscured. |
| *Poor:* | Now, surface features cannot be readily identified except close up. The sun is usually totally obscured. |
| *Nil:* | Snow surface features cannot be readily identified. No shadows or contrast exist. Dark-colored objects appear to float in the air. The sun is totally obscured, although the overcast may exhibit considerable glare. The glare appears to be equally bright from the surface reflection in all directions. |
| *No Surface:* | Total loss of surface definition due to blowing snow, fog, ice fog, or any other restriction to visibility. |

| Horizon Values | |
|---|---|
| *Good:* | The horizon is sharply defined by sky and snow surface. |
| *Fair:* | The horizon may be identified, although the contrast between sky and snow surface is not sharply defined. |
| *Poor:* | The horizon is barely discernable. |
| *Nil:* | Total loss of horizon definition. The snow surface merges with the the whiteness of the sky. |
| *No Horizon:* | Total loss of horizon definition due to blowing snow, fog, ice fog, or any other restriction to visibility. |

Nil surface definition and nil horizon definition were what ski mission aircrews called flying inside the ping-pong ball. When flying inside the ping-pong ball, it was impossible to judge distance and altitude. Visual cues outside the aircraft were disorienting. Buildings looked as if they were floating.

McMurdo weather observation at 2:00 p.m.:

- Grid winds were from 340º at 28 knots
- The visibility was 200 meters, less than a ¼ mile, with light snow
- Clouds were overcast at 1,000 feet
- The temperature was -15º, and the dew point was -19º
- The barometric pressure was 28.64
- The surface and the horizon definition were both nil

Terra Nova Bay weather observation at 2:00 p.m.:

- Grid winds were from 250º at one knot,
- The visibility was unrestricted
- The clouds were scattered at 3,000 feet with a broken deck at 7,000 feet

McMurdo weather observation at 2:30 p.m.:

- The winds picked up. They were from grid 340º at 35 knots, gusting to 40 knots
- The visibility was 100 meters or about 300 feet
- Terra Nova Bay weather at 2:30 p.m.:
- The grid winds were from 060º at 2 knots
- The visibility was unrestricted
- The clouds were scattered at 3,000 feet, with another scattered deck at 7,000 feet

The weather was good and getting better at Terra Nova, but not at McMurdo. The McMurdo winds were blowing from Herbie Alley.

Sittinger wondered how the forecasters always got the weather so wrong. For the next hour, Mark Doll and Dingman coordinated with the Italians to prepare for their arrival. The weather was clear when they arrived over the Ross Sea but not so good along the coastline. Sittinger descended below the clouds and into the frozen bay area where the runway was located. Dingman guided them in, and they configured the aircraft for landing.

Sittinger saw the runway and lined up on it. He was exhausted. He told Mark Doll, "I'm beat. Take the landing." Mark Doll replied, "What?" Sittinger, "You'll do fine." Doll, "Are you sure?" Sittinger, "Yeah, I'm done. You can tell everyone you landed at Terra Nova. It's yours." Doll set Skier 94 on the runway at 4:00 p.m., and Sittinger was right. He did a fine job.

One of the first things the aircrew noticed when they opened the door was the smell of a wood fire. A woodstove filled the air with a wonderful scent. Tensions subsided. Doll said, "We were welcomed to Terra Nova by a man with a brilliant, beautiful, big, brass and chrome espresso machine."

This was Staff Sergeant Mike Spiak's first flight to Antarctica. He said, "As we left the aircraft, I was greeted by an Italian woman. She took us to the dining hall. When we entered the room, there were bottles of wine on every table." He never wanted to leave.

Dinner had been prepared for Sittinger's aircrew and his passengers. The menu included wine, food, and birthday cake. It was the chef's birthday, but the Raven Gang felt like the party was for them, and more wine was served.

Bill Smith played cards with the Italians all night. Wayne Mussmacher, one of the maintenance guys, walked to his sleeping quarters. It was a large hut-type building with separate rooms and bunk beds. There was a fireplace, and a fire was burning. It was warm and comfortable. They were given a couple of cases of beer and a couple of bottles of wine. The alcohol was gone in a short time.

After a couple of hours, Sittinger was directed from the dining hall to the Italian communication center. Skier 96, JD, was on the way to Terra Nova Bay and wanted to talk with him. Sittinger brought Dingman along. As he walked to the communications center, he noticed the weather had worsened. On the radio, JD questioned Sittinger about how he got into Terra Nova Bay. Sittinger described how he descended over the water then flew below the clouds into the bay, but he followed up by also telling him the weather had gotten much worse. Dingman got on the radio with Major Kurt Bedore, JD's navigator. She said, "You won't see anything until the last minute. Then you'll see barrels on the ground. Trust your instruments." Sittinger listened as JD descended and began his approach. He heard Lieutenant Jason Reape make one last call to report their landing gear was down. Then all communication stopped. Sittinger thought JD had impacted a mountain.

# McMurdo

It was the first Operation Deep Freeze Season without the Navy since 1955. The Raven Gang was now the sole LC-130 support for the mission, following a three-year transition. The season had started early with the rescue of the doctor from the South Pole in early October. Following the rescue, there was a pause in the operation, and then, a couple of weeks later, they started flying again.

It was the typical poor early-November weather in McMurdo. The flying schedule followed the weather patterns. The Raven Gang intentionally planned the Operation Deep Freeze season with a slow beginning, bringing only a few airplanes to the theater. As the season progressed and the weather improved, the Raven Gang built up their armada to fly more missions. Then, as the weather began to deteriorate, the Raven Gang reduced their coverage again until the season ended in late February.

The poor November weather meant fewer missions were scheduled, but there was always a push to fly. This push was caused by the scientists' anticipation for a new science season to begin. It happened every season. The scientists expressed their eagerness to the contractors in Building 165. The Raven Gang was on the back end of all this eagerness and often regretted it. It was about to happen to Major John de Graaf on this cold Antarctic morning, but he saw it coming.

The National Science Foundation started the construction of the new South Pole station. It would be a multi-story structure built on footings, columns, trusses, and a jacking system so that the buildings could be periodically raised to keep pace with the snow accumulation. It wasn't a new concept. The Department of Defense did something similar in Greenland in the late 1950s and early 1960s. The DYE sites were massive structures expected to last ten years, yet they remained in operation until 1989. On multiple occasions, the DYE sites were jacked up to keep pace with the snow accumulation.

The new South Pole station structure was intended to last fifty years. By looking at the snow's drifting, this engineering feat would be constructed in harmony with the wind patterns. Building this structure on "stilts" would allow the strong winds to pass under the station and help scour the building's underside to keep snow from building up beneath it.

De Graaf's mission was to get pictures of the snow drifting for the National Science Foundation so they could orient the station properly.

| **Skier 96 Aircrew** | |
|---|---|
| **Pilot:** | Major John "JD" de Graaf |
| **Copilot:** | First Lieutenant Jason Reape |
| **Navigator:** | Major Kurt Bedore |
| **Flight Engineer:** | Master Sergeant Shad Gray |
| **Loadmaster:** | Master Sergeant Lance Peck |
| **Loadmaster:** | Technical Sergeant Dave Vesper |

Before JD joined the Raven Gang, his first assignment after pilot training was in the active duty as a T-37 pilot at Columbus Air Force Base, Mississippi. He later became a KC-135 pilot at Robins Air Force Base, Georgia. In 1990 he joined the Raven Gang. He started as a copilot in the aircraft, gradually upgrading to become a ski mission instructor pilot.

He wore a Boonie hat when he flew with the sides folded up and his headset wrapped over the top. He had a big smile and a sharp wit with vicious one-liners. He once said of the weather shop people that their recognition of the rapidly deteriorating weather conditions gave him hope they'd become successful weather forecasters someday.

JD learned from very talented pilots like Ray Tousey, Graham Pritchard, Giles Wagoner, Jim Wilbur, Aldo Marchegiani, and many others. His slow upgrade allowed him to fly with all of the Raven Gang pilots and become aware of the mission's challenges. After nine years of flying the mission, he was teaching these techniques to the next generation.

First Lieutenant Jason Reape was his copilot. It was Reape's first Antarctic season, and he was smiling a lot as he prepared for his first mission on the continent. Major Kurt Bedore was his navigator. Bedore was new to the mission, but he was a B-52 electronic warfare officer in the active-duty Air Force before coming to the Raven Gang. Reape and Bedore were about to learn some lessons about Antarctica.

JD, Reape, and Bedore walked down the dirt road to Building 165, Raven Operations' location. When they walked into the office, they were given their mission folder from the supervisor of flying with a synopsis of what they were expected to accomplish throughout the day. Next, they walked to the weather counter and received a briefing on the weather forecast.

The weather was far from perfect, but there was a sense of urgency to complete a mission, any mission, on the continent. For the last week, the Raven Gang had been in Antarctica, and the weather had been awful. No missions had been completed. This morning, however, there was a break in the cloud cover. Conditions were improving, and they were going to the South Pole.

After completing the paperwork, they walked back along the dirt road to Derelict Junction and caught a shuttle down to the ice runway's aircraft ramp. It was about a twenty-minute ride.

When they arrived at their aircraft, Master Sergeant Shad Gray, Master Sergeant Lance Peck, and Technical Sergeant David Vesper were already on the flight line. By the time the other three arrived, they had completed the aircraft pre-flight inspections.

De Graaf gathered his crew together and briefed them on the details of the flight. They were to make a quick flight to the South Pole, take some pictures, and return to McMurdo. There was no expectation for them to land. When the briefing was completed, the crew strapped in their seats, started the engines and taxied to the fuel pits.

A good ballpark minimum fuel requirement was about 35,500 pounds of AN-8 for this routine South Pole mission. Typically, the Raven Gang expected to burn 15,000 pounds of fuel on the way to the South Pole. On the return flight, the aircraft would weigh less so they could climb higher and burn less fuel, about 12,000 pounds. If the weather conditions were perfect at McMurdo, they required 8,500 pounds of fuel over the airfield upon their return.

Gray asked JD, "How much fuel do you want?" He replied, "They said the weather was supposed to be good enough all day. But I don't trust'em, Shad. Fill it up. I want every drop."

JD was told the day's mission was simple, but there was an urgency to complete it. The weather was questionable but improving. He knew better. There was no simple mission in Antarctica, and the weather and urgency increased his caution. Gray helped the maintenance people fuel the aircraft. JD gathered the rest of his crew and went to the dining facility on the flight line, where he met his two passengers.

The weather went down while Gray put 62,000 pounds of fuel in Skier 96. When he was finished, he was directed to go to the dining facility. Skier 96 was on hold until the weather improved. Their scheduled takeoff time came and went. Eventually, the weather improved, and the weather forecaster was optimistic enough to convince the military staff in Building 165 that the weather would hold. De Graaf was directed to proceed with the mission. They went to the fuel pits, started the aircraft engines, taxied to the ice runway, and they were airborne at noon.

## South Pole

The flight to the South Pole was uneventful. JD's mission was to orbit overhead the South Pole Station with the cargo ramp open. The aircraft would be traveling about one hundred fifty knots through the frigid air. His two passengers intended to sit on the aircraft's open ramp and take pictures of the station's drifting snow patterns. It sounded crazy, especially with a temperature of -60° Fahrenheit at the South Pole.

The weather was clear skies and unrestricted visibility. It was a beautiful day with light winds. De Graaf descended into the South Pole visual pattern. Two National Science Foundation contractors were on the flight. One was the air operation supervisor. He managed aviation requirements in McMurdo. The other was a photographer. They sat on the ramp of the aircraft and took pictures of the drifting snow as they passed over it. Peck and Vesper, the loadmasters, ensured they wore an airdrop harness that was secured to the aircraft's floor so they wouldn't fall out.

When they were finished taking pictures, the loadmasters closed the ramp and door and prepared their passengers for the flight back to McMurdo. There was talk of landing and giving the Pole some fuel. It wasn't part of the plan, but the aircraft had a lot of fuel remaining. JD had an iron-clad reason for not doing it. The Raven Gang had set a -50° Celsius, -58° Fahrenheit, temperature limit for operations at the camps. It was too cold. He completed what he came to do, and he turned back to McMurdo. En route to the ice runway, he directed Reape to call Mac Weather to get a weather update. The 4:00 p.m. satellite image should have arrived for the weather forecasters. He wanted to know what was happening throughout the McMurdo area and the Terra Nova Bay area. He wasn't surprised to hear the weather was poor, and landing at McMurdo was going to be a challenge. Upon his arrival, he set up a holding pattern and orbited around the area. After about two hours, the weather still didn't look good at McMurdo, so he diverted about two hundred miles south to Terra Nova. He knew Sittinger was there.

## Divert from Terra Nova Bay

Reape called the Italian camp and let them know they were headed their way. JD asked to speak to Sittinger. After several minutes, Sittinger got on the radio. Sittinger and JD talked about the approach into Terra Nova Bay. Sittinger told JD the weather was poor and described how he descended over the water then flew below the clouds into the bay.

When JD arrived over the Italian airfield, the weather didn't look good. He briefed his crew and followed Sittinger's advice. He descended below the clouds. Bedore directed JD toward the bay using his radar. About five miles from the field, his navigation systems and radar overlay were spot-on, but he couldn't pick out the camp's radar signature. The cloud ceilings dropped below five hundred feet. Visibility cues outside the aircraft were white-on-white ahead.

Things quickly became uncomfortable. Later reflecting, Bedore said, "Within three miles of the camp, the navigation system was telling me to continue, but the radar never lies. There was no bright radar return for the camp." He was rattled. He told JD, "Something isn't right. I don't feel comfortable with this. Go around."

De Graaf immediately added power and began to climb. Briefly, the terrain broke out in front of the aircraft. It was Mount Abbott. The aircraft cleared it as they climbed. Any delays would have been catastrophic. Bedore cross-checked his coordinates to see if he had screwed up when he programmed the navigation systems. Perhaps he had the wrong coordinates, or perhaps they lined up on the wrong bay. The coordinates were correct. He didn't "fat-finger" the wrong information into the system. He couldn't find anything wrong. Reape mentioned he saw clear skies below. Gray said, "JD, we're at bingo fuel." De Graaf responded, "Okay, we're going to Siple Dome." He had had enough of Terra Nova Bay.

The direct line to Siple Dome from Terra Nova Bay took them across the north side of Ross Island. This allowed Reape to talk with the weather people. The skies were clear at Siple Dome, and it was a beautiful day. One of their passengers, the civilian air operations supervisor, took the opportunity to talk to his people in Building 165 and let them know he would be going to Siple Dome. The camp hadn't been opened for the season. No one had been to Siple Dome since the previous season. The Siple Dome camp manager was still at McMurdo. She got on the radio and explained where to find the survival food storage and the aircraft fuel pump.

## Siple Dome

Siple Dome was 81°39' South, 149°04' East. The design of the Siple Dome skiway was much like other science camps on the continent. It was 10,000 feet long and 200 feet wide. It had a taxiway arc along one end of the skiway that allowed the aircraft to taxi off the skiway; drop off fuel, cargo, and people; then return to the skiway.

The flight was just under two hours. Bedore picked up the camp on the radar and guided JD toward it. The weather was clear, and the winds were mild. JD picked up the skiway flags from the previous season and landed without incident. The surface was smooth. He taxied Skier 96 alongside the fuel tank upon his arrival. They had been airborne for 11.8 hours. It was approaching midnight, but the sun was still high in the sky.

They had 10,000 pounds of fuel remaining. Gray found the fuel pump in front of the fuel tank. Reape and a couple of others found a Herman-Nelson heater at the camp and dragged it near the aircraft. Gray turned on the heater and let it run for a while. He then opened the valve, and warm air began to blow out of its hose. The fuel pump was moved near the heater to warm it.

The air operations supervisor got out of the aircraft and kissed the snow.[148] The aircrew needed rest. Refueling the aircraft could wait. They had enough fuel to keep the auxiliary power unit, or APU, running all night, which would keep the aircraft warm inside. It was -16 degrees Fahrenheit.[149] Most of the crew slept in their seats. The rest spent the night scattered around the aircraft. Crewmembers took two-hour shifts and stayed awake to watch the APU to ensure it ran smoothly throughout the evening.

## Graham Pritchard

Sittinger's aircrew and passengers had slept in rooms with bunk beds. The accommodations were comfortable considering any other camping alternative. Spiak slept on the bottom bunk with Gifford on the top. Gifford snored, and it was an ungodly noise. Spiak beat on the bottom of Gifford's bed throughout the night, but it didn't do any good. Gifford got a good night's sleep. Spiak didn't.

It was Tuesday morning. Sittinger radioed the McMurdo weather forecasters from Terra Nova Bay. The weather forecasters told him he had a two-hour window to make it to McMurdo. It would be about a forty-five-minute flight, so he decided to give it a try. The weather was good where he was, so he could always return to Terra Nova.

De Graaf woke up in the morning and radioed the McMurdo weather forecasters from Siple Dome. He was told there was a two-hour window to make it back. It would be a two-hour flight to McMurdo. He decided to stay where he was. He wasn't interested in playing any more games.

Colonel Graham Pritchard was in McMurdo. He was on the flying schedule all week, but no one had been flying due to the poor weather. He was nearing retirement and wanted to be a crew dog one last time. Earlier in the season, Pritchard was with Major George Rob on the rescue flight to get the doctor diagnosed with breast cancer from the South Pole. Now he was planning to fly to Siple Dome to help out JD.

Pritchard knew Bob Sittinger's crew was at Terra Nova Bay, and they were well taken care of by the Italians. JD's crew was facing a different situation. The camp hadn't been opened up for the season ahead. The weather was improving enough in McMurdo for Pritchard to get airborne. John Bartow told Joe Axe he should come along on the flight. This was Axe's first week in Antarctica. Axe found the scheduler in the dining facility. The scheduler agreed it was a good idea.

| Skier 92 Aircrew | |
|---|---|
| **Pilot:** | Colonel Marion "Graham" Pritchard |
| **Copilot:** | Lt. Col. Alan Ross |
| **Navigator:** | Lt. Col. Ginny Reilly |
| **Flight Engineer:** | Technical Sergeant Dustin "Dusty" Larsen |
| **Loadmaster:** | Technical Sergeant Marty Spier |
| **Loadmaster:** | Technical Sergeant John Bartow |
| **Loadmaster:** | Staff Sergeant Joe Axe |
| **Crew Chief:** | Master Sergeant Joe Butler |

Pritchard, Ross, and Reilly arrived at the flight line. Larsen had completed the preflight of the aircraft, Skier 92. Spier, Bartow, and Axe loaded the passengers and cargo in the back. Master Sergeant Joe Butler was Skier 96's irascible red-headed crew chief. He flew along with Pritchard to see if JD was taking care of this airplane. He had his survival gear, Newport cigarettes, a bottle of rum, and a six-pack of Coke.

Some people called this flight a rescue mission, but Pritchard knew it was intended to get the camp manager and several other camp personnel to Siple Dome. If the weather didn't improve, at least Pritchard could get the camp opened up for the aircrews, and they would be able to utilize all of the camp's resources. Not long after Pritchard was airborne, Sittinger landed in

McMurdo. While Pritchard was on his way to Siple Dome, the weather at McMurdo went down again. He wasn't surprised. In the back of his mind, he expected to spend the night at Siple Dome. He had seen a lot. The flight was uneventful.

Graham Pritchard graduated from pilot training in 1969. His first assignment was Alaska. He flew with the Firebirds for three-and-a-half years, occasionally going to Greenland to support the ice cap's DYE sites. In 1972, he was on alert status and flew to Greenland when "Frozen Assets" crashed on the ice cap. After he left active duty, he arrived in Schenectady, New York, when he heard the skibirds were transferred there. Now in 1999, as the Commander of the 109th Airlift Wing, he was spending a quiet night on the ice, one last time. The camp manager had prepared a nice feast. After dinner, he pulled a tent from the survival gear in the back of the aircraft and set it up under his aircraft's wing.

He was with two aircrews, and most of them had no experience camping out on the ice. He wanted his aircrews to recognize they could make themselves comfortable camping out with the gear available in the aircraft, one last lesson before his military flying days ended. But it didn't work. Boredom set in for Bartow and Axe. They eyed the snowmobiles they had just brought to the camp. They started them up and raced up and down the skiway, finding moguls for jumps and playing. It was good stress relief until the camp manager caught Bartow and yelled at him.

Butler was arguing with Shad Gray, JD's flight engineer. Gray kept Skier 96's APU running all night, and Butler didn't like it. JD defended Shad Gray. He argued, "The APU is a constant speed and constant load engine. As long as it has oil, it will run without any problems." It was nothing Butler didn't already know, but he didn't like it.

Dusty Larsen, Pritchard's flight engineer, had his APU shutdown. Ginny Reilly, Pritchard's navigator, was cold. She walked into JD's aircraft and asked Gray if he was going to keep his APU running all night. Gray said yes. So, Reilly walked back to her aircraft, grabbed her sleeping bag, and walked into Skier 96, and stayed the night.

Larsen went into Skier 96 to talk with Shad Gray. He asked Gray if he intended to keep his APU running all night. Again, Gray said yes, so Larsen went back to his aircraft and started his APU. Butler was livid, but there was nothing he could do. He went to the back of the aircraft, dug into the survival gear, then went outside and set up a tent under the wing of Skier 92. He climbed into his sleeping bag for the night.

Raven Operations called Dusty Larsen while he sat in his seat, keeping an eye on the status of his APU. The deployed commander was looking for Joe Axe. Axe got on the radio, and he was told he was AWOL. He had not been put on the flight orders to go on the mission. Pritchard listened to all the chaos. Some things still needed to be worked out, but this wasn't the sound of people fearing for their survival. He knew his people would be okay in their new mission. He tucked himself into a sleeping bag and went to sleep. The next morning was uneventful. De Graaf called back to McMurdo and got a weather forecast. It looked good. He got his aircrew together. They started their aircraft engines and returned to McMurdo. Pritchard followed a short time later.

CHAPTER 25

# THE POINT-OF-SAFE-RETURN

*Author's Note: Below is the story of three aircraft going to McMurdo at the end of the Operation Deep Freeze Season. The quotes are from radio transcripts of their flight.*

It was 22 February 2000. Snow was beginning to appear on the Southern Alps, the mountain range that splits New Zealand's South Island. February in New Zealand is late summer. It was a mild morning when Skier 92 departed Christchurch. The temperatures were around 60° Fahrenheit. There were fluffy cumulus clouds in the sky, with little wind. You could see for miles. It was forecast to remain this way all day. It was in stark contrast to where Captain David Panzera's aircrew was going when they departed Christchurch on this beautiful summer day.

There is no summer in Antarctica. When the sun begins to set in mid-February, it gets cold rapidly. It is probably most accurate to say there is only autumn and winter in Antarctica. And autumn was gone. The Raven Gang was wrapping up another Operation Deep Freeze season. Before they could return to New York, they needed to bring the remaining people who were scheduled to return home out of McMurdo. Those that remained would stay throughout the harsh Antarctica winter. Three aircraft left Christchurch that morning. Panzera was the aircraft commander of the last southbound LC-130 aircraft for the season.

The Raven Gang culture bred bold aircraft commanders. They were opinionated and confident. There was always the potential for any of them to get stuck on the snow and spend a significant amount of time on the ice cap awaiting assistance or rescue. They had to be able to make decisions on their own. They had to be confident to survive on the ice cap.

| Stogy 91 | |
|---|---|
| **Pilot:** | Captain Danny Lincoln |
| **Copilot:** | Lt. Col. Tim Thomson |
| **Navigator:** | Major Fabio Ritmo |
| **Flight Engineer:** | Chief Master Sergeant Mike Cristiano |
| **Flight Engineer:** | Staff Sergeant Joe Neale |
| **Loadmaster:** | Senior Master Sergeant Billy Nolin |
| **Loadmaster:** | Staff Sergeant Bruce Lassiter |

| Skier 96 | |
|---|---|
| **Pilot:** | Lt. Col. Joel Mayron |
| **Copilot:** | Lt. Col. Virginia Holland |
| **Navigator:** | Lt. Col. Paul Jeffries |
| **Flight Engineer:** | Master Sergeant Brian Alix |
| **Loadmaster:** | Technical Sergeant Randy Williams |
| **Loadmaster:** | Technical Sergeant Tim Macauley |

| Skier 92 | |
|---|---|
| **Pilot:** | Captain Dave Panzera |
| **Copilot:** | First Lieutenant Jason Reape |
| **Navigator:** | Major Ron Ankabrandt |
| **Flight Engineer:** | Technical Sergeant Chris Hoffman |
| **Loadmaster:** | Master Sergeant Tim Putman |

Captain Danny Lincoln was the aircraft commander of Stogy 91. He was young and cocky. His auburn hair, round glasses, and big smile shaped a very affable personality. Danny enjoyed smoking cigars, so on this flight, he changed his call sign from the traditional "Skier" moniker to "Stogy."

The second aircraft, Skier 96, was commanded by Lt. Col. Joel Mayron. He had a narrow frame, dark hair, although thinning on top. Joel loved to laugh. He was more knowledgeable of the Antarctica mission than anyone else in the squadron. Before arriving in New York, he was a pilot in the Navy's VXE-6 squadron, flying Operation Deep Freeze missions. He had the newest aircraft at the 109th Airlift Wing. It was an LC-130H3 model. The configuration of this aircraft had some differences from the older ones. The modified HF, high frequency, radio antennae would give him some difficulty on this particular day. Newer isn't always better. Lincoln's aircrew would relay much of McMurdo Center's information to him and from him throughout the day.

Captain Dave Panzera was Skier 92's aircraft commander. Panzera had a powerful frame. He was deeply religious, conservative, and outspoken. He was also incredibly caring and devoted to his family, which included the Raven Gang. He came to the squadron as an enlisted man after serving several active duty years. The Raven Gang gave him a commission then sent him to pilot training.

## Staff Members

When the 109th Airlift Wing took over Operation Deep Freeze, the deployed staffing was kept very small. The person in charge of the LC-130 flying operation was the deployed commander. However, the commander of all military forces was the CODF, the Commander of Operation Deep Freeze. This included the Coast Guard ice breaker and the Navy personnel who on-loaded and offloaded the cargo ship when it came into port in early February.

Colonel Richard Saburro was responsible for two operations, or as they say, he wore two hats. He was the Detachment 13 Commander in New Zealand, and he was the CODF in Antarctica. Saburro came from the Raven Gang. He was of average height, skinny, blond hair, and blue eyes. He was a single father of three girls in the early 1990s and a General Electric manager in Schenectady. He enjoyed taking a couple of weeks each year to go to Greenland. He eventually became the squadron commander for the Raven Gang and was the first commander of Operation Deep Freeze from the New York Air National Guard. Over the previous forty years, the Navy ran the show. Saburro was in McMurdo.

Major Danny Dunbar, who worked as the operations officer at Detachment 13, was Saburro's assistant in McMurdo. He worked closely with the flying squadron throughout the day to close out the Operation Deep Freeze season. Dunbar was a navigator and the current operations officer for the Raven Gang before taking the job in New Zealand. He was an affable man who liked to laugh and play. He knew the people in the flying squadron, and he knew the mission.

# Christchurch

The weather was beautiful at McMurdo throughout most of the evening hours, and the sun was only setting for an hour or so at this time of year. The winds started picking up a bit by 3:00 a.m. By 4:00 a.m., the visibility had dropped significantly due to blowing snow. An hour later, the cloud ceilings were down to one thousand feet above the ground, and visibility was down to a mile.

The three aircrews were alerted in the morning. They followed their standard guidelines. The navigators received an Air Force computed flight plan and an OPARS flight plan.[150] The advantage of an OPARS over the Air Force flight plan was it provided a computed point-of-safe-return time. Navigators computed their own point-of-safe-return and compared it to the OPARS. It was a good backup check.

The scheduled takeoff times were 9:00 a.m. for Stogy 91 (Lincoln), 10:00 a.m. for Skier 96 (Mayron), and 11:00 a.m. for Skier 92 (Panzera). Stogy 91 ran a little late. Skier 96 was close to on time. Skier 92 was early. The consequence was all three aircraft were given the same weather forecast for their departure:

- Cloud ceiling of 8,000 feet
- Visibility was expected to be five miles
- Winds were expected from a grid 220-degree direction at 8 knots.
- A temporary condition was expected to drop visibility to ½ mile

- Winds were expected to increase to 12 knots.

Due to the hazardous nature of the mission, flying in and around Antarctica, the Raven Gang had created weather criteria for their aircrews before the season began. Before they left Christchurch for Antarctica, the weather forecast must have a one thousand-foot cloud ceiling and three miles of visibility, or better, for the arrival time at McMurdo. The forecast easily met these restrictions.

This weather briefing was significantly different from the weather forecaster's trend data throughout the early morning hours. Still, after reviewing his limited data, he anticipated improving conditions later in the day. The most recent satellite picture showed a clearing over the Ross Ice Shelf, to the east of McMurdo, and he expected it to arrive overhead by the afternoon.[151]

In short, the weather briefing indicated the crews should expect good weather in McMurdo for most of the day with some visibility issues through parts of the day. Williams Field's primary skiway direction was 250° and 070 °. There was going to be a quartering headwind on landing. There was also a cross-skiway. Its direction was 330° and 150°. Seven miles away, Pegasus Airfield was their alternate location with an ice runway. Its direction also was 330° and150° degrees.

The temporary weather conditions were noteworthy, but they wouldn't keep the aircrews from departing Christchurch. Before crossing the point-of-safe return, they were required to get an updated weather forecast for McMurdo. The point-of-safe return was their decision point on whether to continue to Antarctica or turn back to New Zealand.

Two of the three aircraft were empty since the final southbound missions from New Zealand were to preposition three aircraft in McMurdo, Antarctica, to fly passengers and cargo back to Christchurch on the following day. This was one of the few bright spots of the day. This meant two of the three aircraft could add more fuel for the flight southbound, which they did. Panzera's aircraft had 9496 pounds of timbers in the back of his aircraft. They were stacked in two layers. This extra cargo meant Panzera had less fuel than the other two aircraft, which would impact the day's events.

An en route eight-knot headwind was forecast throughout the flight's duration; therefore, it would take 8½ hours to get to McMurdo. The equal-time point was four hours and fifteen minutes into the flight. Their point-of-safe return was about five and one-half hours into the flight due to the additional fuel they had onboard.[152]

Stogy 91 departed Christchurch at 9:35 a.m. Skier 96 departed at 9:45 a.m. Skier 92 departed at 10:25 a.m. Paul Jeffries, Skier 96's navigator, told Mayron he didn't like taking off immediately after Stogy 91. But Mayron was concerned that his HF radios would give him problems throughout the day, and he wanted Stogy 91 to be close enough to hear him and relay his information to the air traffic controllers.

## The Weatherman's Bluff

The first few hours of all three flights were uneventful. Mayron had problems with his radios, and Lincoln relayed his information. A couple of hours before Stogy 91 reached their point-of-safe return, a C-141 aircraft was scheduled to arrive at McMurdo. The C-141 was much larger than the LC-130. It carried enough fuel to be within an hour of McMurdo before reaching its point-of-safe return.

**11:25 a.m.**

The C-141 aircrew received a point-of-safe-return weather forecast with a 4,000-foot cloud ceiling, but only a one-half mile of visibility for their arrival, with forecast winds from grid 340-degree direction at twenty-five knots, gusting to thirty knots. Their landing runway was Ice Runway 33 at Pegasus Airfield. The C-141 aircrew returned to Christchurch due to the high winds and poor visibility.

Twenty minutes before Stogy 91 (Lincoln) was scheduled to cross their point-of-safe-return, Lt. Col. Ted Bell, in McMurdo, watched the weather closely. He was the deployed commander of the Raven Gang. Every time he looked out the window, it seemed worse than before. The current weather conditions sucked, but the forecast indicated the weather would improve soon.

He wanted to turn the aircraft back to Christchurch, so he walked downstairs to Danny Dunbar's office and talked things over. Dunbar decided to recheck the weather and talk with the forecaster before turning the aircraft around. Together they went to the weather shop. For the last several hours, the forecaster had no new satellite imagery to tell him what the weather was doing in the local area. Every day, from about 9:30 a.m. until about 4:30 p.m., sun-glint from reflections off of the snow blinded the satellite. Therefore, the forecaster was working off data that was several hours old. However, he didn't tell Dunbar and Bell.

The forecaster showed Dunbar the old satellite imagery. It was the same satellite imagery used for the Skiers' Christchurch departure weather forecast. The only new information he had was the trend information throughout the day, but Dunbar and Bell were not aware of that.

The forecaster still had faith in his old data even though the current weather conditions were not supporting his earlier prognostications. He expected the weather to improve, although the C-141 aircrew had already turned around and gone back to Christchurch. He convinced Dunbar the weather still looked good for the aircrafts' arrival times.

Therefore, when the southbound aircrews requested an updated weather forecast, the forecaster gave them rosy expectations, and the aircraft commanders pressed on to McMurdo.

## Stogy 91's Point of Safe Return

The Raven Gang created their own criteria for the point-of-safe return. They needed an updated weather forecast for McMurdo within an hour of crossing their point-of-safe return. The McMurdo forecast needed flight conditions of a five hundred-foot cloud ceiling and two miles visibility or better before an aircrew was authorized to fly past their point-of-safe-return. The forecast they received easily complied with these requirements. McMurdo weather forecast for their arrival time was expected to be the following:

- Cloud ceiling of 2,000 feet
- Visibility was expected to be five miles
- Winds were expected from grid 310° at 12 knots.

McMurdo's current weather observation stated the following:

- Cloud ceiling of 1,500 feet
- Visibility was three-fourth miles
- Winds currently from 60° off of skiway heading at 16 knots
- The surface and horizon definition were both nil

The surface and horizon definition were important considerations for landing. It gave the pilots a mental picture of what they would see when they transitioned from near vision to distance vision; precious seconds from when they transitioned from aircraft instrumentation to outside visual references to land their aircraft. In this case, it sounded as if they would be landing inside the ping-pong ball.

Stogy 91 (Lincoln) passed their point-of-safe return at 2:30 p.m. The weather was challenging due to the visibility and winds, but Lincoln was a skilled aviator, and even this weather didn't cause him much concern.

At 2:57 p.m., Dunbar spoke to the incoming aircraft on the McMurdo Center frequency using the call sign "CODF."

**Dunbar:** "Stogy 9-1, Stogy 9-1, CODF."

**Thomson Stogy 91's copilot:** "CODF, 9-1, go-ahead."

**Dunbar :** "And 9-1, uh, just, uh, to let you know that, uh, the conditions are not improving as fast as we would like them to improve and also wanted to let you know that, best guess, on new accumulation of snow out at Willy Field is two to three inches of snow at this time. We're unable to get people out to Willy Field to sweep the runway or groom the runway prior to your arrival. We will continue to work that, uh, but that's what you're looking at, is two to three inches of new snow. The winds predominantly all day have been down Runway (Skiway) 3-3. Understand you don't have an approach to 3-3, but (Skiway) 2-5 does have some drifting on to it, and the preferred runway (skiway) probably for your arrival will be 3-3, over."

**Thomson:** "9-1 copies, Dan. We've been talking about that and also, maybe, Pegasus, if need be."

There was nobody at Pegasus. After the C-141 returned to Christchurch, Dunbar pulled all the airfield personnel out because the weather conditions were so poor.

**Dunbar :** "Roger, and, uh, we understand. That certainly is a backup plan, but just to let you know, we cannot get out to Pegasus. We've actually got two vehicles stuck on the road between Pegasus and Willy."

Stogy 91 (Lincoln) was committed to continuing to McMurdo. They no longer had fuel to turn return to Christchurch. Skier 96 (Mayron) still had an opportunity to turn around. Skier 92 (Panzera) definitely could turn back to Christchurch, but they kept the faith and continued on.

## Skier 96's Point of Safe Return

Skier 96 (Mayron) had the same optimistic weather forecast for their arrival at McMurdo, and they received the same current weather observations as Stogy 91 (Lincoln). Again, radio reception and transmission were a problem, so Stogy 91 relayed the information.

> "Mac Center at 3:02 p.m.:
>
> "Attention all Skiers. Attention all Skiers. Mac Center with the Willy (Williams Field) 0-2-0-0 (Zulu time; 3:00 p.m. local time) weather and Pegasus. Willy weather as follows for 0-2-0-0:
>
> - Grid wind 3-2-0 (direction) at 2-5 (knots);
> - visibility 300 meters, blowing snow;
> - sky obscured, vertical visibility 1,000 (feet);
> - temperature minus 1-4;
> - dew point minus 1-7;
> - altimeter (pressure altimeter setting) 2-8-9-5;
> - surface definition: poor;
> - horizon definition: nil

"Pegasus ASOS[153] weather reporting:

- Overcast 4,000 feet (cloud ceiling);
- visibility a quarter-mile;
- temperature minus 1-2;
- dew point minus 1-3;
- grid wind 3-6-0 (direction) at 3-3 (knots), gusting to 4-4.

"Mac Center out."

Stogy 91 (Lincoln) and Skier 92 (Panzera) acknowledged. Stogy 91 passed the information to Skier 96 (Mayron).

All three aircraft were communicating with each other on their VHF radios and were discussing the weather. Mayron was the most experienced of the three aircraft commanders. He was familiar with forecasts from Navy weather forecasters but not civilian-contracted weather forecasters. He assumed there was no difference, and he told Lincoln and Panzera the weather usually improves when they say it will.

No one could have anticipated what was to come. However, Mayron had confidence he had the fuel to hold overhead if the weather remained poor and they had to wait a while before landing. If the weather didn't improve, he assured his aircrew that he could land in the white-out area without difficulty. Skier 96 continued past their point-of-safe return.

The new current weather observation was no better than the previous one, but the forecast was good, so Skier 96 pressed on.

Mac Center at 3:29 p.m. announced,

> "Attention all Skiers. Attention all Skiers. Mac Center with the 0-2-2-5 Willy weather, followed by Pegasus ASOS weather.
>
> "Willy weather as follows, 0-2-2-5:
>
> - Grid wind 3-2-0 at 1-9;
> - 600 meters and blowing snow;
> - vertical visibility 1,000;
> - temperature minus 1-4;

- dew point minus 1-6;
- altimeter 2-8-9-7;
- surface definition poor;
- horizon definition nil.
- Remarks: Visibility fluctuating between 200 and 1200 meters.

"Pegasus ASOS weather, as follows:

- Overcast 1,000;
- visibility 1 and a ½;
- temperature minus 1-2;
- dew point minus 1-3;
- grid wind 3-6-0 at 3-9, gusting 4-6.

"Mac Center out."

Again, all aircraft acknowledged.

Mac Center at 3:42 p.m.:

"Stogy 9-1, Stogy 9-1, Mac Center, yes sir, I just received the first skiway condition for (Skiway) 2-5, as follows: They're reporting that snow is drifting from the outboard side (Skiway) 2-5, 10 to 12 feet; 3 to 4 inches deep. The rest of the runway, correction skiway, is looking good. They'll keep monitoring that. Right now, we don't have one for (Skiway) 3-3 due to the winds picking up. And they weren't able to get out there, but that is their priority, to get back out there and check it consistently. Over."

# Skier 92's Point of Safe Return

About four hours into Skier 92's flight, an hour before reaching their point-of-safe-return, Panzera received a weather forecast for his aircrew's arrival at McMurdo. At 2:44 p.m. local time, it stated the following:

- Cloud ceiling 2,000 feet
- Visibility of 6,000 meters, or 5 miles
- A direct 12-knot crosswind

The forecast was good, and the crosswind was manageable. The hourly observations were crappy all day, but the two previous aircraft were beyond their point-of-safe-return, and they were pressing on to McMurdo. The most recent weather observation improved slightly. Perhaps this was the improving conditions they were waiting for.

Panzera felt confident he wouldn't have any difficulty continuing to his destination. If things didn't work out, he'd follow the lead of the other two aircraft. Panzera's copilot, Jason Reape, didn't like it. Reape was a young lieutenant, but he knew a bad situation when he saw it. He had been tracking the weather trends all day. None of the observations showed any significant improvements, and they showed little indication the weather would improve by the time they arrived at McMurdo. He wanted to turn back; however, it was too late.

Skier 92 passed their point-of-safe return at 3:44 p.m. Although they took off from Christchurch forty minutes after Mayron, Panzera's aircrew passed the point-of-safe-return within fifteen minutes of Mayron due to their lighter fuel load.

Mac Center at 4:03 p.m.:

> "Stogy 9-1, Skier 9-6, Mac Center with 0-3-0-0 weather at Willy Field and Pegasus, as follows.
>
> - Willy grid wind 3-3-0 at 2-5;
> - visibility 300 meters, blowing snow;
> - sky partially obscured, vertical visibility 1,000;
> - temperature minus 1-4;
> - dew point minus 1-7;
> - altimeter 2-8-8-6;
> - surface definition poor;
> - horizon definition nil.

"Pegasus ASOS, as follows:

- Grid wind 3-6-0 at 3-4, peak gust 4-3;
- sky condition overcast at 4,000;
- visibility three-quarters of a mile;
- temperature minus 1-1;
- dew point minus 1-3;
- altimeter 2-8-8-8.

"Mac Center, out."

The aircrews began to slow down and were reducing their power to conserve fuel, no longer confident the weather was going to improve before their arrival. They continued to communicate with each other on the VHF radio. They needed to ensure separation from one another. Stogy 91 (Lincoln) was the lead aircraft, so they took charge of the situation. They had a plan, but there were changes and updates as they approached McMurdo. Mac Center eventually cleared Stogy 91 to flight level 280 (Lincoln), Skier 96 to flight level 300 (Mayron), and Skier 92 to flight level 320 (Panzera).

Radio traffic was heating up, and for most of the flight, aircrews talked with either Auckland Radio or McMurdo Radio on the HF radio. When aircrews couldn't contact either of them, South Pole Radio would help relay information. As the aircraft came in McMurdo's range, they were asked to tune to frequencies on the VHF radio. This was in addition to the aircrews communicating with one another on their other VHF radio.

The aircrews stayed aware of their relative position to one another and kept receiving updated weather information. As they monitored their dwindling fuel status, they needed a plan for how to proceed. They spent a lot of time talking about landing in the white-out landing area. The aircraft commander, the pilot of each aircrew, briefed their people on expectations, and they coordinated separation between each aircraft for landing in the white-out area.

In 1998, the Navy squadron had two aircraft land in the whiteout landing area minutes apart. That was a tricky situation. Three aircraft in the white-out area had never been done. There were a lot of big questions. How were they going to maintain separation in the white-out area after the first aircraft landed? How was Skier 96 going to be assured he wasn't about to land on top of Stogy 91? How was Skier 92 going to be assured he wasn't going to land on the other two aircraft?

Then there was the question of the three ASOS weather transmitters the weather shop just reported were in the white-out landing area. Where were they located? Why were they there? Who put them there? The white-out area was supposed to be clear of obstacles. And finally, there was the crosswind. It was last reported at thirty-four knots, gusting to forty-three knots. All previous white-out landings were successfully done due to fog. The fog was associated with little to no wind. The maximum crosswind component for an LC-130 landing was fifteen knots. This was challenging on a clear day.

Lincoln and Panzera were young aircraft commanders with limited experience. Challenged with up to a forty-three-knot crosswind and three-quarters of mile visibility, landing in an open snowfield with two other aircraft and other obstacles in the same white-out area was getting to be an interesting day.

## Emergency Landing Options

Dunbar was also concerned about landing three aircraft in the white-out landing area and was looking for options. He knew there was a search going on for a suitable alternate location. In January 1999, two Royal New Zealand Air Force C-130 aircraft were inside their point-of-safe-return on a flight to McMurdo when an unexpected fog bank rolled into the McMurdo Area. They landed safely at Pegasus, but this was the incentive for Rich Saburro to start the search for an alternate landing site. However, on 3 January 2000, a month and a half ago, there was still no answer. Joel Mayron landed in the white-out landing area when a fog bank rolled into McMurdo unexpectedly. The search started in earnest. On 14 January 2000, Saburro sent a Detachment 13 representative, via helicopter, to a potential alternate location named Far Western. It wasn't a suitable place to land an LC-130. On 26 January 2000, a Detachment 13 representative flew via helicopter to a blue ice glacier near Brimstone Peak. That wasn't suitable either. On 2 February 2000, Saburro sent Lt. Col. David Fountain to fly, via helicopter, to Odell Glacier near Wyandot Ridge. This site had potential. It was very old blue ice that was hard, solid, and flat.

Fountain was a maintenance officer for the 109th Airlift Wing. He was a prior-enlisted man who, in later years, became an officer and was sent to pilot training. He had been with the unit for nearly twenty years. Fountain was in McMurdo; more accurately, he was at Williams Field closing the maintenance facilities for the end of the season. Dunbar gave him a call.

Fountain decided to see Dunbar at Raven Operations instead of giving him the details over the telephone. Williams Field is located seven miles from McMurdo. His drive along the snow road was hazardous in the current weather conditions. Several times he had to stop due to a loss of all visual cues. When he finally arrived in town, he went to Building 165 to see how he could help with the recovery of the aircraft. Dunbar filled him in on the situation, then asked for recommendations.

Fountain recommended Odell Glacier near Wyandot Ridge. After providing some details, Dunbar agreed Odell was a good option; however, Ted Bell and his staff were opposed to the suggestion. Odell Glacier had not been surveyed, and a fixed-winged aircraft had never been there to test it. Certainly, no LC-130 had been there before. There were no markings for landing at any specific location there. Dunbar agreed the weather needed to be clear for an aircraft to land there. The pilot would overfly the site and determine if he wanted to give it a try. He decided Panzera's aircrew should look because he had less fuel.

# McMurdo Arrival

McMurdo airspace was Class E. The surrounding airspace was Class G. There was no radar coverage to identify aircraft. Therefore, the aircrews told the air traffic controller their position, and the controllers kept the aircraft separated by altitude or distance to avoid conflicts.

**5:37 p.m.**

Lincoln's aircraft was one-hundred-six miles from Williams Field. Mac Center cleared them to hold on the 116-degree radial, from overhead Williams Field out to ten miles, using left-hand turns.

**5:53 p.m.**

He reported they were established in the holding pattern.

**6:01 p.m**

Mayron reported 100 miles from Williams Field. Mac Center cleared him to fly to Byrd and set up a holding pattern to the grid southeast, between thirty-five and fifty miles from the Williams Field TACAN. Byrd was a reporting point grid-east of Williams Field. Its location would keep them clear of Lincoln.

**6:06 p.m.**

Mac Center cleared Lincoln to lengthen his holding pattern out to fifty miles.

**6:09 p.m.**

Mac Center gave Mayron the same holding pattern as Lincoln; the 116-degree radial, from over Williams Field out to fifty miles; left-hand turns. Lincoln was at flight level 280, and Mayron was at flight level 300. There was no conflict. This allowed both aircraft to overfly Williams Field and gave them the chance to look below and see if they could find an opportunity to land. Stogy 91 and Skier 96 remained in the holding pattern. They were waiting for either the weather to improve or run out of fuel, whichever came first. The weather didn't cooperate.

**6:12 p.m.**

Panzera was given the same holding instructions. They were at flight level 320.

**6:21 p.m.**

Before Panzera arrived over Williams Field, Dunbar passed the following information to them:

**Dunbar:** "Ok, Skier 9-2, we have some coordinates as follows: South 76º 38" 05' at (East)160º 01' 3." Would like you guys to basically put that in your SCNS for a place to go and hold. You'll get your clearance here in a moment; uh, it is near Wyandot Ridge, north, uh, grid northwest of the Dry Valleys.

It's a blue ice area that was surveyed. You guys need to go over, stay at your altitude and look at that area and see if it's VFR (visual conditions). It may be a possible divert."

**Skier 92:** "OK, we copy that, now, uh, but not too hot on going someplace first time, like that. We have pretty much a solid deck all around us. We'll put that in and take a look at that area and call you back."

**Dunbar :** "Yeah, you need to get a clearance to go over there and, uh, what I want you to do is stay at your altitude and take a look at it. The only way I can put you in there is if it is VFR."

Fountain got on the radio with Panzera and spent a lot of time talking over the things he remembered about this location; the 1.3-degree rise; the dimpled surface conditions; and the sastrugi, large frozen wave-like formations of solid ice, in the area. Afterward, Dunbar asked Fountain to return to Williams Field to provide field conditions to the aircrews as they arrived.

So, Fountain risked another hazardous drive back to Williams Field. Due to the weather, he spent the rest of his night there and slept in the chow hall with his maintenance folks.

Soon after these conversations between Panzera and Dunbar and Panzera and Fountain, Mac Center gave Skier 92 clearance to proceed to the specified coordinates.

**6:24 p.m.**

Dunbar called Lincoln and Mayron.

**Dunbar:** "Don't know if you had your HF (radio) still up. I gave some coordinates to Skier 9-2, and I'd like to pass them on to you as a possible divert if the weather is VFR (visual conditions) there."

Immediately following, Mac Center cleared Stogy 91 to those coordinates. Lincoln questioned the clearance, and Mac Center apologized. They had jumped the gun. Stogy 91 and Skier 96 remained in holding over Williams Field.

**6:29 p.m.**

**Lincoln to Dunbar:** "What efforts are being made to get someone out to Pegasus?" It was quite likely the weather conditions at Pegasus were the same as Williams Field, but the runway's orientation was more in line with the wind conditions. Dunbar replied, "The current condition of the road going between Willy and Pegasus at this time is impassable. We would have to get the SAR (search and rescue) vehicle in order to get anybody out there." Lincoln wanted "eyeballs" out there, and Dunbar said he would "work the issue."

## Divert to Wyandot Ridge

Panzera flew to the coordinates Dunbar gave him.

**6:48 p.m.**

**Panzera:** "And, uh, Mac Ops, Skier 9-2, we're going to need ten minutes of silence here. No attempts to contact. We'll be airborne, thinking about what we are going to do over the blue ice area." Seconds later, they requested a descent to flight level 200. Mac Center had no radar. There was no way to confirm the location of Stogy 91 and Skier 96, so the air traffic controller called each aircraft to verify their position before he gave Skier 92 an answer.

**6:50 p.m.**

**Mac Center:** "Skier 9-2, remain outside of 80 DME (nautical miles) from Willy Field. Expedite your descent through flight level 2-7-0; after that, your discretion."

Lincoln was at flight level 280, so the air traffic controller wanted Panzera to expedite his descent to get below him. Panzera did so. Two minutes later, Skier 92 reported to Mac Center they were passing flight level 270.

**Mac Center:** "Roger that, understand you want no comms for ten minutes?"

**Skier 92:** "That's affirmative."

Four minutes later, Panzera had a plan.

**Panzera:** "Skier 9-2 request descent below controlled airspace to 10,000, cancel and go VFR at that time."

Mac Center granted the request. Panzera was now in clear weather and wanted to descend to look at the glacier. VFR, visual flight rules, meant Mac Center would no longer control where they were going. They had free rein to do as they wished.

**6:59 p.m.**

**Mayron to Mac Center:** "Here's what I'm going to do. Going to maintain a holding pattern on the 116 (radial), flight level 3-3-0, but going to orbit the 50 DME point in that area to be a comm relay for 9-2, if he needs it. Also, perhaps, if I decide to go to those coordinates, it will be quicker for me to go there."

# Stogy 91's Descent to Williams Field

**7:10 p.m.**

Lincoln had been airborne for over nine and one-half hours, and his aircraft was low on fuel. He needed to do something, now. The visibility at the ski-way was poor, and the wind was blowing from a 340° direction.

**Stogy 91:** "OK, just want to give you our plan. We're at (flight level) 2-8-0. We're 4-5 DME. And want to commence the TACAN One (approach) Skiway 7. Wanna come down, take a look at it, and if we can get a circle out of that, we're going to circle to (Skiway) 3-3. If that doesn't look good, we're gonna then break off, go out to stay on the approach, uh, go out to the arc. We'll take the ARA (airborne radar approach) and try and get a circle out of that."

**Mac Center:** "9-1, Roger, standby."

**Stogy 91:** "OK, 9-1, uh, with the fuel, we need to start the approach. We're leaving 2-8-0, now, descending."

Lincoln was low on fuel. He knew where all the other aircraft were, and he knew where the terrain was in the area. He didn't declare an emergency, but the air traffic controller knew they were in trouble. If Lincoln did declare an emergency, nothing would have changed. Stogy 91 and the air traffic controller knew what the other was doing. The air traffic controller would give Lincoln any clearance he requested as long as it was clear of terrain. They were in sync.

Moments later Mac Center replied.

**Mac Center:** "Stogy 9-1, cross Byrd at or above 10,000, cleared TACAN One Skiway 7, circle 3-3. Report Byrd, inbound."

**7:14 p.m.**

**Stogy 91:** "And Mac Center, 9-1. Just to double-check. I'm sure the light you, uh, the light apparatus at the approach end of (Skiway) 3-3 just wanted to double-check that it is operational."

**Mac Center:** "9-1, that's negative, sir. The REILS (runway end identifier lights) were removed earlier and moved into Pegasus. And the field electrician hasn't been able to get out to the PAPI (pilot approach path indicator) on 3-3 yet."

A weather observer had just arrived at Pegasus. He needed a few minutes to get set up and look at the field, but he had already notified Mac Center that the wind was blowing the snow fifteen to twenty feet off the surface. Above twenty feet, the skies were clear.

**7:22 p.m.**

Mac Center passed on the weather observation for Pegasus Field.

**Mac Center:** "OK, he gave me plain language. 1,800 to 2,400 meters (visibility) with the airfield. Been in sort of a hole there, surrounded by blowing snow throughout the circumference of the airport. Appears to be worse visibility there, low level, blowing fifteen to twenty feet high. Surface definition, fair. Horizon definition, good."

# Odell Glacier

Panzera flew to the coordinates he had been given. The aircrew knew there was a risk in landing there. They placed their emergency gear near the crew entrance door in case they needed to make a quick exit from the aircraft. Odell Glacier, the blue ice glacier near Wyandot Ridge, was at an elevation of about six thousand feet, higher than Denver, Colorado. He overflew the area at different altitudes surveying the area. The last pass was at five hundred feet. Panzera and Jason Reape, his copilot, agreed on a location to land.

**7:22 p.m.**

**Skier 92 reported:** "Yes sir, we made a go-around on this last pass, and we'll be landing the next pass and call you safe on snow." On their first landing attempt, Panzera tried to ease the aircraft onto the snow. The waves of ice were very firm. As the skis impacted the waves of sastrugi, the crew rattled around the inside of the aircraft.

Hoffman was wondering if the aircraft was going to break up from the repeated impacts. Anything not strapped down in the cockpit became a flying projectile. Even the heavy sextant case broke free and flew through the cockpit. It was unbearable, so Panzera aborted the landing and went airborne again. They made another pass, and Panzera and Reape noticed another area that looked as if it had fewer sastrugi. They were committed to trying again.

Like many flight engineers, Hoffman had a habit of sitting at the front edge of his seat as close to the instruments and engine controls as possible. His seat belt and shoulder harness were loose. On one of the last violent jolts on the landing, he slid through his shoulder harness and hit the aircraft's ceiling.

**7:25 p.m.**

Skier 92 reported to Mac Center.

**Skier 92:** "Skier 9-2 would like to report with a lot of relief, safe on snow. We'll call you when we recover." They kept their engines running and asked Mac Center to get the CODF. Dunbar got on the radio.

**Dunbar:** "9-2, go ahead, this is CODF."

**Skier 92:** "CODF, this is a very bumpy place."

**Dunbar:** "Say again."

**Skier 92:** "No systems are giving us problems. Some serious bumps in this area. We're gonna get out and take a look at the airplane."

Ron Ankabrandt, Panzera's navigator, remained on the radio with Dunbar. Dunbar wanted to ensure they landed at the coordinates he had given them. He was trying to work out a landing plan for Mayron. Lincoln was committed to land in the McMurdo area; Williams Field, Pegasus Field, or the White-out landing area. They didn't have the fuel to get to Wyandot Ridge. But Mayron still had a chance.

It wasn't supposed to be a bumpy landing from what Fountain told him. Ankabrandt went in-depth, verifying their location, and finally decided it was the right place. Panzera got out of his seat and left Chris Hoffman, his flight engineer, to keep a watchful eye on the aircraft. He was the aircraft systems expert, and he had a severe headache; both good reasons for him to stay put.

# Missed Approach

Panzera was safe on the snow, but the air traffic controller was still worried about the two additional aircraft. Tim Thomson, Lincoln's copilot, reported overhead Byrd. From Byrd, Lincoln flew directly to Williams Field. He could see the field from overhead, looking straight down. However, the aircraft couldn't drop vertically to land. Lincoln needed at least a mile of slant range visibility on his approach to Skiway 07 to enable him to circle to Skiway 33. It looked dicey.

He had arrived overhead the airfield from the opposite direction of his intended landing direction. Therefore, he overflew the field, turned thirty degrees to the right, and flew outbound for ten miles, then made a slow left turn and arced around until he intercepted the final approach course, inbound to Skiway 07.

**7:28 p.m.**

**Mac Center:** "Stogy 9-1, I have the condition for the ice runway at Pegasus."

**Thomson:** "I tell you what, we're busy right now. I'll call you inbound."

Lincoln rolled out of the arc and intercepted the final approach course to Skiway 07. On short final, he intended to cheat to the right of the course and maneuver to align the aircraft with Skiway 33 if the visibility was good enough. This would allow him to land into the wind. Mount Terror was close, and in that direction, so Fabio Ritmo, Lincoln's navigator, remained focused on his radar to guide Lincoln and keep the aircraft clear of the terrain.

**7:34 p.m.**

**Mac Center:** "Stogy 9-1, check wheels down, correction skis down, wind 3-4-0 at 2-1, cleared to land any skiway of your intention."

**Stogy 91:** "OK, any skiway."

**Thirty seconds later, Thomson called:** "OK, Mac Center, 9-1, uh, we didn't see much at all 'til we got over the field. We're gonna come—actually, we'll talk to you in a second. We're climbing out in VFR conditions."

## Damage Assessment

Soon after they stopped, the aircrew of Skier 92 started to assess their situation. While the air traffic controller worked with Lincoln, Dunbar continued to chat with Ankabrandt.

**7:35 p.m.**

Panzera was back on the radio.

**Panzera:** "Danny, this is Dave."

**Dunbar:** "Go ahead, Dave, and by the way, what is your fuel status?"

**Panzera:** "We're looking at about 11,000 (pounds) on the gas. We have damage to the fairings forward of both mains (skis). Uh, we're operable. Want you to know that's how rough it was. We're going to taxi a little bit over to the left of us and take a look at what appears to be the area you're talking about. From our viewpoint, the three circles that we made, this is the best area that we could put down in."

**A few seconds later, Panzera added:** "I'd also like to point out that we are having an APU (auxiliary power unit) problem. We cannot keep our APU running. What's the weather back home?" Dunbar responded, "The weather is not good at this time. What I would suggest is that you, basically, keep at least one engine running and work it that way to minimize your fuel."

The APU was used during ground operations. It burned less than 1,000 pounds of fuel per hour. An aircraft engine, running in low-speed ground idle, burned less than 2,000 pounds of fuel per hour. Keep an engine running, or preferably the APU would allow Hoffman to keep air-conditioned heat blowing in the aircraft.

**Panzera:** "Are the other two planes thinking of coming here?"

**Dunbar :** "Negative, both still in the air."

**Panzera:** "OK, we're gonna survey for them. Be back shortly."

**Dunbar :** "Appreciate that as soon as you can—we'll be standing by."

# Pegasus Landing

Stogy 91 was running out of fuel. Lincoln needed to decide what they were going to try next.

**7:36 p.m.**

**Thomson called Mac Center:** "We're gonna go over, take a look at Pegasus, and then if we decide we're gonna try it there. We'll call you back."

**Mac Center:** "9-1, Roger."

**A minute later, Mac Center notified them:** "Stogy 9-1, 0-6-2-3 (Zulu time) Pegasus weather, as follows, grid wind 0-1-0 (direction) at 4-2 (knots)."

**Stogy 91:** "And Mac Center, we're interested, right at the moment, just the condition of the ice runway that he (the weather observer) drove up and down in."

Lincoln hadn't decided exactly what they were going to do, but there were really good indications he was about to give Pegasus Ice Runway 33 a shot. Fuel was critical, and options were narrowing. Mac Center confirmed the ice runway was in good condition. The runway had bare ice and an inch of snow.

Next, Stogy 91 wanted to know what the winds were. They were grid-direction 340 degrees at forty-six knots. The winds were coming straight down Herbie Alley, and fortunately, Runway 33 was aligned with it. They then asked for the barometric altimeter setting and were told it was 28.90. Finally, they wanted confirmation the runway was clear and learned that it was.

For the next few minutes, Lincoln took time to talk over their options with his crew. He was flying over Pegasus Field in visual weather conditions, but the winds were crazy high. However, they were aligned with a runway, and the runway was clear of obstacles. Landing with such a high headwind would mean their ground speed would be very low. That was a positive thing for an icy runway. They should be able to stop in a hurry if Lincoln could get the aircraft on the ground.

**7:43 p.m.**

**Thomson reported:** "OK, we are lined up for a final (approach) to Pegasus."

**Mac Center:** "Stogy 9-1, cleared ARA Runway 3-3. Report safe on deck."

**Thomson,:** "Understand, uh, cleared for landing at Pegasus for 9-1, is that correct?"

**Mac Center:** "That's affirmative."

**Thomson:** "OK, 9-1 will call you safe on deck."

**Mac Center:** "Stogy 9-1, check wheels down. Wind 3-6-0 at 4-1, gusting 5-1."

**Thomson,:** "9-1, wheels are down."

For the next minute and a half, the radios were silent. Everyone kept the frequency open until Stogy 91 reported their status.

**7:45 p.m**

**Thomson reported:** "Mac Center, 9-1 safe on deck."

The silence was deafening. You could hear their relief over the radio. So far, two aircraft down, one to go.

# Skier 96

Mayron had been airborne for ten hours. He hadn't decided whether to go to Odell Glacier or give Pegasus a try. They were still orbiting around fifty miles from McMurdo at flight level 300. Lincoln called Mayron and told him a sucker hole was still over Pegasus.

Chris Hoffman, Panzera's flight engineer, talked on the frequency with Brian Alix, Mayron's flight engineer, about his APU's condition. Hoffman had it running steadily now.

Dunbar got on the radios. He wanted to know more about the damage to Skier 92. The aircrew confirmed the damage was to the fairings only. They also suspected snow had fallen over the last few days and created very hard sastrugi, which may not have been present when Fountain was there.

Panzera said, "I'm not so sure if sending another Herc here is a good idea." That cleared up any questions for Mayron. At 7:50 p.m., he requested, "Mac Center, Skier 9-6 presently at 4-6 DME, flight level 3-0-0, request a descent for an approach into Pegasus."

Mac Center cleared him to start a descent toward Pegasus, but the air traffic controller hadn't heard from Lincoln's aircrew for a while. He couldn't clear Mayron to land until he knew whether Lincoln was clear of the runway. Making two 360° turns, Mayron dropped the aircraft from 30,000 feet to 1,000 feet. Thomson reported Stogy 91 was clear of the runway a few minutes later.

At 7:56 p.m., Mac Center gave Skier 96 the current observation at Pegasus:

> "Grid wind 3-6-0 at 2-9, gusting 5-1; visibility 24 hundred meters, blowing snow; sky obscured, few (*clouds*) at 1,500 (*feet*), broken (*cloud ceiling*) at 5,000 (*feet*); temperature minus 1-4; altimeter 2-8-9-1; visibility is fluctuating between 200 and 8,000 (*meters*); surface definition, fair; horizon definition, fair. How copy?"

Mayron copied, and several minutes later, he reported ten nautical miles from Pegasus.

**8:02 p.m.**

**Mac Center:** "Skier 96, check wheels down. Winds 3-6-0 at 3-1, gust 4-2. Cleared to land Runway 3-3, Pegasus."

**8:04 p.m.**

**Mayron:** "Skier 96, gear down."

**8:07 p.m.**

**Paul Jeffries, Skier 96's navigator:** "Mac Center Skier 8-9-6, on HF, safe on the runway at Pegasus."

Immediately after landing, the visibility dropped. When Mayron touched down, the far end of the runway was already obscured. He slowed the aircraft to a crawl. As he tried to taxi clear of the runway, the high winds caused his aircraft to slide sideways. Mayron stopped the aircraft. He then took his hands off of the aircraft controls. "You guys don't mind if I just sit here for a minute." Then finger-by-finger, he slowly tugged each flight glove off of his hands, to pause, and as a means to keep his composure. Nobody objected.

After a few minutes, Mayron tried again to taxi the aircraft off the runway, but the winds were too strong. With every attempt to turn, the aircraft weather-vaned. He directed his copilot, Virginia Holland, to lower the skis. Holland lowered the ski control switch, and the skis came down. They created a more stable platform. Mayron taxied his aircraft next to Lincoln with the nose of the aircraft facing the wind. Both aircrews remained there waiting for transportation. But it would be another 5½ hours before they arrived in McMurdo.

The winds were howling all night. The nose strut was at full extenuation most of the time. The wind and the turbulence made it feel as if they were flying on a low-level flight. Alix ran Skier 96's auxiliary power unit until it was warm, then shut it down and went to sleep. The cold woke him up, and he started it again. He didn't know how long the storm would rage, so he conserved the remaining fuel for as long as he could.

## Skier 92 Update

Everyone was relieved the three aircraft were on the ground and safe, but there was still a big recovery effort ahead. Two crews were at Pegasus, and the road was impassable. One crew was over one hundred miles away on a six thousand-foot high glacier near Wyandot Ridge. The aircrews at Pegasus were eventually picked up and brought to McMurdo.

Panzera hadn't decided whether he would risk flying to McMurdo. Dunbar wanted to get him back. He let Panzera know that Pegasus was still a possibility. He suggested Panzera get airborne within the hour. The other two aircraft made it into Pegasus, and he hadn't seen a significant change in the weather. The only other option was for Panzera's aircrew to spend the night on the blue ice glacier.

**8:37 p.m.**

**Panzera called McMurdo:** "CODF, based on the assessment of all the crew members, we're calling it a night."

He let Dunbar know he didn't feel comfortable taking the aircraft airborne until a maintenance team took a look at the aircraft. Hoffman may have found more damage to the aircraft. He had enough fuel to keep the APU running through the night. He told Dunbar if he started a takeoff roll and didn't get airborne within the first two miles, it was possible the aircraft would fall off a nearby cliff. He wanted to spend some time clearing a path free of sastrugi before he started. Furthermore, they were safe on the ground. There was no reason to go airborne again until the weather cleared.

About 15 minutes later, Panzera called again. He already had three engines shut down to conserve fuel. He had about six and a half hours of fuel remaining with one engine going. He was going to shut down the last engine and just keep the APU going to make the fuel last longer. He wanted Dunbar to know if the APU failed, he'd lose his radios. If he lost his APU, it was also going to get very cold, very fast; however, the APU kept running. Dunbar told Panzera to check in every four hours throughout the evening and give a status check.

Panzera passed his fuel status on to Dunbar.

**Panzera:** "We do not recommend, in the present state, that we bring another (LC-) 130 in here. That is bar none. We really believe that …that it is gonna be necessary to have a crew of people come here, and I mean quickly to get going on a partial clearing, and I don't know how you will get fuel to us in that condition."

**Dunbar :** "Roger that. Copy all that and will work that issue at this point."

Dunbar signed off of the radios for the evening. He needed to work out a recovery effort before he went to bed for the evening.

# Rescue Plan

Richard Saburro was surprised when he heard the news of the three crews that evening. Frequently throughout the day, he had tracked weather on his computer. The weather outside was poor, but the forecast continued to look good. Now, Saburro needed a plan to rescue Panzera's crew.

They went down their list of resources. The Canadian Twin Otter aircraft's crew were on their way home for the season. They had departed McMurdo two weeks prior, and there was no chance of getting them back. The McMurdo helicopter contractors had moved all their aircraft into a hangar the week before and closed up shop for the season. Many of the pilots and maintenance people had already left Antarctica.

The Coast Guard icebreaker had left the McMurdo area four days earlier. It had two helicopters, but it would be a logistical nightmare to get the ship to return. And if they did return, it would take days before they could fly out to Wyandot Ridge. Panzera would run out of fuel by then, and no fuel meant no heat for the aircrew.

The risk needed to be assessed to determine whether landing another LC-130 at Wyandot Ridge was a good idea. The temperature was a big factor because the days were getting shorter, and the temperatures were getting colder. If they went, a maintenance team would need to go along to assess the damage on Skier 92, in addition to the potential damage to the rescue aircraft.

But, risking another LC-130 was the best immediate answer. It could bring additional fuel, a maintenance team, and provisions, and Panzera's aircrew wouldn't be out there alone. This was the plan, but Saburro needed a contingency plan if this didn't work out. The only real option was to let the aircrews come up with a plan.

On 23 February 2000, the leadership made an excellent decision. Knowing that an aircraft had been damaged when it landed on Odell Glacier, and the potential for it to happen again if they sent a second LC-130, and the Twin Otters and helicopters were no longer available, Major George Rob was chosen to pilot another LC-130 to rescue the aircrew of Skier 92.

Rob had rescued the doctor from the South Pole at the beginning of the season. She had been at the South Pole through the previous Antarctica winter to provide medical support for the camp. She diagnosed herself with breast cancer, and she needed to be rescued from the South Pole to get medical help. Her emergency rescue was flawless.

Leadership didn't like to acknowledge that Rob was the best ski pilot of the Raven Gang. George Rob was gritty and raw. He loved to laugh. He laughed at jokes and pranks. He liked his wine and beer, and he laughed when he drank. But Rob wasn't laughing now because he had mentored Panzera and wanted to get him home.

The plan was for two crews and one aircraft to fly to Odell Glacier. Rob had been part of Ted Bell's staff in Raven Ops, so he was well-rested for the flight. Dave Fountain was questionable to fly. He had slept in the chow hall at Williams Field, but he was the only one who had been to Odell Glacier. He would be Rob's copilot. The second aircrew, commanded by Bob Jinks, would be in the back of the aircraft.

Once Rob landed on the blue ice glacier, he would turn the aircraft over to Bob Jinks. Jinks was also part of the staff in Raven Ops, and he would be well-rested. He was a new ski aircraft commander, but he had years of experience flying C-130s in the active-duty Air Force before coming to the Guard. Joel Mayron would be his copilot. Jinks and Mayron would fly Rob's aircraft back to McMurdo, with Panzera's aircrew in the back.

Rob's aircrew would remain at Odell Glacier with a maintenance team until Skier 92 was ready to return to McMurdo.

# The Rescue

McMurdo and New Zealand people worked late into the evening hours, coming up with the rescue plan. The recovery aircraft needed to have maintenance personnel, tools, repair parts, heaters, snowmobiles, ice-cleats for walking, and food and fuel.

It took more than 5½ hours for one Hagalund tracked vehicle to transport both Lincoln's and Mayron's aircrews from Pegasus to McMurdo due to the road's condition. Paul Jeffries thought the Hagalund ride was the worst part of the day.

Throughout their awful experience, Mayron could not shake the feeling he had let the young people in the other airplanes down. He regretted his cavalier attitude earlier in the day. They arrived in McMurdo around 2:00 a.m. and needed rest. Dunbar needed some of these crewmembers, like Mayron, to be part of the rescue aircrew; therefore, it would be late afternoon before the rescue attempt could be made.

Panzera checked in with McMurdo every four hours throughout the evening. Hoffman was injured while getting jolted around during the landing and his neck was in pain. Ankabrandt was concerned about him because he kept talking about walking back to McMurdo. Perhaps the six thousand-foot altitude, or the stress, or hypothermia, or a combination of it all, was taking its toll on him.

Panzera needed to clamp down on this sort of talk. He identified a location for the rescue aircraft to land, and he tasked his people to knock over sastrugi and drifts to provide a more suitable landing for their rescue aircraft. The by-product of this work detail was it kept everyone from focusing on their predicament.

Putman checked the back of the aircraft for damage. Every galley door and drawer was opened. The shelves on the metal book rack were bent. The left paratroop door emergency light was over by the right paratroop door. The LC-130 aircraft was equipped with an entrenching tool, a small, pointed metal shovel. The head of the shovel could be bent and locked at ninety degrees. Panzera's crew used the entrenching tool as if they were splitting wood. When they hit a mound of snow, it disintegrated and blew away. The work was difficult but easier than they expected. Every crewmember took a turn swinging the shovel except Hoffman, who later commented, "I was inside nursing my head and the APU."

They worked throughout the night. It was cold and windy work. The blowing snow felt like sand grains hitting their faces. Putman put on his new gauntlet mittens, and it was the first and last time using them because the extreme cold cracked them. At one point, he yelled at Panzera while they were working, saying, "We can't do this here."

Surprised, Panzera asked, "Why?"

Putman responded, "We don't have a building permit for this."

Both Panzera and Ankabrandt paused, then laughed. Their situation sucked. The weather was getting worse, Hoffman was hurt, and they didn't know when they would be picked up. It was remarkable they found something to laugh about. By morning, they had cleared an area about five hundred feet long and seventy-five feet wide. They were tired, and the thin air was adding to their fatigue.

The ski-equipped C-130 aircraft was designed with special modifications to aid aircrews stuck on the ice cap. One example was the source of fuel to the APU. The typical C-130 fed fuel to the APU from the #2 fuel tank. When the #2 fuel tank emptied, the APU stopped. The skibirds fed fuel to the APU through the crossfeed manifold. All fuel tanks can feed the crossfeed manifold; therefore, the APU could continue running until all aircraft fuel tanks were empty.

Hoffman kept the APU running, and this allowed hot bleed air to flow through the air conditioning system and keep the aircraft warm throughout the night. When crew members weren't swinging the entrenching tool, they were inside the aircraft napping and staying warm. Putman used the timbers in the back of the aircraft as a bed for the night.

In the morning, Panzera removed some webbed seats from the back of the aircraft. The seats were red and stood out on the clear Antarctica afternoon. He positioned them in the snow to mark the area they had cleared throughout the evening to help Rob identify the area when he arrived overhead. The seats blew away soon after they were put up. Then they used the Kool-aide packets from their survival meal kits to mark their makeshift landing zone.

Rob and his crew had no difficulty finding Panzera's aircraft. They talked over the radio and pointed out the area his crew had cleared. Rob made one more pass and lined up on a final approach, and completed the appropriate checklists. He intimately knew the technical manual of the aircraft. Chapter Five recommended how to land on bomb-damaged airfields. The blue ice glacier wasn't bomb-damaged, but from what Panzera told him, it was the next closest thing.

He touched down on the glacier and stopped abruptly. His purpose was to minimize the landing roll, thus minimizing aircraft damage. On touchdown, he stomped on the brakes and reversed the throttles. Everyone was hanging in their seat belts and shoulder harnesses. It worked. The aircraft stopped. There was no damage to the aircraft or the crew.

After landing, Rob spent forty minutes taxiing around the area. When he completed his survey, he taxied to Skier 92. He aligned his aircraft in the opposite direction of Skier 92. Another aircraft modification to the LC-130 was an aircraft-to-aircraft refueling kit. This allowed the aircrews to refuel one aircraft from another aircraft parked nearby.

When the wingtip of his aircraft was past Panzera's wingtip, he stopped. The refueling panels, located on the copilot's side of the aircraft, were aligned. Rob's aircrew had the refueling kit, and when he stopped the aircraft, the loadmasters from both aircraft opened their paratroop doors and extended the refueling hose between the aircraft. The flight engineers worked the refueling panel, and Rob's aircraft transferred fuel to Skier 92. It was cold, and the wind was howling. The maintenance folks swarmed Skier 92.

| Maintenance Team | |
|---|---|
| **Master Sergeant** | Robert Thivierge– Crew chief |
| **Technical Sergeant** | Steven Radz—Crew chief |
| **Technical Sergeant** | Daniel Beachler– Electrician |
| **Technical Sergeant** | Mike Craig—Engine mechanic |
| **Technical Sergeant** | John Stiles– Hydraulic specialist |

The specialists carefully inspected the aircraft to ensure the systems were still functional. Crew chiefs are jacks-of-all-trades. They refueled Panzera's aircraft from the fuel tanks of the other aircraft and helped out where necessary. Master Sergeant Bobby Thivierge was the overall authority to recommend whether the Skier 92 was safe to fly to McMurdo. A flight doctor from McMurdo also came along with Rob and looked over Panzera's crew to ensure no one required medical attention before going back to McMurdo.

A power cart was pulled from Rob's aircraft and moved to Skier 92. It would be used to start the aircraft engines when the time came. The fierce cold wind tried to blow the power cart away, down the glacier. So, Technical Sergeant Steve Radz took an aircraft crash ax and slammed it into the ice.

Next, he got an aircraft chain and secured the power cart to the ax to hold it firm.

*Bobby Thivierge*

Jinks and Joel Mayron, with Panzera's aircrew, returned to McMurdo. The maintenance team spent hours pulling panels and checking systems. They did a thorough inspection of the aircraft. There was no damage except to the fiberglass ski fairings. Rob flew Skier 92 to McMurdo a few hours later.

# Return to Christchurch

By the end of the day, all the aircraft and people were back at McMurdo. It was time to plan for the final northbound missions to close the season. The day was spent packing up tools, equipment and loading the aircraft to go home. Skier 91 and Skier 96 flew back to Christchurch on the same evening as the rescue.

While refueling Skier 92, Steve Radz noticed the aircraft's nose radome was billowing smoke. Something was on fire. Radz pulled the fuel hose from the aircraft and stopped the refueling operation. He then ran to the front of the aircraft and helped put the fire out. The cause of the fire was radar receiver/transmitter, and its mount had been packed in snow during its time at Wyandot Ridge. Maintenance needed another day for repairs. Later in the evening, Saburro had the C-141 aircraft fly to McMurdo with parts needed to fix Skier 92. They returned with the last of the people who were scheduled to leave Antarctica for the season.

On 24 February 2000, Rob flew Skier 92 to Christchurch with the gear down. Over the next couple of days, maintenance performed additional checks on the aircraft before it flew back to New York. The maintenance people took their time and did a very thorough job in the beautiful, sunny, late summer weather of Christchurch, New Zealand.

CHAPTER 26

# MAINTENANCE AIRCRAFT RECOVERY PROGRAM

During the 1995 Greenland Season, two broken aircraft at Camp Century sparked the beginning of the Maintenance Aircraft Recovery Program. The Raven Gang was operating out of Thule Air Base, Greenland, to support the National Science Foundation objectives.

| **Skier 92** | |
|---|---|
| **Pilot:** | Lt. Col. Giles Wagoner |
| **Copilot:** | Lt. Col. James Blakney |
| **Navigator** | Major Michael Spina |
| **Flight Engineer:** | Senior Master Sergeant Michael Cristiano |
| **Loadmaster:** | Senior Master Sergeant Dennis Morgan |

Lt. Col. Giles Wagoner's day began with an open snow flight to the Greenland ice cap. He landed and offloaded his cargo. As he tried to take off, the snow was very challenging, and the aircraft wouldn't accelerate. He tried multiple times to get airborne, but he couldn't get the acceleration he needed. On his last takeoff attempt, he reached forty-five knots. He decided it was now or never, so he directed his flight engineer, Senior Master Sergeant Mike Cristiano, to fire the ATO bottles. Skier 92 accelerated further, and he was able to pull his nose ski off of the snow. His takeoff slide continued for several more miles. He was exhausted when he finally got airborne.

On their return leg, Major Danny Dunbar from Raven Operations asked if they would fly a maintenance team to rescue the aircrew of Skier 91.

Skier 91 was disabled at Camp Century, located about one hundred miles from Thule Air Base. They couldn't extend the aircraft skis because the ski control valve malfunctioned and needed to be replaced. Wagoner and his aircrew agreed. Skier 92 landed at Thule, picked up four maintenance workers and a ski control valve. While they were on the ground, Lt. Col. Jim Blakney moved to the left seat, and Wagoner moved to the right seat, and Blakney flew the mission to Camp Century.

## Camp Century

The weather was questionable, and the winds were unpredictable. However, Blakney decided to descend. He was inside the ping-pong ball, with no surface definition and no horizon. Outside the aircraft, everything was a dull white. As they approached the surface, Cristiano made altitude calls from the radar altimeter. The radar altimeter sent radar signals to the ground and bounced back to the aircraft giving the height above the ground to an indicator on the pilot's instrument panel.

Typically, pilots liked to hear the flight engineer call when they were at 100 feet, then "50…40…30…20…10…." However, Skier 92's radar altimeter wasn't accurate. Immediately after Cristiano said, "40," the aircraft impacted the ground. Blakney fought to keep control of the aircraft. It became airborne again and went into about a sixty-degree left bank. Technical Sergeant Brian Bik, sitting in the back on the left side of the aircraft, was "looking straight up" at the other side. While the aircraft was still in a left bank, the aircraft made its second impact on the ground.

The #1 and #2 propellers went into the snow. The #2 engine started to wind down, and the aircraft made an arcing turn. Blakney gained control and stopped the aircraft. He directed Wagoner to shut down the #2 engine. Only speculation can explain why the #2 engine, the inside engine on the left wing, failed, but not the #1 engine.

After taking a few moments to gather his composure, Blakney tried to taxi closer to Skier 91, but he was stuck in the snow, and the #2 engine wouldn't restart. This was the second aircraft of the day to be put out of action at Camp Century.

The maintenance people on Skier 92 repaired Skier 91, then both crews and the maintenance people flew back to Thule. The maintenance contingent in Thule formed a team to fly back out to Camp Century to repair Skier 92. When they returned, they slept in tents and fighter trenches topped with parachute material and ate canned Spaghettios™ and ravioli for the next eight days.

## Maintenance Aircraft Recovery Program

The 109th Maintenance Group realized they lacked proper survival training. Unlike in the past, the DYE sites were no longer available to shield them when the environment became too raw. They needed to develop a survival program to prepare them for future mishaps. They needed funding to build a camp with shelter, food, water, and equipment. This sparked the creation of the ski mission's Maintenance Aircraft Recovery Program.

The Raven Gang aircrews' life support shop, or aircrew flight equipment shop, had developed a barren land arctic survival program, Kool School, in the early 1990s to survive in Greenland and Antarctica. There are no trees on the ice cap, so unlike the arctic survival school in Fairbanks, Alaska, the school in Greenland was designed so crewmembers could survive without an external fuel source to keep them warm. Arctic survival instructors from Fairbanks, Alaska, attended the 109th Airlift Wing's Kool School to accredit the course for those who attended it. Their curriculum taught techniques for evasion, resistance, and escape from the clutches of an enemy.

However, Master Sergeant Joe Butler had a different concept of what his survival maintenance program should be. He wanted instruction on the physical and psychological stresses of the cold weather; a discussion of cold weather clothing, shelter requirements, fire; the procurement and storing of water; medical concerns related to cold weather. This was the standard stuff. But unlike a combat scenario, on the polar ice cap, people wanted to be found.

Before the 1995 Camp Century incident, few maintenance members attended Kool School. It had a lot of value for survival but didn't quite meet their needs. Butler's vision of what they needed included a three-day survival course on the Greenland ice cap. First of all, each maintenance member needed to be issued mandatory survival clothing.

On day one, his people needed to dig and sleep in a fighter trench in the snow. On day two, they needed to build a camp from their supply inventory; this included a polar haven and tents. On day three, he wanted them to become familiar with track vehicles, such as snowmobiles, piston bullies, and bulldozers, which were necessary to repair the aircraft.

Between 1995 and 1998, Butler worked on his concept. He trained recruits on how to survive and fix airplanes in harsh polar environments. He obtained funds to purchase the camping equipment he needed. Then, he convinced Mr. Steven Dunbar, a National Science Foundation survival and recovery contractor, to attend his class on the Greenland ice cap to certify the camp and the curriculum.

Dunbar witnessed what Butler had done, and he wrote a stellar letter to the National Science Foundation, certifying the aircraft recovery team was one hundred percent self-sufficient. In doing so, Butler's team no longer needed to rely on support from the National Science Foundation before his team went out and recovered an aircraft.

From November 1998 through early January 1999, this recovery team pulled an aircraft out of a crevasse and repaired it at Upstream Delta. In late February of 2000, they recovered an aircraft from Odell Glacier, near Wyandot Ridge. In December of 2003, they encountered multiple challenges.

## The Mission

Earlier in the day, on 4 December 2003, Lt. Col. Chris Penno's crew had left McMurdo, Antarctica, with pallets of fuel drums destined for Ford Range. These were to become a fuel cache for the Twin Otter aircraft operating in the area later in the season.

*Joe Butler*

However, before going to Ford Range, Penno's aircrew was scheduled to fly to the Flood Mountain Range in Marie Byrd Land, Western Antarctica.

| Skier 91 Aircrew | |
|---|---|
| **Pilot:** | Lt. Col. Chris Penno |
| **Copilot:** | Captain Erik Srokowski |
| **Navigator:** | Major Cheryl "Sam" Olszowy |
| **Flight engineer:** | Technical Sergeant Chris Collins |
| **Loadmaster:** | Senior Master Sergeant Billy Nolin |
| **Loadmaster:** | Staff Sergeant Patrick Newton |

# Mount Moulton Site Analysis

An open snow site was generally an open snowfield where no one had been before. Scientists wanted to go to these locations because of their scientific value. Following the disaster in a crevasse field at Upstream Delta in 1998, the Raven Gang had built a robust site review analysis of all the National Science Foundation's selected sites. It was required before they landed anywhere.

The site-review analysis typically began the year prior at the National Science Foundation. Once the National Science Foundation's Office of Polar Programs identified where they wanted to go during the next Antarctica season, they would get satellite imagery, followed by an assessment from specialists of the imagery. In turn, the Office of Polar Programs provided this information to the Raven Gang.

After the Raven Gang received the satellite imagery and analysis of these sites, their Antarctica Shop would review the data. They created a repository of information for these sites before the upcoming Antarctica season and prepared a briefing for the commanders to review. The intent was to minimize surprises when landing at a new site.

During the season, an aircrew overflew the intended location and visually observed the site before landing. They surveyed it from different sun angles to identify crevasses, ridgelines, or any other potential hazard. A photographer snapped photos throughout the reconnaissance for review after they returned to McMurdo.

Flood Range was a range of large snow-covered mountains extending in an east-west direction for about sixty miles, and Mount Moulton was located there. The aircrew planned a reconnaissance flight of the Mount Moulton science site. The lead scientist, the camp manager, a mountaineer, and a photographer would go along. This was the standard operating procedure of the Raven Gang before landing in an open snow area.

The science value of the Mount Moulton site was to investigate the changes in the West Antarctic climate. Scientists did this by collecting ice cores from a blue ice glacier up to 480,000 years old. They identified the age of the layers of ice in the cores. The trapped air within the ice core gave them an understanding of the climate during that period.

This part of the mission was a success. The photoreconnaissance of the sight appeared to be safe for LC-130 landings. After a close review of the photos, the Raven Gang would send another aircrew to land at Mount Moulton with the science team.

After the reconnaissance flight, they flew to Ford Mountain Range to drop off the fuel drums. Ford Range was about one hundred sixty miles west of Mount Moulton, along the route-of-flight back to McMurdo. It took half an hour to get there.

## Ford Range

The Raven Gang was familiar with the Ford Range area. During the 1998–1999 Antarctica Season, they had set up a skiway and flew multiple missions there. At the time, the project's lead scientist described the area this way:[154]

> *"We are headed into the abyss of Antarctic weather. Gale force winds and driving snow are what Marie Byrd Land has in store. Just as likely are moisture-laden ice fogs that shroud everything in eerie silences for days on end. We believe the Ford Ranges are fault-block mountains developed after the onset of West Antarctic glaciation, 20 million years ago or even earlier. Polished, glaciated surfaces on mountain summits, once part of a continuous plateau, are cut by glacier-filled valleys."*

That occurred five years before. The skiway was gone now, and their intended landing location was a windswept ice sheet again.

Ford Range was east of the Ross Ice Sheet, in an area known as the West Antarctic Ice Sheet. Their landing location was approximately six-hundred fifty nautical miles from McMurdo. It was a vast open area with mountains and nunatak[155] surrounded by glacial fields in all directions. Satellite images showed a five-square-mile area free of crevasses and obstacles, true east of Cody Nunatak and true west of Mount Jones and Mount Atwood.

Penno landed Skier 91 in the open snowfield at 77°13.0' South, 142° 44.43' West. He expected to be on the snow for about ten minutes. The surface conditions were six inches of soft snow over hard-packed snow. He did not intend to stop but taxied very slowly. The aircraft was moving at a snail's pace until the loadmasters were ready in the back to offload the pallets. When Senior Master Sergeant Billy Nolin called for power, Penno pushed up the throttles and accelerated the aircraft to create momentum for the pallets to move back. Nolin and Staff Sergeant Pat Newton pushed the pallets of fuel as they were exiting out of the back of the aircraft. Nolin called "Load Clear" when the last pallet exited, and Penno slowed again. The loadmasters closed the ramp and door when they were finished.

They were ready to return to McMurdo. After briefing how he would conduct the takeoff slide, Penno pushed the throttles forward, and the aircraft began to accelerate slowly, too slow. He was limited on how far he could slide. He was in a five-mile box known to be safe from crevasses. As he approached the end of the safe area, he pulled the throttles back and slowed down, turned around, and tried again.

He tried several times with no success. He needed better snow and more headwind. The crew felt a significant bump on the slide. Penno aborted the takeoff and stopped. Something was wrong. The nose of the aircraft was sitting lower than normal. He suspected the nose strut needed to be serviced.

Penno tried four more times to get airborne before the utility hydraulic pressure went to zero. He stopped the aircraft. "Chris, go out and take a look." Technical Sergeant Chris Collins, Penno's flight engineer, was the systems expert on the aircraft. He climbed out of his seat and walked down the stairs of the flight deck.

Nolin opened the crew entrance door, and it fell open ninety degrees. Typically, the door swings open until the door's back comes in contact with the aircraft's fuselage, but now the door was resting on the snow. The nose of the aircraft was very low. This was the first week of Collins' Antarctica career. He scrambled outside and walked to the nose gear area of the aircraft. He told Penno, "I know what the problem is. The nose gear cylinder snapped." When it broke, it moved aft. The beginning of the cargo compartment above was resting on the nose ski. They weren't going anywhere.

Major Sam Olszowy made a radio call back to Raven Operations in McMurdo.

**Olszowy:** "Skier Ops. Skier 91. Be advised we're on the ground at Ford Range with all four engines shut down. Everyone is safe, no injuries."

There was a long pause on the other end. Colonel Verle Johnston replied.

**Johnston:** "Roger, #4 engine shut down."

**Olszowy corrected him:** "Negative; all four engines are shut down."

Then, an even longer pause.

**Johnston:** "Roger, all four shut down."

She heard a heavy sigh.

They were going to spend the night on the ice. Penno turned the aircraft's nose into the sun before he directed the engines to be shut down. He wanted the radiant heat of the sun to keep the aircraft warm through the night. The crew slept in the aircraft. The Mount Moulton four-person science team set up tents outside.

## Rescue, Recovery, and Repair Plan

On 5 December 2003, a Twin Otter aircraft picked up the aircrew and the science team and flew them to Siple Dome Camp, two hundred seventy-five nautical miles south of their location. In 1997, scientists from the Desert Research Institute in Reno, Nevada, conducted various climate studies at Siple Dome. When the research was finished, the National Science Foundation considered shutting down Siple Dome, but it was still a key location as a link for operations taking place in the Western Antarctica Ice Sheet. A fuel cache was kept there, and Twin Otters frequented this location to refuel or spend the evening.

It also turned out to be a splendid location for the Twin Otter pilots to bring stranded aircrews to await transportation back to McMurdo. Olszowy made a radio call from Siple Dome as she did the night before to let Raven Operations know they were ready for transportation back to McMurdo. Later in the afternoon, an LC-130 flew to Siple Dome and brought everyone back to McMurdo. Master Sergeant Robert Thivierge and an aero-repair specialist flew out to Siple Dome on the LC-130. That afternoon, a Twin Otter flew them to Ford Range to survey the damage to Skier 91 and determine how to fix it.

Thivierge was in charge of the LC-130 Maintenance Aircraft Recovery Program after taking over the program in May of 2002, and this was his first major recovery effort. The maintenance team he hand-picked for the recovery effort had either attended the Maintenance Aircraft Recovery Program or were students in his most recent class. It turned out to be a very interesting challenge.

It was obvious at first glance that Skier 91 would need a complete nose gear and ski assembly. The front nose gear spindle was broken. The following day, an LC-130 arrived at Siple Dome, picked up the two maintenance people, and flew them back to McMurdo.

Upon his return to McMurdo, Thivierge talked with Chief Master Sergeant Robert Podbielski, the maintenance supervisor in McMurdo. Thivierge planned to remove the nose gear assembly from Skier 01 when it arrived in Christchurch, then have the assembly brought back on the next southbound aircraft. Podbielski liked the plan and approved it.

It was Saturday morning, and Skier 01 was already on its way to Christchurch. This was the standard 109$^{th}$ Airlift Wing weekly rotation. Most of the people on board were on their way home to New York. Upon landing, the maintenance team in Christchurch removed the nose gear and ski assembly from the aircraft.

On Sunday, 7 December 2003, Skier 96 departed Christchurch for McMurdo with the nose gear assembly. Captain Mitch Stevens was the aircraft commander and was one of the younger ski mission aircraft commanders in the Raven Gang. He was going to have an interesting week.

Thivierge was asked to attend a senior staff meeting in the conference room of Building 165. It was a daily meeting of National Science Foundation representatives, contractors, and military personnel. The purpose of the meeting was to discuss the missions for the week.

Thivierge didn't think it was a friendly meeting. He discussed what he needed to bring the aircraft back to McMurdo. Then the questions started. The contractors failed to understand the significance of what Thivierge needed to do to repair the stranded aircraft.

The contractors had a myopic view of what it entailed and only seemed concerned about getting the Raven Gang to deliver fuel caches to the Western Antarctica Ice Sheet. They weren't interested in a maintenance team's efforts to repair the stranded aircraft. Dangers and hazards were not in the contractors' scope of work. They couldn't grasp what Thivierge and his team might face while at Ford Range. Instead, they questioned how much space Thivierge and his team would take with their parts and tools. One comment Thivierge found particularly aggravating was, *"They don't need that much food; they're only going to be there 24 hours."*

Thivierge held his tongue, but he was angry and walked out of the room. His boss followed him out in the hallway. "What's wrong?"

Thivierge said he wasn't going out to Ford Range with the limited food and equipment. He already had a skeleton tool kit. His team had trained for these instances, and he wasn't going to shortcut their needs. His commander walked back into the room and got Thivierge everything he asked for.

# Snowed In

Thivierge and his team flew out to Ford Range.

| Maintenance Team | |
|---|---|
| **Master Sergeant** | Robert Thivierge (team lead, crew chief) |
| **Technical Sergeant** | Chris Wren (crew chief) |
| **Technical Sergeant** | Dave Crouch (crew chief) |
| **Technical Sergeant** | John Stiles (crew chief, formerly a hydraulic specialist) |
| **Technical Sergeant** | Scott French (repair and reclamation; aero-repair and hydraulic specialist) |
| **Technical Sergeant** | Gene Haller (repair and reclamation; aero-repair specialist) |

On 9 December 2003, the first of several aircraft arrived at Ford Range with 9,272 pounds of cargo, Thivierge, Haller, and four passengers.

Two of the passengers were survival mountaineers to assist with camp functions. One was a Raytheon services employee to assist with camp maintenance, food preparations, and inventory of all the National Science Foundation supplies. The fourth was also a Raytheon service employee to operate the ground power equipment.

Later in the day, Captain Carlyle Norman dropped off the nose gear assembly with the rest of the maintenance team. I was flying on the night shift. We arrived later in the evening with additional food and supplies. Night and day are relative at this time of year in Antarctica. The sun is always up. The weather was sunny and clear for the first 40 hours while they repaired Skier 91. The maintenance team set up a base camp and removed the nose gear assembly from the aircraft in their first few hours. French and Haller put an uninflated airbag beneath the fuselage of the aircraft. They used an air compressor to inflate the bag. The nose of the aircraft rose high enough for them to install the aircraft nose jacks. With the jacks installed, the damaged nose gear was disassembled and pulled out from under the aircraft with a snowmobile and muscle. It took everyone to push the new strut and ski assembly into place.

The aircraft jacks were on sleds, which caused them to constantly shift in the soft snow while raising and lowering the aircraft, making it unstable. Instead of lowering the aircraft onto the new nose gear strut and ski assembly, they decided to raise the aircraft's strut and ski assembly. Thivierge had a floor jack he bought from an auto parts store in New York. His jack worked perfectly. The new strut slipped into place, and they attached the strut and hydraulic lines.

In the early morning hours of 11 December 2003, the maintenance team finished their work. They were ready to return to McMurdo, but this was going to take some time. The weather turned bad at Ford Range, and no aircraft could land and pick them up until the low cloud ceiling cleared. Overnight the winds howled, and the visibility dropped. Using a handheld wind speed anemometer, Thivierge and one of the mountaineers recorded eighty-two knots during the storm. Throughout the blizzard, everyone constantly cleared snow from their two-man tents' walls to keep them from collapsing inwards. Their pieces of equipment would be buried by morning, so they stuck bamboo poles nearby with flags to locate them after the storm.

*Skier 91 Jacked with Nose Gear in Foreground*

By the morning of 12 December 2003, the storm had abated, but the camp was in a fog bank, and the aircraft was buried in snow. The weather didn't improve throughout the day, and they spent their time digging the aircraft and their equipment out of the snow. They spent another day and night at Ford Range, and their camping trip was turning into a survival situation.

I flew to the South Pole Friday evening and returned in the early hours of Saturday morning. After my return, I went to Building 165 to debrief the mission. Chris Penno was there, and he told me I was now the deployed commander. The former deployed commander was boarding an aircraft to go to Christchurch in a few hours. There would be no official change-over.

Penno couldn't be the deployed commander because he was under investigation for leaving the airplane at Ford Range. It was a formality, but he couldn't do any official duties until the investigation was completed. He told me to get some rest and return by noon. He kept an eye on the operation while I left and rested.

I returned to Raven Ops around noon, and Colonel Verle Johnston was with Penno. Johnston was the acting commander for Operation Deep Freeze. It was Saturday afternoon. Typically, we only flew Saturday morning flights and, the maintenance people got Saturday evening off. Typically, there would be no one on the flight line after the last Saturday morning line returned to McMurdo. But this wasn't a typical Saturday.

Johnston wanted to talk to me about rescuing the six maintenance people and four civilians stuck at Ford Range. He gave me an update on the situation, telling me the weather was clearing over Ford Range. The weather forecasters expected a hole to open up, and there was a window of opportunity to land an aircraft there to bring everyone back.

As the deployed commander, I was in charge of the LC-130s flying operation on the continent. Penno had no official responsibilities, but he had already worked out a strategy to get the airplane and maintenance guys back. Johnston and Penno were looking for my approval to start the rescue operation.

Johnston asked me, "Joe, do you want to risk sending an aircraft out there?"

Without hesitation, I said yes.

"The weather may close up, and we may lose our chance this weekend. Are you sure you want to risk it?"

"Absolutely."

"So would I."

That was the go-ahead.

The maintenance teams were still on the flight line with an aircraft ready to launch. Penno already had aircrews in crew-rest ready to go.[156] They were in an alert status waiting for the call.

**4:00 p.m.**

Penno alerted the aircraft commanders and told them they had the mission's go-ahead. He told them to get something to eat before showing up at ops, "A hungry pilot is a stupid pilot." Nobody wanted to fly with a hungry stupid pilot. The aircraft commanders, in turn, alerted the rest of their crewmembers.

Captain Mitch Stevens and Captain Carlyle Norman were the aircraft commanders. We planned to use both aircrews and one airplane. Stevens was the aircraft commander of Skier 95, the first crew. He would land at

Ford Range and return to McMurdo with the maintenance team. Norman would travel to Ford Range in Skier 95 and fly Skier 91 back to McMurdo.

| Skier 95 Aircrew | |
|---|---|
| **Pilot:** | Captain Mitch Stevens |
| **Copilot:** | Lt. Col. Tim Thomson |
| **Navigator:** | Major Cheryl "Sam" Olszowy |
| **Flight engineer:** | Technical Sergeant Chris Sherman |
| **Loadmaster:** | Technical Sergeant John Bartow |
| **Loadmaster:** | Staff Sergeant Kevin Zenner |

| Skier 91 Aircrew | |
|---|---|
| **Pilot:** | Captain Carlyle Norman |
| **Copilot:** | First Lieutenant Richard Hoss |
| **Navigator:** | Captain Seth Barrows |
| **Flight engineer:** | Master Sergeant Keith Ardrey |
| **Loadmaster:** | Technical Sergeant Carmelo Modesto |
| **Loadmaster:** | Technical Sergeant Scott Seeberger |

# Things Never Go as Planned

The enlisted people went to the flight line to pre-flight the aircraft. The officers came in and started flight planning around 5:00 p.m., Saturday afternoon. It was going to be a busy night. The weather created doubts for everyone, and they knew it was going to be challenging. After the flight planning, the officers went to Derelict Junction and caught a ride to the flight line. Skier 95 was ready to go. They taxied to the fuel pits. After fueling, they taxied to the ATO loading area. When they were ready, they re-started the engines, taxied out to the ice runway, and Stevens took off. They were airborne at 8:00 p.m. The two-and-a-half-hour flight to Ford Range was uneventful.

Upon Skier 95's arrival at Ford Range, the weather was worse than they expected. Stevens couldn't see the surface below. He decided to remain at altitude to conserve fuel until the weather improved. Sam Olszowy set up a holding pattern in the navigation system, and Stevens put the aircraft in orbit. He then called me at Raven Operations and told me the weather wasn't cooperating.

Stevens orbited for two hours before a sucker hole opened up in the clouds, and he saw his opportunity. It was his best chance to get beneath the clouds and down to the snow below. When he saw Skier 91, he flew a couple of low approaches to look at the snow surface and set up his landing approach. He made an open snow landing, and the snow was not too rough but not that smooth either.

He stopped and kept his aircraft engines running. He sent Zenner out the crew entrance door. Zenner extended the communications cord of his headset to create a nominal barrier. Its purpose was to remind people to turn away from the spinning propellers as they exited the aircraft. Captain Carlyle Norman's aircrew departed the aircraft and walked over to Thivierge. Skier 91 was ready to go.

The maintenance team had been digging the aircraft out of the snow all day. Shovels were the only thing they had available to do so, and they were exhausted. Thivierge gave Norman and Master Sergeant Keith Ardrey, Norman's flight engineer, a briefing on their replacement of the nose gear and ski assembly. Together the maintenance team and the aircrew spent a couple of hours looking over the aircraft and pre-flighting it. They verified they had enough fuel to return to McMurdo. Then they mounted the ATO bottles on the side of the aircraft and installed the ignitors.

The plan was for Norman to depart first to ensure Skier 91 got airborne before the maintenance team left the ice. Norman's aircrew started the engines and taxied straight ahead. When he was clear of the camp, he increased the throttles to takeoff power. As the aircraft accelerated, Norman said, "ATO—Now!" Ardrey fired the bottles, and Norman pulled the aircraft off the snow, and they soon disappeared. He was airborne at 2:30 a.m.

Thivierge's team with the recovery equipment boarded Skier 95. When everything was secured in the back of the aircraft, Stevens pushed up the throttles to takeoff. He couldn't break free of the ice. The friction created from the surface of the skis sliding along the snow generated heat. This heat melted the snow beneath the skis and as the aircraft remained idle the water layer froze and bonded the skis to the ice. The depth of the ice beneath the skis depended on how hot they were when it stopped. It was deep enough to hold the aircraft in place while Stevens applied maximum power to Skier 95's four engines.

Stevens sent Thivierge and his team out to dig snow from beneath the skis so he could break free. After digging, everyone boarded the aircraft, but Stevens still couldn't break free. Several times the maintenance people were sent out to dig. Stevens wanted to lighten the weight of the aircraft. He had two pallets on board. One of them was the pallet with the broken nose gear from 91. The other pallet had the camp equipment and the civilian's personal gear on it. He told the loadmasters to push the pallets out into the snow. It wasn't a popular decision; however, it was enough to break the aircraft free. The only things remaining in the back of the aircraft were a snowmobile and the ten passengers.

Stevens now had another problem. The time struggling to break free of the ice burned a lot of fuel. They couldn't make it back to McMurdo. As the aircraft accelerated, Stevens fired his ATO bottles and was airborne at 3:30 a.m. The aircrew talked over their problem and decided to go to Siple Dome to refuel before returning to McMurdo.

## Siple Dome

The flight time to Siple Dome was 1.3 hours, and the weather was beautiful when they arrived. Stevens set the aircraft down on the skiway and taxied to the fuel tanks. The fuel specialists hired to run the fuel pump at the camp guided Stevens to where they wanted him to stop the aircraft. There was plenty of fuel hose; however, they preferred to move the aircraft closer to the fuel pits to make it easier for them to retrieve the fuel hose after the refueling was completed. After they stopped, Thomson raised the skis. Stevens kept the aircraft engines running.

Senior Master Sergeant Chris Sherman left his flight engineer's seat and went outside. He walked around the aircraft and searched for any potential problems following their struggles at Ford Range. Then, with the fuel contractors' help, he attached the hose to the aircraft and loaded 15,000 pounds of fuel for the flight back to McMurdo.

When the fueling was completed, everyone returned to their seats. Stevens directed Thomson to lower the skis. Once the nose ski was down, he pushed the throttles up, high into the flight range. He intended to create a surge of momentum to break the aircraft free from the ice. It was the typical technique.

Once the aircraft broke free of the snow, Stevens pulled his throttles back to flight idle. As he did so, Skier 95's #1 propeller remained at a higher power setting while the other propellers went to flight idle. The #1 propeller's high-power setting caused the aircraft to pivot aggressively, ninety degrees to the right, toward a large metal fuel storage tank. Olszowy, the navigator, yelled, "We're going to hit! We're going to hit!" Zenner, the loadmaster, shouted, "Everyone, hold on! We're going to hit!" In the rear of the aircraft, John Stiles had fallen asleep as the aircrew fought to break free of the ice. When Zenner yelled, he jumped up out of a dead sleep. He thought they were airborne and were about to crash. As he tried to get oriented, the aircraft went dark. Gene Haller also had fallen asleep. When the aircraft went dark, French shoved him to wake him up to be ready to evacuate the aircraft if needed. Haller's reaction was the same, "Are we airborne?" he asked.

Thomson reached forward and shut down the aircraft engines. This sudden action caused the aircraft to lose all power. Inside everything went dark. Moments later, Sherman turned on the aircraft battery. Electrical power was restored, and lights came back on.

The aircraft stopped short of hitting the tank, but they were only twelve feet away. Stevens evaluated his situation. The orientation of the aircraft prevented him from being able to move it. The C-130 was designed to taxi in reverse; however, Stevens's aircraft was on skis. Any attempt to back away from the tank, using reverse thrust, had the potential to pitch the aircraft's nose up in the air and cause the aircraft to fall back on its tail. This was not a good option. Fortunately, Stevens had the maintenance recovery team with him.

## Skier 91's Return

Seth Barrows, Norman's navigator, called Raven Operations and notified me they were one hundred miles, about twenty minutes, from the field. I called the flight line people to notify them of his arrival. No one answered. I tried to contact the SOM, supervisor of maintenance, also. No luck. They had gone back to town. I went down to the flight line and into the maintenance tower. No one was there. Norman arrived overhead at 5:00 a.m. I cleared him onto the parking ramp. The supervisor of maintenance arrived and took over. I went back to town and into Building 165.

It was about 6:00 a.m. when I returned. Chris Penno was back in the office after a night's rest. He had a wicked smile on his face when I arrived. He told me, "Skier 95 is broken down at Siple Dome."

In disbelief, I said, "No."

He kept smiling and said, "Yep."

Verle Johnston showed up in the office. Penno filled us both in on what was going on at Siple Dome. He said Mitch Stevens called from Siple Dome. He explained how Stevens's aircraft pivoted ninety degrees to the right when he pulled out from the fuel pits, and he was now stuck with the nose of the aircraft within a few feet from a large metal fuel tank containing JP-8.

Johnston sent me to bed. I left the building, and Johnston and Penno began working on the Skier 95 rescue. Stevens's aircrew went into crew-rest at Siple Dome, while Thivierge and his team came up with a game plan and coordinated it through the maintenance folks at McMurdo.

# Siple Dome Recovery

Thivierge contacted Mac Ops on the radio. He wanted to talk to the supervisor of maintenance, Chief Master Sergeant Bob Podbielski. Johnston and Podbielski talked with him. The first thing Podbielski asked, "Bob, do you want me to send another maintenance team?" Thivierge said no. His team wanted to stay and help out, but he needed the bridled assembly to pull the aircraft backward. Johnston commented, "Hopefully, we have it in the supply building."

The bridle assembly was stored in New Zealand when the LC-130s were not in Antarctica. At the beginning of the season, it was brought to McMurdo. Thivierge told Podbielski he'd find it packed in purple boxes at the supply warehouse. Podbielski walked down to the warehouse and found the boxes.

The bridle assembly was part of the CDDAR, crash-disabled-damaged aircraft recovery equipment. It was an elaborate tow-line system created to pull Skier 95 from a crevasse in 1998.

Two orange-colored chains connected either side of the ski. The chains were extended behind the ski, and each chain connected on either end of an orange-colored bar. The bar was the width of the ski. Both chains then continued further behind the bar and connected to one end of a second bar. The other ski had the same setup—both chains connected to the other side of the second bar. The second bar had two large black rubber grommets, which raised the bar out of the snow. Two thick cables were also attached to either end of the second bar, extended for about twenty feet, and attached to a bulldozer.

*Bridle Assembly, Chris Wren Pic*

The bridle assembly was brought to the flight line and loaded in the back of Major Bruce Jones' aircraft, Skier 92. After the loading was completed, Jones taxied to the fuel pits, filled the aircraft full of fuel, started engines, and took off from Ice Runway 25. He brought an engine mechanic along, Technical Sergeant Eric Carlo, to look at Skier 95's engine.

The weather was clear when he arrived at Siple Dome. He landed the aircraft without any problems and taxied near Skier 95, stopping the aircraft but kept the engines running. Stevens' aircrew swapped out with Jones' aircrew. Stevens took Skier 92 and returned to McMurdo with the passengers. Jones' aircrew and Thivierge and his team remained behind to fly Skier 95 back.

| Skier 92 Aircrew | |
|---|---|
| **Pilot:** | Major Bruce Jones |
| **Copilot:** | Captain Leroy King |
| **Navigator:** | First Lieutenant Kelly Davey (Person) |
| **Flight engineer:** | Chief Master Sergeant Al Stahl |
| **Loadmaster:** | Master Sergeant Glen Preece |
| **Loadmaster:** | Staff Sergeant Jerome Schmidts |

Master Sergeant Glen Preece knew what the problem was at Siple Dome before he left McMurdo, and he knew what was in the boxes. He knew he needed plenty of wooden planking to use beneath the skis and ensured he had it. He also insisted on bringing a cordless power drill. No one understood why. En route to Siple Dome, he spent most of his time unscrewing the hundreds of screws securing the purple boxes' lids, holding the bridle assembly. When Skier 92 arrived, Thivierge was happy to see Preece had most of the screws removed.

Thivierge and his team attached the cables from the bridle assembly to the main skis of the aircraft. Five years earlier, the bridle assembly was designed to pull Skier 95 forward out of a crevasse. In their current predicament, they did the exact opposite. The leading extensions of the assembly were attached behind the aircraft, then to a bulldozer.

Thivierge climbed in the bulldozer and began pulling on the cables. The aircraft didn't budge. They needed more power, so he got a second bulldozer lined up in tandem behind the first bulldozer and connected them with chains from the aircraft. Now two bulldozers pulled the aircraft, but it still wouldn't budge.

Chief Master Sergeant Al Stahl and Preece talked to Thivierge about Plan B, which was to put wood under the Beaumont "Beau" Buck, Sr. wheels. With wooden planks under the main landing gear tires, they would evenly distribute the wheels' bearing pressure over a larger surface on the snow to prevent them from sinking in. They wanted Thivierge's team to drag the aircraft backward with the bulldozers while it was riding on its wheels along the wood planking. Haller and French agreed. This was another part of their training in CDDAR.

Thivierge considered it. The snow around the camp was firm. Camp personnel had been grooming it throughout the season. With wood under the main landing gear, the snow would remain a solid, even surface, but Thivierge was concerned dragging the nose gear in the snow could damage it. The nose ski needed to be isolated.

The LC-130 could isolate individual skis from the hydraulic system. With the nose ski isolated in the down position, they could raise the main skis. Stahl went back to the ski isolation valves and isolated the aircraft's nose ski while it was down.

The maintenance people placed plywood shoring below the main tires. When everything was ready, Captain Leroy King raised the skis on Jones' command. The main skis came up, and the nose ski stayed down. The main tires were resting on the plywood. Thivierge got in one of two bulldozers and pulled on the cables. The aircraft moved backward, but not much. More shoring was added to give the main landing gear a surface to ride on, and Thivierge tried again. And again, the aircraft moved only a little.

Jones paced the distance from the aircraft's nose to the fuel tank and paced the distance to the tip of the aircraft's wing. He estimated how much distance the aircraft needed from the tank to enable him to spin the aircraft around. Then he marked a spot in the snow that was visible from his seat in the aircraft. Thivierge asked Jones if the aircraft was far enough away from the tank to spin the aircraft around. Jones agreed to give it a try. They disengaged the chains from the skis of the aircraft and the bulldozers. Stahl went to the cargo compartment and opened the nose ski isolation valve, and the nose ski came up.

Jones and his aircrew got in their seats, ran the appropriate checklist, and started the engines. When everyone was ready, he directed King to lower the skis. When the nose ski was down, Jones added power, and as the aircraft began to move, he pulled #1 and #2 engines on the left wing of the aircraft to reverse and pushed the #3 and #4 engines on the right wing forward, while the main skis came down. The result was immediate. The aircraft turned well clear of Jones' mark in the snow, and it was clear of the large metal tank.

Jones stopped the aircraft. It was time to talk about the #1 engine. Eric Carlo knew the engine was a problem the previous week. While Thivierge connected the bridle assembly, he pulled the ladder from the cargo compartment, opened the #1 engine cowling, and searched for obvious leaks and linkage problems but didn't find anything amiss. However, he knew the propeller needed to be changed. He talked it over with Thivierge, Jones, and Stahl. There were no aircraft hangars, and the weather in Antarctica was unpredictable. Low cloud ceilings were moving in. If they changed the propeller at Siple Dome, it would take several days, waiting for parts and perhaps the weather to clear. The aircrew and maintenance people would be in a survival situation without the food and supplies they required.

They talked about the pros and cons. Before Jones agreed to fly it back to McMurdo, he performed some engine checks. He taxied the aircraft to the skiway and stopped. Running up the engines, Stahl took a good look at them. Jones then increased the throttles and taxied up and down the skiway several times. When Stahl was satisfied, Jones taxied back to parking. Thivierge signed off the write-up in the aircraft forms, and Jones was ready to go. The boxes with the bridle assembly cables and chains were loaded in the aircraft's cargo compartment. Thivierge and his team climbed in too. Preece closed up the back of the aircraft and ensured everything was strapped down. Jones taxied to the skiway and pushed up power. He lifted the nose off of the runway, and Skier 95 returned to McMurdo.

CHAPTER 27

# SURVIVAL

Two major events changed the dynamics within the Raven Gang. The first event happened on 11 September 2001. The aftermath left the airline industry bankrupt and wiped out much of the airline pilots' retirement savings. The furloughs at the airlines didn't happen immediately. It took time for the airline industry to deal with the impact of the crisis. This brought a lot of talent into the Raven Gang.

The second major event happened on 13 May 2005. The Pentagon released its proposals of base realignments and closures (BRAC). Stratton Air National Guard Base was on the closure list because the runway did not meet Air Force standards. A federal commission was set up to review the list, and on 8 September 2005, a new list was submitted and later approved. With the aid of the National Science Foundation and the local community, Stratton was removed from the list.

On the surface, it seemed simple to close the base and move the unit to a different location. However, the impact on the community was huge. In Scotia, New York, and the surrounding area, the impact would have been devastating to the area's small business communities. Stratton Air National Guard Base employed about 1,200 full-time and part-time people.

The National Science Foundation's loss would have been very significant, also. Not all of Stratton Air National Guard Base employees were willing to move their families to a different location and continue to fly the ski mission. In most cases, people were willing to find other employment within the Schenectady community or the surrounding area. In other words, after years of building a credible LC-130 ski mission program for Antarctica, the National Science Foundation would need to find another ski mission flying organization. However, none existed.

The 109$^{th}$ Airlift Wing needed the National Science Foundation as much as the National Science Foundation needed the Raven Gang.

## Last of the Old Guard

After 11 September 2001, nine very experienced airline pilots, who were traditional guardsmen, drill status guardsmen, also known as part-time guardsmen, were absorbed into the Raven Gang's full-time active duty, Air Guard-Reserve, also known as the AGR force. During this uncertain period, Lt. Col. Mark Sakadolsky and a couple of other airline pilots took leave from their airline job and joined the Raven Gang's full-time force. Many other airline pilots were furloughed and joined the full-time force out of necessity.

Sakadolsky was the last of the old Guard with more than twenty years of ski mission experience. He joined the Raven Gang in 1985. As a lieutenant, he flew the DYE site resupply missions with Pritchard, Tousey, Wagoner, Wilbur, Marchegiani, etc. His upgrade was slow and methodical. It took him years to learn the ski mission, and he became a master at it.

In contrast, over the past several years, the Raven Gang had upgraded pilots as if on an assembly line. Pilots would upgrade to aircraft commander before they were ready to upgrade to ski aircraft commander. This expedited the upgrade process; however, it didn't ensure these pilots received the ski mission experience they needed. In some cases, it extended the time for them to upgrade because they missed opportunities to go to the ice.

The training office ran the instructor pilot meetings. Often these meetings were contentious. Sakadolsky wanted to delay aircraft commander upgrades until pilots were ready to become ski mission aircraft commanders. This would slow down the upgrade process, and it also ensured pilots didn't upgrade to aircraft commander unless they went to the ice.

Sakadolsky had overwhelming support. There was no reason to continue an upgrade policy when there was a high demand to upgrade pilots. Those days were gone. With the flood of airline pilots into the squadron, more than enough qualified ski mission aircraft commanders could fly the line. The Raven Gang returned to the Old Guard's way of doing business. The pilots' upgrade process slowed.

## War

The base was spared from the 2005 base-realignment-and-closure by the intervention of the National Science Foundation. However, it clearly showed a vulnerability. The New York Air Adjutant General told the 109th Airlift

Wing they needed to get their four airplanes without skis into the war or they would lose them. The war effort demanded more aircraft.

The Raven Gang pilots decided, if the airplanes went to the war, then the aircrews would go to the fight. No one liked the idea of other people flying their airplanes. Every guard unit in the country felt the same way. The rental car analogy weighed heavily in the discussion. How well would the other people treat their airplanes?

Getting to the war zone wasn't as easy as it sounded. The standard rotation for other Guard units was a four-month deployment, every fifteen months. That didn't work for the Raven Gang. At times, the fifteen-month rotation cycle would land in the middle of Operation Deep Freeze, and that was a problem. The ski mission was their operational mission, not the combat mission. They weren't authorized to relinquish their responsibilities in Antarctica. Therefore, instead of becoming a part of a standard fifteen-month rotation cycle, they deployed with whatever Guard units were scheduled during the spring and summer months, during the Greenland season when their commitments were less.

The paint scheme on their airplanes was another problem with getting into the war. The wheeled airplanes were painted with the same color scheme as the skibirds, more silver than gray, with orange highlights. The design was intended to help identify a disabled and stranded aircraft on the ice cap. This color combination was not well-suited to the war zone. They needed to be painted to meet the Middle East's Central Command theater of operations requirements.

The greatest challenge the aircrews had was to be combat-ready. They needed significant amounts of training if they were going to Afghanistan. Four aircrews spent the spring months of 2007 training and preparing to go to Bagram, and during July and August, they flew into Afghanistan for the first time. They deployed an incredibly experienced aircrew force. Of the eight pilots that went on the first rotations, seven of them were instructors. The Raven Gang considered the flying schedule in Antarctica more challenging than in Afghanistan.

The Bagram leadership was uncertain about this group of aviators who had no experience in the combat theatre. The C-130 missions included short-field takeoffs and landings on unimproved surfaces, flying in the dark evening hours using night vision devices. By the end of their rotation, the Bagram leadership had a significantly different and positive opinion of the Raven Gang.

The Raven Gang went to Afghanistan again in 2009 and 2012. At other times individual Raven Gang aircrew members flew with other squadrons around the country to get into the fight.

Despite their efforts to save their aircraft, the 109th Airlift Wing lost two of its wheelbirds. The USAF took 83-0486 and 83-0488 from their inventory.

CHAPTER 28

# GREENLAND ICE CAP SURVIVAL

The Raven Gang was operating out of Kangerlussuaq, formerly Sondrestrom Air Base, again. Thule didn't like frequent flights in and out of their airbase, and their operating hour restrictions were a hindrance on the Raven Gang operation. In 1997, negotiations were finalized to move the operation back to Kangerlussuaq. The Greenlanders were willing to contract their services to support the 109th Airlift Wing.

Despite the wheel birds and aircrews going to war, the skibirds never stopped flying to the polar icecaps. The Greenland Season continued throughout the spring and summer months. Scientists still wanted to complete their science projects. Aircrew training still needed to be completed for the next Antarctica season. The Europeans still wanted support to move their science camp.

In 2007, Lt. Col. Steve Yandik was faced with significantly different challenges than his squadron personnel in Afghanistan. Working at a surface altitude of 10,000 feet above sea level, in sub-zero temperatures, during severe snowstorms was the Raven Gang's bread-and-butter mission. However, that didn't mean it was easy.

Three aircraft with crews arrived in Kangerlussuaq on Monday, 18 June 2007, and they were scheduled to return to Schenectady on Friday. By the end of the week, two missions needed to get to North GRIP or North Greenland Ice Core Project camp.

North GRIP was a European camp located at 75.1° North, 42.32° West, on the Greenland ice cap. The plan was for Yandik's aircrew to deliver Dr. Joergen Peder (JP) Steffensen and his team, then return to Kangerlussuaq. It would be the first flight scheduled into North GRIP in three years. The second aircraft was scheduled to go there the following day to drop off additional supplies.

Multinational European organizations funded the North GRIP Project. The Centre for Ice and Climate at the Niels Bohr Institute, University of Copenhagen, Denmark, managed the logistics. The institute sent scientists to Greenland to drill and analyze the ice cores. This was Steffensen's job. His camp started drilling at North GRIP in 1996. They finished their work when they reached bedrock in July 2004. They closed down the camp when they were finished, but they left their camp and equipment there. Now following a three-year break, they were back.

Steffensen had a six-person team. Steffen Bo Hansen was his technical and logistics expert. Sverrir Hilmarsson was his mechanic who would prove instrumental throughout the coming days. There also was an electrical engineer and two junior researchers on the team.

Inside the North GRIP garage, there was a Caterpillar bulldozer, three Alpine snowmobiles, and two tracked vehicles called flexmobils. These were the German's version of a small piston-bully snow groomer. Steffensen and his team's mission was to evaluate the status of their equipment at North GRIP, then traverse the ice cap and build a new camp. The new camp would be called NEEM or Northern Greenland Eemian and was the site for a new drilling project. NEEM was located at 77°27' North 51°3.6' West.

The ice cores had global climate significance. Within the ice cores were tiny pockets of air, bubbles trapped in time. The bubbles gave scientists a look at the Earth's atmosphere from the period when the ice formed. It was a record of the environment from many thousands of years past. The Earth is currently in an ice age interglacial period named the Holocene. The North GRIP ice cores gave scientists a record of the atmosphere throughout this period. The scientist's intention at NEEM Camp was to find ice cores dating back to the previous interglacial period, the Eemian Period.

| Skier 96 Aircrew | |
|---|---|
| **Pilot:** | Major Steve Yandik |
| **Copilot:** | Lt. Col. Pete Thalheimer |
| **Navigator:** | Major Joe Zotto |
| **Navigator:** | Major Blair Herdrick |
| **Flight Engineer:** | Senior Master Sergeant Brian Alix |
| **Loadmaster:** | Chief Master Sergeant Dennis Morgan |
| **Loadmaster:** | Staff Sergeant Caspar Buchanan |

Major Steve Yandik was the ski instructor aircraft commander scheduled to fly to North GRIP. He had no illusions about the mission. Weather and snow conditions were always a challenge for the first flight of the season into a camp. All the better for his student, Lt. Col. Pete Thalheimer who was upgrading to ski mission aircraft commander.

Greenland was the Raven Gang's ski mission training location. Thalheimer was an aircraft commander, but he had limited experience in the ski mission. Yandik's job, and that of the rest of the Raven Gang's instructor pilots, was to ensure new pilots, like Thalheimer, understood the mission, and he was capable of landing an aircraft on skis before sending him out with his own aircrew.

Major Joe Zotto was a navigator flight examiner. He was going to sit back and watch Major Blair Herdrick throughout the flight. It was Herdrick's initial ski mission evaluation. If Herdrick did a good job, Zotto would allow him to fly missions without an instructor watching over his shoulder. Zotto had a racquetball game scheduled when they returned from the mission, but he would miss it.

Senior Master Sergeant Brian Alix was a very experienced ski mission qualified flight engineer. Brian Alix started his military flying career in 1980. In 1989 he joined the Raven Gang. He was a workhorse and would certainly prove his worth on this mission.

Chief Master Sergeant Dennis Morgan and Staff Sergeant Caspar Buchanan were the loadmasters in the back of the aircraft. With them was a Chief Master Sergeant from the Air National Guard Bureau in Washington DC. He came along to see what the Raven Gang did on the ice cap, and he was about to participate in the challenges of these extreme cold weather air lifters.

Every aircraft is unique and has a personality of its own. Overall, Skier 96 was solid. It was a good aircraft for the mission ahead.

# Survival

**Wednesday, 20 June 2007**

The weather wasn't good on Tuesday, so no flying took place. However, on Wednesday, Yandik and his aircrew took off from Kangerlussuaq. In the back was the science team with much of their baggage for the traverse from North GRIP to NEEM. They had more cargo scheduled on a second aircraft before the traverse could begin.

Thalheimer's landing at North GRIP would be an open snow landing. He was going to land the aircraft in an open snowfield without a prepared landing surface. This wasn't a unique situation. The Raven Gang frequently dealt with this at every camp at the beginning of the season in Greenland and Antarctica.

Although not unique, North GRIP was special. The field elevation was 9,570 feet. The high altitude was always a challenge. The aircraft engine performance was not as efficient at altitude due to the thin air. The thin air was a challenge for people also. Everyone needed to watch one another for hypoxia symptoms. Headaches were a problem if they stayed for extended periods of time. Acute mountain sickness, high-altitude pulmonary edema, and high-altitude cerebral edema were also concerns.

Another challenge was the Greenland snow. The climate was different than Antarctica. Antarctica was a desert, and the snow was very dry. Greenland snow had a higher moisture content. Ski takeoffs were much more challenging. If you were good in Greenland, Antarctica was a walk in the park.

Yandik knew there was a good chance they'd be spending the night at North GRIP. It wasn't part of the plan, but he was a realist, and he'd been flying the ski mission for fourteen years. He had ATO on board which helped but wasn't a panacea for ski takeoffs. En route to North GRIP, a two-hour flight, Yandik talked with Steffensen. For years the scientists and aircrew had worked together to accomplish the mission. It was a symbiotic relationship, and the people had grown close. Yandik told Steffensen he might need his help to groom a skiway. Steffensen understood, but the garage with the grooming equipment was buried deep in the snow. Steffensen would need some help from the aircrew to dig it out. They left the conversation open-ended until they were on the ground.

*NGRIP in 1996 (Sverrir Hilmarsson Pic)*

It was a beautiful Greenlandic day when Thalheimer touched down the skis on the snow. It was 10:50 a.m. The sky was clear, and the visibility was endless. There was little to no wind. The temperature was -4° Celsius or 25° Fahrenheit. While they were overhead, they could see the old camp. The camp's structure looked like a large black soccer ball on a pedestal. It was three stories high. Inside, a staircase in the middle of the ball allowed access to each floor.

The "soccer ball" was built on a wooden foundation and firmly anchored in the snow. Annual snowfall at North GRIP was about two feet per year; however, standing structures collected much more snow due to snowdrift. Once the snow drifted up to and was flush with the top of the ball, accumulation at the top would stop until the ice sheet's surface around the rest of the camp reached the same level. Eventually, all camp structures collected so much snow that the entire camp would become an elevated hill.[157]

Due to the snow accumulation over the last few years, the ball now looked like a dome. Snow drifts had built up and buried the first two floors of the structure. Now, the only access to it was from the top hatch. The other entrances were buried in the snow. The only windows not buried in the snow were on the third floor of the camp.

Around the camp, other structures were not yet buried. Many structures were still visible. A large metal pipe was sticking out of the snow. It was the casing pipe from the North GRIP ice core borehole 10,105 feet or 3,080 meters deep. Some of the flags from the old skiway were still visible. The flagging was made of black radar reflective material mounted on bamboo poles. The design was well thought out. The navigator could pick out the reflective material using the aircraft's radar and guide the pilot to the skiway in poor weather conditions. The bamboo was frangible. If an aircraft slid off the side of the skiway, the flag poles would break but wouldn't damage the aircraft. Some of the old skiway flags were still visible from years before, and Herdrick guided Thalheimer to them, and he landed.

Yandik knew this beautiful day would be a problem. The radiant sunlight reflecting off the snow created heat which made the snow surface soft. After he landed, Thalheimer needed 13,000 inch-pounds of torque on all four engines to taxi at ten-knots of speed. This was two-thirds of the available engine power. The aircrew ski combat offloaded the pallets of cargo. The ski combat offload was a variation of the typical C-130 combat offload. One big difference was the aircraft never stopped moving during the ski combat offload.

After the pallets rolled out of the aircraft, Chief Master Sergeant Dennis Morgan walked onto the aircraft's ramp and looked at the ski's tracks in the snow. They were deep. Thalheimer taxied to the desired parking location and stopped to drop off the passengers. Caspar Buchanan opened a paratroop door to allow Steffensen and his team to depart. The snow was up higher than the belly of the aircraft.

Steffensen and his team exited the aircraft and walked over to their camp. It was standard practice for the aircrew to wait until Steffensen established radio communication before they left. It was a safety measure for the science team. During the wait, Morgan notified Yandik about the aircraft tracks in the snow. He knew there was no chance they were getting airborne until the snow firmed up. When Steffensen checked in, Yandik asked him to groom a skiway. This was going to take all day and into the night. The word "night" is a relative term when the sun is up twenty-four hours a day in the high Arctic.

Before he shut the aircraft down, Yandik knew the aircraft was stuck in the snow. He wanted to get it unstuck. The skis cooled in the snow, and ice bonded to the bottom of the skis. Taxiing on snow created friction. The friction created a layer of water between the skis and the snow. Thalheimer needed high-power settings to taxi the aircraft, so he created a lot of friction.

Morgan, Buchanan, and the chief from Guard Bureau alternated jumping out the paratroop doors located on either side of the aircraft's cargo compartment and shoveled beneath the skis. The engines were running, and the propellers were turning, so they needed to be careful.

Yandik cycled the skis up and down as they shoveled. When the skis were up, the belly of the aircraft was lower in the snow. The tires of the aircraft protruded between the skis and sunk deep in the snow. When the skis were lowered, the aircraft raised above the snow, and the tires rose above the skis. When the skis were down, the loadmasters shoveled snow into the depressions the tires made. They spent a lot of energy filling in the depressions, then climbed back in the aircraft and deeply breathed on the oxygen hose. They continued this routine for an hour until the tires no longer sunk into the snow, and Yandik was satisfied they could move. He then shut down the aircraft's engines.

While the aircrew dug the aircraft out of the snow, Steffensen's people worked on opening the camp. The science team had brought a five-kilowatt diesel generator to run power to the main dome for light, cooking, and melting snow for water. It was cold inside, perhaps colder than outside the camp. When the aircraft engines shut down, Steffensen's team was ready to dig. Before a skiway could be groomed, they needed to access the garage located near the "soccer ball" to get the flexmobil. The aircrew became part of Steffensen's team working toward a common cause.

Steffensen divided everyone into shovel teams. The teams alternated digging, which allowed everyone to take a break and get some oxygen after expending their energy at the high altitude. When they were finished, they had dug a path about eight feet deep and wide enough for the heavy equipment to leave the garage.

Sverrir Hilmarsson, from Iceland, and Steffen Bo Hansen, from Denmark, were Steffensen's mechanics. Their task was to start the equipment in the garage and keep it running. This was in line with Brian Alix's flight engineer job. He was the systems specialist of the aircraft. He went with Hilmarsson and Hansen to see if he could be of any assistance. The garage was a large white tent structure. It was torn in several places due to the weight of snow accumulation over the years, and there were abrasions on the frame, but everything in the garage was in good order.

By 3:30 p.m., the garage was open, and Hilmarsson had all of the vehicles running using a Herman-Nelson heater he also had stored in the tent and a small generator and a battery charger he brought with him. That evening, Alix told Yandik, "It should have been a commercial for Ski-Doo™. After sitting for three years, Sverrir gave the starter cord one pull, and the snowmobiles started right up."

Grooming of the skiway began at around 4:00 p.m. and continued until midnight. Occasional breaks were necessary to refuel the driver and the machine. Behind the flexmobil, Steffensen dragged a large metal beam. This beam groomed a firm even surface in the snow. He spent the evening riding up and down a two-mile swath, two hundred feet wide between the old skiway flags.

Yandik needed to wait until the temperatures cooled down. He called Raven Operations in Kangerlussuaq to get an update on the weather forecast. He wanted to know when the coolest time of the day was going to be. Raven Ops told him three o'clock in the morning. So, he decided to wait until morning to depart. A couple of hours after the coldest part of the day, time to allow the molecules of snow to bond, would be the best time to try to get airborne again.

They spent the night in the aircraft. They were tired after a long day of digging. Each of them had an overnight bag for just this occurrence. In it was food for the evening and any personal items they would need.

The headaches weren't a surprise, but it difficult to rest. Breathing in pure oxygen from an aircraft oxygen mask cleared it up immediately. The aircrew kept an eye on one another throughout the night. High altitude sickness could kill any of them if left unattended. Yandik learned about a problem first-hand that evening with a new Life Support Shop initiative.

Before the Greenland Season started, they decided the aircrews no longer needed sleeping bags in their survival gear. Instead, sleeping bags were kept in the aircraft. That night Yandik found there were more people than sleeping bags in Skier 96.

He spent the night in the flight deck without a sleeping bag so everyone in the cargo compartment would have one. Initially, the sun was in his face, and he was comfortable using his parka as a blanket. However, as the Earth continued to rotate and the hours passed, the sun moved around the aircraft, and the radiance was no longer reflecting in the flight deck. This resulted in Yandik nearly freezing. Throughout the evening, Steffensen continued grooming the skiway.

# Inside the Camp

**Thursday, 21 June 2007**

It was early morning and time to wake up. Several crewmembers briefly put on an aircraft oxygen mask, and their headaches disappeared. They strapped in their seats, ran the appropriate checklists, and started the aircraft engines. Thalheimer taxied out to the skiway for departure, and Skier 96 attempted their first takeoff at 5:45 am. The skiway was oriented to a 300°/120° magnetic heading. The winds were coming from 220 degrees magnetic heading. The wind velocity was fifteen to twenty knots, a strong crosswind. Thalheimer set all four engines to maximum power. As the aircraft accelerated down the skiway, the wind hit the rudder and caused the aircraft's nose to pitch to the left. The only way to counteract it was to pull the #4 engine back. Reducing the power on one side of the aircraft allowed him to stabilize the direction and keep the aircraft on the skiway, but it robbed necessary power to accelerate. The 9,570-foot altitude also was a contributing factor for the lack of acceleration. The high altitude had a thinner atmosphere and didn't provide the air density to allow the engines to reach maximum power.

He tried different flap settings hoping to accelerate. He tried going down the skiway in the opposite direction to see if that would have any effect. He looked for spots of faster acceleration along the skiway. After several attempts, Yandik realized it was useless to continue skiing up and down the skiway because they were burning up their fuel. The temperatures were too close to the melting point, and the snow was so soft, the aircraft wouldn't accelerate. Ten degrees cooler would have been perfect.

Steffensen had prepared a good surface for the aircraft to slide, but it needed time to set. Waiting more time allowed the sintering process, the molecular bonding, to take place. However, waiting also meant the sun would begin to shine, and radiant heat would warm the skiway, further softening the snow.

They didn't have any cargo in the back of the aircraft to give them an aft center-of-gravity. A two thousand pound pallet on the ramp of the aircraft would have been perfect. The aft center-of-gravity would allow the nose to ride higher in the snow, and Thalheimer would have been able to "pop-a-wheelie" as he continued to accelerate down the skiway. There were too many environmental elements working against them. A change in any one of these conditions may have allowed them to get airborne, but it wasn't going to happen. The only positive effect of sliding up and down the skiway was to improve the surface conditions. Yandik decided to conserve their remaining fuel and allow Steffensen to continue grooming the skiway.

The aircraft no longer had enough fuel to make it back to Kangerlussuaq. They needed a fuel stop on the way back. Thule Air Base was a consideration, but it was in the wrong direction. Yandik decided they would go to Summit Camp, an American camp on the Greenland ice cap, about forty-five minutes south of North GRIP.

After returning to the parking ramp, they shut down the aircraft engines and waited for better conditions. Yandik called Raven Ops in Kangerlussuaq and coordinated the fuel stop.

The aircrew was going to spend another day at North GRIP. This was Buchanan's first ski mission. He hadn't been to Kool School yet. The Guard Bureau chief hadn't either. Throughout the morning, as they waited for better surface conditions, Morgan decided to pull out the survival gear from the boxes in the aft of the cargo compartment, and he started a mini Kool School for Buchanan and the chief.

Kool School was the 109th Airlift Wing's variation of the Air Force Arctic Survival School. Unlike the Arctic survival in Fairbanks, Alaska, the

Raven Gang operated on the polar ice cap. The ice cap didn't have trees for warmth and shelter, so the Raven Gang needed to survive on the ice cap with only the tools they had in the aircraft.

Morgan started with the stoves. Alix helped him. He went to the aircraft fuel drains and siphoned some fuel. He attached the proper ignitors to the stove. Different ignitors were available based on the fuel type. After changing out the ignitors, he lit the stove. The aircrew needed more water. Morgan put a large, metal, rectangular-shaped container over the stove and filled it with snow. Once the snow was melted, they poured it into the aircraft's five-gallon water igloo and immediately recognized the large amount of work necessary for so little gain.

Morgan pulled out the Polar MREs, meals-ready-to-eat, in case they chose to eat them. Each of these polar MREs was loaded with 6,000 calories. Survival on the ice cap required a lot of work. Each aircrew member was expected to eat one of these a day. Next, they decided to set up tents off the right wingtip. The wind started to blow, so before they set up the tents, they built a wind wall from snow blocks. It was difficult work because the snow was soft.

*Damn!* The weather began to deteriorate. Steffensen continued to groom the skiway until the weather rolled in. By 11:00 a.m., the wind was blowing thirty knots, and the temperature was -5 degrees Celsius. The sky was an overcast cloud ceiling. The snow surface and the horizon blended together. The visibility dropped to a one-half mile.

Looking out in the distance, Steffensen couldn't find a horizon due to the surface being the same color as the sky. He took a break from grooming and went inside the camp to rest and eat some food. He got on the radio and talked with Kangerlussuaq to give his people there an update and, in turn, got a weather update.

He left the ball and told the aircrew of an impending storm. It was going to be a massive and dangerous one. Steffensen didn't want anyone outside the camp until the weather cleared. Everyone, including the aircrew, needed to stay inside the science camp throughout the storm. Each aircrew member had an arctic survival bag with cold-weather gear. These bags and their personal overnight bags needed to be carried into the camp before the storm hit. Morgan was the first one at the dome entrance. As he started down the ladder, he slipped and fell about ten feet. He was very fortunate that he landed flat on his back, on a table below. It broke his fall and collapsed. If he had fallen two feet to the left, he would have continued down the staircase to the next floor below.

At 1:30 p.m., the weather worsened, and the wind changed to a 280° magnetic heading, more in line with the skiway, and the snow began to fall. It covered the freshly groomed skiway, one step forward, two steps back. The visibility dropped to a one-fourth mile. At times, no one could see the plane from the dome of the camp.

Everyone was miserable and very cold inside the dome. They sat around looking for something to occupy their time and take their mind off the cold.

Zotto asked, "Why don't lobsters share?" Everyone looked around.

Alix: "What?"

Zotto: "Why don't lobster share?"

Alix: "I don't know. Why don't lobster share?"

Zotto: "Because they're shellfish."

Everyone laughed and began to relax. Zotto continued with the jokes. Alix thought Zotto might be having hypoxia symptoms due to the altitude or hypothermia because of the cold and hard work. He didn't find out until years later Zotto had a cheap joke book.

For water throughout the day, they opened the door on the bottom floor of the camp. Outside the door was a wall of snow. They carved out snow from the wall and melted it in the kitchen. Yandik approached Steffensen about starting the main camp generator for warmth; however, he was hesitant. One of the reasons Steffensen didn't start the generator was because he was concerned about using all of his camp's fuel. They had a limited supply until the second resupply aircraft arrived. The second aircraft hadn't arrived because Yandik couldn't get airborne. There was no reason to have a second aircraft stuck at the camp.

Also, Steffensen hadn't started the main generator because he was concerned about carbon monoxide poisoning. He knew the story of Admiral Byrd's solo adventure in Antarctica. After spending several months alone, Byrd began sounding unusual over the radio. Fortunately, he was rescued before succumbing to the carbon monoxide fumes. Steffensen insisted on preparing the camp before starting the main generator.

One last concern before they fired up the generator, Steffensen wanted a secondary exit from the dome in case of fire. Currently, the only available exit was from the top of the ball. Sverrir Hilmarsson found the means to address all of Steffensen's concerns. He had closed down the camp and turned off the generator in 2004. He had prepared it to be fired up again before he left. The fuel tank was full with enough fuel for four days. The cooled ethyl-glycol for the generator was in a container beside it, and the exhaust vent was already sticking out at the top of the dome.

The generator was at the bottom of the building structure, some twenty feet below the snow surface. A path needed to be cleared for the generator's intake shoot. This intake vent was buried in the ice cap outside the camp. They needed to create a solid flow of air from the surface to the generator. This required going outside the dome and digging more snow. Hilmarsson knew the location of the intake vent.

They cleared the snow down to the intake, and as they did so, they also cleared snow from the second-floor window in the radio room. This provided Steffensen's secondary exit. When they finished their trench to the intake, they needed to extend the intake pipe above the snow surface to prevent it from getting buried again. Before they could do that, they needed to locate a suitable pipe long enough for the job.

North GRIP was an abandoned ice-core drill site. Years earlier, the scientists built a workshop beneath the snow. They found several vent pipes from the workshop poking out of the snow. They dug them out, carried them to the camp, and placed them in the trench down to the original intake.

With the air intake in place, Hilmarsson, Hansen, and Alix went to work. A Herman-Nelson heater with a hose was in the garage. It was still in good working order. They dragged it out to the dome and extended the hose through the second-floor window. They cut a hole into the floor and extended the heater's hose to the lower level. The heater blew hot air onto the generator and warmed it up.

The battery to start the generator was dead, so Hilmarsson needed to recharge it. Fortunately, he had charged the vehicles' batteries the day prior. They went back out into the snowstorm and to the garage. They got the battery from the bulldozer and carried it inside the camp. They shoved the dead battery out the second-floor window, and Herdrick pulled it up the trench and left it on the surface. Hilmarsson carried it to the garage and recharged it. At 6:30 p.m., Hilmarsson started the generator.

It was a hard day of work for everyone. It was cold, uncomfortably cold. The storm rolled in with greater force. No one had any inhibitions and undressed out of their sweaty clothes into dry clothing. During dinner, everyone needed gloves as they ate chicken and rice soup. It was so cold, ice started to glaze over the soup as they ate it. Everyone went to sleep on metal bunkbeds or the floor. They bundled up in their survival gear. It was the beginning of another very cold night of sleep. Steffensen assigned people throughout the night to exit through the top of the camp, to ensure the intake remained clear as the snow continued to fall. The generator provided power to the small electric heaters inside the camp. It ran throughout the evening hours while they slept.

# Normalization

**Friday, 22 June 2007**

As the night wore on, people threw off their blankets and opened their parkas. The aircrew woke up in the morning wearing only their flight suit. They didn't remember shedding layers of clothing throughout the night as it warmed up. The ceiling was leaking due to the condensation. It was almost 15° Celsius, 60° Fahrenheit inside the camp. It had been a difficult couple of days, but now they were more comfortable, more relaxed. Everyone sat around the dining table eating breakfast and laughing. It was a new day.

By Friday morning, the weather had improved outside the camp. The skies were clear, the winds were light, and the temperature was -8° Celsius, 18° Fahrenheit. Snow covered the skiway Steffensen had groomed. He spent the early morning hours, alternating with Morgan, grooming the skiway again. A path also needed to be groomed for the aircraft to taxi to the skiway. They started grooming at 8:00 a.m. and continued until 4:00 p.m.

*(left to right) Joe Zotto, Pete Thalheimer, Steve Yandik (hat), Brian Alix, Blair Herdrick*

The aircraft was buried in snow. They shut down the engines early on the day before, so the aircraft was cold before the snow came; therefore, no ice compacted in the inlets of the engines, only snow, but it was compacted all the way to the first compressor blades.

The snow had drifted around the nose of the aircraft, and it looked as if it had a beard. The aircrew grabbed their shovels. They spent hours preparing the aircraft for flight, including the top of the aircraft, which needed to be cleared of snow. Performance of the aircraft relied on the aerodynamic lift of the wings. An aircraft can accelerate to high speeds on the ground, but the aircraft was just a snow bus without the proper lift characteristics. They cleared off everything that added drag to the aircraft. If the drag coefficient was inaccurate, then the takeoff and landing speeds and distances were inaccurate, which could be fatal.

Yandik called Raven Operations in Kangerlussuaq to get a weather update. The weather was good at North GRIP. The weather was good at Kangerlussuaq. But now, Summit was in the midst of a snowstorm. Yandik had no other option but to stay another night at North GRIP because there was nowhere else to get more fuel for the aircraft.

Steffensen spent hours thinking about his options while grooming the skiway. The plan he wanted to execute had fallen apart. After the second aircraft arrived, he wanted to pack up his supplies, load them on his tracked vehicles, and start the traverse to NEEM. But now, it was Friday. In Kangerlussuaq, the Raven Gang was preparing to go home. The second aircraft never came to North GRIP, and it wouldn't be coming. The LC-130s were leaving Greenland for New York, and they wouldn't return for weeks.

Yandik also had spent a lot of time thinking about Steffensen's situation. If Steffensen remained at North GRIP, his science team would be left with limited supplies. His aircrew had used a lot of the science team's resources. One LC-130 had already left Greenland for New York. A second aircraft would leave for Schenectady when Yandik returned to Kangerlussuaq. Upon Yandik's return, he would leave for New York after a good night's rest. They were scheduled to return in two weeks, on 9 July 2007.

Yandik and Steffensen talked things over. In years past, it was possible to negotiate with the 109th Airlift Wing to get what Steffensen needed. But those days were gone now, and everything was highly political. Money was tight due to the Global War on Terrorism, and the bean counters had taken over the negotiations.

Whether he returned to Kangerlussuaq or stayed at North GRIP, Steffensen would be several weeks behind schedule. His science team continued the inventory of the camp throughout the day. They had already accomplished much of what Steffensen intended before their departure for NEEM. There was no reason to remain at the camp. Steffensen decided it was best for his team to return to Kangerlussuaq with Yandik.

There was little for the aircrew to do while they waited for things to improve at Summit Camp. Steffensen had a satellite phone. Throughout the day, he allowed everyone to call home and talk to their family and let them know they wouldn't be home on time. It was a generous thing to do, but that was Steffensen's nature.

They spent their day inside the camp playing card games. As the afternoon passed into the evening, they decided to cook a final feast. There was no reason they wouldn't leave in the morning. The aircrew found some wine in the camp's storage facilities from years before. It was frozen, so it needed to thaw. In the meantime, they cooked a pasta dinner.

Friday evening, everybody enjoyed a candlelight dinner. Their shared experience of the last few days created a special bond between the science team and the aircrew. This was Dennis Morgan's last trip to Greenland. After more than twenty-five years of flying the polar ice cap missions, he was about to retire from the military. The dinner turned into a celebration. The wine and pasta dinner were fabulous, and the shared feelings of the adventure were bountiful. It was a wonderful party and spirits were high. They went to bed that evening, prepared for the day ahead.

# The Return

**Saturday, 23 June 2007**

Yandik woke up tired. He had spent three nights at altitude, and his body was adjusting, but he still felt worn out. One aircraft and one aircrew remained in Kangerlussuaq. It was an airdrop aircrew. They were ready to drop fuel drums at North GRIP if Yandik couldn't get airborne. They would need to collect the bundles and break them down to access the fifty-five-gallon drums and move them near the aircraft. Alix would refuel the aircraft. Steffensen's science team would help, but it probably meant another night at North GRIP. This was the backup plan.

For three days and nights, Yandik had gone through his options. Everyone was in good spirits following the dinner last evening. Now everyone was looking to him to get the aircraft airborne. It wouldn't be a problem if the conditions were right. It wouldn't be a problem if the aircraft's engine and propeller seals didn't leak after spending three days and nights on the ice cap.

The time for Thalheimer's training was over. Yandik decided to do the takeoff. The aircraft needed to get airborne on the first slide. A second attempt was questionable due to its fuel status. He thought to himself, "*Thalheimer can have the takeoff at Summit.*" Saturday at 4:00 a.m. the weather was good. The winds were blowing at fourteen knots from 320° magnetic heading, almost down the skiway. The skies were clear, and the temperature was -13 degrees Celsius, perfect temperatures for skiing. They shared one last meal and shut down the camp.

The aircrew pre-flighted the aircraft and called Kangerlussuaq to file a flight plan in the system. Alix installed the ignitors in the eight ATO bottles hanging on the sides of the aircraft.

Morgan intended to give Yandik as much aft center-of-gravity as possible. The aft center-of-gravity would help Yandik get the nose off of the skiway. It was an empty airplane, with only five passengers and their luggage. Morgan directed the passengers to sit on the ramp in the back of the aircraft. A cargo strap secured the passengers to the floor.

The main skis made a four-inch depression as the aircraft taxied onto the skiway. At the end of the skiway, Yandik turned the aircraft 180 degrees. The aircrew completed their checklists, and Alix armed the ATO. Skier 96 accelerated easily down the North GRIP skiway in their first attempt, so Yandik didn't use the ATO. When they were airborne, Herdrick contacted the Greenlandic air traffic controllers and let them know Skier 96's intentions. Once they were level at their assigned altitude, Yandik thought through the next challenge. Summit Camp was located at 72°34'28" North, 38°27'20" West, and its field elevation was 10,600 feet above sea level, higher than North GRIP.

It was a short flight. Summit was at the apex of the Greenland ice cap. It was an American year-round science research camp. The weather was forecast to be a good day at Summit, but the skiway was questionable due to the snowstorm the previous day. The airfield flagging was good, so finding the skiway wouldn't be a problem. Even if weather conditions were poor, Herdrick shouldn't have difficulty identifying the skiway on his radar, and he could guide Yandik there.

They landed at Summit at 7:05 a.m. and taxied to the refuel location. The skiway and ramp were in poor condition. Refueling from a camp meant robbing the camp of its fuel reserves. The fuel they took would need to be returned on the Raven Gang's next rotation to Greenland. Yandik worked with Zotto and Herdrick to determine how much fuel they needed. Alix on-loaded the fuel. After refueling, they were ready for departure.

Thalheimer started the engines, and the aircrew completed the required checklists. Alix armed the ATO system. The acceleration was slow on the skiway. The fresh snow made it stickier than Yandik's departure at North GRIP. Thalheimer didn't waste any time. As he accelerated through sixty knots, he called, "ATO—Now!" Alix fired the bottles. The takeoff was spectacular from the passenger's point of view, strapped to the aircraft's ramp. In the words of Steffensen, "Very nice view of the ATO flames through the windows of the paratroop doors."

CHAPTER 29

# EXCEPTIONAL BECOMES ROUTINE

There was no question the Raven Gang had a unique culture. They flew unique airplanes to unique locations. Therefore, they needed unique techniques to succeed. Young pilots practiced the aircraft's unique capabilities, and they learned to fly it at its limits. They were excellent at what they did.

The instructor pilot corps delineated good ski mission techniques from the bad. In 1995 they collected these specific techniques for the aircraft commanders to use when they were having difficulty on the ice cap. This publication became known as the *"Ski Handbook."* It was kept current through the years. When new pilots were assigned to the Raven Gang, their upgrade to ski mission aircraft commander was calculated, methodical, and slow.

Through the years, the Raven Gang's travails became less dramatic as the aircrews matured in the mission. They diverted to other locations, dealt with broken aircraft on the ice, and spent nights in unusual places. They knew Antarctica and what it was capable of, and they knew the weather forecasters and their limitations.

Within the squadron, they had built exceptional planning sections. The Antarctica section worked with the National Science Foundation's Office of Polar Programs to determine mission requirements and examine each camp's landing surface requirements throughout the season. The Greenland section coordinated with the National Science Foundation and PICO contractors. They also worked with the European science community to support their needs.

The tactics section consisted of three branches; the polar tactics branch, the combat tactics branch, and the aircraft modification branch. The polar tactics branch managed the polar airdrop program. This organizational structure fulfilled the needs of Antarctica and Greenland. The combat tactics branch began creating ski mission methods for supporting combat operations in the Arctic. One example was determining the usefulness of night vision devices while landing on the Greenland ice cap.

The aircraft modification branch worked directly with Lockheed Martin, the maker of the C-130 aircraft, and the Air National Guard C-130 Functional Area Manager to modify their aircraft with eight-bladed propellers. They oversaw the test and evaluation of an eight-bladed propeller for the LC-130 aircraft. This propeller gave greater acceleration to the aircraft during takeoff, which was the greatest challenge for the ski mission.

*Eight-Bladed Propeller, 109 Air Wing Pic*

The Raven Gang sent navigators to TERPS school. When they returned, they designed approaches to different locations throughout Greenland and Antarctica. Loadmasters traveled throughout the country to help contractors determine how to break down large pieces of equipment so they could fit within the LC-130 cargo compartment.

Most of the aircrews didn't have active duty experience, so flying the ski mission was all they knew. They had never received any special recognition, and consequently, they didn't realize they were special.

# Weather Forecasting

Despite the resources available between the National Science Foundation, SPAWAR Systems Atlantic, National Aeronautics and Space Administration or NASA, and Pacific Air Command Air Forces or PACAF, the Raven Gang could not get an accurate weather forecast with any certainty. Unfortunately, too many people considered the white-out landing a routine procedure.

In 2011, the ski mission profile was removed from simulator training because it cost too much. Every Operation Deep Freeze flight was a "close-watch" mission due to its hazards, yet most of them were treated as routine. It was inevitable. The aircrews were highly skilled. Their training was demanding. No pilot became a ski mission aircraft commander unless the Raven Gang's instructor pilots agreed to it.

When the 109th Airlift Wing took over the Navy's mission in 1996, the National Science Foundation agreed to provide *"...timely and accurate local and regional weather forecasts, warnings, flight forecasts, and Terminal Aerodrome Forecasts for all stations in Antarctica that operate aircraft and support ship operations."*[158]

On 13 September 1996, at a meeting at National Science Foundation Headquarters, they contracted SPAWAR, Charleston, to provide aviation weather forecasts supporting the United States Antarctica Program. SPAWAR, Charleston hired contractors to do the job. A SPAWAR, Charleston meteorology administrator provided government oversight of these contractors. For over twenty years, this remained the primary source of weather forecasting for aircrews.

The SPAWAR Systems Atlantic website stated:

> *"Frigid temperatures, strong winds, crystalline snow, glaciers, mountainous terrain, snowstorms, white-outs, icebergs, fog, and blizzards all presented unique challenges and hazards to*

*the weather forecasters. Extreme elevation changes had to be factored in also. Flights departing from McMurdo Station's sea-level airfields may land at stations or camps at altitudes of 10,000 feet or more."* [159]

## Satellite Blackout

Time is relative when the sun is up twenty-four hours a day. In Antarctica, the clock can be adjusted to any time zone. Through trial-and-error, the best time period to fly from Christchurch, New Zealand, to McMurdo, Antarctica, was in the middle of the day New Zealand-time. New York-time and Denver-time had been considered for Antarctica operations, but ultimately New Zealand-time made operations out of New Zealand easier.

Using the New Zealand clock provided the best flying weather. Landing earlier in the day resulted in greater potential for fog in McMurdo. Landing later in the day had greater potential for unstable weather in McMurdo. However, a satellite blackout period occurred throughout the flight when the aircrews flew during this time period.

Aircrews flew from Christchurch to McMurdo while reflections from the ice blinded the satellite. The weather forecasters could not see any changes in the weather patterns until the aircrews were past their point-of-safe return. They got their best look at satellite imagery just before the aircrews departed Christchurch, and they wouldn't get another until just before the aircrews landed in McMurdo. The aircrews' point-of-safe-return weather forecast was generated from the 10:00 a.m. satellite image coupled with current observations, automated weather station information, and trend data. The aircrews called it "now-casting" instead of forecasting.

## Pegasus Airfield

Through the years, the National Science Foundation looked for ways to save money. They stopped carving out an ice runway in the McMurdo Sound and ran flying operations at Pegasus, a fourteen-mile drive from McMurdo. On a good day, this was a forty-five-minute drive one-way, which increased an air-crew's workday. They wanted a single airfield operation, but the 109th Airlift Wing objected. There needed to be an alternate airfield, or Pegasus would be considered a remote location. Remote locations required the Raven Gang to increase the amount of fuel they carried for their flights. More fuel in the aircraft meant less cargo moved.

They agreed to keep Williams Field as an alternate airfield. As long as the weather forecast remained in accordance with Air Force guidance and the Williams Field TACAN approach was available, it was a legal alternate. Besides, the aircrews used the Williams Field instrument approach for the white-out landing procedure. Both the 109th Airlift Wing and the National Science Foundation agreed, the Williams Field Skiway didn't need to be groomed. This helped offset the cost of keeping it open.

Now that flying operations were conducted on a full-time basis from Pegasus Ice Runway, contractors built a ninety-degree perpendicular skiway. The Pegasus Ice Runway was preserved for C-17 aircraft. Pegasus Skiway became the primary landing location for the Raven Gang. Pegasus Skiway was parallel to Williams Field Skiway. Therefore, the Raven Gang's primary landing location was parallel to the alternate landing location. They were only seven miles apart. The Pegasus Ice Runway was still available in an emergency.

In 2012, an unusual wind event blew dirt onto Pegasus. These tiny particles of dirt collected on Pegasus Ice Runway. Solar heating warmed the tiny particles. Tiny puddles of melted ice grew over time into pockets of melted ice and eventually into potholes. In efforts to protect the ice runway, the National Science Foundation closed it during the middle of the Operation Deep Freeze season and covered it with piles of clean snow to reflect the sun's heat. The snow was cleared, and the runway was opened for the much larger C-17 aircraft in October when the science season began and again in February and March when it was time to stop operations. The ice runway was no longer available as an emergency airfield from late November through mid to late February.

By 2015, the National Science Foundation moved their primary flying operations to Williams Field Skiway, and Pegasus Skiway became the alternate location. This shortened the drive to and from the airfield, but it didn't solve their alternate location limitations. The weather people believed Pegasus was a good alternate landing destination. The Raven Gang aircrews disputed it. When "Herbie" blew, the crosswinds exceeded the limits for both locations. "Herbie" was the aircrew's nickname for a severe high wind event that blew between White and Black Island from the South Pole's direction.

## The Reckoning

SPAWAR continued to report they were ninety-three to ninety-seven percent accurate. The Raven Gang also disputed this. PACAF weather specialists were asked to intervene on behalf of the aircrews, but PACAF supported SPAWAR Systems Atlantic. It was absurd! In January 2012, Lt. Col. Seth Barrows, the chief of standardization and evaluation for the Raven Gang, found a website that showed the United States had the best weather forecasting in the world. When the United States weather forecasters predicted instrument flying conditions, they were 64% accurate.[160] Something didn't add up.

For over twenty years, SPAWAR Systems Atlantic reported their phenomenal forecasting accuracy. When confronted with the United States' accuracy, SPAWAR Systems Atlantic confessed they were using different metrics to develop their statistics. Nothing was done to improve the forecasting, but the conversation began to change. SPAWAR Systems Atlantic stopped reporting how accurate they were.

During the 2013–2014 Operation Deep Freeze Season, these concerns received very serious attention. A New Zealand 757 aircraft, a modern and technically advanced aircraft with one hundred twenty passengers on board, landed at Pegasus Airfield below recommended weather minimums after holding for several hours.

*The Press*, a newspaper in New Zealand, reported the incident on 3 May 2014:

> *"On October 7 last year, New Zealand's Foreign Affairs Minister entered the cockpit of an RNZAF aircraft heading to Antarctica. The pilot, says Murray McCully, looked 'extremely grim.' Not*

*long after, while the aircraft maintained a holding pattern at altitude, McCully and a 22-year-old female 'staffer' were run through impact procedures. The RNZAF flight attendant briefed the pair on their front-row obligations. In the event of an impact landing, they would have to open the Boeing 757's emergency doors and chutes and let people pass. [The flight attendant] said: 'This is my seat here. If I am incapacitated or killed, the first thing you need to do is move my body out of the way.' There is no sugar-coating on those occasions,' says McCully."*[161]

The news article continued with details of the incident.

The modernization and technological advancements of the 757 aircraft did not help the pilot. However, four days before this incident on 3 October 2013, a similar flight had been made in beautiful weather conditions. A third pilot on board the flight had taken pictures of the approach. Fortunately, he was also on this flight on 7 October 2013. On their final approach into Pegasus, the pilots reviewed the pictures and found the approach's centerline was offset fifteen meters to the right. On the next approach, the pilot flew fifteen meters right of the centerline. The copilot saw the lead-in flags and guided them in. The pilot landed the aircraft safely.[162]

As typically happened, the Antarctica season ended in late February, and nothing was done to improve the weather forecasting for the following season. Because there was no loss of life, permanent injuries, or damage to the aircraft, the 757 aircraft incident was forgotten.

# White Out, 11 January 2015

White-out conditions were originally associated with visual conditions without definition, visual conditions without shadows, and visual conditions with no depth perception. It was like flying inside a ping-pong ball. Buildings seemed to float in the air. Many viewed a landing in visual white-out conditions as not much different than landing in a fogbank. Before long, commanders considered it a viable landing procedure when the weather was poor.

During the 2014–2015 Operation Deep Freeze Season, the weather forecasting was worse than usual. Eight days apart, two aircraft landed in the white-out landing area. On 11 January 2015, Major David Zielinski landed Skier 81 there. Another aircraft was two hours behind him.

Zielinski was lucky. A cloud had settled over both Williams and Pegasus airfields bringing the weather down to zero-zero. After a couple of approaches into Williams Field, Zielinski decided to land in the White-out landing area.

| Skier 81 Aircrew | |
|---|---|
| **Pilot:** | Captain David Zielinski |
| **Copilot:** | Major John Patton |
| **Navigator:** | Lt. Col. Kurt Bedore |
| **Flight Engineer:** | Technical Sergeant Christopher Dumond |
| **Loadmaster:** | Technical Sergeant Jason Bull |
| **Loadmaster:** | Staff Sergeant Dan James |

Fortunately, the white-out landing area was clear of clouds, and the wind was calm. Zielinski landed in the open snow and taxied over to the Williams Field parking area. There was an investigation, and it cleared the weather forecaster of any failures. The weather event happened so quickly there was nothing he could have done to prevent the incident. A brief small area of fog developed over the airfields. As luck would have it, this occurred at the exact time Zielinski arrived from Christchurch. The fog lasted for sixteen minutes, from 5:30 p.m. to 5:46 p.m.

The cloud base had risen to a six hundred-foot ceiling at Williams Field after Zielinski landed in the white-out area. With better tools, the weather observers could have told him to wait out the fog bank, and Zielinski would have landed on the skiway. The weather increased to six thousand meters, or five miles, of visibility and scattered clouds by 5:55 p.m. It was beautiful weather by the time the next aircraft landed.

The law of percentages dictates that if you continue a risky practice and get away with it without doing anything to alleviate the risk, something bad will inevitably happen. Accident investigations have shown there are usually multiple warnings before a major disaster occurs. Every white-out landing on record, up to 19 January 2015, had been due to fog. The winds were calm. The aircrews were able to fly straight into the white-out landing area and make a blind landing.

Things were different on 19 January 2015. The crosswind was strong. Landing blind with a significant crosswind wasn't possible on an open snow-field, even for the most skilled pilot. Skill wasn't the only thing that saved the aircrew and passengers that day. Lt. Col. Steven Yandik wasn't a rookie. He was the main factor that contributed to a successful landing. He had over twenty years of experience in the mission and had been flying white-out landings in the simulator for years.

# Recourse

Yandik's near-catastrophic flight brought the funding back to the ski mission simulator profile, but it would take several more years to develop it. In the meantime, the Raven Gang rewrote their standard operating procedures to address the poor weather forecasting. Their Blue Book changed to state the following:

> *"When faced with unforecasted deteriorating weather, ACs can be put in a position where they must land in the McMurdo whiteout landing area. When such a condition exists, ACs are authorized to commence an approach with weather reported below minimums to help them better judge their available options. If during this approach, they are able to make positive contact with the skiway markings and are in a safe position to land, they may do so."*

This provided top cover for what the aircrews were already doing. The only reason more white-out landings didn't happen was that these pilots were very good cheaters. It had become common practice for the Raven Gang to fly below the instrument approach procedure's minimum altitude. They never bothered to declare an emergency.

Following the events of 19 January 2015, and with PACAF's weather forecasters' help, SPAWAR Systems Atlantic formalized a standardization and evaluation program. They measured their people's performance and removed them from providing forecasts if they were incapable of doing the job. However, the aircrews didn't see any improvement in the forecasting because the forecasters didn't have the necessary tools to improve their accuracy.

During the 2015–2016 Operation Deep Freeze Season, the 109th Maintenance Group's new commander, a former C-5 pilot, witnessed Major Aaron Lancaster landing below the approach minimums. She walked up to him afterward and said, "That was illegal!"

He laughed and simply replied, "Yeah," then walked away. He was more disturbed by the poor box lunches his crew received for their flight than the blown forecast. He was resigned, knowing nothing would be done about the weather forecasting, but something might be done about the food service.

CHAPTER 30

# WHITE-OUT, 19 JANUARY 2015

The day's mission was routine. Lt. Col. Steve Yandik's aircrew was alerted at 6:45 a.m. They ate breakfast at the Commodore Hotel and arrived at the Christchurch International Airport flight line. The day's future events were inescapable and inevitable. There were multiple indications through the years that the flight from New Zealand to Antarctica had the potential for a large-scale tragedy, but nothing was ever done to prevent it.

| Skier 82 Aircrew | |
|---|---|
| **Pilot:** | Lt. Col. Steve Yandik |
| **Copilot:** | Captain Nicholas "Justin" Garren |
| **Navigator:** | Captain Jefferson Wood |
| **Flight Engineer:** | Senior Master Sergeant Kevin Hubbley |
| **Loadmaster:** | Technical Sergeant Michael Wallace |
| **Loadmaster:** | Staff Sergeant Logan Brennan |

Yandik was a farmer, grew mostly apples, and had a farm store. Every Monday from late summer to late autumn, he brought leftover pies that he didn't sell over the weekend to the squadron. He was a coarse man with a dour personality, but he liked to laugh. He loved airplanes and loved to fly. He was a rare pilot who also had FAA certifications to work on aircraft. Yandik had seen his share of unanticipated events throughout his flying career. There were few pilots better suited to deal with what was to come.

The flight was the second LC-130 flight of the day going to Antarctica. It was scheduled for a routine 7½-hour over-water flight to Antarctica. It was typically an eight-hour flight, so the shorter flight time indicated there was a significant tailwind. Captain Jefferson Wood, Yandik's navigator, computed a point-of-safe-return point which was the last point along the route of flight where the crew could turn around and return to New Zealand, with the minimum required fuel reserves arriving at the airfield.

Wood was now on the third flight of his Operation Deep Freeze career. This was his second flight from Christchurch to McMurdo. On his first flight to McMurdo, Major David Zielinski was the aircraft commander on the aircraft two hours ahead of him. The weather caused Zielinski to land in the white-out landing area. Fortunately for Wood's aircrew, the weather had cleared up before their arrival. It was quite an interesting insight into the mission for which he had just signed up. It was all the more interesting because he was the senior forecaster at the National Weather Service office in Buffalo, New York. Before that, he worked as a national weather service forecaster in Anchorage, Alaska, and Marquette, Minnesota.

Captain Justin Garren was Yandik's copilot. He also wasn't a rookie on the mission. He had been a loadmaster in the squadron for six years before becoming a pilot and was about to take part in a flight that loadmasters only get to witness. It was going to be a very different and interesting day.

Senior Master Sergeant Kevin Hubbley was the aircrew's flight engineer. In 1998, he was on a flight into Upstream Delta, Antarctica, when his aircraft ended up in a crevasse. That didn't keep him from continuing his career with the Raven Gang, but after more than twenty-five years of flying, he was nearing retirement.

The loadmasters, Technical Sergeant Mike Wallace, and Staff Sergeant Logan Brennan were young airmen. Wallace had been with the Raven Gang for about eight years. His bright carrot-top head and big smile made him stand out everywhere he went. He was the belly-flop champion of Ballston Lake, New York. Brennan had about four years in the squadron. He was a Guard-bum; he earned his part-time paycheck taking whatever jobs were available in the loadmaster section. He flew a lot and was fast gaining experience. This flight would steepen his learning curve.

Hubbley, Wallace, and Brennan went to the aircraft while Yandik, Garren, and Wood went to the operation building to plan the flight. At 7:30 a.m. Yandik received a weather briefing via a satellite link from Charleston, South Carolina. The weather forecaster used a 4:00 a.m. satellite image. It was a standard weather briefing. Over McMurdo, the forecaster anticipated they would have a twelve thousand-foot broken cloud ceiling with unrestricted visibility. The grid wind was forecast to be from 290° at fifteen knots, gusting to twenty knots. This indicated a quartering headwind for Williams Field's Skiway 25 landings.

Just after 10:00 a.m., the weather forecaster received an updated satellite image of the McMurdo area. It was the last satellite picture the weather forecasters received before Yandik passed his point-of-safe return. Satellite coverage over McMurdo was always limited throughout the day. For the crew of Skier 82, from 9:08 a.m. to 03:45 p.m., the reflection of snow from the earth's surface blinded the weather satellite. This was a 6½ hour window void of vital weather, cloud movement, winds, and precipitation information.

Yandik received a revised forecast for McMurdo. The cloud ceiling would be five thousand-foot overcast skies and unrestricted visibility with snow in the vicinity by their arrival time. The winds changed to grid 290° at twelve knots. This new forecast indicated there would be much lower cloud ceilings than the previous forecast. It came as no surprise their alternate airfield, Pegasus Skiway, was forecast to be much the same as their destination, Williams Field Skiway.

Deteriorating weather conditions were in the forecast, but no lower than fifteen hundred-foot broken cloud ceiling and two miles of visibility. The winds were expected to die down to grid 060° at 9 knots, well within minimum limits. These worsening conditions weren't expected until three hours after their scheduled arrival.

Hubbley conducted the preflight inspection of the aircraft, and everything was in good shape. Wallace and Brennan received their cargo, forty passengers, and their baggage. The cargo weight was less than the maximum allowed for the flight, so Yandik directed Hubbley to add additional fuel.

When Yandik, Garren, and Wood arrived at the aircraft, the flight crew strapped in their seats, ran the appropriate checklists, and started the engines. It was a beautiful summer's day when they left Christchurch. Skier 82 was airborne at 11:04 a.m. New Zealand-time.

## Safe Return Point

The first half of the flight was uneventful. None of the weather trends piqued any of the aircrew's interest. It was another boring flight southbound. Weather forecasters in McMurdo did not have weather radar. To address this shortfall, they provided aircrews hourly weather observations. Aircrews received them via Iridium text or HF, high-frequency radio. This gave the aircrews the ability to make more informed decisions about continuing past the point-of-safe return or turning back to Christchurch.

Throughout the flight, the weather observers in McMurdo sent them more current observations than most flights received. The official name given to these observations were meteorological reports, METAR, and special observations. The only difference between the METAR and special observations was the time they were given. The METAR was given at the top of every hour, whereas special observations were given at any time. It usually took about five minutes to generate the report and send it to the aircrews, and they started arriving soon after takeoff.

Current observation for Williams Field, 11:25 a.m.: The winds were calm, and the visibility was unrestricted; there were a few clouds at twelve thousand feet and a broken cloud ceiling at approximately twenty thousand feet; the temperature was -9° and the dew point was -14°; the barometric pressure was 29.10. In the remarks, it reported fata morgana[163] (a mirage) to the grid east-northeast direction; the surface definition and horizon definition were good.

They received an observation at 11:55 a.m. and another at 12:25 p.m.: The winds were from 350° grid direction at four knots; the visibility was unrestricted; there was a broken cloud ceiling at seven thousand feet; the temperature was -7° and the dew point was -12°; the barometric altimeter was 29.11. Remarks: The surface definition was fair, and the horizon definition was good.

Clouds were moving in the area. In the last half-hour, the cloud ceiling had dropped from twenty thousand feet to seven thousand feet. It wasn't a surprise because it coincided with their updated weather briefing. The winds were light, but they were coming toward Williams Field from Herbie Alley. Herbie Alley was a nickname the aircrews gave the area from which high crosswinds and bad weather typically came from, between White and Black Island, to the grid north of Williams Field.

They received a current weather observation at 12:55 p.m. and another at 1:25 p.m.: The winds were from 290° grid direction at eighteen knots; the visibility was unrestricted; there was a broken cloud ceiling at sixty-five hundred feet and another broken deck at twelve thousand feet; the temperature was -7° and the dew point was -11°; the barometric pressure was 29.12. Remarks: The surface definition was fair, and the horizon definition was good.

The winds were picking up as Yandik neared his decision point, whether to continue to McMurdo or return to New Zealand. The increased amount of fuel Hubbley put on the aircraft shifted the point-of-safe-return point further down the flight path, allowing them to turn back to Christchurch farther along the route if necessary.

Within an hour before passing the point-of-safe return, every Raven Gang aircrew contacted the McMurdo weather forecaster to get the most up-to-date forecast. Yandik's aircrew received their point-of-safe-return forecast 4.5 hours into the satellite blackout period.[164] At 1:32 p.m., Skier 82 received the following updated weather forecast for their scheduled arrival time of 5:35 p.m.:

Between 5:00 p.m. and 7:00 p.m., the weather was expected to be:

- Sky condition, few clouds at 1,500 feet
- Scattered clouds at 3,000 feet
- Cloud ceiling was broken at 5,000 feet
- Overcast clouds at 8,000 feet
- Visibility was expected to be unrestricted with snow in the vicinity
- Grid winds were 290° at 12 knots
- Temperature -6° Celsius; dew point -11°
- Pressure altimeter setting 29.16
- Remarks: Trace rime icing between 7,000 feet and 15,000 feet

The Pegasus forecast was identical. A low-pressure system, which spins clockwise in the Southern Hemisphere, was moving through the Ross Sea, north and east of McMurdo. It was forecasted to impact the McMurdo area later in the evening between 9:00 p.m., and 11:00 p.m. Clouds were expected to roll in and bring snow. This would further reduce visibility. The snow and low visibility would remain in the area until a pressure ridge building in Victoria Land, west of McMurdo, forced the low-pressure system to move further east.

Jefferson Wood received this information on his laptop. A three-knot decrease in the wind was the only difference between this forecast and their updated 10:00 a.m. weather briefing. Wood noted the forecast was viewed with some misgivings by Yandik. He was puzzled because he didn't see anything in the forecast that suggested they should turn around and return to Christchurch. He continued to monitor the current observations for the field. The significant difference in the next two observations was the cloud ceilings dropped to five thousand feet.

Current observation for Williams Field, 2:25 p.m.:

- The winds from 300° grid direction at thirteen knots;
- the visibility was unrestricted;
- there was a broken cloud ceiling at five thousand feet and another one at seven thousand feet; the temperature was -7° and the dew point was -11°;
- the barometric pressure was 29.13.
- Remarks: The surface definition was fair, and the horizon definition was good.

The 10:00 a.m. forecast remained on target. The current observations, although trending down, were well above what was necessary to continue to McMurdo. At 2:32 p.m., they passed the point-of-safe-return, their commitment point. They were going to McMurdo, and no longer had enough fuel to return to Christchurch.

Jefferson Wood switched the aircraft navigation system from magnetic orientation to grid. Grid helped aircrews deal with the longitudinal lines as they converged and joined at the South Pole. Grid navigation was originally a U.S. Army creation. It was based on a flat earth map. On a small scale, this made navigation simple. In aviation, this created some interesting results. By flying the prime meridian northbound over the North Pole and continuing on the same track, grid navigation had the aircraft heading grid-north while heading to the South Pole.

While flying southbound out of New Zealand, south of sixty degrees south latitude, Skier 82 was on a 327° grid course line, almost directly grid-north. East was west, and west was east. North was south, and south was north. Lewis Carroll, the author of *"Alice in Wonderland,"* would find this amusing.

Current observation for Williams Field, 2:55 p.m.: The winds were from 300° grid direction at fourteen knots; the visibility was unrestricted with light snow showers; there was a broken cloud ceiling at three thousand feet and an overcast cloud deck at forty-five hundred feet; the temperature was -7° and the dew point was -11°; the barometric altimeter was 29.13. Remarks: There was icing in the area; the surface definition was fair, and the horizon definition was fair. The weather started to deteriorate, and it was going to get much worse.

## McMurdo Arrival

Soon after passing the point-of-safe return, Wood realized Yandik's misgivings were well-founded. The weather observations started trending downward. The low-pressure system over the Ross Ice Shelf that was expected to hold off until later into the evening hours came in faster than forecasted.

Yandik voiced some choice words about the weather forecasters. However, they bounced around the inside of the aircraft but never escaped their confines. The surface and horizon definition started deteriorating. The clouds were dropping lower, and the visibility in different sectors of the sky was worsening.

Current observation for Williams Field, 3:38 p.m.: The winds from 310° grid direction at twelve knots; the visibility was four thousand meters, about 2½ miles. A broken cloud ceiling was now at two thousand feet, and an overcast cloud deck was at three thousand feet; the temperature -7° and the dew point was -9°; the barometric altimeter was 29.15. Remarks: Visibility to the grid east was at sixteen hundred meters or one mile; the surface and horizon definitions were poor.

The temperature and dew point spread was narrowing, an indication for potential fog to form. The cloud ceilings were dropping, the visibility was falling rapidly, and the winds were increasing sharply out of the grid north/northwest. A full-blown "Herbie" hit the McMurdo area.

Jefferson Wood remarked, "By three hours out from McMurdo, we knew that we were going to be in for a tricky approach and landing."

At 3:45 p.m., the weather forecaster received an updated satellite picture. He never saw the bad weather coming until it was too late for Yandik to turn back. The cloud ceiling and visibility continued to drop, so did the surface and horizon definition.

Current observation for Williams Field, 3:55 p.m.:

- The winds were from 340° grid direction at five knots;
- the visibility was down to thirty-two hundred meters, two miles, with light snow;
- there was a broken cloud ceiling at fifteen hundred feet, and an overcast cloud deck was at two thousand feet;
- the temperature was -6° and the dew point was -9°;
- the barometric altimeter was 29.15.
- Remarks: Visibility was sixteen hundred meters, 1 mile, to the grid north-northeast; the surface and horizon definitions were poor.

The weather conditions the forecaster had anticipated for later in the evening had arrived early, and it was much more menacing. His next 4:00 p.m. terminal area forecast reported the weather would be bad but manageable for their arrival time. He sounded optimistic, but the aircrew knew otherwise.

Williams Field forecast at Yandik's 5:35 p.m. arrival:

- Sky condition, scattered clouds at 500 feet
- A broken cloud ceiling at 1,200 feet
- Overcast cloud deck at 2,000 feet
- 2,000 meters, 1¼ miles, of visibility with light snow showers
- Wind from 320° grid direction at 15 knots
- Altimeter 29.16

Pegasus forecast at the time of their arrival:

- Sky condition, scattered clouds at 1,200 feet
- A broken cloud ceiling at 2,500 feet
- Overcast cloud deck at 4,000 feet
- 4,000 meters, 2½ miles, of visibility with light snow showers
- Wind 320° grid direction at 15 knots
- Altimeter 29.15

There was a temporary forecast line beginning at 4:00 p.m., with one thousand meters of visibility for the next four hours. This included Yandik's arrival time, and if it were accurate, it would prohibit them from seeing the skiway on their final approach to landing.

Time became compressed for Jefferson Wood, and everything accelerated. An hour and a half out from McMurdo, Yandik started talking to his aircrew about a white-out landing. He wanted everyone's input. He intended to fly the TACAN approach to landing to Skiway 25. If he were unable to land there, they would execute the published missed approach and try again. He intended to keep trying until either the weather cleared and he landed, or the aircraft ran low on fuel, and he needed to put it down in the white-out area.

Current observation for Williams Field, 4:23 p.m.:

- The winds were from 350° grid direction at fifteen knots;
- the visibility was down to two thousand meters, 1¼ miles, with light snow;
- there was a broken cloud ceiling at fifteen hundred feet, and an overcast deck at two thousand;
- the temperature was -6° and the dew point was -9°;
- the barometric altimeter was 29.15.
- Remarks: Both the surface and horizon definition were nil.

This was very similar to the 4:00 p.m. forecast. It was obvious the forecaster was "now-casting." The wind had increased and was now blowing up to fifteen knots. A fifteen-knot direct crosswind was the Raven Gang's limit for landing on skis. They decided on fifteen knots to prevent the skis' sides from digging in the snow and causing the aircraft to dip and drag a wingtip, then cartwheel.

Seven minutes later, another observation. The only difference for the 4:30 p.m. observation was the visibility was down to one thousand meters, less than a mile. The legal weather minimums required at least a mile of visibility for aircrews to fly the Williams's TACAN approach. When Pegasus wasn't available, the Raven Gang ignored the minimums. It was the only option remaining.

# Souza's Landing

Lt. Col. Cliff Souza's aircrew, Skier 81, left Christchurch at 9:35 a.m., about an hour and a half ahead of Yandik. Souza was the deployed commander for the Raven Gang. On Saturday, he was short a pilot to fly to Christchurch, so he flew the mission. He intended to be back on the continent the following day. On Sunday, the weather rolled into McMurdo. The weather forecast was poor, so he spent another day in New Zealand.

It was now Monday. The weather forecast wasn't great, but it was good enough to return to the ice. It was a routine flight until he arrived in McMurdo. He passed the point-of-safe return and committed to land in Antarctica. His options were limited. When he arrived, Williams Field Skiway 25's winds were barely within limits, and the cloud ceilings weren't an issue either. It was the visibility. Although the one thousand meters was forecast to be a temporary condition, the last observation said it was one thousand meters.

The surface and horizon definitions couldn't get worse. There were no shadows as the horizon disappeared and the dull white clouds blended with the dull white snow. On the ground, as people walked around, it looked as if they were walking on clouds. Aircrews equated this condition to operating inside a ping-pong ball. The weather observer was working overtime.

Current observation for Williams Field, at 4:55 p.m.:

- The winds were from 350° grid direction at eighteen knots;
- the visibility was down to one thousand meters, less than a mile, with light snow;
- there was an overcast cloud ceiling at fifteen hundred feet; the temperature was -6° and the dew point was -8°;
- the barometric altimeter was 29.15.
- Remarks: Visibility was sixteen hundred meters, one mile, to the grid north-northeast; the surface and horizon definition was poor.

Current observation for Pegasus Field at 4:55 p.m.:

- The winds were from 330º grid direction at eighteen knots;
- the visibility was down to thirty-two hundred meters, two miles, with light snow;
- the cloud ceiling was at two thousand feet, and there was another overcast deck at 3,000 feet;
- the temperature was -6º and the dew point was -8º;
- the barometric altimeter was 29.16.
- Remarks: Visibility to the grid east was nine thousand meters, more than seven miles. The surface definition and the horizon definition were nil. To the grid east, the horizon definition was poor.

Souza chose to fly the MLS, or microwave landing system, approach to Skiway 25. In his gut, he felt if he didn't get the aircraft on the ground on this approach, the winds would get more challenging on the next one. His options weren't good, so he told Captain Pat Newton, his copilot, "If at decision-height, you see the lights, and I think I can control the drift, I will land." When Souza started his approach to landing, there was a seventeen-knot direct crosswind. The maximum limit was fifteen knots. He knew the reason for the limit but also knew he could probably handle the extra two knots. There weren't better options available. The visibility was still one thousand meters, less than a mile.

Another Pegasus observation came in ten minutes after the last one.

Current observation for Pegasus Field, 5:05 p.m.:

- The winds were from 330º grid direction at eighteen knots;
- the visibility was thirty-two hundred meters, two miles, with light snow;
- the cloud ceiling was at two thousand feet, and there was another overcast deck at three thousand feet;
- the temperature was -6º and the dew point was -8º;
- the barometric altimeter was 29.17.
- Remarks: Visibility to the grid north-northeast was unrestricted, clear skies. The surface definition and horizon definition were nil. To the grid north-northeast, the horizon definition was fair.

Bands of weather were sweeping through the area. It was a tease; on one observation, the weather seemed to improve; on the next, the weather was significantly worse. The weather observer reported Pegasus observations more and more often. Aircrews had gone to Pegasus Ice Runway in the past during a similar instance. It was aligned with the high winds. But it was no longer available. It was closed and covered with snow. The only option was the Pegasus Skiway. The skiways at Williams Field and Pegasus were seven miles apart and parallel to each other, so the crosswind affected them both the same way.

To the grid northeast of Pegasus Airfield was the Royal Society Mountain Range with mountains as high as fourteen thousand feet. There was no viable approach to Pegasus Skiway from the northeast that would allow Souza to descend and see it, in the event he wanted to try his luck with a crosswind landing there, instead of Williams Field. Furthermore, no one was at Pegasus, and there were no emergency vehicles, so it was unlikely anyone could get there. The current weather reports were from an Automated Surface Observing System or ASOS. There was no tower or ground support. If he needed to go to the white-out area, there was no approach to get there from Pegasus. The approach for a white-out landing was based on an approach to Williams Field. There were no advantages in going to Pegasus.

The sky had fallen to the ground. The visibility was below the requirements to fly the approach to land at Williams Field, so Souza cheated. At decision height, Newton picked out the lead-in lights to the skiway. Souza put the aircraft in a crosswind landing attitude. As he transitioned from looking at the instruments inside the aircraft to outside, he couldn't differentiate the surface from the horizon. The buildings on the airfield looked as if they were floating. The skiway flags gave him his only sense of orientation. He landed at 5:10 p.m.

As he touched down onto the snow, he "split the throttles" as he slid out. He used differential power by pulling the #1 and #2 engine on the left wing toward reverse, and #3 and #4 throttles forward, to maintain directional control of the aircraft. He couldn't see anything but the skiway flags as they passed. It was a challenge to taxi to the parking ramp. In the back of his mind, he thought, *I wonder what Steve is going to have to deal with? If we were another 15–30 minutes later, I would have been in the white-out area!*

# Yandik's Arrival

Yandik received a third Pegasus observation within twenty-three minutes. The weather continued to get worse.

Current observation for Pegasus Field, 5:18 p.m.:

- The winds were from 330° grid direction at seventeen knots;
- the visibility was twenty-four hundred meters, or 1½ miles, with light snow;
- there were a few clouds at one thousand feet, scattered clouds at two thousand feet.
- The cloud ceiling was an overcast deck at three thousand feet; the temperature was -6° and the dew point was -9°;
- the barometric altimeter 29.17.
- Remarks: Visibility to the grid north-northeast was unrestricted. The surface definition was poor, and the horizon definition was nil. To the grid north-northeast, the horizon definition was fair.

Yandik had a long career with the Raven Gang. He began pilot training in 1993. On his first trip to the Antarctica ice cap, he was with Dick Bayly helping to repair an aircraft in January 1995. He went to Siple Dome and picked up the aircrew that taxied into a crevasse in 1998. He had spent several nights with the scientists on the Greenland ice cap in 2007. Now in 2015, he was faced with the most serious challenge of his career. He was fighting for the survival of his aircrew and the forty passengers in the back of his aircraft.

Current observation for Williams Field, 5:22 p.m.:

- The winds were from 350° grid direction at nineteen knots;
- the visibility was down to one thousand meters, less than a mile, with light snow;
- there was an indefinite cloud ceiling of about eleven hundred feet;
- the temperature was -6° and the dew point was -8°;
- the barometric altimeter was 29.16.
- Remarks: The surface and horizon definitions were both nil.

The McMurdo area lost a defined cloud ceiling. Now the weather observer was looking straight up to see how far he could see. It was a guessing game—another Pegasus observation at 5:35 p.m., seventeen minutes from the last one. The difference was the visibility increased by one-half mile.

Williams Field observation at 5:37 p.m., fifteen minutes from the last one. The difference was an increase of one knot of wind, and the cloud ceiling improved one hundred feet.

Williams Field observation at 5:55 p.m., eighteen minutes from the last one. The difference was the surface definition improved from nil to poor.

All the radio chatter was becoming meaningless. Upon reaching one hundred miles from their destination, Skier 82 had twelve thousand pounds of fuel remaining. This gave Yandik enough fuel to descend from altitude and attempt a couple of instrument approaches.

The most recent forecast indicated they would have two thousand meters, or 1¼ miles, of visibility for their arrival, but the four-hour temporary condition of one thousand meters of visibility was more accurate. The two thousand meters gave Yandik legal authorization to fly the approach. It was a subtle gift from the forecaster, but it didn't matter; Yandik would have tried anyway. He had no other options.

The weather was below the minimums for every approach to Williams Skiway and Pegasus Skiway. There were no other suitable airfields within flying distance. The wind also increased to a twenty-knot direct crosswind. Yandik's first approach into Williams Field held little hope for a better outcome on the next approach. He chose to fly the TACAN approach to landing. The sustained crosswinds on the surface were strong, and the cloud ceiling and visibility were below minimums for the approach. Yandik's concern wasn't the cloud ceiling; it was the visibility.

The winds at altitude were stronger than the winds on the surface, gusting up to thirty-five knots. The nose of the aircraft was pointing into the wind. This caused the aircraft to track about twelve degrees left of where the nose was pointing. The aircraft's large tail, sticking up from the rest of the aircraft structure, acted like a weather vane as the aircraft flew around the rectangular pattern. Jefferson Wood's recalled Yandik's approach to the airfield:

> *"The drift was bouncing between 12 to 13 left. I will never forget that moment, though, as we broke out from the clouds. We were crabbed way off-center due to the drift; descending rapidly, likely in an attempt to dive below the cloud deck; from my perspective, seemingly pointed right at the ground, GPWS was screaming at 'sink rate' and 'pull up.' All the hairs on the back of my neck went up, everything seemed all wrong, and it did not seem like a safe landing was possible given our configuration, the weather conditions, and our distance from the ground, so I called 'Go around!'"*

Wood's gut told him that the approach was not good and continuing could lead to disaster. He reflected, *"I have occasionally wondered if I made the right call. Is it possible that Steve could have landed the aircraft out of the configuration we were in?"*

No one will ever know. Yandik responded immediately and executed the go-around procedure. He added power and pulled the nose of the aircraft back into the clouds and flew the missed approach procedure into the clouds.

## Math Problem

Wood was scared and extremely focused. He kept himself busy, constantly cycling the navigation system to new waypoints. He cleared all previous approaches he had loaded in the navigation system and instead built the white-out area and displayed it on the radar. This allowed the pilots to have some visual guidance on their radar screen. He monitored the Morse Code identification of the navigation aid constantly to verify they were still functioning. He also monitored the radar and the moving map display on the navigator's laptop to ensure that they stayed away from the terrain below. It helped keep his fear at bay.

On Yandik's TACAN approach to Skiway 25, the winds were significantly out of limits. It was time he went to the white-out landing area. This area had been surveyed and certified to be free of man-made objects before the beginning of the Operation Deep Freeze mission. This gave Yandik and his crew some confidence the terrain in the area was safe.

The procedure to land in the white-out area was written in the McMurdo instrument approach book. It was designed to fly the TACAN approach and continue overhead past the navigational aide. After passing the TACAN, the procedure required the pilot to fly within specific radials to remain within the white-out landing area's confines. It was in the shape of a pie. Yandik was facing a complex math problem. He intended to fly along the area's left side, on the 247-degree radial from the TACAN. At approximately 8½ to 9 miles past the TACAN, he intended to turn the aircraft 90 degrees to the right, facing the wind. By turning into the wind, he eliminated a major portion of his problem, the crosswinds. There were thirty-one radials, between 247 degrees and 278 degrees, to the other side of the area. Using the sixty-to-one rule, eight miles away from the TACAN meant every 7½ radials equaled a mile. Therefore, he had four miles to set the aircraft onto the surface before he went outside the area.

The aircraft would be traveling at a ground speed of about one hundred twenty knots, which was two miles per minute across the ground. Yandik had four miles from one side of the area to the other, so he had about two minutes to set the aircraft on the snow. Once he rolled out of the turn, he intended to start a gentle descent rate of two hundred feet-per-minute. The aircraft would be about two hundred feet above the ground descending at two hundred feet per minute. He expected to land one minute after he rolled out of his final descent. Yandik wasn't computing any of this math, though, because he had already flown it in the simulator, and he knew what he was doing.

## Final Approach

Justin Garren, Yandik's copilot, suggested attempting a circling approach to Skiway 33, which was a good idea most days. However, when the visibility was good, it was intimidating to fly this circling approach. Legally, the visibility needed to be at least a mile to give Yandik some awareness of the mountainous terrain in that direction. But, Yandik was beyond legalities. He was desperate and was looking for any means to get the skis on the snow. There was a lot of risk flying toward the terrain in bad weather. After some discussion, Yandik decided he preferred the white-out landing risk to the risk of the circle. He didn't need to see to land in the white-out area. Jefferson Wood, *"Given the near-zero ceiling and visibility, the lack of an instrument approach, and a strong wind that would be blowing us towards the precariously close higher terrain of Ross Island, that was ruled out."*

Fuel was at a critical point. It was clear the weather people wanted Yandik to go to Pegasus. The forecasters didn't understand there was no legal way to approach the field, nor an illegal way to guarantee they would be clear of terrain. Although Pegasus was considered a viable alternate location, the 109th Airlift Wing danced around the legalities of what an alternate required. It had no emergency equipment available, and because the airfield wasn't in use, no one was there. Legal or not, if Yandik could have landed there, he would have done so. He flew over Pegasus when he went missed approach, but he never saw it.

The weather observer began giving observations over the radios every fifteen minutes.

Current observation for Pegasus Field at 5:55 p.m.:

- The winds were from 330° grid direction at twenty-one knots;
- visibility was twenty-four hundred meters with light snow;
- a few clouds were at one thousand feet, and scattered clouds were at two thousand feet.
- The cloud ceiling was an overcast deck at three thousand feet;
- the temperature was -6° and the dew point was -9°;
- the barometric altimeter was 29.18.
- Remarks: Visibility to the grid northeast was unrestricted. The surface definition was poor; the horizon definition was nil. To the grid northeast, the horizon definition was fair.

Current observation for Pegasus Field, 6:10 p.m.:

- The winds were from 340° grid direction at eighteen knots;
- the visibility was twenty-four hundred meters with light snow;

- there were a few clouds at one thousand feet and scattered clouds at two thousand feet.
- The cloud ceiling was an overcast deck at three thousand feet;
- the temperature was -6º and the dew point was -9º;
- the barometric altimeter was 29.18.
- Remarks: Visibility to the grid northeast-east was unrestricted. The surface definition was poor; the horizon definition was nil. To the grid northeast-east, the horizon definition was fair.

Current observation for Pegasus Field, 6:25 p.m.:

- The winds were from 330º grid direction at twenty knots;
- the visibility was twenty-four hundred meters with light snow;
- there were a few clouds at one thousand feet and scattered clouds at twenty-five hundred feet.
- The cloud ceiling was an overcast deck at three thousand feet; the temperature was -6º and the dew point was -9º;
- the barometric altimeter was 29.19.
- Remarks: Visibility to the grid northeast was unrestricted. The surface definition was poor; the horizon definition was nil. To the grid northeast, the horizon definition was fair.

Current observation for Pegasus Field, 6:40 p.m.:

- The winds were from 330º grid direction at twenty knots;
- the visibility was twenty-four hundred meters with light snow;
- there were scattered clouds at twenty-five feet, and the cloud ceiling was a broken deck at three thousand feet.
- There was an overcast deck at thirty-five hundred feet; the temperature was -6º and the dew point was -9º;
- the barometric altimeter was 29.19.
- Remarks: Peak winds were blowing up to twenty-seven knots. Visibility to the grid northeast was unrestricted. The surface definition was poor; the horizon definition was nil. To the grid northeast, the horizon definition was fair.

Current observation for Williams Field, 6:55 p.m.:

- The grid winds were from 340° at eighteen knots;
- the ceiling was an overcast cloud deck at fifteen hundred feet;
- the temperature was -6°, the dew point was -9°, and the barometric altimeter was 29.19.
- Remarks: Surface definition and horizon definition were nil.

Current observation for Pegasus Field at 6:55 p.m.:

- The grid winds from 330° at eighteen knots;
- visibility was nine thousand meters with light snow;
- scattered clouds at twenty-five hundred,
- the cloud ceiling was a broken deck at three thousand, and there was an overcast deck at thirty-five hundred feet;
- temperature -6°, dew point -9°, barometric altimeter 29.20.
- Remarks: Peak winds were blowing up to twenty-seven knots. Visibility to the grid northeast was unrestricted. The surface definition was poor, and the horizon definition was nil. To the grid northeast, the horizon definition was fair.

Every METAR and special observation came across the radios, and the chatter was constant. Clearly, the weather people thought Pegasus was an option, with a peak crosswind gusting up to twenty-seven knots. Little changed from one special observation to the next. It was not helpful, and it became an unnecessary distraction. Yandik was having difficulty focusing on his approach.

# Emergency Response

Cliff Souza and his aircrew debriefed their aircraft problems with maintenance. They then caught a shuttle ride up to Mac Town. Souza walked into Building 165 about an hour after he landed. He stopped in Raven Operations and told Lt. Col. Joe DeConno, his deputy, to follow him. They went into Mac Center, the air traffic controllers' office, just in time to monitor Yandik's last approach.

"We heard Steve make his last approach attempt and announce they were going to the white-out area. I recall telling the controller to let them be and stop calling them." Souza listened as Skier 82 flew toward the white-out area, then all communication stopped. He waited. He tried to get hold of Yandik on the radios. He couldn't get verification the aircraft was on the snow.

McMurdo's emergency operations center was activated, and Souza went downstairs to be a part of it. DeConno remained with the air traffic controllers. The National Science Foundation representatives and their contractors, including Mr. Steve Dunbar, gathered in the briefing room. Souza and Dunbar discussed their options. "I figured they were about ten minutes from touchdown. About fifteen minutes later, Center tried to call them to confirm they were down safely but got no answer. After twenty minutes of not hearing anything, I hoped they were down safe and taxiing in. But after more than thirty minutes, I said call the fire department."

Initial responders went in search of the aircraft and aircrew. Williams Airfield's fire department deployed toward the white-out area, however within a quarter of a mile after departing the airfield's prepared surface, they were stuck in the snow. The rescuers needed rescuing. Souza and Dunbar talked about the next step. It was difficult for Souza to remain detached from the issue while wondering if his squadron members were injured or worse.

## White Out Landing

Yandik knew this was his last chance because his fuel was critical. He had over twenty years of ski mission experience. The white-out landing was something he had practiced in the simulator for years until the ski mission training profile was deemed no longer necessary.

Other aircrews had successfully accomplished a white-out landing. Landing blind in an open snowfield was impressive. There was always the risk of impacting someone or something the pilot couldn't see. But Yandik was faced with an additional challenge. He wasn't simply going to be flying four miles beyond the skiway and touching down into a snowfield, blind. He didn't have an eight-mile limitation, and if he failed to land, there wasn't more open snow outside the confines of the area.

Yandik first had to address the strong crosswind. He needed to turn the aircraft ninety degrees at a low altitude. After he rolled out of his turn, he had two minutes to land, and if he failed, his missed approach would take him toward the twenty-five hundred-foot mountainous White Island. He had one shot. On Yandik's final approach to landing, there was some confusion. The wind had blown them across their intended course-line toward McMurdo and Mount Erebus. Wood closely monitored the radar and knew where they were, so he directed a left base turn away from the terrain. Garren asked if he meant a right turn.

Wood firmly replied, "We need to turn left to get to our waypoint."

Yandik complied. He could see the Coast Guard cutter in the distance, but as they approached the airfield, the weather went from bad to worse. They reached the initial approach point and turned left again, towards Skiway 25.

Wood felt a grave sense of finality on the final turn towards Williams Field, thinking, *"We could end up a flaming pile of wreckage in a blizzard at the end of the earth, but even greater than that was a fear that we would end up in that flaming pile of wreckage because I screwed up."*

The landing gear and skis were down, and the flaps were set at fifty percent for the approach. Yandik maintained one hundred-forty knots of airspeed. As he flew over the airfield, he considered going below the minimum altitude for the approach but, if it resulted in a high descent rate and made the rest of the aircrew uncomfortable again, they would direct another "go-around," which would cause more distraction on his way to the white-out area.

Perhaps he could duck-under, perhaps he could circle, perhaps there were better options available, but he didn't see them. He considered everything, but the weather wouldn't cooperate. Perhaps it would this time. Perhaps, perhaps! His decision came down to one cold, hard fact. He didn't have any more fuel. If he didn't get the aircraft on the snow, the aircraft engines would begin to flame out, one-by-one. This would make things exponentially more difficult. He couldn't see the airfield as he crossed his missed approach point, so he climbed up to five hundred feet and continued to the white-out area. He overflew the TACAN and continued another four miles. He was now within the white-out area confines.

Yandik needed his people to concentrate and focus on the immediate problem, so he told everyone to turn off their radios. Wood recalled later:

> *"As we flew out the radial that marked the edge of the whiteout area, the weather continued to deteriorate. We flew roughly two-thirds of the way into the whiteout area boundary to maximize our distance available to land, which was a good thing since visibility and ceilings were nil. The tower was constantly pinging us on the radios, so we turned off the VHF radio to minimize distractions."*

Yandik flew up the left side of the designated area. About 8½ miles from the TACAN, or 4½ miles into the area, he began a right ninety-degree turn. Garren was looking outside for anything to guide Yandik in the storm. The only thing he saw was white, just white, no shadows. White forward, white to the right, white to the left, white down. No point looking up. The white snow flying toward the windscreen was like a kaleidoscope, dizzying.

Yandik had descended below three hundred feet. The turn caused the aircraft to extend deeper into the area. He rolled the aircraft out of the turn about nine miles from the TACAN. The width of the white-out area was now about five miles. The math only got better the deeper he went into the area.

Wood kept Yandik aware of his distance to the other side. All extraneous conversations had ended long ago. Both pilots and Wood were focused on Yandik's progress. Hubbley remained focused on the aircraft systems. Wallace and Brennan ensured the passengers were strapped in and prepared for landing.

The aircraft was now pointing into the wind, and this made things much simpler. Garren dropped the flaps to one-hundred-percent on Yandik's command. Yandik slowed the aircraft to the skiway threshold speed. He knew he was traveling less than two miles per minute due to the headwind. He started a slow two-hundred-foot per minute descent. Wood recalled:

> *"As we descended into the whiteout area, I made the standard radar altimeter callouts. The last one hundred feet went by very slowly, the last 50 feet even more slowly—30 feet...30*

*feet…20 feet…20 feet...and so on. That last 10 feet went by even more slowly. With about three miles to go, we made our initial touchdown. I say 'initial' because we bounced pretty hard, not because of bad flying, mind you, but because of the rough, ungroomed nature of the white-out area. We bounced back into the air for what seemed like an eternity."*

Yandik knew the aircraft would float as he approached the snow due to the aircraft's lightweight and the ground-effect as the large wings approached the ground. Ground-effect created a cushion of air below the wings, and the aircraft floated on it. Yandik needed to force the aircraft through ground-effect. When the aircraft touched down, it bounced back into the air. It was quite likely he hit Zielinski's ski tracks which rutted the area during his landing in the area the previous week. There was no way to avoid them.

Yandik had the experience and discipline to maintain the aircraft's landing attitude. He watched his airspeed and let the plane settled back onto the snow. It impacted firmly and then slowed. They were safely on the snow at 7:00 p.m. Jefferson Wood felt a wave of elation as Yandik slowed the aircraft, knowing that the most dangerous part of their journey was behind them. However, there was still the significant challenge of navigating the airplane across nine miles of snow in a blizzard.

He built a radar approach into their navigation system to guide Yandik back to the centerline of Skiway 07 at Williams Field. The weather conditions were zero-foot cloud ceiling and zero miles of visibility. The color of the snow was the color of the horizon. There were no shadows; therefore, the crew was effectively blind looking outside the aircraft. They were taxiing inside the ping-pong ball, which resulted in a zig-zag pattern.

Jefferson Wood: *"The winds were frequently gusting over gale force, making Steve and* Justin *work hard to keep the plane going in a straight line. Every time they relaxed their grip, even for a few seconds, the plane would get blown sideways. Flying over the tracks a couple of days later, it looked like we were drunk! We eventually saw the firetruck lights through the gloom, somewhere off to our right."*

Garren realized what had happened. On the radio, he contacted Mac Center and reported that they were safe. When Yandik saw the rescue vehicles, he chuckled and shook his head. The aircrew's focus on where they were going exhausted them. The tension inside the aircraft remained high throughout their taxi to the ramp. Finally, Yandik stopped the aircraft an hour after they landed. They shut down the aircraft engines with about thirty-nine hundred pounds of fuel.

Hubbley talked with Yandik about the landing. It had been firm, and there were no injuries, but Hubbley thought it was a good idea to log a hard landing into the aircraft forms. The landing registered 3.9Gs on the G-meter. According to the book, a hard landing was 4.0Gs. Yandik agreed it was worthwhile to get the aircraft checked out. In the following days, the maintenance team contacted Warner-Robbins to determine where to search for signs of a hard landing. They were told to look at the landing gear and skis. If no damage was evident, then no other maintenance was required. The aircraft was fine.

They piled into a shuttle and returned to Mac Town. Jefferson Wood later recalled, *"There was much cursing of the forecasters as we rode up into the town as we felt that they were responsible for placing us in a very dangerous situation, but at the end of the day, I privately thanked God that we made it safely home."* It was quite the introduction to Antarctica.

CHAPTER 31

# CRAZY SCIENCE

*Author's Note: Year after year, more scientists arrive in Antarctica with a ground-breaking project of our time. Their scientific results are crucial, and there's no time to lose. They rush to bring their projects back home but never seem to consider what they will do if things go awry. If the scientific data is critical and must safely return to the United States, perhaps they could wait until December to bring the project home. There is a greater chance of the aircrew spending the night on the ice cap in November and February at some remote location. The weather forecasting tends to be more reliable when the weather patterns are more stable in December and January.*

The first image of the supermassive black hole at the center of our galaxy, Sagittarius A, was expected to be produced in April 2017; however, it wasn't. The South Pole Telescope's raw data wasn't available because it was still at the South Pole. On 15 February 2017, the Raven Gang flew their last flight to the South Pole for the season. No flights occurred from February through October. Access to the disks would not be possible until the Raven Gang returned in late October or early November to start another Operation Deep Freeze season.

Disks from the South Pole Telescope needed to get to the Max Planck Institute for Radio Astronomy and the Massachusetts Institute of Technology's Haystack Observatory. Its data would be combined with data of seven other telescopes from around the world. This combination of data would be converted into an image of the event horizon of the black hole.

The other telescopes that contributed to this project were ALMA[165], APEX[166], the IRAM thirty-meter telescope,[167] the James Clerk Maxwell Telescope,[168] the Large Millimeter Telescope Alfonso Serrano,[169] The Submillimeter Array,[170] and the Submillimeter Telescope.[171] These were telescopes located at high-altitude sites around the world and formed an "Earth-sized virtual telescope. The EHT [event horizon telescope] represented decades of observational, technical, and theoretical work with expectations of providing unprecedented sensitivity and resolution."[172]

The data from each telescope had been precisely timed using atomic clocks and stored on high-performance helium-filled hard drives. The South Pole greatly increased the north-south extent of the event horizon telescope, and therefore its resolution."[173]

Small amounts of test data were sent, via satellite, to see if the experiment was working. And it was. But, there was too much data to transfer everything via satellite. It would be the first time a project like this had been accomplished. The science community was excited to have the data. This excitement meant getting the disks from the South Pole was a priority for the National Science Foundation while the science community waited.

## The Weather Forecast

In mid-October, the Raven Gang left New York and flew their aircraft to Christchurch, New Zealand. By late October, the aircraft was in McMurdo, Antarctica.

| Skier Aircrew | |
|---|---|
| **Pilot:** | Captain Brandon Caldwell |
| **Copilot:** | First Lieutenant Brian Alexander |
| **Navigator:** | Lt. Col. Ron Ankabrandt |
| **Flight Engineer:** | Senior Master Sergeant Michael Messineo |
| **Loadmaster:** | Master Sergeant Dave Vesper |
| **Loadmaster:** | Senior Airman Ryan Rhoads |

The weather was poor throughout the following week. No flights had left McMurdo since they arrived. Captain Brandon Caldwell hadn't flown all week. Raven Ops alerted his aircrew. They were going to fly. His flight engineer, Senior Master Sergeant Mike Messineo, and his loadmasters, Master Sergeant David Vesper and Senior Airman Ryan Rhoads, caught a van at Derelict Junction for the forty-five-minute ride to the aircraft to perform preflight inspections and load cargo on the aircraft for the mission ahead. Caldwell, his copilot First Lieutenant Brian Alexander, and his navigator Lt. Col. Ronald Ankabrandt walked along the dirt roads of McMurdo to Raven Ops, in Building 165, to plan for the flight.

McMurdo is reminiscent of an old Alaska gold mining town built on a mountainside. This particular mountain was Mount Erebus, an active volcano. People are usually seen walking around town in red parkas and sunglasses. It's a civilian community of workers who maintain the town and take care of the scientists. Most buildings are painted wood or tin on the outside. The highest building is three stories high.

The National Science Foundation runs McMurdo. Its sole purpose is science. The main operating location for Operation Deep Freeze is the Department of Defense's logistical support to the United States Antarctic Program. Antarctica's harsh, unforgiving, and unpredictable weather makes every flying mission on the continent a high-risk, close-watch mission.

In the early hours of 9 November 2017, and throughout the evening hours the day before, the weather was forecasted to be poor for most Antarctic locations. Therefore, the next day's original plan was to fly local area orientation missions for the multiple new crewmembers on the station. However, when Lt. Col. Seth Barrows, the Raven Gang's deployed commander, arrived at Skier Operations that morning, the weather was beautiful and was forecasted to remain that way all day.

Barrows checked the weather. The forecaster told him he thought Shackleton Glacier Camp had potential. A crew might be able to take a look. If they couldn't land at Shackleton, they could return to McMurdo. This was the plan Barrows gave to Caldwell. Caldwell checked the weather with his crew an hour later and came to the same conclusion. It sounded like a solid plan.

Caldwell, Alexander, and Ankabrandt left the building and caught a van to the skiway. Meanwhile, Barrows took another look at the weather. He furrowed the brow on his bald head, holding his glasses, as he often did, and walked into Skier Ops and told his director of operations he wanted to speak with Caldwell when he got to the flight line. Shackleton weather was going down again, but the weather was improving at the South Pole. He needed to get people and cargo out of the South Pole, and he wanted Caldwell to go there instead of Shackleton.

# McMurdo Weather Systems

The weather forecasters were contracted through the Space and Naval Warfare Systems Center. For years the Raven Gang said that the weather forecasters in Antarctica needed better tools. They lacked twenty-four-hour satellite coverage. They had no Doppler weather radar and only limited automated weather observation stations. They were always working on better computer modeling when they had the funding.

McMurdo is on Ross Island off the coast of Antarctica. A permanent ice shelf connects the island to the continent. Along this ice shelf were the two McMurdo airfields, Williams Field Skiway and Phoenix Ice Runway. McMurdo airfields were at sea level, surrounded by high terrain. The Ross Ice Shelf bumps against the McMurdo basin. It's deeply frozen glacial ice, with a layer of ice crystals as a surface base.

As the frozen McMurdo Sound's ice melts, open water begins to loop around Ross Island. Meso-high weather patterns north of McMurdo can cause fog to form. The forecaster's lead-time to notify the aircrews can be as little as thirty minutes. Gusty winds cause light surface snow to drop visibility from unrestricted visibility to less than a mile for hours. This low visibility lasts as long as a moderate wind flow funnels through the region.

Lee-side low weather patterns, north of McMurdo, formed within a few hours caused heavy snow or fog conditions. These explosive weather conditions frequently lasted for days when deep polar lows moved in from the Ross Sea. Lead-time for the forecaster to notify the aircrews was five to seven hours.

The funneling effect from mountainous areas, south, and west of the island, occasionally caused winds above hurricane strength. The forecaster's warning time was a few days to twelve hours out. Sometimes they are surprised and get no warning at all. These were ongoing challenges for the weather forecaster and, more importantly, to the aircrews.

*South Pole (coolantartica.com)*

# South Pole

Caldwell called Raven Operations and got the word to go to the South Pole. He received an updated weather briefing. Vesper and Rhoads loaded the cargo on the aircraft. The aircrew taxied the aircraft to the fuel pits to take on as much fuel as possible. The Raven Gang typically departed McMurdo at the aircraft's maximum weight limitation of 155,000 pounds. Excess fuel would be given to the South Pole.

Skier 42 was loaded, fueled, and ready to go. Caldwell called for the checklists to be run. The aircraft engines were started, and the required briefings were completed. He taxied out to the Williams Field Skiway and started his takeoff slide. He pulled the nose ski off the snow at about sixty-five knots and waited for flying airspeed before pulling the rest of the aircraft off the snow.

Once airborne, Caldwell turned the aircraft grid-north to fly to South Pole station. The flight was about three hours. The direct flight from

McMurdo to the South Pole, over the Trans-Antarctic Mountain Range with mountains exceeding fourteen thousand, over the cold, barren, and unforgiving landscape was stunning. The sun is always up from mid-October through mid-February in this part of the world.

Along the flight path and tracing the Beardmore Glacier backward, its blue glacial ice rises from the Ross Ice Shelf to the Antarctica ice cap, the source for this frozen flowing river. There are no trees or flowers to break up the stark grays, blacks, whites, and browns that cover the continent's surface. Antarctica is rock, snow, and ice.

It was an uneventful flight until they arrived. Before descending, the crew got a weather update. The ceiling and visibility were both low. The crosswinds were at their maximum allowed for a ski landing. The wind chill temperature was -65 degrees Fahrenheit. Caldwell briefed his aircrew on how he intended to fly the approach to the South Pole skiway, and all procedural checklists were done before the final approach. The Ski Airborne Radar Approach, or Ski ARA, is the only weather approach available into the South Pole.

Ankabrandt, Caldwell's navigator, guided him down the final approach path, backing him up with wind-drift information and distance to landing. The aircraft descended one hundred fifty feet per mile. The approach was designed to be very shallow in case the radar altimeters were inaccurate. Based on the aircraft's speed, Caldwell had a three hundred foot-per-minute descent rate.

Alexander, Caldwell's copilot, kept his eyes focused outside to pick up the skiway approach flags, but he also backed up Caldwell on airspeed and descent rates. This was his first flight in Antarctica, but he had received extensive training during the previous Greenland Season.

Alexander didn't pick up the skiway approach flags as Caldwell leveled at the minimums, three hundred feet above the snow. At the missed approach point, Ankabrandt called, "*Go-Around,*" and Caldwell added power and climbed back up to pattern altitude. They tried it again a second time and failed.

On the third attempt, Alexander saw the skiway flags just before the skiway. This would be an interesting landing. Caldwell descended and landed two-thirds of the way down the skiway. The aircraft wasn't going to stop in time. The aircraft had slowed, but as they approached the end, Caldwell told his aircrew, "I'm going to the left of the skiway flags on the opposite skiway." And he did.

He went off the end of the skiway but didn't stop. Instead, he added power and made a left turn, two hundred seventy-degree turn, and taxied to the parking area by manipulating the throttles. He stopped in the fuel pits area. People on the ground were stunned, except for Chris Penno. Penno had been the chief pilot for the Raven Gang. He now worked for the National Science Foundation's Office of Polar Programs." He smiled as he saw people's reactions.

The aircrew kept the aircraft engines running. Caldwell received an updated weather forecast for McMurdo. The forecaster called for better than visual meteorological conditions or VMC. It was a beautiful day at McMurdo and was expected to remain so until after their return. With this information, Caldwell decided to offload fuel from his aircraft to the South Pole station.

When Caldwell was ready, Alexander got out of his seat and positioned himself at the bottom of the flight deck stairs, at the crew entrance door, to be a safety observer as the loadmasters moved cargo out, then into the aircraft. He maintained interphone communications with the pilot. Ankabrandt put on his cold-weather gear, exited the aircraft, and positioned himself off the aircraft's nose to be the external safety observer for the fuel offload operations and the cargo offloading and on-loading operation. He maintained interphone communication with the pilot and the flight engineer. Vesper and Rhoads put on their cold-weather gear and offloaded the 14,710 pounds of cargo and the nineteen people that flew from McMurdo with them. They then loaded six people and 15,142 pounds of cargo. Some of it was sensitive equipment.

Messineo, the crew's systems expert, was responsible for offloading the fuel from the aircraft fuel tanks with the fuel system specialists' help at the camp. He put on his cold-weather gear, exited the aircraft, and did a walk-around of the aircraft before ending up at the aircraft's aft copilot side. This was the location for the single-point refueling. He checked in on the aircraft interphone to ensure good two-way communications with Caldwell and Ankabrandt. He offloaded 6,692 pounds of fuel based on the updated

McMurdo weather forecast. Had the forecast been poor, he would have left more fuel in the aircraft.

# Unforecasted Weather

After the cargo was on-loaded and the fuel offloading was completed, Caldwell was airborne much like he was on his departure from McMurdo. The weather was still very poor when he got airborne; however, he easily climbed to cruise altitude.

One hour into Skier 42's return flight to McMurdo, they got their first indication something was wrong. After flying an hour over the broad, open, snow-scape of the Antarctica ice cap, the Trans-Antarctica Mountain Range was just ahead. Although the transmissions were garbled, McMurdo asked the aircrew how much fuel they had on board.

Messineo said, "Ask them why they're asking?" And Alexander did. McMurdo seemed to be having the same difficulty receiving Skier 42's transmission because they asked again how much fuel they had on board.

Caldwell got on the radio and asked, "Why do you want to know?"

McMurdo was in the middle of an unforecasted wind event, a "Herbie." These winds exceeded the crosswind limits for Caldwell to land at Williams Field or Phoenix. To make matters worse, the wind was blowing snow which drove the ceiling and visibility to zero-zero. Both Williams and Phoenix were in whiteout conditions, with zero ceiling and zero visibility.

Caldwell certainly didn't want to return to the South Pole due to the poor weather. Shackleton Glacier Camp was not an option. It's located in the Trans-Antarctic Mountain Range. The weather had to be significantly better than it was before they could descend into the mountains. Messineo knew immediately they were in trouble. He was a New Yorker with Italian ancestry, and he had a lot to say. He recommended Caldwell climb the aircraft higher into less dense air and pull back power to conserve gas, which Caldwell did. Through the garbled HF communications, Skier 42 was notified an unforecasted wind event made both McMurdo airfields unsafe to land.

Caldwell talked over his situation with his aircrew. He told them he was considering the white-out landing procedure. The crew needed to prepare. Emotions began to build. For the younger crew members, Alexander and Rhoads, they knew they were in for some excitement. The remaining older crew members were frustrated and angry.

The white-out landing area is an open snowfield between the mountainous Ross Island to the left and White Island to the right at roughly twenty-five hundred feet in height. The area was surveyed at the beginning of the season to ensure it was free of crevasses. This gave the aircrew a degree of confidence the terrain in the area was safe. But there was no guarantee the area was free of manmade obstructions like igloos or natural obstructions like hard ridges of snow and ice called sastrugi.

The white-out procedure was written in the McMurdo approach book. It was designed to fly the TACAN approach and continue overhead and past the navigation aide. After passing the TACAN, the pilot must fly within specific radials to remain within the white-out landing area. The area was eight miles deep, from four to twelve nautical miles from the TACAN, and between the two hundred forty-seven-degree radial and two hundred seventy-eight-degree radial. Therefore, its width got wider the deeper an aircraft went into the area.

If Caldwell needed to fly this procedure, the crosswind would be the greatest hazard, so he would need to fly deep along the left side of the designated maneuvering airspace then make a right ninety-degree turn into the wind toward White Island. It was extremely risky, but it had been done in the past. He had never practiced it, although a new ski mission simulator profile was coming.

## Divert

Before Skier 42 arrived in McMurdo, they received some good news. The weather at Mario Zucchelli Station, an Italian research field one hundred ninety-two miles past McMurdo, had VMC weather conditions. This was a piece of luck. It was November. Later in the season, the Italians closed their camp, and their airfield would no longer be available. But going there had its own dangers. If he committed to going to the Italian camp, there was no possibility of returning to McMurdo for a white-out landing. If the weather dropped at Mario Zucchelli Station and he couldn't land, his only remaining option would be to fly over the mountains with the hope his fuel lasted in a last-ditch effort to land on the ice cap.

When Skier 42 arrived overhead McMurdo, the crew was informed that the winds had slackened slightly and that visibility was up to one-half mile. The microwave landing approach system minimums were one-half mile at Williams Skiway. After calculating his fuel, Caldwell determined that if he descended and flew an approach to Williams Skiway and the weather became worse, he would need to fly the missed approach procedure. He would have to declare an emergency and land in a blinding snowstorm in an empty snowfield, four miles from Williams Field, with 12 people on board. Knowing the weather at Mario Zucchelli Station was still beautiful VMC conditions, Caldwell decided going there was his safest course of action.

## The Cargo

Caldwell landed safely at the Italian camp. He taxied to parking and shut down the engines. The Italian reception was a pleasant one. Food and drink were ready for the aircrew when they entered the camp. Caldwell notified Raven Operations in McMurdo that they were set for the evening. In response, he was notified that the aircraft's sensitive cargo could not be tilted and could not be frozen.

The sensitive cargo were disks for the Event Horizon Telescope. Losing the data on the disks would be a horrible disappointment for the science community. If the disks were damaged, the science wouldn't be just the loss of South Pole telescope data but a significant loss to the Event Horizon Telescope. The data on the disks was invaluable to the science community.

Vesper and Rhoads went back to the aircraft. Over the next two hours, and with the help of the outstanding people at Mario Zucchelli Station, they carefully offloaded the equipment and stored the science cargo in a warm warehouse overnight. The next morning Caldwell's aircrew retrieved their passengers and cargo, fueled the aircraft, and returned to McMurdo. The disks were immediately flown to New Zealand.

The Event Horizon Telescope status update was given on 15 December 2017. It stated:

> *"Over the past two months, the EHT team has been working hard on processing a preliminary data set that does not yet include any data from the South Pole station. Using this data set, the team has refined the data processing pipelines that will be used to calibrate the data and also tested many of the analysis tools that will be used to make images and search for signatures of strong gravity effects at the event horizons of supermassive black holes."*
>
> *In early November, the EHT data disks were sent from the South Pole Station on a journey by air, sea, and land going through McMurdo Station on Antarctica's coast through Christchurch in New Zealand and Port Hueneme in California.*
>
> *On Wednesday, December 13, the long-awaited shipment of hard disk drives from the South Pole finally arrived at the MIT Haystack Observatory. Half of the data was soon on its way to the Max Planck Institute for Astronomy in Bonn, Germany. After the disks are warmed up, they will be loaded into playback drives and processed with data from the other 7 EHT stations to complete the Earth-sized virtual telescope that links dishes from the South Pole to Hawaii, Mexico, Chile, Arizona, and Spain. It should take about three weeks to complete the comparison of recordings, and after that, the final analysis of the 2017 EHT data can begin!"*[174]
>
> *The stunning new image showed the shadow of the supermassive black hole in the center of Messier 87, an elliptical galaxy some 55 million light-years from Earth. The black hole is 6.5 billion times the mass of the Sun.*[175]

For Caldwell's aircrew, this flight was nothing new, no hype, no thanks, no "job well done." He spent the afternoon after his return planning his next day's mission. But his extraordinary success could not be overstated.

# EPILOGUE

The Raven Gang is a non-traditional LC-130 squadron. There are many stories yet to tell. We have dined with princes and princesses. We have flown kings, senators, congressmen, ambassadors, generals, and entertainers.

Some things are not covered in this book. Perhaps someone else will write of them someday. There are stories of aircraft engine flame-outs, meteorites, dinosaur bones, and snow angels. There is the story of Dunbar's air bridge after the Navy's last Antarctica season, the Raven Gang's first aircrew spending the night at an outlying camp called Shackleton Glacier, and returning to Christchurch at the point-of-safe return, better known as boomerangs. There were flat tire takeoffs on skis, more ping-pong ball stories, many white-out landing stories, including one at Siple Dome. There have been many broken aircraft at outlying camps, including a story of how a soup can repaired a bleed air duct; and another about the use of coffee stirrers to manually lower skis. Stories of near collisions at the camps; adventures at Kulusuk and dirt strips on the Canadian north coast; and someone sticking their tongue to a piece of frozen metal, just to see if it's true.

It's time to bring my stories to an end, but before I go, here are a couple of summaries of other significant events.

## Greenland Expedition Society

In the early 1990s, the Raven Gang supported the Greenland Expedition Society, a civilian organization's efforts to recover World War II aircraft from below the Greenland ice cap. Two B-17 and six P-38 aircraft made an emergency landing on the ice cap, south of Kulusuk, Greenland, in July of 1942. Everyone survived, but the aircraft were left behind. Major Norman

Vaughan went back to the aircraft and recovered the Norton bombsights from the aircraft a few weeks later.

Fifty years later, Ray Tousey, with the assistance of the legendary Norman Vaughan, built a ski landing area to allow the Raven Gang to deliver the heavy equipment for the support of the Greenland Expedition Society.

# Eight-Bladed Propeller

The Raven Gang spent more than nine years testing the eight-bladed propeller. They put four of these propellers on aircraft 83-0492. On the first attempt to fly to the South Pole, all four propellers sprung a leak. The aircrew returned the aircraft to McMurdo. All four propellers had lost all of their fluid but kept running. Maintenance repaired the propellers with replacement seals, and the Raven Gang flew the aircraft back to New York. New propeller seals were designed and installed.

For more than the next nine years, the 109th Maintenance Group needed two supply chains for parts, two sets of maintenance procedures, and different training programs put a great deal of burden on them. It wasn't until 2019 the rest of the skibirds were fitted with eight-bladed propellers.

*Sondrestrom Flight line*

The 109th Airlift Wing still has two aircraft with four-bladed propellers, but the maintenance challenges have been reduced. When they deploy to Antarctica and Greenland with the skibirds, they only need the eight-bladed propeller supply chain.

## Aeromedical Squadron

The 109th Airlift Wing also has an aeromedical squadron. It's made up of nurses around the local Schenectady, New York, area. Aeromedical squadron aircrews put on their military uniform, and they fly around the world and rescue wounded soldiers from war zones. In the case of the 109th Aeromedical Squadron, they save people on the ice caps also. The nurses and medical technicians are the true heroes in these adventures.

There are two notable rescues from the ice cap I'll discuss here. Perhaps the most well-known rescue was of the female medical doctor at the South Pole during the Antarctic winter. Three aircraft and three Raven Gang aircrews arrived in New Zealand in early October of 1999. Two of the aircraft and aircrews departed Christchurch, New Zealand, and flew to McMurdo, Antarctica.

The day after they arrive in McMurdo, Antarctica, the rescue was scheduled. The skies were clear, but the extremely cold temperatures at the South Pole delayed the mission for a day. The following day the weather was poor at the South Pole, but the temperature warmed to -50° Celsius or -58° Fahrenheit.

With the substantial support of his aircrew, Major George Rob flew through the high winds and low cloud ceilings and successfully landed at the South Pole. The cold temperatures and lack of moisture in the snow made the surface feel more like sand as he taxied the aircraft to parking. The aircrew didn't chance shutting down the engines at these temperatures. The propellers' seals would immediately freeze, leaking hydraulic fluid, and the aircraft would become a hazard to fly. Chief Master Sergeant Mike Cristiano watched the engine instruments. Senior Sergeant Kurt Garrison and Technical Sergeant Dave Vesper opened the crew entrance door and guided the stricken doctor aboard the aircraft with its engines running. The flight nurses took over her care.

The gritty snow conditions created a difficult challenge for Rob. He got the aircraft airborne, firing the ATO or assisted takeoff bottles. They returned to McMurdo, where the doctor and the medical team were taken to a C-141 aircraft that flew her to Christchurch, New Zealand.

Years later, a lesser-known rescue but perhaps the longest rescue on the books occurred from 29 October 2008 through 5 November 2008. The chef at Davis Camp, an Australian camp in Antarctica, crashed his four-wheeler bike and suffered multiple fractures on October 20, 2008.[176] He fractured his pelvis and broke both his ankles. His friends called for an ambulance; however, the nearest one was in New York, sixteen hundred miles away so, it was going to take a little time.[177]

Originally, the Aussies intended to bring the chef home onboard a ship, but they determined he would not survive the trip. Through a series of phone calls, they asked the Raven Gang to rescue him. Major Dave Lafrance and his aircrew, including a 139th Aeromedical Evacuation Squadron member, were selected for the mission before their deployment to Operation Deep Freeze season.

They flew in a commercial airliner from Albany, New York, to Christchurch, New Zealand, where they picked up their LC-130 aircraft. The following day they flew to McMurdo, Antarctica. They delayed a day in McMurdo because Davis Camp was located on the other side of the continent, and the weather was forecast to be poor.

On 3 November 2008, the aircrew boarded their aircraft and flew to Davis with a medical team. Davis Runway was carved out of the ocean's ice surface. When LaFrance landed, the aircraft's weight created a bow-wave on the ice ahead of him and another behind him, but the ice held. The surface was very slick, and the winds were blowing. LaFrance left the throttles in the flight range until the aircraft hit a layer of snow. He was afraid he would lose control if one of the propellers delayed going in the ground range. Lafrance remarked, *"Once we hit the layer of snow, we immediately gained some control back, and I gingerly went into the ground range and reverse."*

He used differential power, manipulated his throttles to create asymmetric thrust to guide his aircraft to a stop. The aircraft was parked, and the aircrew was fed and then went to bed. In the morning, the camp manager was sitting outside Lafrance's room with coffee, a weather update, and current information from McMurdo. Lafrance thought, *"What a way to wake up."*

The camp manager asked Lafrance if he trusted his navigator. He wanted to be sure Lafrance didn't return to Davis Camp once he left. The camp manager said, "Here's the deal; once you declare that you have passed the point-of-safe-return, the ice runway will be destroyed by the ship in the harbor to bring in supplies to the camp." Lt. Col. Marc "Sipowitz" LeCours, the navigator in question, looked at the winds and briefed the rest of the aircrew they weren't going to fly directly north. He intended to use the tailwinds to his advantage and boomerang around the weather front. Later in the afternoon, Master Sergeant Jamie Hill and Technical Sergeant Joe Axe brought the patient and the medical team on board.

LaFrance took off from Davis Camp. They initially flew east for the first couple of hours before turning north. They had tailwinds for the rest of the trip. It was a ten-hour flight to Hobart, Tanzania. Sipowitz shaved an hour off of the flight. They landed on 5 November 2008, at 1:00 a.m. The patient survived. For LaFrance, it was the most memorable flight of his career. He and his aircrew then flew to New Zealand to support Operation Deep Freeze. As frequently happens, by the end of the season, the rescue was forgotten.

# Current Arctic Efforts

When the 109th Airlift Wing initially took over the Operation Deep Freeze mission, they put variants of their ski operations on hold, including operating on the frozen Arctic Ocean. They are now reviving these capabilities. In 2011, the 109th Airlift Wing started a dialog with senior military commanders throughout the country. The LC-130s are included in the Air Force Arctic Strategy Talking Points, dated 21 July 2020. Their unique capabilities provide America a power projection capacity other countries lack.[178] They have demonstrated their capabilities in recent years during exercises supporting the United States and Canadian military ventures.

The 109th Airlift Wing is working with the Department of Defense to recapitalize the ski mission. The Wing continues to work with commanders, educating them on the aircraft capabilities as they update their operational plans and strategies. They have also worked closely with Canadian military forces in the Arctic. The Raven Gang is again building skiways on the Arctic Ocean and conducting operational exercises from them.

The warming climate has allowed greater access throughout the Arctic Ocean. It's actually made the northern passage waterway a reality. Undiscovered natural resources in the Arctic and northeast Greenland have created a great deal of global interest.[179] The average estimate of undiscovered oil and gas in the Arctic are *"approximately 90 billion barrels of oil, 1,669 trillion cubic feet of natural gas, and 44 billion barrels of natural gas liquids."*[180] The Arctic has the potential to supply around one-quarter of the world's needs.

Russia has always seen the Arctic as their backyard. In the 1930s, they were mapping their coastline and building drifting ice stations long before any other nation was interested in doing so. They are currently *"securing economic interests, expanding their military presence, and investing in new offensive and defensive technology."*[181]

China's "One Road" policy demands access to the Arctic, although they have no natural border with the area. China seeks to normalize its presence in the region, enhance polar operating capabilities, and gain a regional governance role.[182]

# Current Antarctica Efforts

Over the last few years, Pegasus Airfield has closed. Pegasus never fully recovered from the damage to the ice runway caused by dust particles blown onto its surface years before. Instead, the National Science Foundation built another ice runway called Phoenix. Phoenix is a mile closer to Williams Field than Pegasus. Now the Rang Gang's alternate airfield is six miles from their primary landing location.

McMurdo is being rebuilt. Many older buildings are being torn down and replaced by more modern structures. The National Science Foundation is significantly improving McMurdo's communications capabilities. Black Island and Ross Island Earth Station, or RIES, are being reconstructed. This will provide the Raven Gang better bandwidth for their own communication needs.

There is hope for improved weather forecasting in Antarctica. The 557th Weather Wing at Offutt Air Force Base may have a high-resolution weather satellite imagery solution. This will address the satellite blackout periods the weather forecasters have been challenged with for over twenty-five years.[183] It may provide timely weather updates over all areas of operation in and around Antarctica. Improved weather forecasting will fix half of the challenges the Raven Gang faces every year. Landing options are the other half.

*McMurdo Flight line*

Italy is also rethinking how to operate in Antarctica. The Italians operate out of Mario Zucchelli Station from mid-October to mid-February. Their location is essential for supporting continental air transport of personnel and freights to and from Concordia Station, a French-Italian research base on the ice cap, during the summer months in the southern hemisphere.[184] Italy is interested in building a gravel airstrip near Mario Zucchelli Station. After an evaluation process that considered the environmental impact. They chose a location called Boulder Clay. It's located at 74°45' South, 164°17'

East.[185] Boulder Clay could become a true alternate location, two hundred miles from McMurdo. It will dramatically increase the safety of the aircrew and its passengers. However, it's undetermined how far into the Operation Deep Freeze season the Italians will keep the airfield open.

Piedmont Glacier is another potential location during emergency operations. Piedmont Glacier is across the McMurdo Sound on the coast of the continent. It's about fifty miles from Williams Skiway. Its proximity to the mountains along the coast will never allow it to be a viable alternate for flying operations. However, an emergency location fifty miles from McMurdo could provide one more landing option for the aircrews.

# FINAL THOUGHTS

While the future of the Arctic and the Antarctic will continue to evolve, bringing changes and improvements, the history of the missions and adventures of the courageous men and women who have gone before will forever offer insights into the unique conditions and challenges that await the coming generations. Their indomitable spirits and clever solutions to seemingly insurmountable challenges serve to be an encouragement to those who will follow in their "ski tracks." Serving with the Skibirds has been the highlight of my career, and telling their stories has been an honor indeed.

THE END

# INDEX

# ENDNOTES


1 109th Airlift Wing History

2 https://www.criticalpast.com/video/65675041185_Distant-Early-Warning-Lines_glaciers_Arctic-terrain_Control-Tower?fbclid=IwAR1D3dgkUSkUEWbcsWx8bTzd9CgrkTyKmiTfJm-t9geUaTeNgcMQs-BSIok

3 Email communications with Mr. Brian Jeffrey, a former DEW Station Operator, http://www.DEWLine.ca,

4 Greenland: Security Perspectives, Taagholt and Hansen, 2001

5 Task Force Slide USAF C-130 Ski Tests, by Kent A. Mitchell, http://www.firebirds.org/menu1/pslide1.htm

6 Skibirds on the Ice Cap, by John H. Cloe, American Aviation Historical Society Journal, Summer 1977

7 314th Troop Carrier Wing (Medium) Historical Report, 1 Jan–30 June, 1959, p. 4.

8 Skibirds on the Ice Cap, by John H. Cloe, American Aviation Historical Society Journal, Summer 1977

9 Ibid

10 Encyclopedia Britannica, Edition 15, 1987; Vol 23 page 763

11 http://www.firebirds.org

12 http://www.c-130.net/aircraft-database/C-130/mishaps-and-accidents/year/1972/

13 Aircraft crashes on Greenland's ice cap, in the Sourdough Sentinel, June 9, 1972; the description of what happened The Destruction of C-130D 70-495 at DYE III; and The C-130 Fin Stall Phenomena, by Tim Brady, U.S. Air Force, bradyt@erau.edu

**14** Aircraft crashes on Greenland's ice cap, in the Sourdough Sentinel, June 9, 1972; the description of what happened The Destruction of C-130D 70-495 at DYE III; and The C-130 Fin Stall Phenomena, by Tim Brady, U.S. Air Force, bradyt@erau.edu

**15** Firebirds' Sondrestrom Daily Log; http://www.firebirds.org/menu10/57-495_p1.htm

**16** Record of Certificate of Damage

**17** USAF Skibirds and the NYANG 109th Tactical Airlift Group, by Chuck Sloat

**18** Ibid

**19** Aviation Investigation Report A13F0011, Canada, Aviation Investigation Report A12F0011

**20** "Wind, Sand and Stars," Antoine de Saint-Exupery

**21** Transport Topics, November 1974 issue

**22** New York State General Karl_Doll, retired Raven Gang navigator

**23** Bobby Dawes, retired Raven Gang Pilot

**24** Wayne Tobiasson, Cold Regions Research and Engineering Laboratory structural engineer, retired

**25** Email communications with Mr. Brian Jeffrey and http://www.DEWLine.ca

**26** DYE-2 and DYE-3 – A 30 Year Engineering History, by Stewart Osgood and Daniel Bornstein

**27** Wayne Tobiasson, Cold Regions Research and Engineering Laboratory structural engineer, retired

**28** Ibid

**29** Skibirds on the Icecap, by John H. Cloe, JOURNAL American Aviation Historical Society, Summer 1977 Journal American Aviation Historical Society

**30** Lt. Col. Eric G. Wiener, retired Raven Gang Pilot

**31** Mission Commanders' Book

**32** Mike Trefzger, retired ski maintenance Senior Master Sergeant

**33** Colonel Jon Adams, Retired Raven Gang Pilot

**34** Email communications with Mr. Brian Jeffrey and http://www.DEWLine.ca

**35** Skibirds on the Icecap, by John H. Cloe, JOURNAL American Aviation Historical Society, Summer 1977 Journal American Aviation Historical Society

**36** Mr. Wayne Tobiasson, CRREL structural engineer for DYE-2 and DYE-3 performance studies, retired

**37** Transport Topic, 1977

**38** Mr. Wayne Tobiasson, CRREL structural engineer for DYE-2 and DYE-3 performance studies, retired

**39** New York State General Karl_Doll, and retired Raven Gang navigator

**40** Mission Commanders' Book

**41** https://www.109aw.ang.af.mil/About/History/

**42** "Structural Analysis of DEW Line Station DYE-2, Greenland 1983-1988," by Michael R. Walsh and Herbert T. Ueda

**43** DYE-2 and DYE-3 – A 30-Year Engineering History, by Stewart Osgood and Daniel Bornstein (Structural Engineers, Metcalf & Eddy, Inc.)

**44** Mr. Wayne Tobiasson, CRREL structural engineer for DYE-2 and DYE-3 performance studies, retired

**45** Encyclopedia Britannica, Edition 15, 1987; Vol 23 page 763

**46** New York Times article, by Richard Halloran, April 26, 1985

**47** https://aviation-safety.net/database/record.php?id=19850420-1

**48** We Were to Freeze to Death, by "Hisham," PLO Fighter Accusing USA After Plane Crash in Greenland

**49** Aircraft registration per http://www.planecrashinfo.com/1985/1985-28.htm

**50** https://aviation-safety.net/database/record.php?id=19850420-1

**51** https://aviation-safety.net/database/record.php?id=19850420-1

**52** https://aviation-safety.net/database/record.php?id=19850420-1

**53** Telex message: 301245Z May 85, From: Sondrestrom AB GL, Subj: Aircraft Crash on Greenland Icecap

**54** Ibid

**55** We Were to Freeze to Death, by "Hisham," PLO Fighter Accusing USA After Plane Crash in Greenland

**56** Mission Commanders' Book

**57** Telex message: 301245Z May 85, From: Sondrestrom AB GL, Subj: Aircraft Crash on Greenland Icecap

**58** Ibid

**59** Chief Master Sergeant Michael Cristiano, retired Raven Gang Flight Engineer

**60** We Were to Freeze to Death, a document written by "Hisham," PLO Fighter Accusing USA After Plane Crash in Greenland

**61** Chief Master Sergeant Michael Cristiano, retired Raven Gang Flight Engineer

**62** Lt. Col. Elliot "Aldo" Marchegiani, retired Raven Gang Pilot

**63** Chief Master Sergeant Michael Cristiano, retired Raven Gang Flight Engineer

**64** Sue Hamilton, in her January 2013 article "The Inuit Dog"

**65** Ibid

**66** Ibid

**67** The National Guard's "On Guard" article, July 1988

**68** https://naalakkersuisut.gl//en/About-government-of-greenland/About-Greenland/Politics-in-Greenland

**69** NICOP IX International Conference on Permafrost; University of Alaska Fairbanks 2008; Session 28: Cold Regions Infrastructures and Transportation; "Permafrost in Marine Deposits at Ilulissat Airport in Greenland, Revisited"

**70** High Arctic Airfield Rehabilitation and "Reconstruction - Thule Air Base," Kevin Bjella, Research Civil Engineer Cold Regions Research and Engineering Lab - CRREL Fairbanks, Alaska, ARTEK-AIC 2018, 3 May 2018

**71** Sue Hamilton, in her January 2013 article "The Inuit Dog"

**72** The National Guard's "On Guard" article, July 1988

**73** "TASK FORCE SLIDE USAF C-130 SKI TESTS" by Kent A. Mitchell, http://www.firebirds.org/menu1/pslide1.htm

**74** Test pilot for Task Force Slide

**75** Ibid

**76** http://firebirds.org/

**77** PICO Bulletin – University of Alaska Fairbanks, Vol. 1 NO 1 April 1989

**78** Ibid

**79** https://earthobservatory.nasa.gov/images/36173/sermersuaq-humboldt-glacier-greenland

**80** Mission Commanders' Book

**81** "Surface elevation and velocity changes on the south-central Greenland ice sheet: 1980 2011," Kenneth C. Jezek; Byrd Polar Research Center and Department of Geological Sciences, The Ohio State University, Columbus, OH, USA E-mail: jezek.1@osu.edu

**82** Drift Stations – Arctic Outposts of Superpower Science by William F. Althoff, pages 8-11

**83** Drift Stations – Arctic Outposts of Superpower Science, by William F. Altho

**84** Arctic Flying, by B.M. Buck, R.W. Corell, R.G. Dickerson, A. Hanson, A. Heiberg, R.K. McGregor, J. Porter, J.F. Schindler, and R.A. Rauch; page 169

**85** Drift Stations – Arctic Outposts of Superpower Science, by William F. Althoff; page 171

**86** Drift Stations – Arctic Outposts of Superpower Science, by William F. Althoff; page 187

**87** Drift Stations – Arctic Outposts of Superpower Science, by William F. Althoff; page 189

**88** Drift Stations – Arctic Outposts of Superpower Science, by William F. Althoff, page 170

**89** Telephone conversation with "Jumper" John Bitters.

**90** Suitability of Ice for Aircraft Landings, by Robert P. Sharp, 1927

**91** http://polarwinter.com/north_pole/north-pole-high-arctic.html

**92** One of a kind DC-3, with three engines and skis, designed by Jack Conroy

**93** Beaumont Manor_Buck. Jr.

**94** New York State General Karl_Doll, retired

**95** Technical Sergeant Greg Doriski, retired

**96** Technical Sergeant Greg Doriski, retired

**97** "Fairbanks Daily News-Miner"- Mike Belrose, Fairbanks, Alaska, Sunday, April 2, 1989

**98** Lt. Col. Paul Bury, retired Raven Gang pilot

**99** crash-disabled-damaged aircraft recovery

**100** Beaumont Manor_Buck. Jr.

**101** Spring to the Ice – A Memoir by Beaumont M. Buck; page 144

**102** Spring to the Ice – A Memoir by Beaumont M. Buck; page 145

**103** Mr. "Jumper" John Bitters

**104** http://www.radiocom.net/vx6/junglejim.htm

**105** https://www.navalhistory.org/2013/02/01/february-1-1955-task-force-43-commissioned-to-plan-and-execute-operation-deepfreeze

**106** https://en.wikipedia.org/wiki/Williams_Field

**107** http://www.puckeredpenguins.org/aboutus.html

**108** http://www.radiocom.net/vx6/vx6roots.htm

**109** Operation DEEP FREEZE 50 Years of US Air Force Airlift in Antarctica 1956-2006, by Ellery D. Wallwork, with Kathryn A. Wilcoxson, Office of History Air Mobility Command Scott Air Force Base, Illinois, October 2006

**110** Wilbert Turk, Colonel (retired) http://www.firebirds.org/menu1/mnu1_p18.htm

**111** Operation DEEP FREEZE 50 Years of US Air Force Airlift in Antarctica 1956-2006, by Ellery D. Wallwork, with Kathryn A. Wilcoxson, Office of History Air Mobility Command Scott Air Force Base, Illinois, October 2006

**112** Bulletin of the United States Antarctic Projects Office, January 1960

**113** Ibid

**114** Air Force C-130 operations in DF-60, https://southpolestation.com

**115** Task Force Slide USAF C-130 Ski Tests, by Kent A. Mitchell, http://www.firebirds.org

**116** Ibid

**117** http://www.vaq34.com/vxe6/vxe6hist.htm

**118** National Security Decision 71, July 10, 1970

**119** https://www.southpolestation.com/trivia/history/321/digout.html

**120** http://www.vaq34.com/vxe6/vxe6hist.htm

**121** Antarctic Journal, January/February 1972

**122** https://www.southpolestation.com/trivia/history/321/digout.html

**123** Antarctic Journal, March/April 1973

**124** "The last moments of 917…." https://www.southpolestation.com

**125** http://www.c-130.net/aircraft-database/C-130/mishaps-and-accidents/airforce/USNavy/

**126** Ibid

**127** Navy Aircraft, vaq34.com

**128** http://stratocat.com.ar/fichas-e/1994/MCM-19941221.htm

**129** Ibid

**130** https://auger.ifj.edu.pl/nowa_en/JACEE/

**131** http://stratocat.com.ar/fichas-e/1994/MCM-19941221.htm

**132** Naval Support Force, Antarctica

**133** http://www.vaq34.com/vxe6/vxe6hist.htm

**134** Navy VXE-6 squadron personnel

**135** Skier Operations was the Raven Gang designation for flight operations. Herc Operations was the name designated for Navy flight operations.

**136** MICAP is an abbreviation for "mission impaired capability awaiting parts." In the Air Force supply system, this comment on the delivery request emphasized its need

**137** The gun box was a metal box used for storage. No guns were authorized in Antarctica

**138** Notes and telephone discussion with Bill Mathews, and the SITREP, situation report, after the mission

**139** "Crevasse Curtails LC-130 Take-off," by Ginny Figlar, The Antarctic Sun, 22 Nov 1998

**140** "Military Hopes for Speedy Recovery of Up D Plane; Ice Trek Passes Halfway Point to Pole" by Ginny Figlar, The Antarctica Sun, 20 Dec 1998

**141** crash-disabled-damaged aircraft recovery

**142** Military wore green parkas, National Science Foundation employees wore red parkas

**143** "Dwight Fisher" - 18 October 1997, The Antarctica Sun

**144** Antarctic Air Operations Planning Summary, 1998-1999

**145** Antarctic Air Operations Planning Summary, 1998-1999

**146** Memorandum of Agreement Between the Department of Defense and the National Science Foundation for the National Science Foundation's Polar Programs, Section IV, A.3.b.(3), 1 May 2007

**147** Mark_Doll notes

**148** "Flight in the White" by Josh Landis, November 7, 1999; The Antarctica Sun

**149** Ibid

**150** OPARS is an acronym for the Navy's Optimum Path Aircraft Routing System program.

**151** It was essential to use grid navigation while flying in Antarctica due to the convergence of the lines of longitude. However, the unusual nature of grid navigation on a southbound flight from New Zealand to McMurdo put the heading systems of the aircraft on a northerly heading.

**152** Typically, the point-of-safe-return is about 15 minutes after the equal-time-point

**153** automated surface observing systems

**154** Antarctica Sun, December 6, 1998

**155** Nunataks were peaks of terrain poking through the snow, similar to islands in the water.

**156** Crew-rest is an aviation term that allowed an aircrew time to get something to eat and drink and allowed them eight hours of uninterrupted rest.

**157** Dr. Joergen Peder "JP" Steffensen, professor, ice core curator, Physics of Ice and Climate and Earth, Niels Bohr Institute, University of Copenhagen

**158** Memorandum of Agreement Between the Department of Defense and the National Science Foundation for the National Science Foundation's Polar Programs, Section IV, A.3.b.(3), 1 May 2007

**159** SPAWAR Website https://www.public.navy.mil/spawar/Atlantic/Pages/news_1-2017.aspx. This site has been removed

**160** http://flightsafety.org/aerosafety-world-magazine/april-2011/why-good-forecasts-go-bad

**161** http://www.stuff.co.nz/national/10004119/Antarctic-passengers-dodged-a-bullet

**162** Inquiry AO-2013-009: RNZAF Boeing 757, NZ7571, landing below published minima Pegasus Field, Antarctica, 7 October 2013; Final Report

**163** A synonym of fata morgana is a mirage or illusion. It's an atmospheric condition that distorts the size of objects, making them appear larger than they are. Often on the drive to the McMurdo airfields, the aircrew would see the aircraft in the distance with very large vertical stabilizers.

**164** SPAWAR Systems Atlantic Quality Assessment Team Analysis of the forecaster performance

**165** https://www.almaobservatory.org/en/home

**166** https://www.eso.org/public/teles-instr/apex

**167** https://www.iram-institute.org/EN/30-meter-telescope.php

**168** https://www.eaobservatory.org/jcmt

**169** http://lmtgtm.org/?lang=en

**170** https://www.cfa.harvard.edu/sma

**171** https://www.as.arizona.edu/arizona-radio-observatory

**172** “Astronomers Capture First Image of a Black Hole” https://eventhorizontelescope.org/

**173** https://arxiv.org/abs/1805.09346

**174** “EHT Status Update, December 15 2017” - Shep Doeleman, EHT Director

**175** Jet Propulsion Laboratory, California Institute of Technology

**176** “Aussie rescued after 16-day Antarctica ordeal,” The Sydney Morning Herald

**177** “Crew from 109th flies Antarctic rescue mission,” by Michael Lamendola, Daily Gazette, December 6, 2008

**178** Department of the Air Force Arctic Strategy Talking Points, July 21, 2020

**179** “Arctic Natural Resources in a Global Perspective,” by Lars Lindholt, The Economy of the North

**180** Ibid

**181** Department of the Air Force Arctic Strategy Talking Points, July 21, 2020

**182** Ibid

**183** Arthur Cayette, Administer of Meteorology, United States Naval Information Warfare Center Atlantic

**184** https://en.wikipedia.org/wiki/Concordia_Station

**185** Multi-Temporal Investigation of the Boulder Clay Glacier and Northern Foothills (Victoria Land, Antarctica) by Integrated Surveying Techniques, by Stefano Urbini, Gianluca Bianchi-Fasani, Paolo Mazzanti, Alfredo Rocca, Luca Vittuari, Antonio Zanutta, Valentina Alena Girelli, Michelina Serafini, Achille Zirizzotti, and Massimo Frezzotti